WE NEED TO HAVE A WORD

WORDS of WISDOM, COURAGE and PATIENCE for WORK, HOME and EVERYWHERE

WE NEED TO HAVE

A WORD

WORDS of WISDOM, COURAGE and PATIENCE for
WORK, HOME and EVERYWHERE

JOHN R. DALLAS, Jr.

HIGH-IMPACT KEY WORDS PROCLAIMED

WEEKLY WORDS from LANGUAGE for LEADING™

Igniting Engagement
Accelerating Results
Stimulating Conversation
Intensifying Self-Coaching

Hillview

Hillview Partners Network LLC | Hillview Institute Press

1133 North Dearborn Street | Suite 3201 | Chicago, Illinois 60610-7197

jrdallasjr@weneedtohaveaword.com | 312.643.8000

http://www.weneedtohaveaword.com

Facebook: http://www.facebook.com/weneedtohaveaword

Concept Testing Digital Version Released 1 March 2011
First Hardcover Edition (Fully Revised) Released 1 March 2012 through 31 March 2013

All Digitally Rendered and Manufactured in the United States of America

First Hardcover Edition ISBN 978-1-105-30520-7

U.S. Library of Congress Cataloguing-in-Publication Data
Dallas, John R., Jr.

We Need to Have a Word
Words of Wisdom, Courage and Patience for Work, Home and Everywhere

John R. Dallas, Jr.
Includes bibliographic references.

Professional Portrait Photography on Book Jacket by Kyle Klug, Ft. Lauderdale

Dedicated to Daughter

JENNIFER GRAY DALLAS

Content

Chapters are dedicated to exemplary individuals who inspire the author. Although these exceptional women and men may not be specifically mentioned within chapters marked in their honor, periodically tributes are posted and updated online through weneedtohaveaword.com, facebook.com/weneedtohaveaword, and twitter.com/JohnRDallasJr.

Exhibits:

"Employ your time in improving yourself by other men's writings, so that you shall gain easily what others have labored hard for." —Socrates

x

weneedtohaveaword.com

Introduction

Peter Koestenbaum, Ph.D.
Business Philosopher, Author, Speaker,
Coach, Top Award-Winning Professor, and
Creator and Owner of The Leadership Diamond®

Words: The Currency of Leadership

"We Need to Have a Word." This book is about being in love with words. And John Dallas knows and loves his words. Words point to things or express attitudes. Words, like the sentences of which they often are a part, make meaning…, mostly, if not always. Everything in this world that is or exists has a word connected with it, even if it is a word about non-words. Martin Heidegger, the influential Twentieth Century philosopher, said, "Language is the house of Being," *i.e.,* "language is the home of being," or "language houses all there is." And similarly, Ludwig Wittgenstein, another of the greats, says that "the limits of my language are the limits of my world."

John adheres to these principles. He is a master wordsmith, and in this book he plays this genius in him to perfection. It's all in a word, all in words, and, as you savor the words, as would a poet, you also savor existence. That is the path also to good business, to effective organizations and to a meaningful life!

John uses as technique to support organizations in business, politics, education and elsewhere the art of enhancing people's linguistic sensitivity. That is a superior way to effectively address communication and growth, both personal and organizational. Current events demand of individuals and organizations that they learn well to manage *change* and develop *leadership*.

This is where organizations ask for help. And the support for business today is ready for it and far more sophisticated than ever before. John is strong and comfortable in understanding these key themes of change and leadership. Cleverly, he assigns them a simple process with a clean solution. The impact of Twitter and Facebook, and more, are ample evidence of the core importance of brevity and breadth in communication to bring about leadership in change through change in leadership in today's world.

In his approach to words through anecdotes, John expects you to use these words to achieve your own highest goals. That vigorous and determined resolve shines through the entire execution of this book: his illustrations, challenges to the reader, instructions, tips, quotations…. John communicates by displaying his characteristically superior creativity, imagination, capacity for innovation, artistic temperament, energy, and unfailing excitement. His capacity for arousing enthusiasm is permanently in evidence. Here the artist's effective genius comes fully into play.

But the heart of the book, its *raison d'etre*, is to show how numerous people in his own active network and life have impressed him, and remind him, daily, of how they themselves have managed, in small ways and large, to come to terms with the fundamental existential questions of life — life in general and their lives in particular. We call the latter the "stuck points" — contradictions, conflicts and paradoxes that are irresolvable, and yet are of such weightiness that one cannot live without answering their relentless demands for solutions. And, what makes it worse, there is a deadline for us, by which time we *must* perform, must *have* performed, period, and we have no excuses!

That, of course is the definition of "stress." But John does not drown you in turgid theory nor in tomes of analysis. He tells you stories, informal tales, as one would during a coffee-and-doughnut break at the office, or a "pit-stop" on the road to refresh for the next stage in the journey, or licking your wounds while resting after a difficult and failed sales presentation, or even reading yourself to sleep after a hard day's work. It organizes your time, your world and it is your daily (weekly) companion on your road of life. The simple life reveals also the eternal structures of the complex human condition. Help here, which this book provides, is for all of us an undisguised blessing.

Another key message in this book, beside interesting and reassuring narratives, is to affirm life's most fundamental point. And that is, no question about it, to *act always on ethical insight, which becomes a life based on ethical principles*. Thus, the meaning of life is to serve — to be of service, to grasp the truth of authenticity that awaits us when we are devoted to giving service. It is to make oneself worthy enough so that, in delivering that service, one has something of true value to offer. Ethics, as he sees it and as is well established in the history of ethical theory, is a matter of making the commitment to do what is *right* — not merely prudential, not only pragmatic, not simply utilitarian (although all these of course, also are matters of great importance), but to be prepared to do what is "right." That may not always be clearly defined or definable, but it is a standard case of "I'll know it when I see it." It represents a higher conception of value. It is central to what John is — or has chosen to be — as a person.

Without getting too technical, allow me to make one quick clarification. There is one key component to an ethical act, one often missed. But not missed in John's way of seeing life and its principal meaning. One consequence of being of service is that we will thereby know oneself as decent, moral, ethical, committed and right thinking, one who is governed by high principle and not just emotion, by careful rational considerations and not just instinct. Anyone who is motivated by conscience, by pursuing fairness and justice, being honorable, trustworthy, reliable — by ideals like that — is also a person one *respects*.

We require respect more than pleasure, respect more than success, respect more than power. Respect touches one's identity, and that is the key. For respect is what makes one worthy, which is what is important, ultimately. That is where John's human stories come from. And that respect, born of giving and of generosity, of dedication to what is fundamentally the proper and decent thing to do — that is the moral person. For historians, that is the real history — not what the *poobahs* and the potentates do, but what the common residents do to survive and make sense out of life. That is the ethics this book celebrates, and such undertaking cannot be self-serving but must be an act of generosity, of acknowledgment, and of sharing the inspiration.

The distinguishing factor lies in the motive, the intent behind the action. The motive has to be good and the motive has to be that it is done for the sake of another and not for myself. The benefit is mine, yes, I try to be a good human being, I am devoted to something other than myself, outside of me. That is the authentic motive. I will then feel better about myself, but that is not the motive, that is at best a by-product.

Satisfaction is not why I do it. What makes an act ethical is that I do it for *you*. If I am honest because honesty is the best policy, then the value of the act derives from the motive. The "best policy" part is self-serving does not make this into an ethical act. The "honesty" part is the ethical component, yes, but only if that is the true motive, and does not show one up as being self-serving in the process. This is a subtle distinction, but it is central to the philosophic history of ethical theory, where respect for autonomously chosen principled ethical motivation is the very heart of morality. Specialists will recognize this as the ethics of the Eighteenth Century philosopher Immanuel Kant, one of the sharpest thinkers ever on this topic.

To his credit, John's ethical commitments are based on the firm view that choosing ethical behaviors defines a civilized human being. On this position John gets high marks. It is at the core of this book. It is what makes it memorable: its essential motivation, its intrinsically ethical message. That is why he wrote it, that is what it says, and this how he hopes it will be used. Words are the vehicle.

What puts it all together for him? What is the inner logic of his life? It is an act of faith; it is his Presbyterian orientation. It is his devotional commitment that is the centerpiece of *his* life. And he means it. And he does not impose it on anyone else, but he does *live* it to show its truth to him and its value to him and, crucial, as a silent model to others. It's teaching by EXAMPLE. It's not evangelism. Making this principled choice is the heart of his ethics. We need to recognize this in order to understand the higher value of this book.

John is the best friend you will ever have. The people in this book become his friends by the very act of their inclusion. He is a person on your side, when you need someone, the most reliable companion you will ever have. He will fight for you.

John is merciless with the demands he makes on himself — strong to a fault, perhaps. That may be hard on him but it is good for his product, *i.e.*, service. He is riveted to his topic, his subject matter, his calling — "words aligned on a hill."

The entire project of experiencing a year of weeks as a set of words, each of which is examined, turned around, held, applied, fingered, in a word, appreciated, poised to expand our sense of the world and its possibilities, is a gifted idea, an appropriate thought, and something that can easily be incorporated into a person's life — for the betterment of self and community. That is the uniqueness of this book, its power and its strength, and makes reading it, especially in small and thoughtful doses, exciting and absolutely delightful.

Let us not forget, We Need to Have a Word shows how words are the currency of leadership.

Peter Koestenbaum
1 March 2012
Carmel, California

Peter Koestenbaum, Ph.D. is Founder and Chairman of both The Koestenbaum Institute and PiB Inc. (PiB for Philosophy in Business). To organizational leaders around the world, he brings deeper and wider definitions, descriptions, and deployment strategies from his legendary studies of 4,000-plus years of leadership philosophy. His Leadership Diamond* is globally recognized for its balance of simplicity and depth (see page 405).

Dr. Peter Koestenbaum earned degrees from Stanford University (physics and philosophy), Harvard University (philosophy), and Boston University (philosophy); his B.A., M.A. and Ph.D. respectively. He also studied at the University of California, Berkeley. He continues to learn and lecture at top universities and other institutions.

For 34 years he taught in the Philosophy Department of San Jose State University, in California, where he received the Statewide Outstanding Professor Award. For over 25 years Dr. Koestenbaum worked closely with psychologists and psychiatrists. While developing breakthrough seminars, lectures and books, other subject matter experts and he collaborated to explore relationship between healing powers of psychiatry and philosophy. This vast amount of work informs guidance he offers colleagues and clients.

Dr. Koestenbaum's business books include: The Inner Side of Greatness, a Philosophy for Leaders, The Heart of Business, and Freedom and Accountability at Work: Applying Philosophic Insight to the Real World. Among his philosophic books: The Vitality of Death, The New Image of the Person, Managing Anxiety, Choosing to Love, and Is There an Answer to Death? His books are sold in bookstores and through online booksellers.

John Dallas clockwise from top left: while President of ETX (1981, photo by Bachrach), with dear friend Kathryn Wood Madden, Ph.D. and his daughter Jennifer Gray Dallas (1986), with friends and former colleagues Andrea Kneuss and Scott E. Squillace, Esq. (1982), with daughter (2004), with former Chicago Mayor Richard M. Daley (2011), and as Co-Founder and President of CreditComm Services (1996).

Preface

"All the great things are simple and many
can be expressed in a single word . . ." —Winston Churchill

Readers and words are top-of-mind. For this book you remain No. 1. While writing I recall persons who exemplify valued qualities of words. Chapters are inspired by and dedicated to people who personify words.

The legacy of King Henry VI also influences the letter and spirit of this volume. Henry V's only heir was nine months of age when he became the youngest monarch to ascend England's throne. Following the death of his father, the infant prince became king. Just-right words were served to the toddler-in-command. Surely influenced by coroneted respect for power, promise and pain within words, at age 17 HRH founded Oxford University's All Souls College, and later started Eton College and King's College, Cambridge. Evidence suggests His Majesty loved his words.

Eventually words failed Henry VI. While awaiting his fate in the Tower of London, perhaps the king said to his executioner, "We need to have a word." Which? Words are action. Words are power. Words are work.

From 1878 until 2010, the once peaceful, pious and benevolent king's All Soul's College administered what was called The Hardest Exam in the World. To applicants for their coveted Examination Fellowship, with *gravitas* a proctor would say only two words. For three hours, in writing, an aspirant was to expound upon one word. As a relevant example, "Wisdom" would be said, simply followed by, "Expound."

All Souls College inflicted all-stress essay tests. The test is called by one word, "Essay." Handling of one word formed the basis for this world-renowned school's make-it-or-break-it examination of a brain's core programming, operating system, and storage capacity. In similar ways your and my expounding upon each of this book's 52 high-impact key words allows us to do wisdom's work. This way we qualify for success.

Good, bad and other blood, sweat, tears, and hopes were shed. This form of exposition was easier said than won. Now the storied hardest exam is history, suggesting a downward shift in higher expectation.

In 2011 the University of Iowa's Tippie School of Management did away with the traditional essay in favor of would-be students using Twitter to write a 140-character application. And Columbia Business School is fairly similar in asking applicants, "What is your post-M.B.A. professional goal?" and limiting to 200 characters their responses — not 200 words, 200 characters. Surely Oxford's All Souls dons (*i.e.*, teachers) are asking, "What is this word coming to?"

Words are characters appearing on the stage in our minds. Standing alone "A" has impact of one or many words. When in 2011 the United States lost its "AAA" rating from Standard & Poors, we were reminded how three As mean top-most quality. "Yes" and "no" teach children to honor and fear power and pain in single words. "Charge" and "retreat" begin and end battle respectively. "Start" and "stop" can do both.

Individual words deployed with just-in-time precision work wonders. Single words used in wrong ways, or at wrong times, can wreak havoc. With thoughtful and thoughtless single words I have started, built, nurtured, destroyed, recovered, enriched and sustained personal, business, and other types of human relationships. "Sorry" works.

Yes, single words work. One word can unlock floodgates. Somewhat as a way of testing myself, I honored timing constraints in taking The Hardest Exam in the World. In 52 weekly three-hour sittings, non-stop first drafts of chapters were written. I set a timer. Over ensuing weeks and months, untimed further effort added, subtracted and clarified text.

You will see edited highlights of what each key word released for me. These words deserve your thoughtful personalization. Your words work.

You. Expound.

This moment we need to have a word. Your given name is the exact word we need. Your first name. Normally forenames are one word.

Do you know your name's etymological or other roots? What does your *name word* mean? Are you fairly certain of its meaning, or are you recalling family folklore? During a lifetime, imagine the untold number of times you hear each of your names. Imagine not knowing what your names probably mean. Why not? You are wise to learn more about any words you often think about, say, hear and feel.

With your vivid imagination for e-readers, or with pen, pencil or marker for hardcover editions, you will want to fill-in your name at the beginning of each chapter of this book. Please. To encourage yourself to have more intimate, productive, beneficial and sustainable relationships with 52 words as action, attach your name to each word.

Throughout this book occasionally the terms letter and chapter are used interchangeably. Please read each chapter as a letter to you from me. As I was writing to you, I could imagine your reactions to my personal letters — from scratching your head wondering what in the world I am trying to say to you, to saying out loud, "Aha!" At a non-judgmental level of inquiry, asking what any author is saying and where she or he is leading ignites and sustains full reader engagement.

Unless you borrowed this book from a library, a dutiful librarian is not going to scold you for writing on these pages. If a friend loaned the book to you, you may discover her or his name is already inscribed. If so, A.S.A.P. you'll want to acquire your own copy. If you are reading *via* a tablet, laptop, PC, smart phone, or from any monitor that does not allow for you to write or type-in your name, please use vivid imagination and visualize your good name in bold block letters.

Try it. Close your eyes for a second or two. Can you see, hear and feel your name? It is essential for you to put your name in the front of your mind and at the top of each chapter. Give it a try. Feel the power and promise of your very own name. Feel your enhanced sense of self. Be in-the-moment. If you are somewhere where you can say your name our loud — just do it! At least whisper it. Please.

At least 52 times you will be writing or imagining your given name. To enrich thought and action behind your good name, you will appear at the beginning of each chapter. Freely insert your name anywhere in the book, please — wherever you want to connect with your good name the words and other thoughts you are experiencing.

From finest calligraphy to chicken-scratch, as you read this book write-in (or imagine) your name as you are prompted to do so. For many years this strategic and enjoyable repetitive action will pay unexpected dividends — starting now. Feel the value of your name.

Insert or imagine seeing your first name: _____.
Please sense the purpose, power and promise in personalizing this
specific message. Ultimately this book is about you and your
openness to sustainable long-term relationships with 52 key words.
You deserve to have your name printed or written in the 52 spaces
provided herein. Just do it. Please. The mental and physical exercise
works. With each movement of your hand, sense the mystery of your
identity's connection to a single word. Your name has influence.

It's about Time for You and Me

It's about time. If timing is everything then everything is about time.
It is high time for us to reach higher places about our sense of timing.

Even before the beginning's Big Bang, timing is everything. In science
and literature we accept all matters of this universe are influenced by
time. Book readers allocate, withhold or withdraw time. Book authors
compete for time. Through respect for time readers and authors relate.

Linguists continue to look for insights into how the mind handles the
challenge of any language. A core question in linguistics is how finite
linguistic rules can generate infinite complexity. Words are something
more. This book's prioritization of time is advanced as a generative
technique so you and 52 words quickly self-identify and deeply relate.
It is my Put Time First Theory for aligning words, minds and action.

In rules of rhetoric, anticlimax indicates a sentence in which the last
part expresses something lower or otherwise lesser than the first.
Quite naturally time is experienced as a first priority. First appealing
to our innate sense of time, therefore, allows chapters in this book to
bring into the moment each of 52 featured weekly words. In
prioritizing time, then thinking, speaking and writing appeals, at a
subconscious level, to our built-in and rapt attention to chronology.
As an example, it is an acceptable style to write, "We are going to
climb a hill today." It is arguably more arresting to say, "Today we are
going to climb a hill?" Time comes first for you and this author.

Needing to re-read a sentence is a wise investment of additional time,
and hardly an automatic indicator of inattentive reading or inadequate
writing. In this and many other books, longer sentences with extended
thoughts are used to encourage and sustain deeper engagement in time.

Periodically choosing to prioritize flow of time over traditional sentence structure requires my intermittently requesting, and your granting, poetic license. A scholar's path toward grammaticality is straight and narrow. You and I will allow for enjoyable scenic detours. Please and thank you.

Time units even smaller than nanoseconds are evaporating as I am writing and you are reading. Keep time in mind. It is here already. Beyond the mystery of 24-hour cycles of circadian rhythm, and man's superimposed mechanical-clock measurement of time in-motion, metaphorically speaking time also has economic importance. "Time is money." Time and money are ours to use and lose. Invest your time.

Delaying until tomorrow something you want or need to do today is called "getting stuck in-time." Allowing yourself to "get stuck" delaying action with too many people and things has a way of stopping the clock; sometimes quite literally stopping life. Getting stuck is unhealthy.

Each weekend you are asked to get un-stuck with the contents of only one chapter about one high-impact word that will improve results at work, home and everywhere. These are words to have for 52 un-stuck weeks ahead. It's about time. Hear the alarm clock. To jog, jab and jolt you into action, perhaps just-in-time these words will echo within you. Words are real. Words are action. Words are time.

From your earliest years your name was associated with someone arresting your attention. In this collection of letters to you from me, your inserting your own name is likely to arrest your attention to this point-in-time, and intensify your brain's endogenous alignment with word views ahead. While reading each chapter, innate power in your attaching your own name electrifies your agile brain's neuroplasticity.

Perhaps before each Monday morning, please read a weekly letter to you from me. If you are already well-connected with a week's featured word, my letter to you will rekindle, stoke or douse fires. If the word is unfamiliar, let the courtship begin! Give it space in your brain and heart. You will not be in love with every word. Rather intimately you will know each word for which you allow ample time for illumination, and then sufficient time for reflection, identification, and even experimental implementation (*i.e.*, immediately using the word at least several times to test its impact). Learn it then launch it. Yes, try it before you *fly* it.

To succeed there is no need for speed. For each person-to-word relationship proposed, give at least a full week of getting-to-know-you time. Each day include the word in your contemplation and during out-loud conversation. Reading weekend-by-weekend you'll take a full year with this book; one-word-per-week. Yearning for learning, in Aristotelian tradition you will call out of yourself deeper wisdom, virtuous courage, and sustainable patience. If you nurture the thoughts and feelings each word triggers in you, I project you'll have life-long meaningful relationships with well over half of the 52 featured words. Please let each relationship begin deep within you.

There is wonder and mystery associated with our emotional and sometimes physical connection to certain words. From first attempts coaxed from our infant mouths, words became expressions of our inner selves. Astonishment, glee, smiles, applause, relief, and a host of other expressions of emotion surrounded most of us when we formed and uttered our first word sounds. Chances are we responded to the emotion of our first word before learning its actual meaning. Thinking back, allow yourself to imagine how thrilled you and those around you were when earliest words started to flow from your young brain, heart and mouth. See if you can feel again at least some of the endogenous joy flowing through your first words. From birth we are blessed with innate ability to find significance in the presence — or absence — of words as action.

Please treat each of 52 chapters as a personal dialogistic letter to you from me. Have robust dialogue with yourself. Listen with a third ear for YOUR thoughts and feelings tucked between this book's words, lines and chapters. Your mind and heart will speak to you. Detail in certain reflections allows for a cumulative Proustian effect. Subtextual messages offer deeper stimulation with higher expectation. Allow the flow. Quickly you'll sense strategic alignment of words, thoughts, actions and results. Sometimes it takes complexity, and perhaps a bit of difficulty, to make words more valuable. Turning to a dictionary intensifies lasting value.

Be these words. These are words to be. By year's end your interactive handbook will be dog-eared, highlighted, smudged, filled with sticky notes, and otherwise marked as abundantly book-loved. You'll carry it with you to read in remarkable places. Acclivity in these 52 key words will lift to higher ground your mind and heart. Enjoy the view.

Judeo-Christian text proclaims, *"We will eat the fruit of our words."* Although manna is enough bread for one day in the wilderness, here you and yours are offered a banquet of ripe and nutritious words from which you will be able to feast for a lifetime. Enjoy every bite!

Thank you for opening yourself to new relationships with 52 words, and with this humble, imperfect and daring author. Each new relationship begins with your name. If you have not already done so, please go back to the top of this section of the book and write your name in the space provided. If it is already there, take another look at your "name word." Feel the power of your given name. Expound.

This is your book. This is our journey. This is about you, me, and those you and I will influence toward successful outcomes. These word stories meet you where you are. For you each word's narrative will range from sparse to labyrinthine. You will find and enjoy a just-right level of complexity that's best for you. From each word story offered, every reader discerns her or his own quantity and quality of resonance, relevance and reward. Ultimately any writing is as valuable as a reader allows it to become. Reading may be a greater skill than writing. Do you agree? The more I realize how much I forget from what I read, the more I admit I may not always be reading at my best.

A mosaic of words, some of the book's pieces are larger than others. As we take this journey, quickly you will discover how brief chapters or extended views are in-place to work to your strategic advantage.

When you scan the roster of Content, you may see a word or more that you need to consider before others. Go for it. Chapter letters are written and formatted to stand on their own. Remember in Content to put a checkmark next to the chapters you read out of sequence. Please try to read all 52 within 12 months of starting this book of letters. Commit, please, to read all 52 chapters over a 12-month cycle.

If you see any word for perhaps the first time, please consider looking it up as an opportunity instead of an inconvenience. Online resources I recommend are onelook.com and visualthesaurus.com.

While reading each weekly letter to you from me, allow your thoughts to expound upon mine. Please. Occasionally coming back to a word to expound some more will be a wise thing to do. Go as far as you want to — or need to — with your thoughts and feelings about each word's upside potential. Enjoy the getting-to-know-you process. Forging relationships with these 52 words is doing wisdom's work.

Word-by-word I am at your side for this wise labyrinth walk. Let's go!

Abundant. Expound.   —JRDjr

Acronym

Chapter Inspired by and Dedicated to
Frederick Ernest ("F.E.") Schuchman (1891-1983)

Please insert or imagine seeing only your initials: _____,

Why in the world of whole words would "acronym" qualify to lead-off our 52-word journey? Among many reasons, we live in a world submerged in acronyms we need to better understand, use more carefully, and enjoy humor embedded in some. This chapter opens our minds to acknowledging complexity and risk within simplicity and jest. In this letter to you from me, there is laughter, seriousness, and somewhat of an acronymic mini-mystery for us to follow to the end. This kick-off chapter is jam-packed with value. Are you ready?

Acronyms can quickly communicate complex messages. Unfamiliar or misunderstood acronyms can add risk to our daily lives. Immediately we acknowledge a percentage of what we do with acronyms. From S.O.S. to L.O.L., here we examine the relative criticality of such abbreviation. Risks and rewards of acronyms are real. A.S.A.P. we need to explore this word's extended significance.

Your reading this book is a **S.M.A.R.T**. goal: **S**pecific, **M**easurable, **A**ttainable, **R**ealistic and **T**imely. During the next 52 weeks of reading together, let's be smart and keep top-of-mind this smart acronym.

Usually designed to be easy to say and remember, the complexity of an acronym's representation of whole words, complex thoughts, robust ideas, and sometimes intricate measurements makes acronym an ideal word with which to start your full-year (52 weeks) journey with We Need to Have a Word. Acronyms appear throughout this book. ROI with this book will exceed your expectations.

Grasping HILL as a frequently used acronym in this book is deemed essential to this journey. HILL represents my employer's High-

Impact Leader Lens™ (HILL) Assessment Model for Viewing and Influencing Movement of People and Things — called The HILL Model™ from Hillview Partners Network LLC. (Refer to page 409.)

Each week this book's 52 "HILL Words" remind us of the featured word's potential for allowing us to (1) see deeper within ourselves, (2) view from a higher plane people and things, and (3) in the broadest possible ways apply the word's real-world value in our day-to-day lives. Indeed expectations are high for your response to these words.

ROI is the three-letter acronym representing Return On Investment. As an utterance or written expression, ROI requires three syllables (r-o-i) instead of six syllables (re·turn on in·vest·ment); perhaps a savings of fifty percent in time and energy. For numbers crunchers, such economy with words is probably good ROI. Comic relief aside, speed of expression and depth of understanding are addressed with use of acronyms. Acronyms do not always get the job done.

Acknowledging the danger of a listener drowning face-first in a bowl of someone else's alphabet soup, we all must remember to at least once explain an acronym's full meaning then use it. I confess to sitting silent as speakers spew forth acronyms without explanation. These days during meetings I might be seen logging-on to a search engine to find definitions of acronyms that are not being offered.

Acronyms are results of intentional acts of lexicalization with strings of letters sometimes formed into pronounceable approximations of whole words. Acronyms are usually contrived from first or other letters within a series of root words. As an example, CEO has become an acronymic word for Chief Executive Officer. Hillview coined CAO for Chief Alignment Officer, the title I choose over CEO. For each presidency I held, CAO tells you what I did. CEO really doesn't. Instead of "The Buck Stops Here" for signs on CEO desks, I suggest – for desks of CAOs who are often also CEOs — a more instructive alternative: Alignment Starts and Stops Here!

The process of creating an acronym is remarkably rich with potential for deeply etching into our minds exceedingly complex thoughts. With an acronym one can say a lot with little verbalized effort, and sometimes with less audible risk associated with completeness. Always-a-Marine D.C. friend Robert Schroeder told me how a stouthearted and proud male U.S. Marine, especially one who is normally known for few words, might not want to be heard among his peers saying poetic imagery such as "End Evening Nautical Twilight" for emphasizing sunset hours, or "Begin Morning Nautical Twilight" for time enveloping a possibly spectacular sunrise. E.E.N.T. and B.M.N.T. respectively easily trip off the most salty tongues. Yet in battle these and many other acronyms can save or destroy human lives. Rob provided from memory a long list.

Have you ever made into an acronym your first, middle or last name? Give or take a word, already Mr., Mrs., Dr., Ms., Sr., Jr., III, Ph.D., M.D., and numerous other prefixes and suffixes are among acronyms routinely applied to your name. Middle names are reduced to middle initials; a single-letter acronym that often prompts the question, "What is your middle name?" Raymond is my answer, not Robert, the name occasional questioners seem to enjoy guessing.

Acronyms used to my face to endear or separate me from the user: JRDjr, JD and JR. As my great grandfather's 1869 name was used for my 1921 dad and 1950 me, yet not given to my 1897 grandfather William McKinley Dallas, technically I am a "III" not a "Jr." My parents had not yet been taught the order of precedence in assigning suffixes for male children who are named out of birth sequence.

For many who join me in finding exceptional value in the Myers-Briggs Type Indicator® (MBTI) tool for assessing personality attributes and likely behaviors, the four letters we earn from our responses to probing questions become an acronym around which we construct broader interpretations of ourselves. Tested three times, ENTJ is the MBTI acronym I earned in 1973, 1988 and 1999: **E** for Extraversion, **N** for iNtuition, **T** for Thinking, and **J** for Judging.

In November 2008, I was retained as a keynote speaker for the annual conference of the Illinois Council for Community College Administrators (ICCCA). Perhaps a majority of the audience raised hands to indicate they too were ENTJ. They and I were startled. ENTJ is the score assigned to the fewest of all tested through Meyers-Briggs. Suddenly I knew a lot more than I expected to know about a large number in the audience. On-the-fly, I adjusted some of my remaining remarks, and a few responses to questions. Applause.

For this complicated talk about strategic alignment, I earned from the audience top-most speaker rankings. Knowing how many fellow

ENTJs were in the room surely helped ENTJ me to connect with them and others. I know the strengths, weaknesses, opportunities and threats (S.W.O.T.) ENTJ represents. An easy search *via* Bing or Google for these four letters will yield insight you may find interesting.

Gallup Organization's StrengthsFinder® 2.0 assessment tool does not use acronyms to express findings for top five themes of strength. My top five themes: Activator, Futuristic, Input, Strategic and Achiever. For private meaningfulness and use, from each of these five words I developed acronyms to help me relate to the personal significance of each word. In other words, I started with the 41 letters represented within these five words and then added 41 more words; resulting in a total of 46 words to support me as I strive to focus on my strengths. When self-doubt, other people, and prevailing circumstances might be over-emphasizing my weaknesses, I summon certain acronyms.

Do you see and feel the importance of acronyms? There's more; much more. Who can forget Natalie Cole's *Unforgettable* album's L-O-V-E. "L is for the way you look at me. O is for the only one I see. V is very, very extraordinary. E is even more than anyone that you adore can love." Could you hear her singing these letters? As I write I am humming the tune. She made an acronym out of LOVE. Let's work harder to love more of life's meaningful acronyms.

From serious purpose to protecting sensitive ears from full expletives, acronyms are a constant in our everyday lives. President John F. Kennedy is quoted as saying, "There's always some S.O.B. at the table who does not get it." I doubt J.F.K. always used the acronym. He remains known by his initials. Think of the way Americans have used shortened names for U.S. Presidents. "Ike" was the acronymic nickname for Dwight David Eisenhower, L.B.J. kept us from having to say Lyndon Baines Johnson, and "W" was the single-letter differentiator between father (No. 43) and son (No. 45) Bush. Learning and taking more seriously certain acronyms will add traction and value to your ways and means of thinking about others and yourself. Yes, Y.O.U.

Take your first name and envision it as an acronym. Choose words for each letter of your name that affirm, inspire, ignite or support you in some way. Have fun with this exercise, yet be sure to allow mindfulness and meaningfulness to resonate within you for each of the words you attach to every letter in your name. Give it a try. Certainly look at the Table of Contents for words you might choose among the 52 represented in this collection. Encourage others to do the same thing with their first or other names, including children who benefit from your fully responsible leadership. In my teens, not too humbly I decided JOHN is Judicious, Original, Honorable and Noteworthy. With an acronym I had set a roadmap for life which I continue to strive to follow.

MARY might be Meticulous, Assertive, Realistic and Youthful. STEVE might be Serious, Trustworthy, Ethical, Valiant and Emotive. Soon create from your name a positive acronym.

At Chicago Title Corporation TRUST was our acronym for:

Truth. Our relationships with our customers and each other will be based on truth.

Respect. We will respect the property rights of our customers, the company, and our fellow employees.

Understanding. We will endeavor to understand the needs of our customers and to try to meet those needs.

Service. We will provide the best service possible consistent with company policies and applicable laws and regulations governing our business.

Trust. We will work to earn the trust placed in us.

For me the concept of "trust within the acronym trust" was more than enough meaningfulness to tip the scale in terms of understanding the intended ethical culture of my new employer. The acronym mattered. This is one of many reasons why acronym is a word worthy of your focus as we jump-start our brains to focus on deeper meaning for words with this book.

A Hillview Team-Strengthening Initiative (TSI) involves asking everyone around a table to choose words that fit with each letter of their first names that illustrate current or envisioned personal or professional strengths. Along with a dictionary, thesaurus and other reference books, HILL Word lists, cards, and other Hillview Alignment Tools (HATs) are used. Participants are encouraged to review strengths named in StrengthsFinder 2.0 and other books and programs Hillview endorses for reversing risk of misalignment with a person's true or anticipated strengths.

When a fire breaks out in a hospital, R.A.C.E. is one of several common acronyms that ignite among employees and others immediate understanding of a compound call-to-action to save lives.

Rescue **A**larm **C**ontain **E**xtinguish

When nanoseconds count, acronyms save more than time and space. Acronymic shorthand can have more impact than longhand. At-the-ready acronyms come in handy for fully responsible leaders. You already know most of the acronyms you need to lead. Nevertheless this chapter will take you where no acronym has taken you before. Herein new acronyms will become part of your way of thinking about strategically aligning language of leadership with sustainable growth for yourself, others, and your organization.

S.O.S. is the Morse Code distress signal ($\cdot\,\cdot\,\cdot$ — — — $\cdot\,\cdot\,\cdot$) for Save Our Ship or Save Our Souls. Photos of hand-scrawled S.O.S. signals made even more poignant photographs and videos of Japan's 2011 earthquakes and tsunamis. Save Our Shareholders seems to be Wall Street's cry for help when financial icebergs are hit. S.O.S. gets the point across at life-saving thinking speed. The acronym S.O.S. sounds more urgent than the words represented. Do you agree? Can you feel the power of this acronym? For some reason we kids of the 60s and much earlier were taught and tested on Morse Code. Hearing "S.O.S." still has a bone-chilling effect on me. Our eighth-grade English teacher, David Mackey, used the nearly unspeakable sinking of the Titanic to get across his points about S.O.S. being a faster way to communicate life-and-death facts. In that Whitehall Junior High classroom, acronyms became important to ship captains and me.

To bring to life for leaders three key words: wisdom, courage and patience (W.C.P.), Hillview uses acronyms to expand clients' views while defining and describing principles and practices of W.C.P. for fully responsible leadership (F.R.L.). Here are a few W.C.P. acronyms we use:

Fully Responsible Leaders Wisely R.E.A.C.T. with

Respect, **E**mpathy, **A**uthenticity, **C**larity and **T**rust

Fully Responsible Leaders Courageously R.E.A.C.H. with

Reality, **E**nergy, **A**scendancy, **C**ommitment and **H**umility

Fully Responsible Leaders Patiently R.E.S.P.O.N.D. with

Rationality, Efficiency, Support, Praise, Options, Numbers and Decisions

Classroom or boardroom grades A, B, C, D, E (or F) are acronyms for levels of performance. Among many meanings, AAA is an acronym for an automobile club and Wall Street's top credibility and reliability ratings. And AA means American Airlines or Alcoholics Anonymous. When heard, read, or used, it is essential for alignment to understand exactly what an acronym means. Imagine the number of times you hear acronyms you do not know, and yet you don't stop the speaker to ask. When another person uses a specific acronym as if absolutely everyone knows precisely what it means, many of us fear a little or a lot asking for clarification.

Within the alphabet soup of acronyms leaders eat, and with my 40-plus years of exposure to esoteric business terminology, I cannot remember nor find acronyms associated with leaders or leadership; letters conjoined in order to discipline leaders to cover bases in how they think and act on-the-job.

Only S.O.B. and SUIT (*i.e.,* "He's a suit") came to a friend's humorous mind when I asked him if he knew of any acronyms to allow quick reference and categorization of leaders and styles of leadership. With laughter a few unseemly expletives were offered for my consideration, but none was an acronym suitable for this book. Searching for acronyms for leadership and leader, Acronyms List (claiming 40,000-plus entries) returned 0 results ("…your search matched 0 acronyms"). Perhaps by the time of this book's publication, some of the acronyms above and below will have been accepted for inclusion within acronymslist.com.

What type of leader are you? Do Hillview acronyms above represent your views about your roles as a leader? Somewhat tongue-in-cheek, also check-in with the following options to see if there is an acronym or more to affirm your identification with the following traits, or an acronym to ignite in you pressing need for change for the better? Among the following do you see yourself with one or more of these acronyms applying to you:

Micro-manager; often called a pain in everyone's assets (PITA for Pain In The Assets)?

Command-and-control, autocratic, authoritarian, unyielding, *etc.* (C&C)?

Machiavellian is when one might use unethical trickery to manipulate outcomes. "Mach" is pronounced "mack," so we say, "Big Mach."

More aggressive than assertive (AGG)? Being assertive is preferable, yet being the first three letters of the word assertive is not acceptable.

Finding fault more so than discovering strengths (FFOS for Finding Faults Over Strengths)?

Passive-aggressive and insensitive toward others' needs (PAIN)?

Stealth-mode; always operating in-secret behind closed doors (SM)?

Laissez-faire or free rein; *i.e.*, almost or completely hands-off (LF or FR)?

Literary license with acronyms above allows this author to draw your attention to these essentially undesirable traits in leadership. What other types of leaders come to your mind, and what acronyms would you craft to signal to others your views? Take a few moments to think about the people around you. How many earn these acronyms?

During consulting or coaching work and in other situations, LID is the acronym used in my confidential mental notes when sadly I hear about or discern a Leader In Distress ("LID"). LIDs are leaders with suspected or known psychological or medical condition(s): depression, addiction, ADHD, bi-polar disorder, possible childhood dysgraphia, disease, illness, or those secretly or openly dealing with other infirmities or something else hidden from view? "Keeping a LID on it" takes on new meaning.

For fully responsible leaders (FRLs) to use among their inner circles or wider audiences, serious or silly acronyms as shorthand for bigger points, help listeners/followers get it quickly. It is, however, essential to ensure that everyone who needs to know knows precisely what the acronym means to (1) the leader, (2) the follower, and (3) anyone else who might be within earshot when the acronym is heard. Hearing acronyms our brains can actually engage at a somewhat deeper level as we instantly complete the words, term, concept, or other longer formulation for which the acronym stands.

A global re-emergence economy requires fully responsible leaders to understand, think, live, breathe, speak, and measure results with knowledge, wisdom, courage and patience embedded within these and other essential acronyms: EBITDA (earnings before interest, taxes, depreciation, and amortization), EBIT (earnings before interest and taxes), EBT (earnings before taxes), ROI (return on investment), ROE (return on equity), P&L (profit and loss), LBO (leveraged buyout), M&A (mergers and acquisitions), SOX (The Sarbanes-Oxley Act), *etc.* In another chapter, Hillview's ROL is discussed, Return On Leadership.

What other acronymic messages come to your mind to help you remember facts or formulae for economic stability and growth? How were acronyms used during your childhood years? Think back to your first acronym. I remember mine.

The first acronym I learned was ACTS, a way of covering all the bases in prayer: Adoration, Confession, Thanksgiving and Supplication. (Indeed "supplication" may have been my first big vocabulary word.) Still I use ACTS to discipline myself in prayer to cover essential steps, and I listen for this acronymous formula when hearing pastors and others pray. Doing so keeps me more engaged in spoken prayers of others.

In 1964 I was 14 when I won first place in a Pittsburgh city-wide poster contest for how I used an acronym to illustrate features, benefits and attributes of home life — H.O.M.E. L.I.F.E. — **H**appiness, **O**rganization, **M**anners, **E**ducation. **L**ove, **I**nspiration, **F**un, **E**ncouragement. It seems that this teen knew what I needed and wanted from my home life. Without high risk of retribution, the acronym allowed me to say a lot to my parents, siblings and others.

Pause. Think about what acronyms allow you to say and do. Hundreds or more other acronyms float in and out of our minds and vocabulary. Oddly very few acronyms relate to leaders or leadership.

Hillview's High-Impact Leader Lens (HILL) for Viewing Strategic Alignment of People, Money, Technology, and other Mission-Critical Resources — central to The HILL Model for Fully Responsible Leadership — may someday be memorialized as a standard for arresting attention to the urgency of clear and panoramic vision; standing on a hill, not on a mountaintop, up in an ivory tower, or on a book shelf. "What is your HILL-view of this issue," a U.S. Senator may someday ask a CEO testifying on Capitol Hill; "Where do you see people, money, technology, and things moving, and what are you doing to influence true-north movement?" Am I dreaming? Y.E.S. One must dream.

Four letters — HILL — mean all this and much more. Trust this compulsiveness about HILL is not your author's ego speaking. HILL is one response to a global modern society's need for a better-to-best way for leaders to see and sense reality and potential; focusing tightly on strengths, weaknesses, opportunities and threats (S.W.O.T.) seen *via* a HILL view. HILL allows *a vantage point to your advantage*; a point-of-view (P.O.V.) from an agile mind's observation platform atop a hill. Get it? Of course you do. This moment your mind is witness to a HILL view.

In the mid-90s I flew from my Orange, California office to Cleveland, Ohio to meet with a top decision-making officer of a major bank. Host and three other officers decided to enlighten a Pittsburgh Pirates-weaned Pennsylvania native by scheduling our lunch in the V.I.P. private club within that city's baseball stadium. (Pittsburgh's claustrophobic Three Rivers Stadium was still standing, so I suppose a point was being made.) Bank bragging began. As a seasoned captain of countless types of B2B conversations, here in Cleveland there was an odd tension at table I simply could not navigate. Flummoxed, eventually two acronyms came to mind about the lead fellow with whom I was hoping to forge a mutually beneficial business relationship: KIA (Know-It-All) and PITA (Pain In The Assets). Later I concluded his fully inflated ego was proving something to his high-on-their-horses colleagues, not to me. I was not at all entertained. Highly engaged I was growing enraged.

Suddenly my declared ignorance toward a banking acronym actually stopped the strange meeting. My not knowing an acronym destroyed the sandy foundation on which I was trustingly investing considerable time and money. Believe when I tell you I was nearly reduced to tears by this man's condescending and otherwise disrespectful and dramatic response to my freely admitting I did not know the meaning of "HELOC" (pronounced "he·lock"). I said I was not yet familiar with the acronym. Ethically I asked what it meant. H.E.L.L. broke loose about HELOC. Clearly appalled he said to me with a sneer, "How could a man of your senior stature and long-term involvement in finance not know HELOC? It is one of the most common banking 'terms'." Alas, again I asked.

To make matters worse, he turned to his colleagues at table and said, "Don't tell him. Let him find out on his own." There were no smiles. I thought a joke was being played. The punch line was a knockout then a lock-out. Shockingly, well within 10 minutes of my HELOC gaffe the lunch was over. A win-win deal was never discussed. Clearly and openly I was judged a fool. I did not know HELOC's words. Son-of-a-banker was not the expletive I exhaled as I entered (alone) the elevator for the parking garage. I struck out in the stadium. An acronym did me in.

Once in the rental car I immediately called and asked the chairman of my company, "Do you know what HELOC means?" He responded, "What? No. Why?" I told him what happened. He and I were not amused. He thought I was making it up and said so. No. Sadly this dark and melodramatic comedy about an acronym's mission-critical importance was too real.

Later, with 22 other leaders in my consumer credit data company, I did not find one person who knew the acronym. On a speakerphone we called a friendly banker at Wells Fargo who said, "I think it stands for …" He wasn't quite sure at all. He fetched the answer. What happened to me in Cleveland remains a startling memory. I was not personally burdened by my ignorance about HELOC, yet I remain unsettled by this banker's perhaps clinical obsession about an acronym. Since this 1995 foolishness, HELOC is probably a more commonly used acronym. Yet this moment I don't recall the last time I heard it.

Did you know what HELOC means? If you did not, you are not alone. Yet the meltdown in the housing market could be based, in part, on root misunderstanding of deeper definitions, descriptions, and risks associated this acronym's key words. Did offending mortgage lenders hide behind acronyms and code names some of their dastardly deeds against public trust?

Many of the acronyms listed above are unknown to many. Perhaps ubiquitous EBITDA (Earnings Before Interest, Taxes, Depreciation and Amortization) trips up more people than we know. At table too often people nod to suggest their grasp of EBITDA and other complex financial acronyms, and yet secretly they may still wonder what it all really means. When relevant clarity is needed, the awkward full-word pronunciation of the acronym EBITDA adds even more mystery. Pause to say it out loud. Easily it trips off of too few tongues. Pause to memorize the words. The whole words matter to business leaders, and so does the acronym.

When six or so years ago the Graham School of the University of Chicago decided it was high time for leaders to delve deeper into esoteric root definitions and history of leadership, wise and affable Dean Dan Shannon reached out for curriculum and teaching expertise to California's highly regarded professor Peter Koestenbaum, Ph.D., a world-renowned business philosopher — now in his fifth decade of focusing on categorizing intricacies of 4,000-plus years of history in leadership studies. Peter created and teaches The Leadership Diamond® to allow students to see, feel and grasp many obscure facets of leadership. In front of appreciative audiences worldwide, he reveals, cuts, and polishes his registered trademark gemstone, The Leadership Diamond®.

There are many robust acronyms within The Leadership Diamond®. Each acronym is worth deeper thought and memorization. PiB is the good-natured acronym Peter uses for one of his business ventures, Philosophy in Business (PiB).

As Peter and I worked together on a Hillview project for National Association of Realtors (NAR), the world's largest professional association with over 1.2 million members (in 2008), I was struck by the liquidity and profundity of response to any and all questions asked by valued friend Douglas Hinderer, NAR Senior Vice President, and by their prior CEO, Terry McDermott. With a steady stream of gently delivered wisdom, courage and patience, Peter unfurled meaning for what I came to call "fully responsible leadership," a term Peter asked if he could adopt for his work as well. Of course I said yes. Because of his tutelage, fully responsible leadership (FRL) came to my mind. We both yearn for the day when thousands or more will embrace FRL for powerful points of differentiation for leading's required competencies and performance.

For upside potential, will you put your mind and arms around worthy acronyms and memorize their significance and embrace their potential for you and those you lead? Long ago I started telling audiences CEO meant Chief Enlightenment Officer, Chief Empowerment Officer, Chief Edification Officer, Chief Engagement Officer, and other illustrative E words. In 2005 I coined CAO to more adequately characterize my role as Hillview's Chief Alignment Officer — until contract-signing time, intentionally side-stepping the less illustrative legal (for ultimate accountability) CEO designation.

Perhaps CEOs are more self-motivated and inwardly mobilized when they think of themselves as CAOs. It works for me. Do you agree?

In some halls of academia the senior academic administrator is known as the Provost. As institutions become more business-like, the Provost is becoming known as the Chief Academic Officer (also CAO). A school's CAO ensures alignment of learning with society's requirements.

Readers on the younger-minded side of today's social media world know precisely what words and images I am communicating when I write: LOL, ROFL, LMAO, OMG, FML, or a few other less polite acronyms of cyberspace. In the early 70s my former wife and I designed an ill-fated line of greeting cards with pop culture acronyms that were much less risqué than a few of the above.

Have you been waiting to solve the mini-mystery of my ill-fated HELOC meeting in Cleveland? HELOC stands for Home Equity Line of Credit. Now we know. Certainly I knew very well the whole name for this debt instrument.

Pause to think about toxicity HELOC grew to represent in a foreclosure-riddled economy. Could this be among the acronyms that should have been repressed in favor of always fully stating the concept, thus making sure borrowers and lenders knew exactly what they were doing with their homes and money?

Perhaps SHELOC (she·lock), for Securitized Home Equity Line of Credit, is quite possibly a better acronym and term for clearer and more ethical truth-in-advertising. The line of credit is securitized by the home. The home itself is the security against default for the securitized loan. The home, therefore, is subject to foreclosure upon the consumer's failure to pay. Before accepting risk, with SHELOC borrowers and lenders might think more analytically and realistically.

Do you remember acronyms that you did not understand? Instantly do you recall not knowing, and when and how you learned? Please pause to list at least a few. You may want to make a list of acronyms you use today, and ask yourself if everyone with whom you use these abbreviations is likely to fully understand their meaning? I suspect there are several HELOCs in your and their daily vocabularies.

TMI? Not all word chapters are as jam-packed. You can unfasten your seat belt during most of the 51 other fast flights to higher views. Yet occasionally oxygen masks may be required. TYVM.

Acronym. Expound.

Acumen

Chapter Inspired by and Dedicated to Eric R. Broughton

Insert or imagine seeing your first name: _____,

Seeing this chapter's title word, what immediately comes to your open mind? Do you already have a working relationship with this word? Somewhere inside of you does this word instantly appeal? As a response to a specific situation at-hand, will this word work to your and others' advantage? For this word to increase in real value, together we must dig, drill and think deeper, so we will reach, climb and soar higher.

Business Acumen. Political Acumen. Financial Acumen.
Intellectual Acumen. Interpersonal Acumen. Leadership Acumen.

Acumen is a noun that puts a name to acquired ability to quickly arrive at good judgments, sound decisions, and right actions. Derived from the 1530s Latin word *acuere*, "to sharpen," today acumen means a strong mind that gets to the point, hence its sharpness, shrewdness, and sometimes its sting. Acumen is acuity and adroitness in thought and action. Acumen is an essential factor in fully responsible leadership. If you make room for it in your busy life, acumen grows.

Acumen breathes life into ideational conversation and project implementation. Yet acumen can amaze and annoy those with less of it than the leader being observed or critiqued. Aspirational and otherwise ascendant people, who are working with leaders with considerable acumen and a track record of results, can choose to respond in awe and strive to learn what they can to accelerate accumulation of their own acumen. Noticeably less secure and emotionally immature observers often choose to be outright disrespectful to those with mastery of wisdom and skills, and may openly and intentionally discount evidence of exemplary acumen. Frequently those threatened by someone's acumen are observed for their myopia and foolishness, and they may not realize how observers will trust them less, promote them fewer times, and otherwise disengage with any person sucking oxygen out of the air with their negativity toward a leader's demonstrated acumen. Acumen needs room to breathe.

A struggling re-emergence economy, teetering venture, threatened household, or even a wobbly one-*with*-one relationship needs steady streams of ever-sharper acumen. Continuously developing levels of business acumen is mandatory for strategic alignment of almost any venture's people, money and other mission-critical resources. From enterprise-wide understanding about how the organization makes its money and achieves profitability, to speaking the same language and heading in the same direction, in these and other ways business acumen is tested for its depth, breadth, and flexibility during constant change. Change is ceaseless. Change must be navigated with acumen.

On a daily basis, do you allow yourself to take note of your and others' escalating levels of acumen? As a fully responsible leader, are you steadily growing more comfortable with your ability to see whole pictures and make comprehensive judgments based on your view? From how high above the fray are you looking? From a hill, I hope. As you survey acumen of those with whom you are working on a project or moving toward a worthy destination, what are you seeing?

> *"If we're going to become the kind of company we talk about in terms of business acumen, we have to have a pipeline of really great business leadership coming through."* —David Murphy

Do you think of yourself as a sharp thinker? Are you intentionally clear and to-the-point in your thoughts, words and deeds? Are you known among peers for your insightfulness? Are you regarded as one who connects life's dots, crosses each project's Ts, and dots each lowercase "i" to ensure high performance — perhaps doing so even before your letters of responsibility are earned or fully formed?

Words count. Your world view is informed by your word view. Fully responsible leaders never stop developing thinking skills and behavioral traits collectively called acumen. Among leaders and their teams, acumen is a robust word for rapt attention and deep focus.

> *"You have to combine instinct with good business acumen. You just can't be creative, and you just can't be analytical."* —Andrea Jung

When hiring new employees, engaging consultants, retaining executive coaches, or choosing friends or life partners, do you allow the word acumen to come to the front of your mind? It must. How does one identify and measure acumen? When I checked indices in several desktop books I keep close at-hand to affirm certain thoughts about HILL Words as they relate to ground-level psychology, philosophy, adjustment, growth, faith, and other disciplines, entries for "acumen" were not to be found. Odd? I think so. Again I discovered a leadership word carefully selected for this book that is not singled out for study by authors for whom I sustain respect. Word-by-word, index-worthy language of fully responsible leadership is unfolding in this book. Feel the book's impact on your acumen. Acumen deserves its rightful place in any index, glossary or mind referring to fully responsible leadership.

"I look for energy, charisma — I look for people who obviously have a level of business savvy and acumen, because this is a show where it's about business."
—Kara Udell

Acumen is Wisdom, Courage and Patience Applied

Through Hillview's High-Impact Leader Lens (HILL) for Viewing Strategic Alignment of People, Money, Technology, and other Mission-Critical Resources (The HILL Model), acumen is discernible when someone takes action in wise, courageous, and patient ways. From your HILL view, do you see yourself surrounded with people of acquired, applied and accumulating acumen?

When Hockey great Wayne Gretzky said, "I skate to where the puck is going to be, not where it has been," did sports reporters and readers call his insightfulness accrued acumen, or did they only perceive a star player's pluck? This quote is validation of the importance of insightfulness through nearly peremptory forethought, here exemplified by studying the accrued mastery of a best-ever player.

Work to use your acumen to "go where the puck is going to be" in your field. Think, act, and stay ahead. Fully responsible leading demands we stay ahead with acumen. Use acumen to invite success.

Anticipating people needs and market wants requires exceptionally fine-tuned and tested acumen. It would be overly simplistic to believe acumen is only derived from diligent academic study and on-the-job lessons. From the shadow side of acumen, many battered children survived abusive households or neighborhoods by learning to anticipate likely behaviors of their abusers, and creating out of thin air distractions or solutions for envisioned problems to come. Perhaps by default many survivors of physical, verbal, and emotional abuse developed acute acumen.

Often I'm asked how I see leadership and strategic matters blocked from others' view. I almost always refer to the "hill view" concept I've used since early years in Renaissance City Pittsburgh. I work hard to mentally rise above it all, not too high; just high enough (*i.e.*, standing on a hill in my mind, but not up on a mountaintop or in an ivory tower), so I can see and react.

Can you feel the value for nurturing your acumen of imagining lifting your fine mind to a hill-level of perspective on life? Can you sense danger to acumen of climbing into rarefied thin air of mountaintops or claustrophobic ivory towers? With a bit of imagery in your mind's eye, surely through creative visualization you see and feel this hill-height point-of-view.

Our toughest younger years can produce early lessons and lasting acumen. This side of acumen is rarely revealed for its truth and value. As an example, when alcoholic and often abusive Dads are late arriving home, and frightened Moms warn kids to "get ready" for likely trouble ahead, fearful anticipation and visualization sharpens senses of all types; mostly preemptive vision.

Often I hear from others how positive I am. I am positive. Acumen comes from each of our unique suites of experiences, strengths, weaknesses, opportunities and threats; personal perceptions and admissions of reality intentionally identified, categorized, prioritized — and dealt with head-on. Failures can teach deeper lessons than success. A lifetime foisted upon us, or chosen by us, that revolved around reversing risk coming our way, often yields exceptional accrued acumen.

As painful as it is for adult me to assess, I know a large percentage of my acquired acumen came from difficult early years. By default, my unsteady years allowed me to stay sharp and ready. Childhood trial-and-error with survival tactics taught me survival strategies and strengths. Strategic alignment of people and things came early in my life. Only in my 50s did I start to publicly claim some mastery of principles and practices of strategic alignment. I continue to align my past, present and future. I will never stop aligning. Trust I will never start whining.

Family, friends, neighbors, and others may recall rather differently experiences that you endured from which acumen developed. Of course they do. They are not you. Only you can express memories of your own feelings. There is wisdom, however, to comparing notes to double-check your memory of precisely the causative factors that led to the feelings and actions you recall. For my early life, maternal Grandmother Shearer was the family historian. Her copious notes in not-too-secret diaries formed a timeline against which I would check memories. She would marvel at how much detail I recalled from exceptionally young ages. What I could not recall she would try to find in her diaries. She would read aloud to me what she wrote, and then sometimes add colorful narrative. Alleged sad circumstances resulting in irreparable nerve damage in my age-four left ear, injury that resulted in 100% neurosensory hearing loss on that side, remain difficult to confirm, contemplate or discuss. With one good ear I coped by listening more intently.

Trust this discussion is not in the least a suggestion that you host for yourself (or me) a pity party. By being up-front I am inviting you to speak similarly openly and candidly — at least with yourself — about what might have happened in early years that brought you to this high, mid- or low point in your unique life's accrued acumen about living. What good, bad, or other pivotal things happened? Do you acknowledge good that came out of bad or any bad from the good?

Somewhat paradoxically, good times remembered may have masked deeper life lessons available for learning. Families who kept-up a front (*i.e.,* a sham) for the kids and neighbors taught the children lessons in smoke-and-mirrors artifice and deception. Some of my friends who inherited great wealth seem particularly low in their acumen, while those who survived poverty, abuse, or other adversity are exceptionally sharp.

There is not only one path to acquiring abundant acumen for your life. Yet I believe it is foolhardy to discount how your life's difficulties may have contributed invaluable fodder for thought that eventually developed into your on-call acumen for on-the-job and full-life success.

"It was all about his business acumen." —Pat Collins

Although the words "business acumen" appear in millions of job descriptions, news releases, annual reports, resumes, and obituary notices, few books or papers are recognized for having adequately defined the term. When I work with clients toward strategic alignment of their business acumen with their personal acumen, the cross-curriculum process is both illuminating and doubly rewarding.

"Business acumen is keenness and quickness in understanding and dealing with a business situation in a manner that is likely to lead to a good outcome."

—Drs. Ray and Greg Reilly

Everywhere we turn there is abundant evidence of insufficient acumen at highest levels of governmental, corporate, organizational, financial, legal, political, educational, spiritual, journalistic, household, relationship, and in other corridors of decision-making. Although I did not list for you a single proper name, for each category you probably already have in-mind at least one inadequate individual. Smoke-and-mirrors often mask low levels of acumen. In each of the above categories it would be productive to pause to list any individuals whose acumen you acknowledge, respect, and may even emulate. Do you include yourself in this A for Acumen A list?

Each of us — as individual leaders and followers — has an extra level of accountability for continuously developing our own acumen. This is a way we will arrive at better and better insights and related choices. Without becoming an insufferable curmudgeon, with age each thinking person must become less willing to accept at face value alleged statements of fact. It is important to apply to what you read, see, hear, and otherwise sense your own acumen for realistic thinking, strategic thinking, big-picture thinking, reflective thinking, and analytical thinking. Think toward steadily increasing your acumen.

Acknowledging need for ongoing self-assessment, you open your eyes, ears, mind and heart to allowing acumen to build and build. Especially for increasing the depth and breadth of your grasp of moral, ethical and intellectual implications related to people and issues you address, be certain you are always employing, deploying and developing acumen. Apply acumen so you and others succeed.

"And wing my words that they may reach the hidden depths of many a heart." —Frances R. Havergal (1872)

Acumen's competence mobilizes this book's Language for Leading. Acumen applied with all 52 featured key words allows leaders to overcome fear of success *and* fear of failure. Acumen unleashes purpose, power and promise in just-right words chosen for impact. Definition, description and delivery of acumen can lift you and others to higher planes for viewing where people and things are moving.

"*We all admire people who display high competence . . .*" —John Gardner

To some leaders calls to put out fires seem to appeal the most. Firefighting has a certain payback some leaders do not find in fire prevention. Acumen is tested during firefighting and fire prevention. Yet misguided leaders who start fires only they can extinguish are of questionable acumen. Fully responsible leaders prevent fires.

"*Critical acumen is exerted in vain to uncover the past; the past cannot be presented; we cannot know what we are not. But one veil hangs over past, present, and future, and it is the province of the historian to find out, not what was, but what is. Where a battle has been fought, you will find nothing but the bones of men and beasts; where a battle is being fought, there are hearts beating.*"

—Henry David Thoreau

Words featured in this book continue to move views, thoughts and actions toward *where the puck is going to be* instead of where "the puck is stuck." On your ice rink are you whacking away at a lot stuck pucks? This book's support for self-coaching allows your words to move you and others to score more goals. Acumen makes it happen.

Pause here to examine your deeper sense of satisfaction with the overall sufficiency of your acumen. Do you have deep comfort with how your acumen allows you to (1) think things through thoroughly, (2) perform at-your-best assigned leadership tasks, and (3) routinely exceed expectations at work, home and everywhere? Considering your accrued-to-date acumen as a touchstone for evaluating your ongoing development as a leader, are you aware of milestones you passed and millstones holding you back? Do you trust your acumen?

Please share with others your thoughts toward their need for intentionality in focusing on their own ever-emerging acumen. Carefully think about and adroitly use and pursue the word. It works.

Thank you for focusing on your and others' ever-increasing acumen.

Acumen. Expound.

Alignment

Chapter Inspired by and Dedicated to Lyman C. Hamilton, Jr.

Insert or imagine seeing your first name: _____,

Seeing this chapter's title word, what immediately comes to your open mind? Do you already have a working relationship with this word? Somewhere inside of you does this word instantly appeal? As a response to a specific situation at-hand, will this word work to your and others' advantage? For this word to increase in real value, together we must dig, drill and think deeper, so we will reach, climb and soar higher.

Here you meet Lyman Critchfield Hamilton, Jr., an all-time grand master of alignment. A few reflections about Lyman are ideal for setting the stage for your success with this chapter's key word. From the mid-1970s LCHjr was among my personal friends — and my No. 1 mentor. I was 26 when we became friends, and I was 30 when we decided to also be business partners. His wonderful all-consuming second marriage, and my untimely and difficult 1990 transfer away from Manhattan to the DC area, caused for us an unintentional and regrettable break in continuity.

Without having in mind a word, framework or context for the composite lesson he was teaching me, since the late 1990s I realize how I learned from Lyman core foundational insight for strategic alignment of people, money, technology, and other mission-critical resources. I am eternally in Lyman's debt for his many lessons and pivotal votes of confidence. Without Lyman's lasting influence in my life, I doubt my company's vision and mission would have emerged.

Alignment plays a central role in Lyman's and my stories. In March 1977 Mr. Hamilton rose to the President and CEO post of the world's largest conglomerate, ITT Corporation, successor to International Telephone and Telegraph Corporation (ITT). ITT was the first client for a New York City-based business I ran for 12 years. My company's success with top *Fortune 500* companies was frequently pegged to this auspicious start with ITT as my No. 1 reference. Indeed ITT put my new business on the world's map.

At its peak, operating in 104 countries with approximately 540,000 employees, arguably ITT was the most technologically advanced corporate entity of its time. As a small yet worthy example, a unit of ITT invented night-vision goggles for military use. Every airport control tower in the world, and every automobile manufactured in any country, contained essential technology and manufactured parts provided by wholly owned subsidiaries of ITT. Telecommunications and postal services of many countries depended on ITT technology and on-the-ground services. ITT was everywhere and in everything.

The so-called Red Telephone between the U.S. President's Oval Office and the Soviet Kremlin was developed by Harris Corporation, yet maintained, under contract to both governments, by ITT. When the CIA turned to ITT for support in a covert overseas mission that went awry, ITT's place in world history became a bit dubious. ITT launched literally thousands of scientific, manufacturing, product and service breakthroughs. It is regrettable that ITT is slipping from memory. Apple and Microsoft readily pop to minds. ITT does not.

In front matter of ITT. The Management of Opportunity by Robert Sobel (1931-1999), published in 1982 by The New York Times Book Company, Inc., Dr. Sobel wrote, *"To John Dallas — whose firm was an unacknowledged co-author of the book. Bob Sobel."* As the Hofstra University New College Professor of Business History, and author of *IBM* and other major works of corporate chronicles, worked to align results of face-to-face interviews of dozens of ITT contributors from around the world, Bob would turn to me to check some of his mostly spot-on conclusions. To help sort through ITT people and detail, Lyman encouraged Bob to rely on my editorial team and me. ITT retained us to support Bob's work. Someone removed my company's name.

Thanks to Lyman, by this point in time I had met almost every key executive interviewed for the book. From cover-to-cover, Bob and I were involved in aligning facts. It was not easy to align ITT history told from different perspectives. Misalignment of ITT memories was common. Frequently Bob and I were amazed by ITT logic and risk we discerned and discussed. By the time the book was released, Lyman had moved on to aligning other initiatives. His successor saw to it that Lyman's starring role in ITT's third phase of emergence would be subordinated on the book's cover and in the major text — almost (not quite) as if Lyman never held the CEO title. He did.

Lyman succeeded. His success noticeably irritated his legendary and powerful predecessor, Harold S. Geneen, who remained Chairman of ITT's Board. Somewhat chilly Mr. Geneen and I enjoyed a cordial acquaintanceship. He earned my respect for his brilliance. For many fair-minded souls, his vindictive act against Lyman wiped clean the slate. Respect was replaced with disappointment. May he rest in peace. If ethical Dr. Sobel were still alive, I suspect now he would regret allowing changes in the book that ITT demanded. If a sequel were published, Dr. Sobel might add a chapter entitled, "Command-and-Control on a Roll."

To protect long-term shareholder value from down cycles of markets that would surely ebb and flow, ITT formed a global safety net that became affectionately known as *International This and That* (the playful description of ITT). To hedge its bets during protracted tech adoption cycles, ITT also owned Sheraton Hotels, Avis Rent-a-Car, C&C Cola, Continental Baking (producing Wonder Bread, Twinkies, and Hostess Ho-Hos), Smithfield Ham, Burpee Seeds, Raggedy Ann and Andy dolls, toys and games, Marquis Publishing (then the true publisher of the real *Who's Who* directories), and numerous other disparate business lines. Imagine leadership, management and communication challenges of aligning 300 or more wholly owned major players in their various fields — and ITT's air force of 126 private aircraft (in 1979) and untold types and numbers of fixed, rolling, and other assets.

Lyman was the right man at the right time to strategically align ITT's many, many moving parts. As Wall Street's favorite master of alignment — whom *Business Week* called a "Hollywood-central-casting perfect CEO" — LCHjr aligned ITT and ITT stock climbed. Following an unthinkable palace coup that remains a case study in boardroom politics at their worst, on 11 July 1979 Lyman resigned.

In its 23 July 1979 issue Time Magazine reported, *"The year's most astonishing management shake-up showed just how little job security there is at the top."* Within three months of Lyman's startling news, my wife and I separated. Two months later I survived a flat-line cardiac arrest. I was 29. My heart, mind and body were hit hard. I never returned home. Accrued wisdom, courage, patience, faith, trust, love, and sense of reality were being tested. I was failing more than passing.

Lyman's loss and pain intensified mine, yet I never revealed to him all that his career catastrophe did to my young life. Deep down I believe he knew. We talked through his confusion. By expressing my personal loss, I did not want to add to his burden. So mostly I kept my own counsel. Nevertheless he and I were strategically aligned.

Without Lyman's alignment skills and sensibilities, eventually Wall Street's top institutional analysts could no longer get their arms (or finite metrics) around such a complex interlocking vision for sustainable value formation. Rather than keep the worldwide strategic alignment of disparate resources dream alive, sadly Lyman's successor dismantled it all; selling-off whatever he could while personally pocketing in the process obscenely large sums. I choose to forget the number of millions he was paid. Not unlike my familiarity with and respect for Mr. Geneen, prior to Lyman's departure I found Lyman's successor Rand Araskog pleasant and bright — and full of surprises.

Harold S. Geneen died two weeks after the company ceased to exist as he and Lyman had built it. Because of the timing of the death, of course Mr. Araskog was questioned, and he assured reporters that "Hal" was in favor of the divestitures. To me it seemed Hal Geneen's life's legacy was pulled out from under his feet, which is precisely what Mr. Geneen did to Lyman Hamilton's place in corporate history. My youngest friends have never heard of Messrs. Geneen, Hamilton or Araskog. Even older friends now struggle and fail to recall very much at all. Character and other lessons are being lost.

ITT PR did as much as could be done to erase Lyman's positive influence, or so it seems to some of us with bias who watched perhaps too closely. Beyond this stage-setting chapter in this book, someday I hope to endow a chair or otherwise honor Lyman for his mastery of strategic alignment of people, money, technology, and other resources. No one "did alignment" better than Lyman.

Not looking back or missing a beat, Lyman went on to head a high-profile leveraged buy-out firm that in 1980 tried and failed to purchase City Investing, itself a miniature ITT-like conglomerate. Later his partners and he made a cash offer for the eventually ill-fated twin towers of the World Trade Center; offering the State of New York $1 billion for both then sparsely occupied buildings. Owners of the buildings declined the reasonable offer, and certainly not because of Lyman's highly valued involvement.

For the hundreds or more first-hand lessons in personal and organizational strategic alignment my all-time hero Lyman allowed me, I dedicate not only this chapter but also all good and other value that Hillview's vision and mission continue to produce.

What Does Strategic Alignment Mean for Your Lifetime's Success?

For the next few minutes we're together with this key word, let the transformative power of thinking about and experiencing strategic alignment speak to every corner of your body and soul, both personally and organizationally. As dramatically overstated as that request may appear to be, you'll find I understated the potential found in a deeper grasp of this word's purpose, power and potential.

"Great things are not done by impulse,
but by a series of things brought together." —Vincent Van Gogh

Alignment is a series of people and things brought together. Through fully responsible leadership, plans, projects, situations, and other circumstances are brought into true-north strategic alignment.

True-north strategic alignment is revealed in the execution of strategy and measurement of results. With true-north strategic alignment as a fully responsible leader's top-of-mind focus, the whole becomes greater than the sum of its parts.

"The task of leadership is to create an alignment of strengths,
making our weaknesses irrelevant." —Peter Drucker

Hillview's true-north strategic alignment is the proper arrangement of the forward-moving force of human, organizational, and other strengths intentionally brought into relationship to and with one another. True-north strategic alignment ("TNSA," verbalized in two syllables pronounced *"tens ə"*) — as Hillview sees, defines, describes, and delivers TNSA — is about forward movement toward a clearly stated worthy destination.

With or without full agreement, a team's individuals are methodically led to follow measurable paths paved with articulated imperatives of many types, and marked with milestones of relevant literacy in nomenclature, verified competency, validated measurement, tested transparency, detailed responsibility, ultimate accountability, and defensible ROI value.

To drive home the importance of TNSA, more TNSA at NASA might have saved the lives of any astronauts who perished due to misalignment of people, money, technology, and other resources.

Acknowledging how change is ceaseless and polarity is omnipresent, TNSA involves vigilance toward potential reward and risk of the dynamic tension of opposing forces pushing against each other.

Not unlike competing tensions of two human arms pushing against each other — called dynamic tension — two competing business priorities, plans, actions, or people are said to be in dynamic tension *with* (*i.e.,* not against) each other. Dynamic tension is a principle exemplified in the managerial measurement concept of the balanced scorecard. Similarly true-north strategic alignment of people, money, technology, and other mission-critical resources must be deeply embedded in teams' implementation plans.

TNSA involves balance of thoughts and actions required for leading people and managing things. Leaders lead people. Managers manage things. Which of the two are you? If you are both a leader and a manager, which function do you prefer? If both are your response, in which are you known to excel? If perfect 50/50 balance of leadership and managing is your response, pause to think and dig a little deeper, so you can reach and climb a lot higher. As with an outward opinion poll, you'll discover internal variance of views with a margin of error of three-to-five percent or more. In decision-making ahead, know your true leadership and managerial strengths, weaknesses, opportunities and threats, and discipline yourself to address these and other required points of clarification.

> *"In matters of style, swim with the current;*
> *in matters of principle, stand like a rock."* —Thomas Jefferson

As leadership style, TNSA is not to be confused with "just another management fad." TNSA is rock-like embodiment of wisdom, courage and patience at-the-ready to be deployed. Nonnegotiable imperatives are vital to understanding true-north strategic alignment. The word imperative and its synonyms have to be hammered home over and over again. Here are 12 prime mission-critical examples (in alphabetical order) of categories of TNSA imperatives:

Brand Imperatives
Cultural Imperatives
Diversity Imperatives
Economic Imperatives
Ethical Imperatives
HR Imperatives
Innovation Imperatives
Legal Imperatives
Performance Imperatives
Personal Imperatives
Political Imperatives
Technology Imperatives

Fully responsible leaders must be able to select any one of the above list and eloquently speak and write toward absolute "must know" qualities in each of these examples of Hillview's concept of Key Alignment Imperatives (KAIs). KAIs are strategically aligned with:

KPI = Key Performance Indicators
KSF = Key Success Factors
ROI = Return On Investment
ROE = Return On Equity
ROA = Return On Assets
ROL = Return On Leadership (Hillview term)
P&L = Profit and Loss

True-north strategic alignment is about forward movement — according to a plan; knowing, understanding, following, meeting, and achieving strategic alignment imperatives related to a set destination or outcome. True-north strategic alignment is intentional creation, ignition, observation, and correction of direction.

To again underscore the point, TNSA is about forward movement. Forward. Movement. These single words are action.

True-north strategic alignment is about envisioning, mapping, initiating, monitoring and sustaining movement toward clearly articulated and worthy win-win-*plus* (a Hillview term) destinations; not necessarily requiring or indicating 100% full agreement. It does, however, require (*i.e.*, mandate) true-north movement.

"Marketplace Value is Ultimately Determined by
Buyers and Never (Ultimately) by Sellers"

"Marketplace Pricing is Ultimately Determined by
Sellers and Never (Ultimately) by Buyers"

Strategic alignment of value and price is essential for sustainable success. Do you think of yourself as being in alignment with your buyers and what they truly value? Do you know what your buyers value about what you sell? Are you sure? Is your organization properly positioned in the marketplace to identify alignment and misalignment with would-be, current, and former buyers? What words would you use to list the top 10 things your buyers value?

On the home front, are you and your spouse or significant other strategically aligned? Are children or other family involved in your sense of alignment or lack thereof? Are toddlers or teenagers top-of-mind as you respond to this question about household alignment? At home and elsewhere, misalignment is both the opposite of alignment and the opposition to alignment. Without too much definition so far, do you already have a sense of alignment as a positive noun?

"Rolling on parallel personal and organizational tracks toward a worthy set destination" is the simple illustration I use to jump-start someone's engagement in the passion and promise of alignment. Alignment is the word to use to test the panoramic all-encompassing view from the hills in your mind's eye. Ask yourself, "Are people, things and I strategically aligned and moving toward success, with or without full agreement of all individuals or other factors involved?" It's about movement.

It is never the right leadership question to ask anyone, "Where do things stand?" Things simply never stand still. Even a project that stops still lives-on in minds alert to applicable lessons from the past. For better or worse, memories about a finished or abandoned project are changing as synapses are firing. Change is ceaseless — as ceaseless as is our need to continually remind ourselves of this fact. Harvard Business School alignment gurus Drs. Robert S. Kaplan and David P. Norton, authors of The Strategy-Focused Organization, The Balanced Scorecard, and Alignment, ask, "Is every part of your organization marching in the strategic direction you've defined?" Alignment.

"That which is to be most desired in America is oneness and not sameness.
Sameness is the worst thing that could happen to people of this country. To make

all people the same would lower their quality, but oneness would raise it."
—Rabbi Stephen S. Wise

During and after a mid-2006 new business presentation to the affable CEO and his less-than-friendly senior managers of a well-known brand-name consumer goods company based in Rochester, New York, for the first time I realized the noun alignment has, for some, environmental toxicity that I had never felt or thought. I was stunned when a mid-50s vice president of the grand old company snapped at me, in front of many executives more senior than he, "I don't like this alignment thing. It sounds to me, John, like you are asking everyone here to get into Gestapo lockstep, and march in Hitler-like conformity. You are suggesting we adopt a concentration-camp culture without leaving any room for individuality or creativity."

His choice of impolitic words sent a chill through me I feel to this moment. He was flat-out wrong. Here I confess I was hurt by his insult to my positive message — and to its positive-minded messenger. Because I was certain my head, heart and words were in practiced alignment, when he concluded they were not, I took it too personally. Perhaps a nanosecond longer than instantly, I yielded to my need to suggest — with a disarming smile — that he must have been dosing-off during my presentation. He did not smile back.

With many years of lessons in platform deportment, especially for when I am under thankfully rare pressure of a heckler or an errant questioner's appearance of disinterest in any response I might offer, I made certain I would not lose my cool. I tried in vain to correct his course with, "Thank you for this wake-up call. No one has ever said Hillview's message was inherently dictatorial, authoritarian, or command-and-control. For all of us, this is a prime example of misalignment in thoughts expressed and words chosen, perhaps by both of us. We are moving in different directions. Your CEO and I met several times before this group meeting, and he pointed us toward the highly likely positive outcome for today's deliberations about TNSA. Yet something I said, or something you thought I said, sent you in a different direction. Let's set this right." It was not to be.

Without a hint at my prior knowledge about this management team's history of resistance to the new CEO's just-in-time vision for changing this company's downward spiral, I posed these questions as a litmus test. I was warned of resentment toward the new boss, yet still I did not expect to encounter such misalignment and bad taste in word choice. Things got worse.

Reversing the PowerPoint slides to one of several with the on-screen message that clearly states "Alignment does not necessarily indicate 100% agreement," I kept an even tone as I said, "Several times I mentioned TNSA is about a team's movement toward an established plan's stated and worthy destination; forward momentum measured by milestones passed and imperatives addressed, but it is not necessarily about 100% agreement. Open disagreement from some team members is expected, respected, and encouraged — especially before the journey begins, and even as a project is underway. Without calling it out for the risk it represents to the favorable end in mind, willful or otherwise intentional movement in a different direction cannot be justified and must not be overlooked.

A fully responsible leader will ask someone who appears to be misaligned what is causing the variance to a set course, just in case there is opportunity for fine-tuning or other correction. If the team leader concludes there is insufficient justification for changing course, the push-back is noted, yet *full-speed ahead* is the only acceptable course of action for the whole team. Team members must move in the same direction, even if one or more disagree with the team captain's direction. This is strategic alignment as Hillview defines and describes it." Uneasily I rested my case.

Mr. Grumpy was not assuaged. He continued to scowl and shake his head sideways. Uncharacteristically I was worn down. To give him a bit more insight about TNSA, I asked if he and I could meet for a few minutes after the meeting adjourned. He agreed. As if heading out for a bathroom break, it appeared he fled the room. I never saw him again.

Before his immaturity was reconfirmed by the above disappearing act of disrespectfulness to his CEO and me, I looked at many of the downcast faces in the room and noted the tense body language. As I continued to field from others less toxic questions, and heard a few words of apology and gratitude, I realized the CEO had on his hands a larger than expected organizational misalignment mess. Thinking back to the CEO's pre-presentation views of his inability to achieve alignment on his own, I realized he was warning me the stage was set for failure. They failed. The CEO failed. I failed. I was very disappointed in them and myself.

The exceptionally competent and otherwise seasoned CEO was embarrassed by his team's resistance to the logic of his and Hillview's TNSA message, and he apologized for their extended myopia. He suggested I meet with his Chief Operating Officer. In a one-on-one private meeting I discovered the COO was the culprit. The COO was covertly encouraging misalignment with the new CEO. He wanted the company to move in a different direction, and others were torn between the CEO and COO. He let this slip, and his face turned beet-red. He tried to back-track. I closed my notebook, set my pen down, pushed my chair back, and declared the meeting over. He was stunned. Then I was surprised when he said, "Are you saying you don't want to work with us? Are you giving up on us that easily?" I was not there to divide and conquer. The CEO had earned my loyalty. The COO was not getting there. I said he and I needed to meet now with the CEO.

With a worried look on his face, the COO went to get the CEO. Too many minutes passed. Sensing I needed to take action, I decided to walk down the hall. I found the two of them in a heated discussion. The CEO spotted me, and he turned and said to me, "John, what is going on here?" It appeared he had been persuaded I was no longer interested in doing business with them. I asked if we three could sit in the CEO's office and talk. The door closed. The air was thick. Gently I tried to explain what had transpired with the COO that required three-way discussion.

The COO denied saying several things I raised from mental notes taken fewer than 30 minutes earlier. He lied when he said I misunderstood him. Even though the detail I offered was hardly borne of misunderstanding, the CEO decided to end the meeting, leave the COO behind, and take me to lunch — which would be our third and final meal together.

CEO was not going to fight his COO, who for 22 years had been a personal friend and business colleague elsewhere. Quite to my surprise the CEO revealed he had been aware of the depth of misalignment. He had hoped the COO and I would bond to help address the push-back felt during the earlier group meeting. If only I had known. Well, bond we did, but not in the way the CEO wished. The COO did not like the solution I represented. He wanted to run the show. I was a threat. I did not trust the COO. He was a liar. The CEO was in error for the way he entrapped me. It was time to move on.

"The shortest and surest way to live with honor in the world
is to be in reality what we would appear to be." —Socrates

After a barely touched lunch, embarrassed CEO drove to the airport crestfallen me. For the short drive I listened as he started to replay the day's history, focusing on the value the majority of his team got from my remarks. He thanked me. Choosing authenticity, I remained silent. Without prompting he reflected back to bygone days when his COO and he were "aligned and moving on parallel tracks." At least I knew the CEO and I were still speaking the same language. Now CEO and COO pals were not aligned, and he declared it was an unspecified personal issue he had to handle himself. I felt doom. Perhaps I gave-up too soon, but I decided he was going to have to ask me to jump in the ring with him. He did not. I did not. We parted ways with warm smiles and firm handshakes. We never again spoke.

> *"He that gives good advice builds with one hand;*
> *he that gives good counsel and example builds with both;*
> *but he that gives good admonition and bad example*
> *builds with one hand and tears down with the other."*

—Francis Bacon

Allow yourself some extra time, please, to immerse yourself in the meaningfulness of alignment, and then extend yourself to embrace the passion, purpose, potential and profit of true-north strategic alignment. Feel the potential in these thoughts and words allied with features, benefits and attributes of true-north strategic alignment:

> Clarity in definitions, descriptions, destinations and deadlines
> Reading from the same page (aligned communication)
> Speaking the same language (aligned communication)
> Seeing each destination as reachable
> Moving forward in true-north direction indicated/mandated
> Shared sense of "we're in this together"
> Knowing "we're in sync" (*i.e.*, aligned) with each other
> Right hand knowing what left hand is doing
> Vigilance toward likelihood of hidden misalignment
> Continuous status validation and refinement
> Updating key people and other resources

With deference to Dr. Steven Covey's *"Begin with the End in Mind"* habit of his Seven, I tell audiences and individuals: *"True-north strategic alignment is means to an end that is always another beginning."*

The word alignment is not a cliché. Perhaps "profit" was once thought of as a buzzword. Profit is a watchword. Alignment is a watchword. Alignment is a call to action. Don't ignore alignment's value. Embrace it. Pursue it. Do it. Alignment reverses risk of misalignment. Align to shine!

In steady life-long pursuit of learning and other success, alignment is a glue word to hold together thoughts and actions. Identification of misalignment is opportunity to cross-check assumptions about true-north strategic alignment. Fully responsible leaders are wide open to possibility that today's symptom of misalignment may be tomorrow's memory of a challenge that clarified views toward better alignment.

Change is ceaseless. And this ceaselessness is the clarion call for your true-north strategic alignment of trusted people and managed things.

Deeply personalize this strategic alignment process. Character, ethics, maturity, emotional intelligence (EQ), intellectual ability (IQ), and your other strengths are tested when you routinely ask yourself these seven self-alignment inventory questions:

1. With **whom** are you frequently out of alignment?
2. With **what** are you often out of alignment?
3. **When** are you most likely to go out of alignment?
4. **Where** do you find yourself out of alignment?
5. **Why** do you allow yourself to go out of alignment?
6. **How** can you correct misalignment you identify?
7. **Does Wow! happen** when you detect strategic alignment?

Those long-ago Journalism 101 classes at Pittsburgh's Duquesne University drilled-in asking alignment questions: "who, what, when, where, why and how?" I added "wow." Indeed "The Wow Factor" adds high-test fuel to our drive to succeed with TNSA.

Presbyterian teachings in orderliness taught eager-to-learn yours truly about thinking and doing things "for the good of the order" — my first encounter with root principles of alignment. Perhaps in pursuit of alignment I failed more than I succeeded. I don't need to be certain of the ratio. I'll not discount any lessons in pursuit of alignment. I am still working to align my authentic self with what's expected of me by fine minds and hearts I respect — people with needs I choose to tend. In the dynamic tension of parts of me pushing against each other, I find self-alignment lessons and value to share. I hope you are reaching-in to the heart of my treasure chest for at least a gem or two. Are you?

Alignment adds depth and breadth to definitions, descriptions and delivery of leadership. Frequently cosmetic and superficial definitions of leadership add unacceptable risk to any organization. Some appointed and elected leaders can't adequately lead their own thoughts, let alone lead people. Illogical thought order trips-up many leaders. A leader out-of-alignment with destinations hits brick walls, rock bottoms, and unemployment lines. Alignment brings clarity.

> *"Words are also actions, and actions are a kind of words."*
> —Ralph Waldo Emerson

Add alignment to your language for leading and you reverse risk. In one-*with*-one Alignment Coaching huddles, MBAs and PhDs often reveal how little they know about history and practice of fully responsible leadership. With a tinge of regret, some admit how their earned degrees qualified them for leadership roles — with or without adequate study or grasp of principles and practices of leadership.

Would you dare to think or say any percentage of the global economic meltdown is attributable to this observation about inadequate lessons about the importance of strategic alignment for fully responsible leadership? With glaring evidence of inadequacy in almost all corners of organizational leadership and accountability, are today's academicians rethinking MBA and other course curricula?

Master of Building Alignment (MBA) would be a more illustrative description for leaders than Master of Business Administration. Building alignment of people, money, technology, and other resources is often what MBAs are really expected to do on-the-job. In today's world, precisely what is business administration? Words for leading people and managing things have lost and gained meaning.

> "How often do the Words lose meaning;
> How seldom are Feelings heard?
>
> We talk, we say, we mean.
> But mostly, we just try to fit in.
>
> It's more difficult for those of us;
> Who would rather 'write down' their feelings.
> They say it's easier to just 'say it out aloud.'

Is it?

I think I've made my choice."

—Kiran

Think, live and breathe intentional alignment of thoughts, words, feelings and actions. I do. Routinely I try to pause long enough to ask myself if my thoughts, words, feelings and actions are clearly aligned for moving in the direction I want and need to be heading. More often they are.

To win wars over inertia, isolation, procrastination, self-centeredness, low self-esteem, myopia, mistrust, addiction, or other counterproductive forces moving against us, the above battle plan is easier read than done. Alignment is armor and weaponry for internal and external conflicts.

Allow your mind to become an echo chamber for each of the words featured in this volume. Hear each word ricochet off of many corners of your mind. With your third ear, listen for each word's value for you and those around you. Listen more hearingly to discern your alignment with each word's purpose, promise and passion. Be ready for clear signals.

When meeting chairs introduce me before I speak to audiences, some say that Alignment is my middle name. I like it.

Strategic alignment for ones wholeness requires deeper thinking toward higher living. There are so many ways to interpret and experience depth and height in bringing to outer life worthy inner thought. Deeply confessing and highly forgiving, I endeavor to think through and align my inner-life and outer-life. At a deeper level I want to know what is really happening with my thoughts, and then be able, thus prepared, to seek and *give* forgiveness at a high velocity (*i.e.*, quickly), and at the highest-possible level of inclusivity. For my peace-of-mind and possible benefit with, for and to others, always I am working with this core definition and on its limitless descriptions.

If I am to be remembered by anyone only as a tireless evangelist for strategic alignment of people and things, I will be satisfied with my legacy. Perhaps so will St. Peter when, at The Pearly Gates, my life's strategic alignment is to be affirmed in its imperfect entirety.

"With best thoughts, words and actions we
align our past, present and future." —JRDjr

Alignment. Expound.

Appreciation

Chapter Inspired by and Dedicated to Pamela Dallas Bardy-Miller

Insert or imagine seeing your first name: _____,

Seeing this chapter's title word, what immediately comes to your open mind? Do you already have a working relationship with this word? Somewhere inside of you does this word instantly appeal? As a response to a specific situation at-hand, will this word work to your and others' advantage? For this word to increase in real value, together we must dig, drill and think deeper, so we will reach, climb and soar higher.

You appreciate me. I appreciate you. These are not brash or egocentric assumptions. Context herein is about our seeing in a new light acts and facts of appreciation. Complex layers of favorable change occur when someone is openly appreciated by someone else.

> *"Appreciation is a wonderful thing. It makes what is excellent in others belong to us as well."* —Voltaire

Let's think about appreciation beyond gratitude; more as an act having economic and societal meaningfulness greater than right-and-proper expression of civil thanks. Appreciation is more than a feeling. Appreciation is what we do to, for, and with each other. In appreciating someone, we make things better than they were a nanosecond earlier.

Lexicographers would probably not mind this additional characterization. Here we are talking about expressing gratitude FOR the sustainable benefit of value appreciation. Good deeds and gifts grow even better by sustained heartfelt expression of thanks. Whether the thoughts or deeds are Divine or human, all good thinking and works deserve to and need to "appreciate in value." Conversely, by our being unappreciative, or under-appreciative by only saying a quick perfunctory "thanks" — and possibly soon actually forgetting the gesture for which we expressed cryptic gratitude — sadly we do damage that devalues each other and the universal need for value to accrue. These are human quality-of-life enrichment aspects of appreciation.

Thanks to appreciated and appreciative friends, I listen to Pandora.com. Pandora and other online providers of content ask on-screen for Thumbs-Up or Thumbs-Down and Like or Dislike expressions of our reaction to what we are hearing or seeing. When on Pandora I choose thumbs-up at the very beginning of a randomly broadcast classical work by geniuses Telemann, Charpentier, Vivaldi, or any of my ten or so other favorite masters, instantly I truly feel more connected to the piece playing. Pause to imagine this impact of appreciation. Can you feel it?

In significant form I gave back something to the experience of enjoying the master's work. I appreciate the work, thus making it better at least for myself. If anyone else is in the room, soon they will learn of my appreciation of the work for which I just cast my yes vote. I might even start conducting the orchestra or humming along. Friends have seen and indulged me as I go under the spell of appreciation for certain classical pieces. Letting them know I am awash with appreciation for the piece, the piece might appreciate in value for them. It happens. I could name many names of appreciative young converts to classical repertoire. Music Appreciation 101.

Quite noticeably I resist myself a tad when I choose thumbs-down. I want to second-guess my reaction. I know I am about to de-value the output of a genius. With a "no vote" Pandora once flashed on-screen "You will never hear this piece again." What if I was distracted or in the wrong mood at the moment to receive the masterpiece in its fullness? That moment, what if I needed an upbeat piece instead of something downbeat and funereal? Indeed, with a "no" I feel I just took away something from the value exchange. Mostly I took away (on Pandora, at least) the prospect of ever discovering I could enjoy that thumbs-down music during a future thumbs-up listening session.

From an Economics 101 point-of-view, in a robust economy our homes, shares in businesses, and other types of hard and soft assets appreciate (*i.e.*, at a steady long-term-investing pace, they continue to grow in market value). Favorable market circumstances must prevail. People selling and buying, at fair rates of exchange, should create sufficient commerce to sustain ongoing appreciation of value.

Especially when economic worries distract us, too few of us do exactly what our faith, society, and economy are crying out for us to do. We must appreciate each other — to make each other stronger, not weaker; build each other up and not tear each other down. People must appreciate. By growing wiser, being more courageous, increasing patience, and otherwise becoming measurably stronger – over the long-haul individuals appreciate in ways not wholly dissimilar to shares of Berkshire Hathaway Inc. Especially in a struggling correction economy, individually We the People must appreciate before expecting our monetary assets to appreciate. This is not the time for organizations to cut budgets for continuing education and other leadership development (*i.e.*, human appreciation). In eras of mandatory cost reduction, such myopia adds even more risk to profit-and-loss imbalance.

Businesses that under-appreciate customers, or their own employees, will find themselves with fewer buyers or none. When I hear of a business faltering or closing, I can't help but wonder if they invested more in ensuring shareholder value (*i.e.*, making dollars stronger) than they invested in appreciating their own people (*i.e.*, making people stronger). People first. Money second. Any correction economy will be defined, described, and challenged by strategic re-alignment of people, money, technology, and other mission-critical resources. Organizations are people. People first. People first. People first. Respecting and appreciating people creates for organizations ever-increasing marketplace value. Ethical tenets and economic logic are sound.

"Encouraged people achieve the best; dominated people achieve second-best; neglected people achieve the least." —Anonymous

Do self-styled manly men have trouble saying "thank you" and mean it? Does saying thanks take something away from such men; their sense of independence, superiority or masculinity? A client in his late 30s chokes when he says thank you to another man, but lavishes on women his expressions of gratitude. Yet with men to whom he thinks himself superior, he is quick to treat them the same way he treats women. I watch in awe at the obviousness of it all. I am yet unable to reach him to suggest a correction of course. I have faith he will come to his senses.

Throughout my career I marvel at a few good men to whom I give meals, bottles of fine spirits, and holiday gifts from some best stores, and a perfunctory spoken "thanks" is the extent of their expression. I don't exactly need the thank you notes few send, but I am aware how an opportunity is lost to appreciate the situation and each other. When I see a tie, cuff links, shirt, or book I gave, once in awhile I wonder if the new owner even recalls from whom the gifts were given. New appreciation *for* appreciation would cure this imbalance.

Each year happily I contribute hundreds of *pro bono* hours of unpaid professional consulting, coaching, and strategic support to organizations and friends with needs I can address — giving acts and intellectual property for which I am normally paid to earn my living. Often the value of what I offer is discounted by a lack of sustained appreciation. Even when I can easily see the recipients personally financially and otherwise benefit from what I freely offered, acts of sustained appreciation are too few and far between. I feel the loss. They suffer loss they don't know about. Only occasionally I speak up.

In the mid-1980s, a good friend's new husband desperately needed highest-level contacts to achieve an ambitious U.S. real estate investment objective for Japanese investors he represented. Giving thought to his formidable challenge, over a tasty lunch I hosted in one of Manhattan's name restaurants, I introduced wife and husband to a top CEO I knew well. Erroneously I thought the meeting did not work at all. There were few smiles at table. I saw no chemistry between the oil-and-water men. To the wife I expressed my regret. No one seemed "to appreciate."

Eight years of silence later, I heard from the wife the two of the unappreciative men went on and purchased and sold together $3 billion (billion with a "b") worth of depressed hotel properties, restored them, and the properties thrived — including one of my favorite resort hotels we talked about during the luncheon. The husband and wife became millionaires, living on 125 acres, in a historic mansion, in elite Northern Virginia horse country. Amazing.

Before deciding she needed to be married to a man instead of her church, the now-gentrified wife had been a Catholic nun committed to vows of poverty. The Hollywood-worthy irony was almost too great to bear. Yet to me it was never funny. Not once did the financier gentlemen, or former-nun wife, thank me for the life-changing introduction, let alone tell me they had formed a business and succeeded beyond their wildest imaginations. The CEO to whom I introduced the couple also kept silent. All along I thought he was blaming me for introducing him to a man he flat-out did not like. This CEO was cut-and-dry about such things. I failed to inquire.

Almost a decade later I learned the bold CEO at least loved the big money the finance man brought from Japan. Nothing in this interim added up to any conclusion I cared to consider. I choose to avoid jumping to black-and-white conclusions about someone's greed or appearance of rank dishonesty. Indeed still I could be wrong. In this case study of appreciation, it all could have been honest oversight. Seasoned deal-making friends suspect intentionality. As a believer, I place such judgment in a higher court. Sure, I feel pangs of regret.

They and I missed opportunities to add even more appreciation to their success. I am certain I would have continued to support them. Character flaws were now so painfully apparent, I chose to sever ties with all parties involved. One of my attorneys suggested a more aggressive response, but I did not introduce the two in order to earn a finder's fee, so I stayed true to my sense of right and wrong. They, however, were quite wrong to deprive us all of appreciation. On a friendship-affirming basis, I would have welcomed a thank you note, and maybe a celebratory lunch at the Manhattan table where I started the ball rolling for them. They kept the ball rolling — toward wealth, yet far away from the ethical behavior of appreciation, as defined herein. I would have continued to appreciate emerging relationships.

When Dr. Peter Koestenbaum had a 2008 audience with the Dali Lama, the security guard ushering him announced he had read two or more of Peter's books about leadership. To me, humble and brilliant Peter seemed more thrilled with the security guard's expression of appreciation for Peter's philosophic work, than perhaps he was with the lofty conversation with the highly revered spiritual leader. Someday I may confirm this observation. Its mere possibility keeps me grounded regarding my focus on Peter's teachings about servant leadership, people-first perspective, and genuine hubris-free humility.

From our first day meeting, I remain thrilled to be able to share and collaborate with Peter. With the quick and natural bond we formed, soon we became fast friends and thinking partners. One year or so later Peter accepted my request to serve as Honorary Chairman of Hillview. I count Peter Koestenbaum among my most cherished friends and colleagues. More than a mentor, Peter is a human measure of true excellence against which I strive to evaluate the depth of my thoughts and breadth of my deeds. Humbly I share Peter's and my conclusion that we appreciate each other in the value-building ways expressed above. This is an example of appreciation at its best. Forever I remain grateful. Peter and I continue to appreciate.

As you and your teams work toward myriad economic solutions, genuinely and authentically appreciate people first, dollars second. On the inside and outside of your organization, who can you demonstrably appreciate today, and in what ways? Where and with whom could you start with a word of heart-felt gratitude?

> *"Gratitude is not only the greatest of virtues,*
> *but the parent of all others."* —Cicero

For the want of a word, are you appreciative? Are you appreciating?

Do you intentionally appreciate (*i.e.*, make better) others? How?

Do you agree it is the right and proper thing for us to acknowledge upside potential in this broader definition of the word "appreciation?" Apostasy, in a religious context, denotes the phenomenon of flouting or abandoning constraining religious views or practices. With lexical apostasy we can flout or abandon simplistic views and uses of such resplendent words that almost beg for their inner light to be released. Appreciation requires and deserves more of us. Let's aim toward higher thinking and use of this electrifying word.

From Through the Looking Glass, by Lewis Carroll:

> "When I use a word," Humpty Dumpty said in rather a scornful tone, "it means just what I choose it to mean — neither more nor less."

> "The question is," said Alice, "whether you can make words mean so many different things."

> "The question is," said Humpty Dumpty, "which is to be master — that's all."

With intentional acts of appreciation, individually and collectively we continue to grow in value. Choose appreciation over depreciation.

Choose to appreciate. I choose to appreciate you. In-the-moment and retrospectively, let us continue to appreciate each other. Please.

Appreciation. Expound.

Ascendancy

Chapter Inspired by and Dedicated to Dr. Dennis Deer

Insert or imagine seeing your first name: _____,

Seeing this chapter's title word, what immediately comes to your open mind? Do you already have a working relationship with this word? Somewhere inside of you does this word instantly appeal? As a response to a specific situation at-hand, will this word work to your and others' advantage? For this word to increase in real value, together we must dig, drill and think deeper, so we will reach, climb and soar higher.

In minds and lives of fully responsible leaders, words applied can take on more meaning and value than any dictionary or thesaurus could capture or represent. Descriptions of words are infinite. Ascendancy and its allies are "HILL Words" that can take us up far beyond definitions: influence, power, control, rule, authority, command, reign, sovereignty, sway, dominance, domination, superiority, supremacy, mastery, dominion, upper hand, prevalence, pre-eminence, predominance…

> *"My words fly up, my thoughts remain below:*
> *Words without thoughts never to heaven go."*
> —William Shakespeare

How comfortable are you with these crystal-clear characterizations of roles, functionality, accountability, impact and measurability of fully responsible leadership? Do such bold words make something inside of you soar or cringe; empower you or devour you? Are you more or less at-ease with knowing your mastery of principles and practices of ascendancy can make or break your career as a leader? Do you feel the promise or peril of your never-ending rise to greater levels of ascendancy in your leadership sensibilities and skills?

When you pause to reflect, can you feel deep down how a fractured or sputtering economy, any unformed or threatened organizational culture, a shaken or otherwise unstable family unit, or an expectable newly exposed set of inner doubts require your full-throttle ascendancy as a leader? Can you possibly imagine sitting back on your heels and waiting for everyone else (or anyone else) to rise to the challenges before you or within you?

Ascendancy is about your and my rising to challenges just-in-time and all the time; under pressure being fit and able to fight fires and always working to prevent them. At times ascendancy may require you to be over-bearing. Sometimes others need from their humble leaders an extra pull forward or a push backward. It takes ascendancy.

Continents, countries, states, regions, counties, cities, neighborhoods, and homes can be viewed for obvious and obscured signs of leader ascendancy or lack thereof. If consumer or investor confidence is low, or societal anxiety and crime are high, astute ascendancy of leaders may be lacking. So boldly we address with this one word — ascendancy — mission-critical need for more acute intentionality in thoughts and deeds of all fully responsible persons in charge of teams at work and home.

Leaders of organizations and/or households must increase their mastery of ascendancy, without forgetting their accountability to their Creator and fellow human beings counting on win-win wisdom, courage, patience, humility, and other acquired expertise. Before touching possibly raw nerves about ascendancy in your organizational life, and later taking a quick look back at ascendancy gone badly in earlier centuries and cultures, let's start with ascendancy in your personal life as a leader of women, men and children. Yes, everyone is watching today's corps of fully responsible leaders. Even other fully responsible leaders are struggling to identify best practices in others' ascendancy.

How socially bold are you? Have e-mail, webcasts, Twitter or Facebook increased or decreased your social boldness? Are you more or less inclined to speak by mobile or land-line telephones, or do you mostly exchange digital text messages with your friends and others? Do you or someone you know hide behind the protective shield of social networking technology? Do you know anyone who abuses the ease with which they can arrest your attention online, only to then waste your time with their ego-driven drivel? Does anyone inflict on you their "web rage" as if protected in a vehicle during bouts of road rage; effectively taunting or screaming at you from safe cyber-miles away?

Should you try to measure or guess how well you are doing in balancing your interpersonal communication? Do you see people face-to-face more than you did 18 months ago? When was the last time you hand-wrote a letter or thank you note? Do you still send *via* snail mail any holiday cards? Are you entertaining in your home more or less frequently, and are you receiving invitations to others' residences at the same pace as two years ago; more or less? How many thoughtful gifts are you buying or receiving *vs.* quick-and-easy gift cards or gift certificates?

Are you one to say hello to neighbors in office or home building elevators or on the street? On highways do you wave a thank you to someone who allowed you to pass or enter? When boarding or leaving a plane, train, bus or boat, do you first greet and later thank those into whose hands you place your life's safety and creature comforts? Are you likely to thank an attendant who handles your cash at a freeway or bridge toll booth? How many times each day do you meaningfully say please, thank you, pardon me, excuse me, or with any words wish someone else an equivalent of health or happiness?

At parties do you almost immediately find a place to sit and "hold court" (*i.e.*, appearing to expect people to come to you), or do you stay standing to circulate to mingle and stimulate conversation and energy? Do you attend events in homes or meeting halls thinking you are the center of attention; waiting to be entertained? Or do you seize opportunities you pitch-in and illuminate and energize the room? Do you smile easily or frown nervously? Is your "look" open and welcoming, or are your arms crossed and closed? Do you breathe oxygen into the room or suck it out? Do you listen? Do you arrive empty-handed, or do you always honor your host with at least a token hospitality gift (*e.g.*, wine, candy, flowers, fruit, *etc.*)? Are you known as a positive influence in social settings, or do you sense people inviting you because of obligation instead of opportunity?

If someone you know tells you she or he is launching a new venture, do you immediately congratulate her or him for obvious courage, intently listen to the plan, then see what you can do to proactively support the quest with introductions, information, investments, time, ideas, or other votes of confidence? Do you have a sense of how your words and acts of encouragement for an entrepreneur may benefit all through job creation, increased purchasing, tax payments, and other value formation? Are you more likely than not to dominate conversation for purposes of self-aggrandizement, or do you intermittently take an interim dominant stance in order to encourage others to pitch-in — collaboratively exchanging with others the control of air space and mind share? Are you socially bold *for the good of the order*, or are you controlling others for your own sense of dominance or hidden insecurity?

Such tough-love questions of this type about ascendancy, from a caring consultant and coach, come from my decades of trial-and-error; lessons learned the hard way. As both an astute observer and contributor to abundant life, I offer the following brief personal glimpse of my early and later grasp of ascendancy. A different "hill" was going to open my eyes wider.

When in late May 1973 a letter arrived in Pittsburgh from Hill & Knowlton's New York headquarters offering me a full Account Executive post with the then first and foremost public relations firm, former wife Cynthia and I were in Williamsburg, Virginia for our wedding trip. I did not see the letter until too late. Mr. Vern Boxell, Senior Vice President of Hill & Knowlton, was rather miffed I had not responded within the week the offer letter allowed. He forgot I told him I was being married and would not return until a certain date. Barely apologetic, he said he had to give the post to the first runner-up of the eight candidates for the job, but he had wanted it to be me. Crushed, of course I asked if he would help find me a post elsewhere in Hill & Knowlton, and he said he'd do what he could. He didn't. Oddly I sensed his unfounded disappointment in me. Perhaps he was simply mirroring my regret.

Goodness knows I was deeply disappointed. I was shooting for the stars and missing by miles. At the same time as this was happening with Hill and Knowlton, I was hedging my career bets with an often promised White House Deputy Press Secretary GS-13 government job that never materialized. I misjudged subtle political exigencies of this desirable appointment. Everything I sought suddenly seemed beyond my reach. Immaturity left me feeling responsible for all factors over which I actually had no control whatsoever. I was 23. With perspective of many years and tears, eventually I saw more of what was happening around me, in me, and through me. Ascendancy played bit parts and big roles.

Fortunately I thought to ask for access to the results from a full day of testing and other examination by Hill & Knowlton's retained psychologist. It appeared he must have reported I passed muster. Within days Mr. Boxell sent me the written results. In a footlocker of mementos from that era, I still have the file. Among many findings, graphical markings on the Guilford-Zimmerman Temperament Survey chart showed me as "ascendant." At that moment I did not feel particularly dominant or any of the other words I found in Webster's, so I needed to know from a pro what all this meant. I asked Hill & Knowlton for permission to speak with the psychologist. I called the good doctor and found a rather warm and chatty professional eager to share his views regarding my strengths. I was both pleased and sad; thrilled to hear how strongly he had recommended me for the high-paying Account Executive post, and very depressed I had missed this perhaps once-in-a-lifetime opportunity (*i.e.,* skipping over the entry-level stages of Junior Account Executive or lower positions).

"Social boldness" is how the good doctor generally explained the significance of my ascendancy. He said I could be counted on to move forward when others would hold back. I connected equally well with males and females. Each dot on the graph showed me in-range for a long life as a successful leader. I was expected to blaze new trails. I was not to be held back. I had a gift for getting ahead against odds. I was not to be denied. I was solid. Wow! With all this good news, why did I feel so, so bad? Later I figured out most of it. Shame was lurking.

Along with rather different presidents Franklin D. Roosevelt and Richard Nixon, the psychologist told me I "scored" E.N.T.J. on the Meyers-Briggs survey he administered. The "E" for Extroversion fit with my ascendancy. He said I relate to others more by extroversion ("E") than introversion. I take in information more intuitively ("N") than only by sensing. I think ("T") more so than I feel. And I judge ("J") more readily than I perceive. I saw hints of weakness in some of what he so glibly told me, and humbly I said so. I was assured time and experience would allow me to see things more clearly. Frankly, I took little comfort in his adroit handling of my angst about losing the Hill & Knowlton job offer. To see where I would land, he wanted to keep in touch with me. Sadly I didn't keep open those clear lines of communication.

After a few more days of licking my wounds, all this upbeat characterization of my suitability for the Hill & Knowlton job eventually served to lift more than my spirits. I learned the hard way the importance to executive success of "keeping up, staying up, being up," and otherwise ascending — *onward and upward!* Even when things for me went down, down, down, the lessons of Hill & Knowlton lifted me back up. I felt unstoppable. I was, however, stopped many times. In retrospect, I was not ready for the responsibility Hill & Knowlton was offering me. I was still too wet behind the ears. Now I am nearly certain I would have failed miserably.

Another job offer in Manhattan was much less appealing than Hill & Knowlton, but I grabbed it anyway. I had to. For many reasons my new wife and I felt very desperate. (I'll spare you the negative impact on our first months of marriage.) I had so much to prove to Mrs. Dallas, in-laws, parents, pals, others and myself. As it happens, I went from the frying pan into the fire.

The six months I survived as a 24-year-old manager of the new consulting division of a trademark licensing business, serving the electric utility industry, knocked me to the ground. Over radical differences of views about ethics regarding public communication related to nuclear energy, and appropriate ways to link the company trademark with 1976 Bicentennial celebrations of 1776, the CEO of that company and I went to the mat. I was beaten to a pulp. My then negligible negotiating skills allowed the Ivy League debate society champion CEO to pulverize me. I lost. Eventually I realized that my views were correct, and I admitted my ego's intransigence was wrong.

From the nasty defeat I confirmed what not to do with the public trust. The debacle opened my eyes to related investor-relations ethics and information-flow challenges on Wall Street. With ascendancy I launched National Business Intelligence Corporation (NBI), the electronic publishing venture I started in 1974, ran for 12 years, and sold in 1986 to a Wall Street firm. NBI clients would include over half of the Top 50 *Fortune 500* companies, and other topmost leaders in almost every major field and industry. Learning high risks and great rewards of my ascendancy, I grew grateful for my early trials.

Perhaps under two years after launching NBI, No. 1 ad agency J. Walter Thompson (JWT) bought Hill and Knowlton. A JWT senior vice president tracked me down in Manhattan. For some reason the HR vice president showed him my Hill and Knowlton file, and he wondered what could have happened that kept me from joining the team. There were breakfasts, lunches, drinks, dinners, and other meetings geared toward trying to get me to change jobs to join his

JWT team, but this time I said no. Rightly or not, I was sure of my calling to lead NBI to new heights. I was not going to stop now. More than a tad of youthful arrogance bubbled-up in my ascendancy.

Five years or so later, one morning JWT's former HR vice president was driving the New York taxi I hailed to get me to LaGuardia. You read that correctly. You may need to read it again. I remember his full name, yet with genuine respect for the gentleman I keep it to myself. He recognized me. I watched him read the luggage tag on the case I placed in his front passenger seat. I recognized him, and confirmed his block-lettered name and clear photo on the taxi operator's license on display. He was so distracted by his embarrassment and perhaps correctly assuming my shock, suddenly we were lost in Queens. He profusely apologized. I suspect we both had teary eyes. I was going to miss my flight. He was a wreck. I was a wreck. Nothing was right.

For weeks I was shaken by seeing this once ascendant man behind the wheel of a yellow cab. *"But for the grace of God . . ."* Imagine the drama. We never spoke again. I called a JWT pal to see what had happened to the former HR VP, and a respectful code of silence was maintained. I regret not finding a good way to reach out to the driver.

Manhattan years were fraught with economic and other challenges. I grew grateful for memory of lessons learned from missing marks and trying again and again. "Being ahead of your time is the same as being wrong" was a lesson I hated learning. As an early adopter of state-of-the-art technology, often I was doomed to spend more money than I could recoup in short order. Having at NBI five early-version PCs (Vydecs built by a subsidiary of Exxon Enterprises) — each priced at $17,000+ in 1975 dollars — my co-workers and I had to struggle extra hard to make our business profitable. To overcome our exorbitant overhead and incurable seasonality of demand for our services required of me unprecedented ascendancy.

During this 1970s era, several overlapping business and personal relationships, with similarly ascendant self-styled *masters of the universe*, shook my confidence in the legitimacy of my ascendancy. At great cost to my development as an adult and as a small business owner, throughout my 20s I was secretly and constantly second-guessing myself. For the better part of a full decade, I was being pushed from all directions. With a wobbly inside sense of my 20s-something self, I doubted my core professional abilities while feigning mastery of it all.

In the late 90s Chicago Title and Trust's retained psychologist, Dr. Luis Baez, reported attributes of ascendancy similar to 1973's pre-screening findings. As I read what Luis wrote to support my candidacy for CEO of Chicago Title Credit, it was *déjà vu*. After 26 years on the front line, it appeared overall I was still ascendant. Certainly I had learned ascendancy is a mixed blessing. Battle scars earned by then, and since Chicago Title days, seem to underscore the essential nature of ascendancy. Ascendancy is exhilarating and exhausting. Ascendancy is empowering and occasionally disabling. Ascendancy includes polarity. Leaders must understand ascendancy.

A month or so after joining Chicago Title, often avuncular Chairman John Rau called me to his office. He had in his hands Dr. Baez's report of my pre-employment psychological screening. John had been Dean of Indiana University's Business School and CEO of LaSalle Bank. So I had more than a tinge of nervousness about what was to come. Fortunately I had a signed contract. With a warm smile on his face he said something like, "You really are a CEO. I just read again what Luis Baez wrote about you, and it's clear you have what it takes to run this business." He seemed to have doubted my history. In-the-moment his affirmation felt like a near-miss with an 18-wheeler. I was not seeing, hearing, thinking of feeling his intentions.

With as much nonchalance as I could feign, I asked why I would have been hired as a CEO if there were any questions about my managerial or leadership abilities. John Rau said "they" thought I was a rainmaker; a super salesman who made big things happen, and so he was ready to have others back me up with strategic and administrative details. As a money-making catalyst I deserved to be CEO, he seemed to say, but perhaps originally I was not really expected to run the show.

This was unwelcome news to me. I was running my show. The Chairman seemed to be pleased. I was conflicted by these mixed signals, but decided against pushing the conversation any further. "It's your baby, John," were his parting words for that meeting. I did not like the feelings I was allowing myself. I was down. I stayed down for quite a long while. Working my way back up proved beneficial.

As I pieced together what would have prompted such a discussion with our chairman, I realized I was not seeing things from a position of internal strength. I felt weak and unsteady on my feet, hardly ascendant.

Surprisingly I had difficulty recovering from that conversation. It felt as if had been hit in the gut by a medicine ball. Mr. Rau did not throw the ball. At age 50 I allowed specific insecurities from my 20s, 30s and 40s to muddle my thinking. It is wise to be introspective, yet I went too far down before I started to climb back up. I allowed self-doubt to nearly cancel out his genuine compliments and supreme vote-of-confidence.

In 2005 Hillview was named to underscore the importance of both good attitude and altitude — being up on a hill to view what's moving below. Ascendancy became a key word in Hillview's High-Impact Leader Lens (HILL) Model for Viewing Strategic Alignment of People, Money, and other Mission-Critical Resources (The HILL Model). The view from a hill is "A Vantage Point to Your Advantage," I concluded. It took awhile to translate these thoughts into trademarks, yet eventually I got there. I was working to think deeper so clients and I could climb higher.

"And remember, no matter where you go, there you are." —Confucius

Today is the day for you and me to make or reaffirm an ascendant choice to avoid seeing things from a flat plain, a lofty mountaintop, or a stale ivory tower. It's wise to choose a panoramic hill view.

Clients and others agree. To clearly see views from positions of strength our minds' hills, all Hillview clients and I take the Gallup Organization's StrengthsFinder 2.0 survey. My five themes for strengths: Activator, Futuristic, Input, Strategic and Achiever. Do you know your five themes of strength from *StrengthsFinder 2.0* (strengthsfinder.com)?

As with any leadership topic, there's a shadow side to ascendancy when practiced only for the sake of ascendancy (*i.e.,* an egocentric leader's desire/need for unbridled dominance over others). From early church school lessons, I recalled how during the 17th, 18th, and 19th centuries (for 300+ years), the Protestant Ascendancy — simply called by Irish-Catholics "the Ascendancy" — collectively characterized perceived and factual political, social, and economic domination by a statistical minority of large landowners, mainline clergy, and learned professionals; all members of the Church of Ireland and Church of England, both being the state churches or the Established Church.

The Ascendancy excluded from all matters of significance Roman Catholics, the clear majority of the Irish population. Yet well into the

1800s, Presbyterians and other Protestant denominations, along with Jews and various non-Christians, were also excluded politically and socially (*i.e.*, treated as if Irish-Catholics). On further inspection, the majority of Protestants were also effectively excluded from the Ascendancy; similarly thought too impoverished and uneducated to cast valid votes. For good reason Irish Catholics and other sects resented and fought the Ascendancy. Presbyterians rarely mention this period of oppression in Ireland. Recalling this dramatic example of tyranny helps leaders keep in-view risks of exclusionary thinking.

In The HILL Model ascendancy is eminently equitable; across-the-board intentionality in full function and fairness. A fully responsible leader is ascendant for right, ethical and moral reasons. Setting the vision and pace for teams is excellent ascendancy in-motion. Do you identify with today's worldwide clarion call for ascendancy?

"Be not careless in deeds, nor confused in words, nor rambling in thought."
—Marcus Aurelius

Intentionally applying ascendancy to your thoughts and actions could catapult you and your accomplishments far beyond your wildest dreams. Imagine in ascendancy yet untapped promise toward success.

"Be bold and greater powers will come to your aid." —Sir Anthony Hopkins

For fully responsible leaders, intentional ascendancy must become and remain a careful, clear, direct, and otherwise intentional way of thinking, leading and living. Ascendancy is a leading way-of-life.

"People who make no mistakes lack boldness and the spirit of adventure. They are the brakes on the wheels of progress." —Dale Turner

Is it too bold of me to outright implore you to rise above temptation to avoid risk that accompanies ascendancy? You expect it of me.

You already know and feel that I am called to lift others and myself to higher ground. Do you think and feel similar purpose for your life?

From hills in our minds we can see ascendancy in movement of people beside and around us. Honoring, emulating and celebrating boldness, we come to this very point in time. As we wrap-up this chapter, let's rev-up our senses to see, hear and feel divine providence drawing us toward ascendancy instead of complacency.

Ascendancy. Expound.

Aspiration

Chapter Inspired by and Dedicated to
Andrew R. McGaan, Esq. and Son Duncan McGaan

Insert or imagine seeing your first name: _____,

Seeing this chapter's title word, what immediately comes to your open mind? Do you already have a working relationship with this word? Somewhere inside of you does this word instantly appeal? As a response to a specific situation at-hand, will this word work to your and others' advantage? For this word to increase in real value, together we must dig, drill and think deeper, so we will reach, climb and soar higher.

"There is no greatness without a passion to be great, whether it's the aspiration of an athlete or an artist, a scientist, a parent, or a businessperson."
—Anthony Robbins

Winning a pro tournament, U.S. Mayor Rudy's son Andrew Giuliani aspires to be a permanent fixture on the pro golf tour. Great Shakespearean player Sir Ian (*Gandalf*) McKellen aspires to be revered for his mastery of a wide range of dramatic roles, but he is comfortable being remembered mostly for *Gandalf's* association with *The Fellowship of the Ring*. Saved and transformed Scott Stapp aspires to regain trust and fame he and his *Creed* band mates once enjoyed. *American Idol* heartthrob Adam Lambert aspires to prove an openly gay man can stay on the top of the music charts of both women and men of any and all persuasions and orientations. Paul Ruben aspires to shake the weight of his Pee-Wee sins of his past and again rise in Hollywood. These are just a handful of vignettes about aspiration in one edition of *Details Magazine*. Aspirations sell copies! Aspirations are very personal and sometimes hot topics for these public people. For you, others and me, aspirations are intensely personal.

Are you aware how often you are reading, thinking, talking and writing about others' strong desire to accomplish great things through acceptance of high calling or by overcoming inner struggle to make the most of their lives? Surely you find compelling most positive stories of aspiration. Is your sense of your own aspirations intensified when you read about aspirational journeys of others? Had you thought this way about your reading interests or habits?

Details is a light-weight, thus easily digestible, magazine about serious, silly, and other types of aspiration. Because its writers focus on quick-take snapshots of aspiration, I subscribe, and fairly regularly I read it. Nearly all publications are journals of aspiration. Subscriptions and newsstand sales of wealth-touting, venture-sprouting, and fitness-spouting magazines are based on reader aspirations to achieve goals that few can or will. From the globe's many holy books to even more abundant self-help guides, and other works of fiction and non-fiction, we need an overabundance of aspiration-inspiring publications from which to choose to glean new insight and other fresh perspective. This book aims to be among your frequently visited resources — if only to scan the Table of Contents for your empowering words.

Pause and think about *above-the-fold* news or feature stories that ignite in you desire to aspire to dig a little deeper so you can reach a lot higher. What words in those stories lift you to new levels of thought and feeling? Do *rags-to-riches* stories do it for you? Journeys from entitlement to enlightenment? How about case studies of corporate turnaround situations? So-called overnight success stories after lifetimes of trial-and-error? Lottery winners? Cancer survivors? Daring rescue stories? Political success? Stories about coming-out from secret lives or other restrictive cocoons? Physical or mental rehabilitation against odds? Near misses? Near-death experiences? Second chances? Lasting-love stories? Second marriages? Stories of atonement? What stories arouse deep in you exceptional feelings of interest or enthusiasm that fuel your aspirational determination to always reach higher for more stars?

Reading *Fast Company, Wired, Inc., The Wall Street Journal, The Economist, Chief Executive, Business Week, Vanity Fair* and *The New Yorker*, I thrive on stories about aspiration. *Black Enterprise* focuses my attention on uphill battles being won by aspirant African-American entrepreneurs eager for a level playing field. Remarkable Adobe Air technology behind "Times Reader," the new online paid subscription service for

The New York Times, allows me to swiftly scan myriad stories and photos revealed by aspirants or investigative reporters; the good, bad, ugly, and uncategorized aspirations true journalists uncover — with or without cooperation of persons whose aspirant journeys they chronicle. DVDs of ABC's mysteriously cancelled TV hit *Brothers and Sisters* features a fictional full-course menu of admirable and not-so-admirable aspirations. Women and men relate to Sally Field's award-winning portrayal of the mother's aspirations for her struggling children, her widowed-self, and those less fortunate than they. Stories of aspiration allow me to breathe easier about pursuing my own high aspirations. I love knowing I am not alone in wanting to figure out ways to achieve bigger and better things. I'm trying. If I don't find stories of aspiration, thankfully somehow they find me.

"Persist. Persist. Persist." —Sir Winston Churchill

If asked "to what do you aspire," how quickly could you thoughtfully and honestly answer? What would you say you are doing today that nothing will keep you from accomplishing? How strong is your will to succeed? What are you so determined to do that you'll continue to refuse to let anyone or anything prevent you? What are your cherished desires you might also call aspirations? Where and in whom are you investing your energy and other resources? Are you enthusiastically and ambitiously pursuing one or more aspirations? Are you directly supporting others in their pursuit of aspirations? How are things going? By the end of this chapter, I believe things will be better.

Quick-Take Exercise in Aspiration Projection

For the next few moments, please immerse your mind in this fast-pace strengths-building thinking exercise about projecting supportive rationale for aspiration. You'll be glad you did. Even though you may not have the following names in the front of your mind, or necessarily care much about all the people or fields covered in this punch list, monitor how often you surprise yourself with how quickly you can project likely top-of-mind aspirations for names and matters in this roster. As instantaneously as possible, what word or words immediately come to mind to finish the following sentences? Try not to over-think or struggle at all with any of these. For a few public and private situations below, there are life-and-death types of responses that may come to your alert and empathic mind:

President Barack Obama aspires to... Former President George W. Bush aspires to... U.K. Prime Minister David Cameron aspires to... Former U.K. Prime Minister Tony Blair aspires to... North Korea's Paramount Leader "Young General" Kim Jong-Un aspires to... Iran's sixth President Mahmoud Ahmadinejad aspires to... Iraqi President Jalal Talabani aspires to... Afghanistan's President Hamid Karzai aspires to... Secretary of State Hillary Rodham Clinton aspires to... Defense Secretary Leon Penetta aspires to... Twice former Defense Secretary Donald Rumsfeld in-retirement now aspires to...

JPMorgan Chase & Co. Chairman and Chief Executive James Dimon aspires to... Microsoft's former CEO Bill Gates aspires to... Apple's CEO Tim Cook, successor to Steve Jobs, aspires to... Warren Buffett aspires to...

Football legend Brett Favre aspires to... New York Yankee pitcher Alex Rodriguez aspires to... Atlanta Falcons' Matt Ryan aspires to... Oprah Winfrey Aspires to... Barbara Walters aspires to... Martha Stuart aspires to...

My boss aspires to... My employer's Mission Statement (*i.e.*, Aspiration Statement?) requires my associates and me to aspire to... My direct reports aspire to...

My spouse/significant other/daughter/son aspires to... My best friend aspires to... The homeless person on the street aspires to... And last yet certainly not least, I aspire to...

How many times did you smile, frown, grimace, snicker, laugh, or scratch your head? Or how many times did you say to yourself "I'm guessing _____," or "Who knows/cares?" Did your level of engagement with this brief exercise underscore insights about your relationship with aspiration? How important to you are aspirations of others and yourself? How seriously did you take this exercise? Did you fully embrace this brief excursion into the might, majesty and mystery of aspiration? Success depends on our altitude, attitude and approach to aspiration — ours and others'. To see how easy it is to discover stories of aspirations of any of the public figures listed above, you may benefit from easy online research *via* Google, Bing, or other search engine.

Aspiration as a word is also defined as the act of breathing, especially breathing in. Breathe-in, hold-in, and exhale thoughts of aspirations of others and yourself. Feel how aspiration fills the body, mind and spirit with excitement and hopefulness. Does this imagined respiratory thinking about aspiration support you as you think more deeply about your own aspiration, and do you care more deeply about dreams and aspirations of others? Climbing to hill heights about aspiration allows fully responsible leaders to breathe-in, hold-in, and then slowly exhale the rarefied air of wisdom, courage and patience. Your life's hills are more alive with clear views of aspiration.

Aspiring to Move from "Wall Street Greed to Main Street Great"

Aspiring to move minds and matter from Greed-to-Great during these taxing days of Wall Street's long-overdue re-engineering, and Main Street's struggle to identify and somehow capitalize on stealth-mode Federal and other stimuli, we need to think and work a lot harder and better before we can breathe at least a little easier. Especially after the near-miss global economic meltdown, and as we nurture the new order of our interdependent *re-emergence economy*, we need to know and support each other's worthy aspirations. By stating and pursuing more selfless than selfish aspirations, we can oxygenate what I pray will become, by 2020 or earlier, a strategically aligned worldwide *collaborative economy*. In their macroeconomics calculations and expansive deliberations, G-20 leaders seem to aspire to a new world economic order.

Let's each remember to breathe oxygen into each room we enter. (You'll note whose egos seem to suck oxygen out of each room.) State your aspirations with carefully chosen words, open body language, genuine smiles, and responsible clarity about upside commercial and societal potential in your aspiring mind's eye. To move from "Wall Street Greed to Main Street Great" in the U.S. economy, we must accept in our vast numbers our strengths, weaknesses, opportunities and threats (S.W.O.T.), and reorient our thinking away from solely selfish or outdated entitlement pursuits. From entrepreneurial or *intrapreneurial* job creation to value generation, celebrate each economic milestone you reach. Doomsday thinking and sorry attitudes of lifeblood-sucking self-styled victims, wallowing in circumstances instead of working toward aspirations, remain parts of the problem.

Sole economic dependency on aspirations of others can be viewed as collective or individual approach-avoidance toward socioeconomic opportunity, individual responsibility, and ultimately discounting any degree of personal accountability for the common good. We all need to aspire higher so we can breathe easier. Even when you'll be gasping out-of-breath following a marathon run toward your goals, each intake of oxygen will fill you in new and deeper ways; getting you ready for your next start-to-finish race.

Is "aspiration" a word that lifts you to new heights in your thinking? It should. It must. Allow this word to lift you. Aspiration is gift-wrapped in your thoughts about faith, hope, positive thinking, prayer, contemplation, experimentation, innovation, revitalization, renaissance, renewal and reward. Please use "aspiration" in speaking with those other trusting souls also counting on your fully responsible leadership. Ask about their aspirations, and let other people know relevant win-win aspirations you are pursuing.

Is it time to re-name organizational and personal Mission Statements? Are they more aptly called "Aspiration Statements?" Breathe-in, hold, and slowly exhale.

Strategically Aligning Social Networking and Social Entrepreneurship

Let's find more ways to use social networking technology — LinkedIn, Facebook, MySpace, Twitter, FourSquare, blogs, e-mail blasts, text messaging, mobile telephones, cloud computing, as well as iPhone and other smart phone apps, *etc.* — to support monetization and profitability of so-called social entrepreneurship. Survival of millions depends on our strategically aligning commercial aspirations with responsible altruism. Kiva.org is the first online peer-to-peer microlending website to which small businesses can turn when banks turn them away. Public-interest sites dedicated to generating grass-roots financial support include change.org, globalgiving.com, and chipin.com. And spot.us enables the public to commission journalists to do investigations and reporting on perhaps overlooked stories.

Costs of both commerce and compassion are to be viewed as long-term and wise investment in our Earth's sustainable future. Dividends will be measured in both Return-on-Investment (ROI) and Return-on-Leadership (ROL); aligned metrics of both money and non-monetary meaningfulness to our planet's people. It's an abundant new world full of interlocking aspirations of many races, religions, and other converging diversity.

> *"For me, commerce is of trivial import; love, faith, truth of character, the aspiration of man, these are sacred; nor can I detach one duty, like you, from all other duties, and concentrate my forces mechanically on the payment of moneys."*
> —Ralph Waldo Emerson

Even from afar, experiencing someone else's almost palpable determination to soar above it all to achieve a worthy ambition lifts us — if we allow ourselves to be moved from the place we were a nanosecond earlier. As the final drafts of this book were being edited, an eagle-eyed corps of carefully selected online readers reported back how their focus on single words allowed them to aspire to new heights with enhanced insight and new ideas. Such a lofty goal is a driving higher purpose of this book; allowing readers and author to intentionally use selected words as stepping stones to climb to a hill-level — but not up to mountaintops or ivory towers.

From the summer of 2011, too many U.K. images of catastrophic misalignment in aspirations are etched in mind. Some commentators said London has not seen such physical devastation since World War II. Devastation of human aspirations is where greatest damage is done.

With these words U.K. Prime Minister David Cameron attempts to reverse increasing risk in cultural misalignment, "The sight of those young people running down streets, smashing windows, taking property, looting, laughing as they go, the problem of that is a complete lack of responsibility, a lack of proper parenting, a lack of proper upbringing, a lack of proper ethics, a lack of proper morals." Toward what are leaders encouraging you to aspire?

Aspirations must run deep in our souls. Aspiring to leadership roles is admirable, yet globally respect for leaders, organizations and governments is rumbling, tumbling and crumbling.

Respect is earned more so than granted or conferred. Two 2011 U.K. royal weddings reminded all of us about societal imbalance in any type of monarchy — in London, Wall Street, or Hollywood. As news cameras were focused on the weddings' grandeur and wealth, I heard from a close British friend how — blocks away in both U.K. cities — homeless subjects (*vs.* citizens) were seen openly urinating on trash-littered shopping streets. Such sad, disgusting, and yet real sights come to mind as civil disobedience, and misalignment of aspirations.

It is foolhardy to think such things cannot happen again on U.S. soil. Leaders in D.C. and all state capital cities must see in London's all-too-frequent combustibility a laboratory experiment in social order gone wrong. As decades-old U.S. entitlement programs are unwound, and personal accountability is returned to top spots in political rhetoric, risk of civil disobedience and copycat crime is quite real for all 50 of the United States.

Strategically aligning people, money technology, and other mission-critical resources requires framework within which new order can form for higher thoughts and actions. Learning deeper definitions and descriptions of the language of leadership facilitates deeper thoughts. Hillview clients are ready for more depth, upon which higher awareness and achievement can be based.

Hillview's Polaris Principle™ for True-North Strategic Alignment™ allows clients to "Dig, drill and think deeper so we will reach, climb and soar higher." This is not only a Hillview motto; it is a six-phase psychoeconomic mandate for the world's survival.

Earliest Dreams and other Aspirations

As a child, what were your earliest dreams and other aspirations? Count how many childhood aspirations you can remember. On a blank sheet of paper, perhaps you'll want to sketch a time line to show when your aspirations changed (if they changed). After your earliest creative visualization of your future, did you envision being a spouse, parent, doctor, lawyer, professor, pastor, teacher, TV anchor, or President of the United States? Rather seriously I considered each of these options, and I can't recall having any other career aspirations.

Various key adults in my life pressed me hard for each of these aspirations, including several seriously encouraging me to run for The

White House. I remain grateful for their voices in my head and those votes of confidence. Regretfully I had so little accrued self-confidence to pursue related opportunities eventually handed to me on silver and plastic platters. I had no macho-man need to be a firefighter, policeman, or sports star. I remain grateful to those who decide to pursue such careers. I march to a different drummer.

From the good Lord above I sensed I was being led in different directions, but I did not always like what I was sensing. I was far too unsure of myself. My career's trajectory reflects too many misfires and misinterpretations, mostly born of a misguided sense of low self-esteem and inadequate self-confidence. Instead of capitalizing on my strengths, now I know I was mostly busy overcoming my right and wrong sense of my weaknesses. This was misalignment in my early aspirations for which I am still paying a price. Truly I am trusting that this whole life of mine is greater than the sum of its disparate aspirant parts.

> *"Add energy, inspire hope, and blow the coals into a useful flame..."*
> —Ralph Waldo Emerson

What do you do to protect your memory of early and evolving aspirations? Do you keep a journal? Allow yourself time for reflection on your true past. Then mostly for relevance to today, work harder to align past, present and future aspirations. Do you see, honor and celebrate milestones and detours along the way? I did and do.

Sharing accounts with each other of our respective simple or complex aspirational journeys has an empowering effect on everyone who cares enough to stop, look and listen with a third ear to what's being revealed. As a very young child I aspired to teach. It was and remains in my blood. I feel it coursing through my veins. Still I regret not pursuing degrees in education. There's still time, I hear. Teachers in their 60s and beyond are teaching and facilitating pursuit of deeper wisdom beneath the higher knowledge they impart.

As my family's adults believed *children should be seen and not heard*, for the most part I kept safely to myself in my room. I lived the 1960s Beachboys song, *In My Room*. Around seven-to-nine years of age, my bedroom was frequently set-up as a mock classroom, with a few old folding chairs I found somewhere, bulletin and chalk boards Grandmother Shearer bought, and a makeshift teacher's desk. I taught imaginary students — using well-hugged teddy bears as stand-ins — English lessons I had learned from first, second and third grade teachers: Mrs. Grogan (brown hair), Mrs. Cain (white hair), Mrs. Larkin (red hair). Yes, 50+ years later I can still see and hear them. Their unbridled word-lover lexical enthusiasm flowed into me.

At perceived risk I began correcting and educating my parents, sisters, and anyone within earshot who would listen to my simple understanding of right and wrong ways to use what I believed to be the King's English. Although hardly a lettered lexicographer, I was transfixed by the power of words. Still I yearn to be better at adroitly using words instead of unknowingly abusing any. I'm getting there. While trying to avoid errors I will always make mistakes. Deceased hero William Safire lamented, yet begrudgingly accepted, the likelihood of his occasional error. I heard his team of eager proofreaders had very little work. Editors and proofreaders for this book remained quite busy. I am grateful for their heeded and unheeded views about right *vs.* wrong.

> *"It takes a certain level of aspiration before one can take advantage of opportunities that are clearly offered."* —Michael Harrington

From age six and before I turned 13, adults in various church, school, and senior-citizen audiences around Steel City, who would listen to my traveling and uncompensated boy soprano soloist voice working hard, wanted me to pursue a career and life in music. Too confidently I told all I was either going to be a minister or an English teacher. For sure I knew God wanted me to be one or the other or both. Far too sure of myself, too often I would say so. I hope it was more amusing than irritating to hear this kid pretend he knew what he was talking about. Of course I knew the high singing voice would change. Perhaps I was hedging my bets.

At age 13 almost instantly I became a baritone. The voice never cracked, it just changed. More than my voice changed. The first year of my teenage life became very adult-like. The day after my older sister was married I endured an emergency appendectomy — aggressively performed on my small abdomen by the Pittsburgh Steelers' overzealous-with-that-scalpel but well-meaning and life-saving surgeon. A close call. Late that year I became a doting uncle to precious niece No. 1, now cherished Mrs. Michelle Bardy Platt. Somehow I knew my life had changed forever. Many things were happening around me I could not understand. Often I pretended I did. I was not exactly displeased with my sudden pseudo-maturity. Far too early I was duty-bound and career-focused. A playful childhood and carefree teen years were not to be.

Very early I had environmentally inflicted self doubts — and a fifty-percent deafness hearing handicap — that kept me thinking about a much brighter adult future. Things had to get better. Before I knew to pursue wisdom, I learned courage and patience. Faith grew. Thoughts about adulthood allowed me to transport myself up and away from my childhood's inadequacies.

In my pre-teens, almost every night I would wrap myself in a blanket cocoon and pretend it was a shiny silver rocket ship. After racing through The Lord's Prayer and Now I Lay Me..., as I fell asleep I would try to fly off to some other land. When mornings came, often I was a pretty unhappy little kid. I did not want to get out of my protective rocket ship. For a short night's sleep, I had escaped stultifying reality, and suddenly I was back at ground zero. Then around my bed I would see symbols of my aspirations to teach, preach and reach. By focusing on evidence of a world beyond my walls, I would try to talk myself into a better mood. I knew to block out what was just outside my bedroom and my household's front door, and almost always I could and would.

Now I believe I lived in a constructive world of aspiration more so than a constrictive and deceptive realm of protective fantasy. To do otherwise would have further depressed, repressed, and otherwise depleted me. Even today in my sleeping quarters I keep in-view a dozen or so upbeat symbols of my aspirations to lift my morning spirits, especially Henry David Thoreau's *"Go confidently in the direction of your dreams! Live the live you imagined."* I will. I do.

In '68 Teachers Aspired to "68"

In 1968 I graduated Baldwin High School. Earlier in that arguably most difficult year in U.S. history, there was a first-ever local teacher unionization movement based on a thinly veiled campaign slogan, "68 in 68." With a degree of embarrassment but noteworthy resolve, aspirant teachers were asking in 1968 for a starting salary of $6,800 instead of $5,400; "68 in 68." Yes, it was appalling they had to beg. In top-ranked middle-class Baldwin-Whitehall school district of suburban Pittsburgh, newly minted teachers wanted at least $567 *per* month to start.

Genuinely I was shocked and disappointed our teachers were making so little. By unwise adults, I was told teachers worked short days and had whole summers off from work, so they should be grateful for their adequate pay. I tuned-out peers and adults who said such rubbish to me.

To this day I remain alert to disparity in a professional's pay earned weighed against value produced and enjoyed by others. Around the same time as 1968's teachers were demanding marketplace fairness, I learned pastors of even the richest churches were also making rather little in stated salary, although good homes, clothes, education, food, books and cars were provided by their congregations.

Being from cash flow-challenged family, I knew I needed to aspire to some financial security. So hearing how little teachers were valued in low dollar-terms, I started leaning more toward a career in slightly more promising church ministry. I planned to somehow teach English from any pulpit to which I might be called. Fortunately for the Presbyterian congregations I never served, they were spared my youthful preoccupation with dangling participles, faulty parallelism, split infinitives, improper use of contractions, and other esoterica I was trying to master.

In junior high school I eyed Houghton College for my Presbyterian education ahead. Then I would be off to study at Pittsburgh Theological Seminary. Somewhat paradoxically, in 1968 I chose Duquesne University, a Catholic school run by Holy Ghost Fathers (now called Holy Spirit Fathers). As discussed elsewhere in this book, by this pivotal time Junior Achievement had helped me decide on a high-earning business career in the public relations side of mass communications. I was assured I could be both a workplace pastor, of sorts, and also a teacher by-example. Far too simplistically I visualized these images of extra value I would bring to my work.

In 1968 Duquesne had Pittsburgh's best journalism department, and so Duquesne was just right for me, at least according to Donald M. Deer (1932-2009), President of the Pittsburgh Chapter of the Public Relations Society of America (PRSA). Don was a grown-up friend and mentor. He was the award-winning Senior Vice President of

Public Relations for Westinghouse Air Brake Company (WABCO). I listened to Don. I followed Don. No regrets. Well, maybe a few.

At age 20 I was the youngest-ever recipient of PRSA's highly coveted "Golden Quill Award for Public Relations Excellence." Without my knowledge, Don submitted my overflowing string book of press clippings for clients of my student-run publicity service. That was mentorship at its best. With all these scrubbed memories of early success, I have nagging regrets from which I hope to someday shake myself free. I did not know what I was doing, yet I was doing it.

From 1967 until 1973 Don Deer was my No. 1 role model in the PR business. Not too secretly I was in awe of him. I aspired to grow up to look, sound, dress, and lead as he did. He was a star. Hollywood central casting would have chosen him as an ideal corporate leader. Everyone loved him, including his CEO. Four decades later, I'm still unsure if he noticed how I learned so much from him. I did not exactly become his clone, yet I certainly mimicked many of his behaviors. Together occasionally we would shop at Brooks Brothers.

In 2009 he died before this book would commemorate his contribution to my career. Don encouraged me to aspire to great things. He was quick to paint pictures of promise for me in New York City. Although he enthusiastically sponsored me to become the youngest-ever (age 21) full member of The Pittsburgh Press Club, Donald Deer was the first adult I recall suggesting I look beyond Pittsburgh to fulfill my career potential. Of course I did.

Manhattan was my aspiration. Simply because of geographic proximity after leaving Pittsburgh for New York, time with Mr. Deer was replaced with the blessing of getting to know ITT's highly admired Lyman C. Hamilton, Jr. Although I missed my times with Donald Deer, I transferred my awe-inspiring allegiance from Don to Lyman, who became my mentor and friend from 1976 to 1990 — until I was obliged to move to the DC area. Both gentlemen seemed willing to teach me — and somehow learn something from me. Today this is called reverse-mentoring. They each thanked me for the smallest lessons I offered. Certainly I frequently thanked them for opening my eyes, ears, mind and heart. My gratitude is eternal for these two specific gentlemen, and also for a short list of other masters of meaningful mentoring — and *reverse mentoring*.

"Mentoring is a brain to pick, an ear to listen,
and a push in the right direction." —John C. Crosby

Each time I am asked how I compare Chicago with NYC, I don't. I can't. I wouldn't. I won't. I really love both great cities. Others I know who lived in both places see nothing substantive (or safe) to observe that deserves compare-and-contrast focus or discussion. In ways that matter to me, they are radically different cities. And I've never been a fan of comparing any major cities. If, however, I am asked to compare what it is like *to live* in Chicago compared to living in Manhattan, truthfully I can talk about why I love living in Chicago, and yet would still thrive in The Big Apple. I want and need both.

Aspirant leaders know perils and promise of thinking outside the box. As we aspire under fire of trial-and-error, we must remember providence is always with us. God called by any name allows us to temper (*i.e.,* strengthen) the steel of our resolve to succeed in and with our aspirations. We articulate dreams and ambitions in order to engage others in true-north journeys toward desirable destinations.

Attributed to Johann Wolfgang von Goethe, German dramatist, novelist, poet and scientist, this call-to-action drives my aspirations:

"Until one is committed, there is hesitancy, the chance to draw back, always ineffectiveness. Concerning all acts of initiative and creation, there is one elementary truth the ignorance of which kills countless ideas and splendid plans:

That the moment one definitely commits oneself, then Providence moves too.

All sorts of things occur to help one that would never otherwise have occurred. A whole stream of events issues from the decision, raising in ones favor all manner of unforeseen incidents and meetings and material assistance, which no man could have dreamed would have come his way.

Whatever you can do, or dream you can do, begin it. Boldness has genius, power, and magic in it.

Begin it now."

Openly I'm self-identified as one who will probably never retire. Unless my brain fails and I can no longer assimilate, calculate and redact data for substantive discussion or publication, I will work.

If people or circumstances have squashed your aspirations, do the above reflections embolden you to think differently about your responsibility to continue to aspire and not retire? Think positively. Dig, drill and think your way up to reaching, climbing and standing on higher ground.

> *"A noble man compares and estimates himself by an idea which is higher than himself; and a mean man, by one lower than himself. The one produces aspiration; the other ambition, which is the way in which a vulgar man aspires."*

—Marcus Aurelius

Not unlike a core message in the chapter for Acumen, Aspiration mobilizes this book's Language for Leading. Aspiration applied with these 52 words allows leaders to overcome fear of success and fear of failure. Aspiration unleashes — in very personal ways — purpose, power and promise in words. Definition, description and delivery of aspiration will lift you and others to higher planes for viewing where people and things are moving.

> *"Words form the thread on which we string our experiences."*

—Aldous Huxley

Imagine how your first breath inspired your mother, and also enriched those blessed to be witness to your aspirational nature. From cradle-to-grave, oxygenating your own robust, promising and rewarding life means also breathing new life into the minds and hearts of other aspirants whose sense of purpose you deftly touch.

Allow your and others' education, inspiration and innovation to inform your aspiration. It is essential, however, to never ever allow finite accomplishments, measurements or views to limit your aspirations. Aspire to always dig, drill and think deeper so you will reach climb and soar higher. Breathe-in deep breaths of aspiration.

If even one word in this book ignites in you deeper, wider or higher aspiration to enhance the quality of your life and the lives of those you influence, I will be grateful and further emboldened to reach higher in all work I am called to do. Let's continue to aspire higher.

Thank you for breathing into my life your responsiveness to my highest aspiration for these words. We need to have a word. Aspire.

Aspiration. Expound.

Assertiveness

Chapter Inspired by and Dedicated to Terri Winfree, Ph.D.

Insert or imagine seeing your first name: _____,

Seeing this chapter's title word, what immediately comes to your open mind? Do you already have a working relationship with this word? Somewhere inside of you does this word instantly appeal? As a response to a specific situation at-hand, will this word work to your and others' advantage? For this word to increase in real value, together we must dig, drill and think deeper, so we will reach, climb and soar higher.

> *"Whatever you can do or dream you can, begin it.*
> *Boldness has genius, power and magic in it.*
> *Begin it now."* —Johann Wolfgang von Goethe

Boldly I dare to say today there is less Goethe-like boldness among leaders than I have witnessed in my more than four decades of one-with-one closeness to senior executives of organizations of all types and sizes; from CEOs with accountability for global empires with more full-time employees than my hometown Pittsburgh has in total residents, to sole practitioners, country pastors, and subject matter experts struggling on their own to consult, coach, speak, and write books aimed toward win-win outcomes. This is one man's view, but it is a clear view from a man who has shaken hands and spent thinking-out-loud time with hundreds or more top-most leaders. The long list of leaders from whom I learn much is distinguished by its variety and lasting impressions. Elsewhere you read vignettes of my blessings of first-hand insight and direct lessons from small-town mayors to CEOs of global conglomerates. I know what I think I know, and I know what I don't know, and yet I know I have much more to learn about both categories of accrued-to-date knowledge and wisdom to come.

Peril of Fear of Litigation, Castigation and Humiliation

Fear of litigation, castigation and humiliation has silenced too many CEOs and other team leaders. To my experienced third ear for listening more hearingly, their collective silence is deafening. Where are the bold voices of today's business leaders? How many top CEO names readily come to mind, and can you discuss virtue or vice of vision they articulate? Perhaps fearing ridicule, or wanting above all else to be seen as scholars who need not speak up and out in order to be heard, a precious few leaders I know rather well barely speak above a whisper. In public forums they rarely speak boldly. Even some of their investors or sponsors, board members, and staff marvel that the individuals hold high posts, without an apparent sense of need for a constant bold, clear, and selfless ascendant voice.

In consulting and executive coaching roles, I am paid to plow fertile client brains to plant and fertilize seeds for fresh thinking. I may ask leaders if they are demonstrating with timidity their humility. Do you? Timidity and humility are not identical or fraternal twins. In the ideational development process toward essential innovation, for too long too many leaders keep to themselves their own ideas. Possibly believing a perilously superficial interpretation of "leaders should listen," they yield to populist psychobabble heard on talk shows and read in business books. Highly rated TV shows and bestsellers are appealing to the maximum number of viewers and buyers of books.

There is possibility a leader's silence is an indication of a paucity — instead of a plethora — of ideas. Even leaders without many ideas of their own must show their hand. For strategically jump-starting others to be assertive with their thoughts and actions, leaders often miss their accountability for mandatory focus, clarity and boldness.

"An idea is salvation by imagination." —Frank Lloyd Wright

There is nothing timid in architectural pioneer Wright's assertion. Many of his ideas became realities during his lifetime. When news editors and we believe the boldest and most newsworthy leadership voices come only from Washington, D.C., state capitals, county boards, city halls, and court benches at all levels of the judiciary, truly I greatly worry we are further shaking the already dangerously compromised foundation of the American Free-Enterprise Way-of-Life. Our imperfect but best-available free-market capitalist system requires bold voices of business leaders. I believe our foundation needs to be shored-up and strengthened in many ways. Philosophic and economic mortar must be made of the molten steel of resolve. Led by trusted business and other organizational leaders, We the People must stand on our own and boldly say, "This, with the help of God, we have done. This is what it means to be an American."

More precisely we need to demonstrate how leaders and followers, of the second decade of the third millennium, did not sit back on our derrières and wait for newly printed U.S. dollars to flow from the nation's political capital city. Economic capital cities New York, Los Angeles, Chicago, San Francisco, Boston, Hartford, Dallas, and other former bastions and bulwarks of entrepreneurial boldness must be released and emboldened to collectively think and dig a little deeper while reaching and climbing a lot higher — without fear of failure.

This is not the time in our society's trajectory, in the arch of world history, for us to yield our individual rights of entrepreneurial and wage-earning independence. In stealth-like political exchange for more healthcare coverage, greener lifestyles, less interference with private acts in bedrooms, and overdue freedom-for-all rights of marriage vows, we appear to be temporarily handing over only to politicians the responsibility for boldly defining, describing and funding our dreams.

Casting votes is not to be the same as casting lots. We are not playing a lottery with our economic future. Indeed economic and personal freedoms must be pursued, pronounced and protected, and violations thereof must be prosecuted to the full extent of the letter and spirit of law and common sense. Heaven's higher authority, rewards, and punishments are to be considered, of course, yet we cannot let spiritual assumption and ecclesiastic mystery muddle our internal messages about the natural order of self-reliance, self-agency, and self-actualization; inherent autonomy *vs.* subjugation in heteronomy.

Arriving in 1999 to work and live in the Midwest, quickly I concluded certain (not all) career politicians here are empowered, by a questionable voting apparatus, to be excessively bold and brash in their public words and deeds. If none of "it" eventually rings true or ultimately valuable, elected officials — who were never expected to tell the complete truth or deliver all the goods — are more or less instantly forgiven. I'm told "it happens" (without the "s" or the "h"). Even when some words and actions are legally actionable as violations of law, trust, and common decency, voters turn the other cheek. Lower cheeks of some politicians need to be addressed by wooden paddles of old-time schoolmarms, and their upper facial cheeks need to washed out with 99.44% pure Ivory Soap. I'm told there are web sites that count politicians' lies told and votes cast because of them. Fact-checkers are kept busy. Infrequently I pause to investigate online accusations of fraud. Instead I search for truth.

While some (not all) politicians count on immediate or protracted forgiveness, public company CEOs fear a perceived wrong word or action will send their company's stock price downward. In such thinking about their own potential financial and other losses, they are paralyzed into inaction. Increasing stock ownership during a CEO's tour of duty may have more negative effects than meet the eye. Once I proposed CEO compensation be tied to their whole industry's success or the Gross Domestic Product (GDP), thus forcing everyone to pay attention to everyone else, cooperate, collaborate, and otherwise compete for the strength of all. Visions of casualties within "survival of the fittest" theory stopped many conversations about this seedling of an assertive idea.

There is an Ear-Piercing Clarion Call for Assertiveness

Indeed this chapter is about the noun **as·ser·tive·ness**. It was important to get here against the above stage-setting backdrop. In fully responsible leadership assertiveness includes, but is not limited to, The HILL Model's Top 10 Assertiveness Markers: (1) intentionally and confidently starting, changing, or ending conversations, (2) proactively sharing with others genuine feelings, views and experiences, (3) making requests; sometimes asking outright for favors, (4) expressing both positive and negative emotions, (5) decisively addressing head-on bothersome people, problems and things, (6) being firm to ensure your and others' rights are respected and protected, (7) challenging traditions or rules that do not appear to be fair or make sense, (8) refusing to conform to arbitrary societal standards, (9) respecting and protecting human and organizational boundaries, and (10) pursuing a lifetime of accruing more wisdom, courage and patience. There are many other HILL examples of assertiveness. These illustrations lay sufficient foundation for the remainder of this jam-packed chapter.

By your peers are you regarded as assertive? Do you think of yourself as assertive? Do you surround yourself with assertive individuals? Or are you thought more aggressive than you may be assertive? Do you surround yourself with in-your-face types of aggressive individuals? Dare I ask if ever you were or are called passive-aggressive? Were you, are you? Are you aware of passive-aggressive people around you? Studying in-depth each of these psychoanalytic terms far exceeds intentions of this book. Online resources will give you more than you may want to know. A Google or Bing search will fill your hopper.

On an imaginary assertiveness scale of one-to-six, with six being "highly assertive" and one being "rarely if ever assertive," where would you put yourself? Where would you rank your boss, a direct report, your significant other or spouse?

For fully responsible leaders, assertiveness is distinguished from aggression and passivity in our communication, strategy, style, and in other thoughts and deeds. Just-in-time I learned considered boundaries are demarcations between and among thoughts, people and actions. Trusted advisor Mike Russell insisted I learn. Aggressiveness is disrespectful of boundaries. Assertiveness acknowledges and respects boundaries. Yet sometimes assertiveness is used to try to expand respected boundaries of others.

Assertiveness allows us to envision a brighter tomorrow in which we all play a more proactive role in addressing strengths, weaknesses, opportunities and threats. Passive sorts of people expect assertive individuals to carry their weight. With the Federal government promising safety nets and bail-outs, the societal burden of dependency and passivity grows heavier and heavier. Is your back hurting? Mine is.

By default, conscious or subconscious desire, passive people are more likely to allow aggressors to manipulate them in bad ways — calling for me to devise a differentiating made-up term I coined many years ago, *"malnipulation."* Mal- is a combining form indicating bad implication of the word it precedes (*e.g.,* malfunction, maladroit, malodorous, *etc.*). The clever little term did not catch-on anywhere but in my mind. Still it works for me as I watch how some assertive people positively manipulate others for win-win outcomes, while aggressive types negatively *malnipulate* to their own advantage unwitting people and pliable circumstances. For questionable, self-aggrandizing, and other less-than-worthy purposes born of self-absorption and other misguided motivators, *malnipulators* are regrettable aggressors.

Until my mid-40s in almost all ways I was just too darn aggressive in my thoughts and actions. Mostly I was assertive, but aggression reared its ugly head when more assertiveness would have achieved the at-risk goal I had top-of-mind. I had little patience with certain types of unengaged personality types and disengaged brains. To offset my over-the-top aggressiveness, I did not know I needed in-depth assertiveness *vs.* aggressiveness training. Aggressiveness topples careers of many leaders. For my aggressiveness I paid a steep price.

Sadly, certain valued colleagues and employees feared my sometimes ruthless aggressiveness, in particular a Vice President of Sales I eventually aggressively kicked out the door. Years earlier during a Cape May off-site weekend retreat for my senior team, in a private setting my associate said to my face that I was the most macho-aggressive man he had ever met. *Macho? Me?* Although said with a smile and with personal-space-invasive locker-room pats on my back I still recall too well, I sensed he did not mean this characterization as any type of compliment whatsoever. When he saw my bewildered or maybe hurt face, the bold fellow said, "That's a compliment, JD!" I did not think so. I was stunned. I listened. I learned. I did not like one bit this characterization of my leading ways. Then indeed I was more aggressive than assertive.

Some 30 years later I still feel the below-the-belt hit of this well-meaning individual's unexpected and unwelcome words. Forever I'm grateful for them. I knew aggressiveness was not my intended *modus operandi* ("M.O."). Early in life I thought of my M.O. as selfless servant leadership of a high-minded gentleman of secular-world distinction; hardly mean-spirited or "macho." Yet for quirky and paradoxical psychological reasons I also relished it. I detested the negative inference I drew from the words, but it still sounded strong to me; manly in my Army dad's post-World War II way. Measurably aggressive actions in business spoke louder than my kindly words spoken to each morning's mirror. My employers and I paid heavy prices for my aggressiveness, while my assertiveness would earn millions of dollars for my companies.

I was a slow learner about the differences between selfish aggressiveness and comparatively selfless win-win assertiveness.

When eventually the Sales VP's own aggressiveness probably started to cost me more money than he was bringing in, and after I did what I should and could to reverse the downward spiral between us, we parted ways. He seemed to be learning from me the traits and practices I was trying to un-learn. Immediately the good man went to work for one of Wall Street's most aggressive *malnipulators*, the infamous Michael Milken, whose crimes against customer trust destroyed great Drexel Burnham Lambert, one of the most exemplary old houses on the Street. Millken landed in jail, served his time, and now teaches at Harvard Business School, and also owns control of Vistage (formerly known as T.E.C.), a national events planning group to support peer-to-peer learning for business owners.

If in the 1970s, 80s and 90s you were one to follow my lead, you would experience me as a prince of a fellow. If you moved a foot in the other direction than I mapped out for you to follow, I could become tyrannical. I said I was protecting my bottom line, but I may have been protecting my ego against any threat to my reasonable quest for sustainable achievement, and my unreasonable pursuit of perfection. As I confess and write for your edification these recalled candid thoughts, I think my few vocal detractors back then were more right than my many fans. Deep inside it seems I had something to prove to someone. With imperfect hindsight I claim overarching ignorance about the difference between man-to-man macho aggressiveness and fully responsible leadership's mission-critical assertiveness. Now I get it. Do you? Knowing then what I know now, with win-win assertiveness I would have proved more to my needy self than with my inferiority-driven aggressiveness. Through this book and *via* other mass communications vehicles and venues, I share some painful yet fruitful lessons. Lessons in assertiveness vs. aggressiveness are still being learned.

Aggressiveness is Taught in Classrooms and on Playing Fields

A widely proclaimed "best professor" I know routinely proudly professes his greatness, and unabashedly encourages all others to follow his lead with unbridled aggressiveness and no humility; with dramatic homiletic emphasis on aggressiveness over true humbleness. He has a clever phrase he extols to much laughter. When somewhere I hear him quoted, I quickly squash the ineptitude of the celebrated cleverness with his incorrect street-wise words and related misguided punditry. He thinks he's so right that I dare not tell him he's quite wrong. In his mid-50s or so, this lettered gentleman's ego is so fully unfurled it is difficult for almost anyone to get a word into his ear or mind. While he is prancing on stage, he is so busy being aggressive that he and a percentage of students fail to detect considerable woeful misalignment in his thinking, chosen nomenclature, and other professorial actions. I believe he means well, but mostly for outside-world ego and financial value accruing toward him and his obvious "chosen ones." Yes, not unlike rock stars, he has groupies.

The professor's fans applaud. As he is sufficiently entertaining when he loudly arrests attention to his mastery of all people and things, routinely he earns loud applause, standing ovations, and high rankings for his Donald Trump-like TV-ratings-driven aggressiveness. Instead he should be evaluated for Steve Jobs' legacy of long-range-value-building assertiveness. This professor's examples of aggressiveness and false humility are ones to not follow. Other more senior and more qualified university faculty than he try to reason with his highly publicized self-image. From higher up I've been forewarned to save my breath. I will. For many reasons he'll probably never reverse his full-throttle frontal assault on leadership logic and civility. He's well-compensated for his showmanship. "It's all about dollars," he might say; "Business is about dollars." Perhaps unknowingly students and others hear and feel, "People be damned. It's about the money." Although he continues to teach, I'm pleased he is no longer the entrepreneurship program's leader.

Introspectively I wish I found all of the above more amusing than disquieting. In part my adverse reaction to Dr. Aggressor comes from my being unsettled by aforementioned memories he evokes from aggressive (*vs.* assertive) missteps in my early career. Today I assert more than I aggress. When and if intentionally I become what I call controlled-aggressive, it is usually to save precious time in making space in someone else's perilously resistant mind. Some people almost beg for aggressiveness. I contend we must all learn to be more assertive. Perhaps digital communication technology and life's fast-beat tempo conspire to encourage aggressiveness.

Many text messages, tweets *via* Twitter, *staccato* e-mail content, spam messages, barked voicemail system greetings, and recorded call-back messages left, demonstrate counterproductive and rude aggressiveness into mind-and-time space of others — resulting a coarsening of our culture, or so it seems to me. To cut through clutter in collective minds, advertising campaigns seem to be growing more aggressive. From pop-ups that pierce through best firewalls and other computerized blocking mechanics, to the on-air screaming huckster trying to pry from our wallets hard-earned cash, aggressiveness is everywhere. Civility and essential assertiveness are being drowned-out by the clamor of loud-mouth, heavy-handed, tight-fisted, unyielding, self-serving, and otherwise corrosive aggressiveness. Are my views too strong? They are assertive.

Boldly stating my views to make a pivotal point, intentionally I am demonstrating strategically aligned assertiveness. There is nothing namby-pamby about assertiveness, so it is overkill to use aggressiveness to prove expertise and practice ascendant leadership. Between words and lines above I trust you felt my feelings about more than one man's lifetime of thinly veiled insecurities. Disguised and displayed in the above professor's aggressive pronouncements of superiority, he finds among followers addicted to melodrama a willing and enabling audience. I pay attention to him so I can learn what to avoid in my thinking and actions. In a large country such as the U.S., there is a sufficient paying audience for almost any side show or main attraction. The Internet proves this theory.

Bestseller and cult classic *The Medium is the Massage: An Inventory of Effects* is a book co-authored and designed by media guru Marshall McLuhan and graphics artist Quentin Fiore, with credit for coordinated by Jerome Agel. In 1967 the 160-page book was published by Bantam Books as an extension to McLuhan's 1964 blockbuster, The Medium is the Message. When this cleverly turned-out work was released, I was 17 and a junior at Baldwin High School in suburban south Pittsburgh. Through my professional (*i.e.*, paid $1.50 *per* hour plus bus fare) poster-boy PR work for Junior Achievement's 50th anniversary promotion campaign, I got the message through the medium of mentoring. A highly regarded mentor, Donald M. Deer, Vice President of Public Relations for Westinghouse Air Brake Company (WABCO) made sure I learned about media and messaging as much as my teenage mind would allow me to absorb. Often I only scratched the surface of Don's deep lessons.

Now smitten with new and youthful perceptions of passion, promise, principles, practices and power of controlling messages and methods of dissemination, at Don Deer's suggestion I went to study journalism and mass communications at Duquesne University. Because of my professional awards in public relations for Junior Achievement, the Chair of the Journalism Department made an exception and allowed me to attend advanced classes. I was thrilled.

After the Dean discovered in my high school records I spoke French and had mastered a Parisian accent — thanks to my Francophile pal Mlle. Evelyn Y. Baxter, the Chairwoman of the school district's foreign language department — immediately he gave freshman me a weekly radio program on the university's 50,000-watt city-wide broadcasting station, "France Applauds with John Dallas," a celebration of French music, poetry and other culture. Great fun. Le programme était très agréable. A number of other terrific things happened that freshman year, including starting off-campus a student-run publicity service for non-profits, Dallas Associates, Inc.

Several weeks of quarantined hospitalization from exhaustion, mononucleosis, and a lesser and common strain of hepatitis slowed me down more than a tad. Okay, I was stopped nearly dead in my tracks. Compared to health hurdles in years to come, relatively speaking this hospitalization was for the equivalent of a common cold. No one knew it took me years to recover from four major health set-backs. Not even closest family or friends would ever hear from me what I was struggling to overcome. Smiles did much to turn away unwanted queries about my health. I was determined to live!

By the time I enrolled at Columbia University to continue my education, I had learned tough-as-nails frontline business leadership lessons. Again I studied the art and science of mass communication, and eventually I revealed to myself how few facts I knew about both. Perhaps I knew more than some others, but then and now I never know all I wish I could. Any lessons I learn make me want more. I pray for time to go back to school to finish my education, earn a Masters and a Ph.D. to crown the value of a lifetime of hard-knocks education. I doubt this will happen. I know of aggressively elitist souls who won't pay attention to any lessons unless a Ph.D. is attached to the name of the instructor. So far I have not encountered any meeting planner or audience with such ivory-tower myopia.

Emotionally secure and otherwise grown-up minds see through thick blue smoke of maladroit aggressiveness. The above examples and other types of lopsided aggressors in classrooms, courtrooms, boardrooms, war rooms, and bedrooms bring real risk to others' developing mindfulness about win-win relationships. Almost totally eclipsing exemplary assertiveness, too many real-world examples of aggressiveness are earning on-screen cyberspace and air time.

Social influence creates or at least exacerbates adjustment problems such as aggressiveness. At home or elsewhere, a young or older child taught aggressiveness against others on wrestling team mats, in ice hockey rinks, on football fields, in rugby scrums, or any inadequately characterized competitive arena or act, is highly likely to struggle in committed one-*with*-one relationships of any variety, including parenthood and boss-and-employee interaction.

In the early 1950s, Presbyterian minister Fred Rogers began his television career at Pittsburgh's KDKA-TV. Later Pastor Rogers went on to create "Mister Rogers' Neighborhood" on the nation's first educational television station, Pittsburgh's WQED-TV. *"Daniel the Tame Tiger"* was the puppet through which he communicated to five-year-old and hungry-for-attention me the importance of assertiveness without aggressiveness. I was to be a tame tiger, not an aggressive tiger. Proudly I joined the Tame Tiger Club, and happily wore at all times my orange membership button: *"I am a Tame Tiger Club Member"* it said, I believe. (Someday I'll search e-Bay to see if anyone has for sale one of those old "Tame Tiger Club" membership buttons. If you have one, please let me know.) I knew in my heart I wanted to be a tame tiger, and then my young life's navigational demands all but stripped away the tame part. Too often my claws were unsheathed — often for basic survival.

At now demolished Pittsburgh Hospital, the umbilical cord wrapped itself tightly around my strong little neck. It was thought to be strangling me. I heard I began fighting for survival — quite literally. The story of the yet unnamed infant Dallas boy screaming and struggling to free himself from the noose is still too difficult for Mom to recount in detail. I no longer ask her. I'll never forget the first time I heard the story. I was transfixed. I saw the pain the story caused my mother. Oddly I noted the curious detachment of my maternal grandmother from her daughter's memory. To this moment I don't recall Dad ever weighing-in on the delivery room scene. Actually he was spared being witness to the infant's strangulation. He was in the nicotine cloud of the fathers' waiting/smoking/worrying room, and probably was not told right away what had just happened to his wife and only son. The year I was born he was preoccupied with other more pressing life-and-death matters, so I'm not sure if he ever knew. Many secrets were kept from and by him. Such were the times.

Since childhood days a chilling phrase from Handel's full *Messiah* haunts me. Dad and I were both "acquainted with grief." One word: grief. I believe deep grief from his childhood haunted Dad until the final days. Within hours of his death he achieved long-denied peace.

Trying to arrest possibly similar negative feelings of despair often coursing through my veins, I too chose aggressiveness. Sadly and regrettably, I ignored many boundaries. Thankfully my Scottish church history included inferred lessons in fair fighting for what's right, proper, and for the good of the order — strategic alignment.

Overtly aggressive people do not respect reasonable boundaries of others. Bankruptcy courts are backed-up with cases brought against aggressive borrowers, lenders, and other originally one-sided aggressors. Family courts are ensnarled with claims for restitution for egregious results from spousal, parental, and dependents' aggressiveness. As we teach youngsters aggressiveness to win on playing fields or in spelling bees, we must remember to place in their minds and souls an on-and-off switch. They and we must remember the differences between assertiveness and aggressiveness.

As this book heads off to the printer, I am more genuine than ever in humbly apologizing to anyone for whom my aggressiveness created more pain than gain. It is never too late to say, "I'm sorry." From my unsteady childhood years I began to feel it was my Superman-like calling to *save the day* — for everyone. Although I still skip the blue suit and red cape, occasionally I instinctively fly through the air and land in someone's face. Less often, still I can come on too strong.

Without pausing to consider long-range impact of putting loudly screeching emergency brakes on a person or thing I believe to be moving in the wrong direction, occasionally my inner-child takes control. Sometimes adult me crashes and burns. Others are negatively surprised by my hot intensity. Now I rarely flare with impatience.

In my formative post-WWII command-and-control years, getting things right required might. Might is *not* always right. Now when rightly or wrongly I sense I have power (*i.e.,* influence) to change someone or something for the better, I act less and less on my own.

Each day more and more I trust God to guide strategic deployment of my wisdom, courage and patience. My outward value increases as my inner child is growing-up. I choose to assert more. I aggress less.

Attuned for years to behind-the-scenes reports of this type of fly-off-the-handle aggressiveness in The White House — particularly during the Clinton years — and now with the headline-grabbing aggressiveness of Chicago's new mayor, allegedly expressing himself with an abundance of fury and expletives (behavior that was forecast long before his campaign began), I am riveted in my place. I want to learn from others' and my mistakes with aggressiveness. I'll remain a work-in-progress. I pray for the Potter's hand to smooth away more of my rough edges.

> *"Language has the power to attract the things we want or things we don't.
> What are you attracting with your words?"* — Yosaif August

Please choose more assertiveness and less aggressiveness. Opt for boldness and not timidity.

Dissuade yourself of the notion that humility is demonstrated through withholding from others news of your greatness in deeper thinking and higher action. The world needs your light.

Perhaps we should all sing to ourselves — and perhaps even in small group settings — the childhood lyrics that were successfully used with Arizona Congresswoman Gabrielle ("Gabbie") Giffords, while she was in music-based speech rehabilitation therapy following an aggressive murderer's 8 January 2011 gunshot wound to her brain:

> *"This little light of mine, I'm going to let it shine . . ."*

Assertiveness lets your inner light shine outward.

Aggressiveness casts a dark shadow inside and out.

Assertively I suggest we each commit to assert more and aggress less.

If need be, however, aggressively I'll defend this book's overarching philosophic and practical premise about preferability of assertiveness.

Assertiveness. Expound.

Authenticity

Chapter Inspired by and Dedicated to
Steven E. Bumpus (1960-2010)

Insert or imagine seeing your first name: _____,

Seeing this chapter's title word, what immediately comes to your open mind? Do you already have a working relationship with this word? Somewhere inside of you does this word instantly appeal? As a response to a specific situation at-hand, will this word work to your and others' advantage? For this word to increase in real value, together we must dig, drill and think deeper, so we will reach, climb and soar higher.

Authenticity drawn from dictionaries includes language such as "undisputed credibility," *etc.* In authenticity there is suggestion and impression of perfection. Inherently and logically, therefore, the word authenticity requires careful consideration and situational clarification.

Perfection only exists beyond this realm. Perfect truth is not yet within our reach. On planet Earth we know one person's perception of perfect truth can be another well-meaning individual's total falsehood. Before we move to the hereafter, there is plenty opportunity for strategic alignment of human and organizational authenticity. For emboldening, empowering, and sustaining people and cultures for fully responsible leadership, deeper and wider understanding of authenticity is essential.

"To contact the deeper truth of who we are, we must engage in some activity or practice that questions what we assume to be true about ourselves." —A.H. Almaas

Real-world working definitions and descriptions of authenticity must include implication of imperfection. By nature or design, an authentic human being is imperfect. Alleged authentic (*i.e.,* indisputable) thoughts of imperfect humans may eventually be found incomplete or erroneous, therefore, imperfect — yet not any less authentic.

Accepting in-good-faith this reality of inherent polarity in authenticity takes off of a leader's shoulders undue burden. At the same time this acceptance of imperfection in authenticity layers-on new levels of accountability for deeper thought toward higher standards.

Expecting anyone or anything to be perfect is folly. We know better. Yet we do not always think about or act upon what we know. Automatically accepting inherent imperfection in our authenticity allows us to always think a little deeper, without burden of cynicism or negativity. Accepting imperfection in authenticity is a positive thing. Why? Well, it's reality. Reality is a good thing, even when it's bad. Dealing with reality is mandatory for true-north strategic alignment of people, money, technology, and other mission-critical resources.

How often do you insist on reality checks? As an alternative, the HILL Model for Fully Responsible Leadership encourages making "reality check marks." Person-by-person and item-by-item, please try to check-off the level of authenticity for which you can sufficiently vouch. Is she, he or it the real thing? How are you making your determination?

Do you and they R.E.A.C.T. with **R**espect, **E**mpathy, **A**uthenticity, **C**larity and **T**rust? Discreetly in meetings I observe key people around the table and try to discern if she or he is R.E.A.C.T.ing to the people and situation(s) at hand. I say to myself or mark in my notes yes, no, or unsure when I ask if each person is:

> Reacting with **R**espect?
> Reacting with **E**mpathy?
> Reacting with **A**uthenticity?
> Reacting with **C**larity?
> Reacting with **T**rust?

Comfort and even a sense of celebration come to me when all five R.E.A.C.T. criteria are met. Concern wells up when I notice lack of any of these, and especially when a wholesale lack of respect signals someone's fully inflated ego (*i.e.,* dangerous personal insecurities). After all, none of us is perfect. We are together in our authenticity.

Authenticity in words chosen to convey authentic meaning may require an extra beat or two of thought and feeling. In writing this collection of letters to you from me I remember lessons in both accuracy and authenticity.

Seek authenticity in all you think, say, write, do or share. Single words startle us with their authenticity from Christopher Isherwood's *A Single Man*, a top award-winning movie destined to become a classic film. When best-actor Colin Firth said, "Waking up begins with saying 'am' and 'now'," the book's original impact on me came full-circle. Am and now.

As I begin each day, I say to myself, "Am. Now." I offer up these single words as prayers of adoration, confession, thanksgiving, and supplication. With those two single words I realize I lived through the night. I'm awake. I'm moving.

Occasionally a prior evening's demands require I say to the mirror a big bold *"Yes!"* Sometimes I'll even whisper, "Go get 'em tiger!" Daily devotions are delayed until I am in the right frame-of-mind to be attentive, reachable, teachable, and sufficiently focused. Am. Now. With these two words are you in-the-moment? Say, "I am. Now."

From cover-to-cover throughout this book you see wisdom, courage and patience. Each time you read these three words, please work to deepen your grasp of their authenticity and meaningfulness to your life's success. Let these key words sink-in deeper and deeper. When you see these three words, you may want to allow yourself to enter a momentary hypnotic-like trance. Chant, pray, sing or whisper them. Really. Try one or more. For you and those you influence, there is incalculable value in each recitation of these words. The three words release a major force for good. Allow these three to remain with you.

Hundreds or more times I tested with others the transformative power of these three single words of authenticity: wisdom, courage and patience. Imagine the peace that can come with a deeply inhaled breath of wise, courageous, and patient authenticity. Hold it. Then slowly exhale. Breaths of fresh air will come with your authenticity.

Authenticity is becoming a modern-day buzz word. Recently I read on a Facebook page, "What you are is what you have been. What you'll be is what you do now." On Fiat TV commercials Jennifer Lopez sings, "I'm right where I'm supposed to be, thanks to where I've been." To me this sounds like promotion of authenticity's value.

Restoration Hardware's Co-CEO Gary Friedman is building his upscale business by discussing his downscale beginnings. Humbly he reveals how his childhood authenticity informs his adult sense of self.

Openly he talks about his mother's influence on his appreciation for words. He published a letter in which he reflects upon hearing his mother sing, in their small apartment, "The Impossible Dream," with highly motivational lyrics from Broadway's hit "Man of La Mancha." During my unsteady childhood years, similarly I used the same play's quixotic words to name, frame and claim my own "knight's quest."

"When we fearlessly fight for what we believe in, and remain hopelessly optimistic about life, love, and the future, we create an authentic connection with all in our path, most importantly with ourself [sic]." —Gary Friedman

This book attempts to narrate and illustrate a multiverse in which you and I might hear, see and feel a quantum theory of authenticity:

"With best thoughts, words and actions
we align our past, present and future." —JRDjr

In this book I write with authenticity. Occasionally literary license is taken in the name of authenticity. From Language for Leading™ all 52 words are seedlings to nurture with your and my authenticity — which is how forests will grow so you and I can see life's green trees.

"Language has the power to attract the things we want or things we don't.
What are you attracting with your words?" —Yosaif August

Fully responsible leaders and those who follow are distracted by and growing weary of word-of-the-day, quote-of-the-day, thought-of-the-day, picture-of-the-day, and other day-by-day deliveries of fast food for thought. One-minute messages may work for texting ones physical whereabouts. For rethinking, rebuilding, rewiring, and reconstituting our collective strengths, more authenticity is required.

Calorific heat of years of economic and related societal meltdowns fried brains, singed spirits, burned bridges, and melted resolve. For healing and recovery underway, this book offers a full year of full-course weekly meals to chew on. Sugary drinks and fast food won't suffice anymore. Our recovering minds, bodies and souls require ripe and nutritious organic words; enriched with deeper thoughts for higher needs. For authenticity we shop at Whole Words Market.

Thank you for digging, drilling and thinking at least a little deeper, so we will each reach, climb and soar higher — all with authenticity.

Authenticity. Expound.

Civility

Chapter Inspired by and Dedicated to Margaret Anderson Wanick

Insert or imagine seeing your first name: _____,

Seeing this chapter's title word, what immediately comes to your open mind? Do you already have a working relationship with this word? Somewhere inside of you does this word instantly appeal? As a response to a specific situation at-hand, will this word work to your and others' advantage? For this word to increase in real value, together we must dig, drill and think deeper, so we will reach, climb and soar higher.

Fully responsible leaders understand and embrace the deeper meaningfulness of ci·vil·i·ty. Etymologically the noun stems from civil, politics; hence "politic behavior." Civility is the act of showing regard for others through disciplines of courteous behavior or politeness. A courteous act or utterance is often a rather formal or perfunctory expression of one's civility. Fortunately for generations to come, etiquette's remarkably unvaried rules of order took the meaning of civility to proportions probably never envisioned by the French or Latin-literate individuals who first embraced the term.

Contents of this extensive chapter may startle you. Please stick with it. The highs and lows this one word brings to this author's mind intensify the importance and vulnerability of civility. Someday a full book may be devoted to these and other nooks and crannies of civility. Please be prepared for a laugh or two, and perhaps even a tear of recognition for human fragility revealed when civility is threatened or absent. This is a word with which fully responsible leaders must reckon.

"One doesn't.
If one does, one isn't.
Since we are, therefore we can't."

In framed needlepoint the tongue-twister above hangs over the south door to my kitchen. Kitchen-curious guests often spot it in its less-than-obvious place and wonder aloud what it means. If time permits, without immediately explaining — and for a moment of impact and fun — I thank them for their interest, suggest they clench their teeth and slowly read it out loud, using what's called Locust Valley Lockjaw ("LVJ"), the colloquial term for a stereotypical upper-class American accent associated with elite residents of Manhattan. In mock Locust Valley Lockjaw, my saying thank you then please are not-too-subtle clues.

For generations those who summer in the hamlet of Locust Valley in Oyster Bay, New York speak in a rather aloof and affected manner, keeping the jaw clenched and thrust forward with their lips tight and barely moving. This is a studied manner of speech designed to elevate, memorialize, and sometimes even mock civility. Can you hear it? Go ahead. You want to. Give it a try. It is not to be easy.

When in the City — as Manhattan is called "the City" in a way as if to say there is no other city in the world — quickly I discovered LVJ affectation I would encounter occasionally masked ignorance to a deeper nuance of a topic being discussed, or more frequently revealed the dramatist's true or trumped-up need to separate self from people thought common. Thankfully most of my exposure to LVJ was among good people who knew better than to deride any fellow human beings, yet still they found in such esoteric humor kernels of truth about themselves or others. Civility matters.

From 1776 onward, We the People struggle to decide what should survive of immigrants' traditions of civility, such that they were. In years leading to U.S. independence, were signs of civility thought marks of a closeted Royalist? Did refined etiquette brand a person suspect of secret unyielding allegiance to the throne? Or did tipped hats, kissed hands, respectful bows, elegant curtsies, and exchange of overly polite words signal a new country's admission of pressing need for rules of engagement between and among the formerly oppressed?

As civility slides to new lows, time-honored rules of engagement seem to be yielding to modern-day pulls toward estrangement. Each year do you think people are more or less polite with each other?

How are you treating others? Civility is learned behavior, a suite of non-cognitive skills. This is good news. There's much to learn.

As for Locust Valley Lockjaw, famous Miss Porter's School taught this elitist accent to Jacqueline Bouvier Kennedy Onassis. Legendary actress Katherine Hepburn perfected the sound, probably quite naturally as the heiress to the Corning Glass founding family fortune, more so than from acting classes. TV's ultra-conservative author and commentator William F. Buckley, Jr. was so locked-jaw in his speaking, at times one could hardly understand him. I was amused.

To humorously underscore a paradoxical aspect of unbridled elitism, mockingly I lock my jaw to make a point or two. What I am saying may not be all that clear to a listening ear, but a message gets through about real-world dexterity, polarity and hilarity within civility.

You probably already know the above-captioned tongue-in-cheek saying, the one displayed in needlepoint, means that if one has class there are certain things one does not do. Heaven forbid! If one does such things that one mustn't, one does not, therefore, have class. And since our illusion of having unquestionable class is a safe assumption or we would not be having such a pithy conversation, we relished how ultimately our joke is on us. Greenwich, Connecticut patron of the social arts Margaret Anderson ("Peggy") Wanick, a cherished and closest friend and I, would discreetly acknowledge each other's over-firm — and devilishly over-the-top — grasp of esoteric issues of civility, particularly what we each knew of Back Country Greenwich etiquette, more or less practiced out of public view at The Round Hill Club and elsewhere.

Less encumbered by pretense, Greenwich Country Club is where Peggy's third husband, Robert Brady, and she were at-ease as highly active members. There they and I would frequently dine and stay overnight. After the Bradys moved to south Florida, on their return trips to Greenwich we would meet, dine, laugh, imbibe the nectar of the Scottish gods (*i.e.*, Dewar's White Label), and sleep it all off in the club's lovely guest rooms — usually chosen by Peggy to be certain our large casement windows would look out over the championship golf course toward the rolling waters of Long Island Sound. I miss those civil days of lavishly lounging-about with laughter and love.

Lovingly and painstakingly, for me Peggy needle-pointed the framed "One Doesn't…" canvas. She is cleverly quoting her first husband, the most humorously pseudo-elitist of the quartet. When out-and-about together occasionally we would witness a minor or major act of unacceptable behavior. With smiles we would whisper to each other, "One doesn't." We tittered privately in good-natured and pretend judgment of someone who should know better than to (1) pick fallen flatware up from the floor of a restaurant, (2) place on top of a used food plate a soiled napkin, (3) season with salt and pepper food from any kitchen without first tasting it, (4) hold a wine or champagne glass by the bowl instead of the stem, (5) avoid sustaining eye contact during toasts, (6) rudely snap orders at service personnel, (7) use foul language, (8) smoke cigarettes, (9) split an infinitive, (10) dangle a participle, or (11) massacre the King's English. Now I imagine the knowing smile on your face. Enjoy it all. Civility allows for laughter.

The "One doesn't" needlepoint art still hangs as a reminder of our self-effacing silliness. It almost always brings any inquisitor to a mild roar of laughter, to which I say, "One doesn't." If glasses are in-hand, then we toast with sustained eye contact and big smiles! The bonding exercise often results in the other person using for years to come all or parts of the saying, mostly, "One doesn't." I try to find and focus on positives and say, "One does." Bonds form.

Peggy, Bob and I informally adopted each other. Cleverly we each filled then current gaps in our family lives. Mommykins, Daddykins and Sonnykins were the whimsical elitist nicknames Peggy assigned to each of us. I was deeply touched. They meant it. The names stuck. Although discreet about where we would use these terms of endearment, friends knew we three were a cobbled-together family of choice: father, mother, and "my son, the entrepreneur." Peggy and I look alike, so few questions were ever asked. Time, distance, and other factors took their toll on our once-solid family unit, yet the love and warm feelings remain from those days of heightened civility.

On a less personal side of civility, indeed it is more than a tad ironic that civility has its roots in politics, and U.S. politics have lost civility. In the 1950s when twice Adlai E. Stevenson ran against Dwight D. Eisenhower, Presidential and other political campaigns and coverage were marked by civility, give-or-take an intentionally planted rumor or two of scandal. CBS-TV News' Walter Cronkite brought civility into our homes, evangelist Billy Graham used civility to shepherd his flock, *I Love Lucy*, *The Dick Van Dyke Show*, and *The Ed Sullivan Show* all epitomized for us Baby Boomers' civility. *Mister Rogers Neighborhood* brought abundant values-based civility to children (and their parents), while *Howdy Doody* taught us to not take too seriously life's frowns.

The Honeymooners seemed to arrest attention to the harsh reality of the downside of marriage, and yet civility was written into the final moments of almost every script. *The Andy Griffith Show* was about down-home southern civility. *The Beverly Hillbillies* was almost 100-percent based on the importance of learning civility in order to function in what was characterized as high society.

Today saying: please, thank you, may I, excuse me, pardon me, I beg your pardon, forgive me, I regret the outcome, shall we dance, dare we leave, hello, goodbye, or enjoy your day are a few examples of thousands of words and phrases of civility. Perhaps dozens of times each day I say please and thank you — and 99.44% of the time I mean it all from the heart.

In every chapter of this book I express my respect for your time by asking with please for your specific engagement in points I make. I thank you for embracing with me the importance of wisdom, courage, and patience. I request and appreciate your engagement in considering views toward how featured words might further enrich your abundant life. In each thought and word expressed herein, I am mindful of civility — a linguistic opportunity to demonstrate, in nuanced style, my highest regard for you and your life's complexity.

This book is a condensed opportunity for me to demonstrate — through turns of phrase, provocative prose, courteous vocabulary, and other good manners — my desire to offer alternative views for you to consider. Lack of civility is shaking institutional foundations, shattering economies, and costing lives. With essential politeness, I demonstrate I care about civility's importance to our emerging global society. Please continue to take seriously civility's higher purpose.

U.S. Civility's Slide

On 22 November 1963 civility took a nearly fatal hit. President John Fitzgerald Kennedy's assassination finished off what scant press coverage of World War II's atrocities failed to bring to our shores about barbaric threats to our freedoms. The days were over for open-top limousines for Presidential motorcades, and that was only a hint of societal changes ahead. Our global reality check happened on the streets of Dallas, Texas. World Wars did not do it. The cost of freedom was felt in hearts of every American glued for days to our black-and-white TV screens. Back then men were not to be seen crying, but they did and they were. I took note of many such lessons.

Jacqueline Bouvier Kennedy was once our democracy's reigning Queen Guinevere of civility. She was 31 when the President was inaugurated. For the sake of her family, her country, and civility's demands on her proper Southampton, New York Republican upbringing, somehow she held it all together. Civility for Jacqueline was tempered steel, not fluff. She made most of the major decisions we remember about civility-in-action during and after her short time in The White House. Son John-John's salute for his fallen father was Jacqueline's gesture of civility toward her son and the whole world watching all of us cope. The toddler's salute was our salute. Talk about tears!

When JFK died the U.S. was only 187 years young. Collectively we felt our country's childhood vulnerability. John, Jr. symbolized both our sadness and hopefulness. If their son Patrick had lived, Jacqueline would have been holding an infant in her arms. Imagine. In these reflections from an author who lived through this messy time, do you feel civility's past, present and future importance and power? Do you sense how today intentionally focusing more of our leadership efforts on incorporating civility into our thoughts and plans would allow us to put people first in our thinking? Civility may be at least one antidote to society's infectious greed and need-for-speed.

History of civility offers us many lessons. When JFK's brief and somewhat surreal *Camelot* era in Washington was replaced with the roughhewn culture of one of the most uncivilized Presidents ever to occupy the Oval Office, a radical societal shift occurred. I felt it. I did not like it. I did not know exactly what was happening. I knew it was not good. I had not yet learned words for these thoughts. I was 13.

As Air Force One hosted the swearing-in of Lyndon Baines Johnson, former First Lady Jacqueline insisted the world see on her clothes senselessly shed blood of her dead American President. She had the high presence of mind to say so, and would not change her clothes. Astonishingly JFK's body's splattered internal tissues were talked about on-air as if carnage was an everyday news occurrence. Until then it was not. This was a tipping point in news coverage. From early years of U.S. journalism, news and photographs of wars and other atrocities were filtered, perhaps with duty to protect civility.

As civility's Commander-in-Chief, LBJ would quickly eschew the classiness and tastefulness of his fallen predecessor and his expensively schooled young wife. As if his sloppy words and disrespectful demeanor were not enough to offend sensibilities, frequently LBJ would ask embarrassed male staff members to join him for conversation while he enthroned himself in his bathroom. From Upstairs at the White House and other books, there are countless validated stories of LBJ's bad taste coupled with bad judgment. Civility seemed destined to remain forever in the past.

Please remember how young I was. At 13 I sensed it happening to us. We deserved better. I knew the country's 200th birthday was 13 years away. I was half-way there. Before a global spotlight would shine on our progress over only two centuries of freedom, we had a lot to do to pull ourselves back up to some semblance of world-class civility.

The Obama Administration rekindled an air of casual sophistication — not too much, not too little, and perhaps just right. Soon history will be the judge of the national and global impact of the Obama family's civility. *The New York Times* concludes Biff and Muffy's traditional preppie clothing and behavior returned to consumer favor. Personal favorites are again doing brisk business: Brooks Brothers (founded in 1818), J. Press (founded in 1902), and Ralph Lauren Polo (founded in 1967). Manufacturers of natural fabrics could not be more pleased with the resurgence of interest in good taste in clothing and more. As one can't judge a book or a leader by its cover, I hope interest in traditional design and finer things is also foreshadowing rise for pondering and practicing thoughts and acts of civility.

In the 1960s civility hit rock bottom, in 1965 (two years after JFK was killed) Malcolm X was murdered. Hate was everywhere. Media-glorified Flower Power of Woodstock-era fame seemed to be accentuated to counter-balance fear of the fire power of guns.

Also in 1968 omnipresent pediatrician and child-rearing-rules author Dr. Benjamin Spock, Dr. William Sloan Coffin, Chaplain of Yale University, novelist Mitchell Goodman, Michael Ferber, a graduate student at Harvard, and peace activist Marcus Raskin were indicted on charges of conspiracy to encourage violations of U.S. draft laws. The 10,000th U.S. airplane was reported lost over Vietnam. North Korean patrol boats captured the *USS Pueblo*, a US Navy intelligence vessel. The North Vietnamese launched the Tet Offensive at Nha Trang. U.S. ground troops from Charlie Company rampaged through the hamlet of My Lai, killing more than 500 Vietnamese civilians from infants to the elderly.

The total number of Americans fighting in Vietnam peaked at 541,000. Pause to memorize that number. I did. We draft-age men were appalled and worried. I remember.

The same year Dr. Martin Luther King Jr. was shot and died. Dr. King's murder sparked rioting in Baltimore, Boston, Chicago, Detroit, Kansas City, Newark, Washington, D.C., and many other cities; at least 46 deaths were blamed on the riots (a fact often forgotten). Dr. King's legacy was accelerated, intensified, and eventually partially mythologized — for the sake of civil rights, civility, and much more for the good-of-the-order. More than four decades have passed. Where are things moving with Dr. King's famous Dream? Dare to speak truth, at least to yourself.

In 1968: "Bloody Monday" marked one of the most violent days of the Parisian student revolt. Andy Warhol was shot in his New York City loft and survived. Robert F. Kennedy was killed. The Soviet Union invaded Czechoslovakia with over 200,000 Warsaw Pact troops. The Democratic National Convention is marked by Chicago police beating unconscious some dissident marchers and sending at least 100 to emergency rooms while arresting 175. Mayor Richard H. Daley's convoluted remarks to the press drew worldwide outrage. Women's Liberation groups, joined by members of New York chapter of the National Organization of Women (NOW), targeted for demonstrations the Miss America Beauty Contest in Atlantic City. Police and military troops in Mexico City reacted violently to a student-led protest and hundreds of the demonstrators were killed or injured. The list of 1968's atrocities goes on and on. How could civility survive all of these direct hits? Damage was done. Still I feel some of this old pain.

How in the world would Americans regain some semblance of civility while the fabric of our society seemed to be torn to shreds? We knew it must. Effort was and is required. Eventually embattled President

Richard Milhous Nixon brought civility back front-and-center to TV screens and our hungry minds. To say the least, RN (as he referred to himself in the third-person) was a rather formal fellow, excruciatingly unyielding in his almost constant coat-and-tie presence — even when photographed kicked-back and relaxing with Scotch in-hand. But his rock-like demeanor seemed to give the country something solid upon which to lean.

President Nixon knew what he was doing to reconstruct a culture of civility for the United States. With good intentions, he went overboard when he ordered uniforms for White House guards patterned after royal sentries of Buckingham Palace. He thought he was giving us what we needed — bold symbols of civility. To a degree that would off-set the barbarianism of the post-*Camelot* years, RN tried to formally institutionalize U.S. civility. Until his catastrophic blindness to Watergate's threat to his vision, the Nixon era was a rebirth of at least the appearance of civility.

Until Watergate, civility's influence on our American culture felt good. From Nixon's visits to China and his daughter's picture-perfect Rose Garden wedding, suddenly Amy Vanderbilt's etiquette was back at center stage. Because of civility we were breathing a bit more easily. Watergate brought us back down. Compared to the Nixon era, handsome and polite President and Mrs. Gerald R. and the Family Ford were simple in their tastes, yet possessed considerable civility.

The deaths of President and Mrs. Ford felt very personal to those of us grateful for their authenticity, trustworthiness and civility.

With ridiculous token gestures of saving money by removing bread plates from dining set-ups at The White House (even for formal state dinners), selling-off the historic Presidential yacht *Sequoia* for under $300,000, and generally exemplifying disregard for tastefulness in civility, President and Mrs. Jimmy (not James) Carter's impact on our collective civility requires no further elaboration. As an ex-President he learned to mind his manners, more or less.

The first Bush White House took civility back up to their at-ease Kennebunkport standards. When Bill and Hillary were elected, more than the Clinton sexual scandal took us back down. Our first-ever CEO "W" allowed his affable wife to rekindle a just-right-for-the-times amount of civility. Since Jacqueline Kennedy's days, The White

House had not been as well orchestrated as a symphony of standards against which keen observers could learn a few things about civility. First Lady Laura's positive impact on civility was overshadowed by headline-holding events.

On the close-to-home tipping point side of things, perhaps when cursive handwriting skills gave way to child-like block printing being acceptable for educated adults, other shortcuts and abbreviations began to be more commonplace; due emphasis on "common." Men no longer bother removing hats or caps when ladies enter elevators. This list goes on.

Efforts to demonstrate civility seem to evaporate with release of each new tech-of-the-moment gadget or smart phone app. Here I am excluding more dramatic specific evidence of questionable taste in books, movies, music and theater, and the virtual ubiquity of off-color humor and triple-x entertainment. Civility is fighting an uphill battle.

Tribute to A.A. Milne's Winnie the Pooh

It is more fun to talk with someone who doesn't use long, difficult words but rather short, easy words like 'What about lunch'?" — Winnie the Pooh

Scholarly humorist author A.A. Milne's original *Winnie the Pooh* books are very much about civility. A careful read of these children's stories for adults reveals countless reminders of right and wrong ways to think and do things. Nine days after they were released to the waiting world, I purchased my first iPad. I was thrilled that Apple chose a *Winnie the Pooh* selection as the only book automatically (*i.e.,* free) on the iPad's virtual bookshelves.

Apple does nothing without careful thought to consequences, and I am enjoying believing the late Steve Jobs was reminding us all to go back to our roots of child-like interest in learning about civility in *The Hundred Acre Woods* of Milne's creation. I read it again on my iPad, and loved relearning a few of these lessons about civility. For smiles and other value, please read to kids and adults the original *Winnie the Pooh* books. Disney's versions of Pooh are clever, but in Disney releases this beloved bear's messages about time-honored civility are barely in-tact.

Without much — if any — thought toward civility or principles of etiquette, Americans of all ages Tweet, text, bump, surf, scroll, scan, plug-in, un-plug, tune-out, check-in, check-out, log-in, log-out, subscribe, unsubscribe, "friend" and "un-friend" (on Facebook and elsewhere), buy, borrow, pay, file bankruptcy, marry, share living space, divorce, embrace, abandon, bear children, beat children, buy pets, abandon pets, eat healthier, weigh more, use profundity, abuse profanity, embrace diversity, remain racist, claim truth, lie, play fair, cheat, give, steal, practice safe sex, abandon in sex all caution, contribute to funds to cure disease, wantonly spread disease, and otherwise play out our lives without pausing long enough to learn basic social graces, or practice ways to move to higher mental places. This run-on sentence takes a toll, but you may want to read it again and feel the weight of each word. Where in this recitation is civility?

Planning toward a day when civility will replace growing societal disenfranchisement, let's think and dig a little deeper while we reach and climb a lot higher. Let's work to bring civility — demonstrations of respect for others and ourselves — back to our thoughts, conversation, action plans, resolutions, and conviction. Putting people first requires definitions and descriptions of civility. As context for strategically aligning people and things, etiquette is a sub-set of ethics, values, standards and behaviors of civility in-practice.

In my long career it remains noteworthy that CEOs, in particular, have been the most civil and otherwise polite with me in conversation, and in expression of their hospitableness during visits to their offices, clubs, homes and yachts. I learned from the best. I watched carefully differences between how CEOs treated their guests and others. It may be difficult to believe, but in my experience CEOs were more quick to offer drinks and other comforts. Here's why.

CEOs know, as fully responsible leaders, they have to make an extra effort to calm their guests in order to have the trusting and open type of conversation required in fleeting moments to come. Rarely does a savvy CEO stay behind her or his desk during meetings. She or he comes around to chairs in the front of the desk, or to sofas and chairs set-up for easy eyeball-to-eyeball conversation. Almost every CEO I meet graciously walks me to the elevator and pushes the down button while winding-up the pleasant conversation we were having. A CEO's final smile and handshake can mean a lot or naught. It depends.

In the late 70s during morning rush hours, often an elevator would be cordoned-off and commandeered by a silent operator to take top officers to their floors in Manhattan skyscrapers. Coats would be taken by receptionists without much of a moment's hesitation. Male servers in tuxedos would bring cups and saucers (not mugs) for fresh-brewed coffee poured from silver pots. Croissants (not muffins), with real butter and fresh fruit preserves, were served with silver tongs. Linen napery was provided instead of paper napkins. At first I thought it was very nice, yet sometimes it was a bit too much.

Later a savvy mentor taught me how these accommodations were often used (*i.e.*, not always) to mark a leader's territory, signal seriousness-of-purpose, identify privilege, and effectively warn recipients that they might never again be treated this wonderful way if they should fall short during or after the meeting. Wow. I knew something was afoot, but I did not guess all of that. In this context, civility has an edge to it. Thankfully I survived dozens of these early tests of my knowledge of etiquette. I enjoyed frequent invitations to be both pampered and tested.

Private corporate dining rooms in New York City routinely astounded me with their formality, yet my hosts and I were at-ease. Yes, it took some practice. I probably could fill a chapter with vivid memories of these places and the lessons I learned — sometimes the hard way.

Recently a colleague and I met with a new president of a major university. We had been with him at meetings and a black-tie gala, but now we three were in his office. Immediately his east coast-honed hospitality was a breath of fresh air. His smile was easy and warm. He was as accommodating and open as we hoped he would be. His relationship with his support team was respectful and friendly. His civility wins applause from students, faculty and administrators. I am fairly certain he'll break all-time records for raising funds from alumnae, foundations, corporations, and other would-be benefactors.

This particular leader is the real thing. His civility is a big part of who and what he is. Did I mention he was all about action and results? When it comes to performance, he always expects A+ work. The seasoned president is a master of words and behaviors of his high office. He communicates his high expectations without command-and-control balderdash. I look forward to our next times together. He already knows I'll do what I can to further his agenda and otherwise support his work. His brilliance and civility won me over.

"Please don't ever write a book." — J.L. Darling

As New Year 1984 began, an author wrote for me in the front of her new release, Outclassing the Competition, *"To John Dallas — Entrepreneur, connoisseur, gourmet cook, and — I suspect — a lot of other classy things. Please don't ever write a book. You would be unfair competition. Fondly, Jan Darling, 4 January 1984."* She wrote the inscription in the book that she gave as a thank you gift for hosting at my New York home a candle-lit meal. I was 33. That age and those halcyon 1980s days are G.O.N.E. Jan never knew how tempted I was to knock her book off the shelves. Etiquette needs a man's perspective, thought I.

Aggressive but polite, I told Jan Darling I was just too busy to give writing a book more than 1,001 or more thoughts. Yes, from my early 30s onward I wanted to write a book, and never seemed to find the time or inner peace to sustain enough concentrated thought and effort in order to be published. And I certainly did not want my first book to address a topic about which so many masters had written.

J.L. Darling was the name on the cover of Jan's book. She did not want a would-be buyer to know she was a woman. I could not understand where she was coming from. I had been weaned on Amy Vanderbilt's *New Complete Book of Etiquette*, *The Guide to Gracious Living*, Charlotte Ford's *Book of Modern Manners*, several etiquette books from Brooks Brothers and Tiffany & Co., and a few books of things to do and not from member-and-guest handbooks of private clubs I was privileged to visit, and some I would eventually join.

From age eight onward I was determined to learn civility's right from wrong, good from bad, tasteful *vs.* tasteless, and other higher-living lessons I needed to balance out what I somehow knew deep-down I needed to know and learn on my own; well, almost on my own. Looking back, I had attentive tutors for learning more than American and European table manners. (I choose European table practices as more logical and practical.)

Three principal factors placed me on this odd track for a young boy to travel, every Sunday amongst the white-gloves and tea-sandwiches civility of First Presbyterian Church of Pittsburgh (founded in 1773, three years before the U.S. Declaration of Independence was signed), total youthful devotion to attending the world-renowned Pittsburgh Symphony Orchestra, and six months of role-playing with Grandmother

Regina Elizabeth (*i.e.*, Queen Elizabeth) Shearer preparing me for an eight-hour 1958 Pennsylvania Railroad train ride from Pittsburgh to Philadelphia and back — to visit in Philadelphia her "proper friends." I had to learn. I did. Grandmother made certain I knew what she knew.

At table in Philadelphia, I made a tiny mistake that I remember as if it were yesterday. It was harmless. It was silly. Again, I was eight years old. Grandmother's stern and impolite reprimand was so humiliating, and yet of the type I later learned proper hosts easily laugh off.

In total it all was just enough to frighten impressionable Johnny Dallas into believing my entire future depended on learning etiquette from *Alpha* to *Omega*, A-to-Z, and finger bowl to demitasse. Thank the heavenly host I did. I am still learning. Are you? Full chapters could be written about each of the above experiences. I won't. I am a natural sponge for learning etiquette. When dealing with fellow human beings and their institutions, there is always a nuance or more to consider.

It was a pleasure for me to be a frequent guest on Chicago's community television program to draw attention to the work of a foundation calling attention to the importance of etiquette. CAN-TV 21 host for the foundation, Sandra Craig, encouraged me to speak plainly, and occasionally humorously, about the promise and peril of my passion for etiquette. On-camera and elsewhere, candidly I admit to many *faux pas* and also to adequate performance. There is always more to learn.

In 2010 an etiquette foundation awarded me an honorary doctorate in the philosophy of etiquette. I am grateful for any foundation and others who are taking the message about the importance of civility – all the way from youngest students in elementary schools, up to senior citizens in assisted living. Young and other ages need reminders and lessons.

There is no need to do any of this with a heavy hand. Empathically and with authentic smiles, by-example instructors must practice what they teach about civility. For lasting impact, they must get it right.

From my being invited by a close friend to dine with an occasional duke, duchess, or other lower British Royal he would host, to planned or chance encounters with politicians and celebrities, my knowing enough etiquette allowed me to mask my nervousness or other forms of unease. Once talking with The Donald's Ivana Trump, suddenly I was being used as a prop as the cameras clicked. Yes, she was posing. The PR handler had signaled her to do what she did best. And thankfully I knew the odd freeze-frame dance that's required to ensure best media photos.

Enjoying extended conversation such varied notables as Barbara Bush, Walter Cronkite, Gloria Vanderbilt (CNN's Anderson Cooper's mother), Tyra Banks, Brooke Shields (and mother Terry), Joel Grey, Senators John Glenn and John Tower, mayors of large cities and small towns, and a few governors, I am so pleased I knew — more or less — what to do and say. Occasionally they did not.

Early I noticed among big names their perhaps feigned humility and endearing awkwardness with required etiquette. Then again, they may never have had the benefit of tutoring in top-hat tips and taboos.

> *"Words have meaning beyond the obvious.*
> *Words have consequences beyond intentions.*
> *Civil words align risk and reward of such unknowns."* —JRDjr

After coming under fire for a churlish slur against gay people, and then unleashing a media torrent of uncivilized thoughts and language on numerous broadcasts about many indecorous topics, in late 2011 Director Brett Ratner submitted his resignation as a producer of the 84th Annual Academy Awards. "He did the right thing for the academy and for himself," Academy of Motion Pictures Arts and Sciences President Tom Sherak said to reporters. "Words have meaning, and they have consequences. Brett is a good person, but his comments were unacceptable. We all hope this will be an opportunity to raise awareness about the harm that is caused by reckless and insensitive remarks, regardless of the intent." Words and consequences.

> *"A civil tongue speaks the language of masters.*
> *An uncivil tongue reveals character flaws of its master."* —JRDjr

At 17 my early lessons in what I later would privately call "gentlemanly etiquette and charm" paved the way for me to enter — for the first time in 1967 and as recently as October 2011 — Pittsburgh's incomparable Duquesne Club. This private bastion of old and new money almost always ranks among the world's top clubs. Duquesne Club experience prepared me for enjoying, as a guest, many elite private clubs throughout the U.S. and in the U.K. I was made ready for c-suite corporate dining rooms, finest restaurants, and formal homes of wealthy and ever-gracious hosts. I had a lot to learn. I made many mistakes. The teen-years foundation of knowledge about a gentleman's behavior in polite society allowed me access to contacts, information and conversations I may never have been permitted. Caring about best etiquette opened for me lead-glass windows and brass-hinged doors.

As Junior Achievement's PR and fund-raising front man to the Pittsburgh business world, it seemed most people assumed I was born with a silver spoon in my mouth. Nope. Two generations earlier Family Dallas wealth mysteriously evaporated. Grandfather Dallas appeared to be the black sheep that caused the run on funds. Yet truly I felt in my heart and soul wealthy beyond measure. I was a youthful believer and a high achiever. The combination of deep faith and high performance kept a smile on my face, and the fork in my left hand and the knife in my right. A steady stream of warm and comforting personal attention and etiquette lessons were offered to me on sterling silver platters.

Quickly I learned politeness is not a sign of a man's vulnerability and weakness. Occasionally bullied for my assumed "snobbishness" (*vs.* my hidden insecurity), with sharp words I julienned offending derrières. Being polite does not mean a gentleman's guard is down. *Au contraire!*

In 1979 I was 29 while staying at a private club in London. By a whispering staff person I was informed H.R.H. Prince Phillip was arriving for dinner. Very discreetly I stepped just outside to observe him and his vintage and Royal Standard-bearing Rolls (with a cracked leather landau roof). There were very few of us. He glanced my way and smiled broadly. I nodded my U.S. head and smiled broadly in return. He beamed as he walked into The Eccentric Club. He probably sensed a Yankee among the crowd, clearly the youngest WASP face among the dozen or so respectful onlookers.

The Eccentric Club was founded as a society for original thinkers. Not insignificantly it closed in 1985. In 2008 it was re-opened. My July 1979 solo dining table was rather close to the Duke's long table of men. I was startled by the constant loud laughter that came from that table. HRH appeared to be the catalyst for much of what was erupting in a normally quiet space. It seemed a bit of a scrimmage.

That evening I learned a few lasting lessons about civility among assumed peers. Prince Phillip (now beyond 90 years of age) is known for his occasionally un-civil tongue. Reports of his many gaffes of incivility are mostly based on generation gaps and other disparity.

*"Civility is not a specific code of behavior as much as it
is a call to unrelenting thought and effort to care."* —JRDjr

Thoughts and acts of civility are paradoxical in their appearance and function. A swordsman screams, *En garde! Touche!* He is being polite, but one must be prepared to parry or perish. Throwing down the glove and all neat clichés of battle are words and acts of gentlemen about to do serious-to-fatal damage to another human being. Polarity noted.

*"Civility is not a tactic or a sentiment. It is the determined
choice of trust over cynicism, of community over chaos."*
—George W. Bush (2001 Inaugural Address)

First dates were unprepared for the ease with which I presented bouquets, opened and closed car doors, yielded to them, handled each *maître d'hôtel*, asked their food preferences, ordered for them, waited to eat until they started, and generally demonstrated my rapt attention to what one does, and studiously avoided what one does not do. I enjoy knowing and doing right things. I try.

Young ladies in audiences who hear me talk about the importance of gentlemanly behavior often nod their heads, immediately applaud, and afterwards thank me for reminding male animals about politeness. Young men hearing my views welcome more than dismiss my perspective. There are notable exceptions. Occasionally someone will dramatically prove my point about men needing a civil tongue.

Recently I read a piece in *The New York Times* suggesting Americans are becoming more polite with each other. Perhaps the protracted economic downturn may have created a tipping point for a return to civility. When almost everyone feels at least a bit more financially vulnerable, perhaps most of us grow more accepting, amiable and amenable.

"Civility costs nothing and buys everything."
—Lady Mary Wortley Montagu

One does.

Civility. Expound.

Clarity

Chapter Inspired by and Dedicated to the
Reverend Dr. John M. Buchanan

Insert or imagine seeing your first name: _____,

Seeing this chapter's title word, what immediately comes to your open mind? Do you already have a working relationship with this word? Somewhere inside of you does this word instantly appeal? As a response to a specific situation at-hand, will this word work to your and others' advantage? For this word to increase in real value, together we must dig, drill and think deeper, so we will reach, climb and soar higher.

Clarity is mission-critical for fully responsible leadership. Clear expression of words, free from obscurity and easy-to-understand, allows comprehensibility and engagement. Through evaluation of clarity, one can assess a leader's ultimate effectiveness.

Judeo-Christian traditions refer to "The Word of God," not words (plural) of God. Collectively, all words, acts, evidence, and educated guesswork about divine wisdom distill to one word. The Word.

One could imagine an All Souls scholar at Oxford arguing in her or his Essay exam the Word of God *is* "God;" the all-inclusive and omnipresent single word. Expound.

When I would return to speak at suburban Pittsburgh's Baldwin High School, I was confronted with a big sign, hanging high in the main entrance, with an unintentionally sexist quote from a speech:

> *"He who is a master of words is a master of men."*
> —John R. Dallas, Jr., B.H.S. Class of 1968

Today my phasing would be more inclusive. When originally I wrote these inelegant thoughts, I had a teenager's sense of the appeal of cosseted words. I knew individual words have their own power.

Words had already freed my spirit. One word can change history. Words can bring clarity and triumph. Words can bring calamity.

Imagine a politician or organization chief saying, "Let me be muddled, muddy, mangled, and otherwise manipulative with my words, hoping you are gullible enough to think you are hearing clarity." With our votes, purchases, and other forms of agreement, we tolerate an overabundance of obfuscation and other murkiness. It's time for change toward more clarity and accountability.

"Let me be perfectly clear" was frequently used by enigmatic President Richard Nixon. Too often Presidents Ford and Carter were unclear. Bill Clinton was not aiming for clarity when he vehemently denied unfitting deeds that led to impeachment. Presidents Bush both seemed to believe they were being quite clear regarding their sense of duty and our best interests. President Obama occasionally channels The Great Communicator, Ronald Reagan. Clear thinking is key.

"Take advantage of every opportunity to practice your communication skills so that when important occasions arise, you will have the gift, the style, the sharpness, the clarity, and the emotions to affect other people." — Jim Rohn

In 1963 Alfred Hitchcock's jaw-dropping thriller *The Birds* was released. Hollywood promoters plastered our telephone booths, door handles, lampposts, and flag poles with ominous black-and-white stickers reading *"The Birds Is Coming."* When Whitehall Junior High School reading teacher Mrs. Dale (Edith) Cleland explained to me the grammatical correctness of this instantly inharmonious construction, for perhaps the first time I deeply realized how just one word could make all the difference in the world. With youthful ardor, wrongly I argued printed promotions should read "The Birds ARE Coming."

"The Birds" IS a movie, I was informed. Instantly, I got it. Clarity.

Especially when dealing with people of other cultures (within the States or globally), such is the never-ending joy and ploy of words. Even now I am still trying to grasp full meaning of how "no" might mean "yes" and *vice-versa*. Clarity denied commands extra effort.

Many times with next-door and overseas negotiations, I learn "yes" means "no" or "maybe." In other cultures and languages clarity requires extra effort. Travel between among regions of the United States often demands extra attentiveness toward ensuring clarity.

Political, organizational and personal clarity comes with time, age and experience. To varying degrees, history often proves we were kept in the dark, by others — and by ourselves; what we thought was clarity was anything but. Focus deeper on ceaseless change to achieve more clarity.

> *"Change is the law of life. And those who look only to the past or present are certain to miss the future."* —John F. Kennedy

In their last years in celebrated urban pulpits, three times over four decades I witnessed breakthrough extra clarity come to Presbyterian pastors. The reverend doctors Robert J. Lamont, Bryant M. Kirkland, and John M. Buchanan each retired from my Pittsburgh, New York, and Chicago churches, after 20, 25, and 26 years of service respectively. Counting their entire ministries, many thousands and I benefited from well over 100 combined years of their ministerial quests for clarity.

As each pastor neared his final sermon, many parishioners would notice extra measures of personal insight and clarity. Perhaps more than each teacher realized, from deeper parts of their giving and grieving souls they were choosing their career-encompassing thoughts and words.

Cynics suspect such enhanced final pronouncements are driven by each ego's concern for legacy. I disagree. I choose to hear lasting resonance of confirmation and affirmation that these teachers were gaining final bursts of clarity as they taught their last lessons about polarity.

> *"Whoever knows he is deep, strives for clarity; whoever would like to appear deep to the crowd, strives for obscurity."* —Friedrich Nietzsche

Listen to yourself. Listen to others. Do you hear clarity? Do you hear muddle? Do you always know the difference? Take a good look at your writing. What are you reading? Are you seeing clarity? Do you expect polarity? Are you known for insisting upon and delivering clarity?

> *"Let us read with method, and propose to ourselves an end to what our studies may point. The use of reading is to aid us in thinking."* —Edward Gibbon

Clarity. Expound.

Collaboration

Chapter Inspired by and Dedicated to Jason P. Jacobsohn

Insert or imagine seeing your first name: _____,

Seeing this chapter's title word, what immediately comes to your open mind? Do you already have a working relationship with this word? Somewhere inside of you does this word instantly appeal? As a response to a specific situation at-hand, will this word work to your and others' advantage? For this word to increase in real value, together we must dig, drill and think deeper, so we will reach, climb and soar higher.

On a day-to-day basis do you collaborate freely and constructively? Are you known as a collaborator? Are you respected by peers and others for your collaborative approach to people, matters and tasks? Would others call you a team player, teammate, fellow traveler, colleague, helper, partner, co-worker, compatriot, associate, or other term suggesting your knowledge, wisdom, courage, patience, and practice of win-win-win collaboration — (1) you win, (2) others win, and (3) the team wins when you collaborate? Or in conversation do you hold back more than you step forward; think your share and say nothing or actually have nothing to say? Far too many of us think or say we are collaborators, and actually we are not as collaborative as we want ourselves and others to think. Do you regard yourself as a giver in collaborative conversation, but suspect others say you are a taker, much less of a contributor than perhaps you want to be?

Seven Sins of Subjugation in Collaboration

Concern for quantity *vs.* quality of your contributions in collaborative settings may trip you up and tie your tongue. Did any of the above questions asked open a pit in your stomach or a spandrel in your brain; an instant sense of fear or opportunity? Fearing you are not going to say something of immediately recognizable high value or impact, and waiting until first you are pleased with your own full and complete thought before venturing forth, are you fearing ridicule, mockery, rejection, subjection, submission, dismissal or worse — irrelevancy? Take an extra moment and re-read these Seven Sins of Subjugation in Collaboration. Are you guilty of subjugating thoughts or ideas from yourself or your associates to premature and sometimes hostile judgment? When others boldly go where their brains lead them, do you act to stop them in their tracks? Or do you try to keep your mind's locomotive engine rolling forward on a parallel, subway or elevated track?

Are fresh and unformed ideas from others intimidating or illuminating; feared or welcomed? Before or on-the-spot, thinking through your personal blocks to collegial collaboration must precede your *thinking outside the box*. When in group settings or with one or more, remember to listen to any little voice or bull horn inside of you whispering or blaring myth and logic associated with wisdom, courage and patience it takes to speak up and out. Hear if any noise is coming from childhood lessons learned that may have shut you up more so than propped you up; silenced your voice instead of giving you voice lessons.

You may have been negatively influenced by misguided misanthropes more so than positively emboldened by thoughtful masters. Don't hesitate to think back to how you may have been stopped from thinking your share — and then sharing with others your words of wisdom, courage and patience.

Grandmother Shearer would tell her only Dallas grandson, "Think your share and say nothing." Then she would say, "Be sure to think before you speak" and "Know when enough is enough." Grandmother was counterbalancing my father's frequent admonition, "Children should be seen and not heard." All these intentionally conflicting messages from our home's live-in 1917 student of Indiana (PA) State Normal School (*i.e.*, a teachers college, now Indiana University of Pennsylvania) were designed, I believe, to give me a sense of my leadership place in society. She expected me to someday live in The White House, and laid claim to the Lincoln Bedroom.

Childhood's psychological remnants of hearing adults say, "Children should be seen and not heard," and similar put-downs to young minds, can carry detritus far into adulthood. If you sit relatively silently in most meetings where your open and clear voice would matter, or you struggle to speak only so you are not seen by others (or yourself) as the one who had nothing at all to say, rethink what makes you hold your tongue when your brain is supposed to be racing. Or is your brain stalled? Are you allowing your electrical synapses to fire at-will, or has someone or something short-circuited the motherboards of your fine mind and good heart?

From "Whatever" to "What if..."

Even if they don't know the name of the singer or the song, disenfranchised or dissembled souls among younger and older generations fall prey to the lyrics in a Doris Day hit single: *"Que Sera, Sera. Whatever will be, will be. The future's not ours, to see. Que Sera, Sera. What will be, will be."* Moving in your mind from "Whatever" acquiescence to "What if..." ascendancy is a mission-critical step for full-throttle collaboration. Recognizing your God-given skills and callings for piecing together life's puzzles, in many different ways, requires unblocking and unlocking engagement of your mind, body and soul.

Collaboration means to give and to take, aggress and regress, approach and retreat, speak-up and stand down, and engage in other genuinely cooperative thoughts and behaviors directed toward favorable outcomes. Even knowing this truth about collaboration, do you feel more power by keeping your mouth shut and snickering at the proceedings while others are clearly struggling with a topic, or do you jump in and swim in uncharted waters with the dolphins and maybe a blood-thirsty shark or two? If you were watching yourself *via* a hidden camera, during most meetings would you see yourself snicker, frown, grimace, roll your eyes, cross your arms across your chest, and let everyone know through your words or body language that you just don't want to — or have to — play this team game called collaboration? Do you let everyone know you are better than they, so why in the world would you (of few superior people) be expected to put on table your flowing fountain of unlimited ideas and solutions? Or would you see yourself leaning into the conversation, physically, vocally; fully attentive and contributive? These roughhewn questions are designed to arrest counterproductive anti-collaboration thoughts and behaviors in anyone who needs this kick in their assets.

Thinking differently about what it means to collaborate will allow the U.S. economy to soar again — in a different upward direction, I hope. "Begin with the end in mind," says author Stephen Covey in his *Seven Habits of Highly Effective People*. In this wise spirit, Internet search engines such as Google, Bing, Ask and others should be called instead — "find engines." Promising their users they will find results seems to be a more compelling value proposition for buyers than saying they can merely search.

"Seek and ye shall find…" is a tried-and-true marketing premise delivered from on high. Seekers and searchers find something, even if paradoxically it is ultimately deemed nothing. Finding gold is more valuable than searching for it, so why not focus on the searcher's desirable end result instead of the search itself? "Find engines" could be thought of as virtual collaborative partners. As you search online, you are collaborating with archived collaborative input of others, correct? Think about how your brain expands as you allow it to respond to what you find online.

Similarly, "social networking technology" and "social media" could be called "collaboration technology" or "collaboration media." The sylphlike word "social" casts a questionable value shadow on Twitter, Facebook, Yammer, Ning, and other online resources with considerable upside potential for facilitating collaboration in the business arena. Today's computing, telephony and mobile technologies contain emerging answers to prayers for those of us who crave more efficient and productive meaningfulness, means and methods for ongoing collaboration with colleagues, customers, prospects, lawmakers, and countless others.

Suppose the above visionary points were made by me in a meeting during which we both had pledged to meet to collaborate to see how we could change industry-standard terminology for search engines to "find engines," or rename social networking to "collaborative networking." How would you have responded to what you might have experienced as my flights of fancy; my trusting shots in the dark when trying to make collaborative progress? How were you responding as you were reading? Were you adding your own ideas to mine? Expound.

If you and I were to agree to collaborate to form a new business, I would expect the two of us to come to meetings prepared to share fairly equally in ideational development, concept testing, and other validation and justification for the proposed venture. Twice in the past three years or so, heretofore respected entrepreneurs suggested we meet to discuss ways of doing business together. In both totally separate instances, neither team's members on the other side of the table from me offered a whipstitch of collaborative input. In both cases, eventually I almost begged the others for at least one of their ideas we could chew on. The only ideas on the table came from me. Eventually I pulled back, withdrew from talks, and reformed in my mind the original relationships to have much less value and potential. Sad.

Lack of ability or willingness to openly and freely collaborate is a big red stop light when traveling down any road toward a business deal or other relationship. Use emergency brakes.

In the name of collaboration, too often annihilation occurs. Oh, the games we play! Over more than 40 years of sitting in meetings with serious, supercilious, and even silly minds, I continue to marvel at passive-aggressiveness, approach-avoidance, self-aggrandizement, delusion, confusion, emotional terrorism, misogyny, misandry, racism, homophobia, anti-Semitism, and other appallingly stupid affronts to goodwill and good-faith of those assembled at table — allegedly seated there to do good (not evil). Bad can happen during such meetings and/or behind closed doors after adjournment. If those walls could talk!

Eleven or so years ago I presented to my team of investors a master plan for a $30-million vision for which I was asking for their collaborative input (*i.e.*, their at least temporary trust, benefit-of-doubt, suspension of disbelief, best-effort creativity, and other confirmation and affirmation during the ensuing discussion). When I finished and collaborative discussion was to begin, the ranking billionaire at table turned to the hidebound human calculator to his left and asked what all this meant in numbers.

Without a moment's hesitation, out loud Mr. Math ran the numbers in his head and concluded my presentation was more than a good risk; the $30 million could turn into $100 million within five years, and there was no end in sight for future revenue and profitability. Without strutting my lesser but adequate analytical math skills, in my presentation I had said as much and more.

Mr. B (for his billions) exclaimed to the arithmetician, "Wow! How in the world can you do all those calculations in your head without a calculator? I am amazed. I'm so glad you are on this team." I tried to arrest Mr. B's attention to the task at hand — collegial collaboration — so we each might have at least some voice, and everyone a rightful sense of ownership with the ideas, relationships, goodwill and other soft assets I painstakingly brought forward for collaborative input. Alas, it seemed only the numbers mattered to Mr. B, not my novel proposed ways of generating new revenue and profits.

Mr. B fell asleep during my high-energy detail-rich presentation. Only big dollar signs could keep him awake; big ideas put him to sleep. Other than "Thank you, John," he said nothing to me; nothing at all collaborative or affirmative in scope. He did, however, immediately write a check for $1.5 million — without a piece of paper from me in his hands. To Mr. B and others, dollars speak louder than words.

Having participated and been otherwise privy to cold-hearted big people acting small, I saw many prospective deals and careers crumble under the weight of bullies unable or unwilling to collaborate. Sad. Shameful.

The above recapitulation from the 1990s is now written with a slight smile, but I confess to discovering as I write a lingering deep pit in my stomach. Absence of collaboration can be painful. Egocentricity of insecure participants in many meetings I moderated destroyed collaboration toward multi-million-dollar deals being envisioned or re-engineered.

Fully responsible leaders must acknowledge then steer clear of the shadow side of why too many of us do not collaborate; why we hold back when stakes are high, why we are secretly fearful of (1) success, (2) failure, or — (3) irrelevance. These weaknesses and there attendant threats must be reversed. Gold stars and battle scars are won by captains of collaboration.

Fully responsible leaders in collaborative situations R.E.A.C.T. exactingly and productively to people and things with:

Respect. Empathy. Authenticity. Clarity. Trust.

Fully responsible leaders in collaborative situations also R.E.A.C.H. high in their thoughts, words, and deeds with:

Reality. Energy. Ascendancy. Commitment. Humility.

Thank you for thoughts and acts toward win-win-*plus* collaboration.

Collaboration. Expound.

Commitment

Chapter Inspired by and Dedicated to Brenda Palms-Barber

Insert or imagine seeing your first name: _____,

Seeing this chapter's title word, what immediately comes to your open mind? Do you already have a working relationship with this word? Somewhere inside of you does this word instantly appeal? As a response to a specific situation at-hand, will this word work to your and others' advantage? For this word to increase in real value, together we must dig, drill and think deeper, so we will reach, climb and soar higher.

Aiming upward toward re-alignment for our economy, we must reach for higher levels of commitment.

Relevant synonyms for commitment: allegiance, commitedness, dedication, loyalty, affirmation, assurance, devotion, faith, oath, pledge, vow, cooperation, earnestness, engagement, involvement, participation, serious-mindedness, seriousness, sincerity, genuineness, authenticity...

From Wikipedia, the free encyclopedia: "Personal commitment is the act or quality of voluntarily taking on or fulfilling obligations. What makes personal commitment 'personal' is the voluntary aspect [*i.e.,* commitment is a choice.] ...it is not necessary that a personal commitment relate to personal interests."

Panoramic view from The HILL: What are you doing today that reflects your commitment to a better tomorrow? At this painfully obvious tipping point in global political and economic direction, oddly some still choose delusional comfort with the past, instead of committing to thinking differently about the future. Forecasting we should or will get back to the way things were means one is outright asking to someday repeat this meltdown. Rather than work to learn from glaring mistakes, and develop and explore un-tethered creative thoughts and ideas about tomorrow's markets and matters, even smart minds sit on their wits and wait. Fully responsible leaders do not wait for others to do all the heavy thinking?

"The significant problems we have cannot be solved at the same level of thinking with which we created them." —Albert Einstein (1879-1955)

Do you agree Wall Street and Main Street will never be the same? Because of this reality check, perhaps unprecedented leader commitment to thinking differently will be remembered as this era's collegial and collaborative state-of-mind that yielded both societal and economic change. Believing individuals are powerless renders us so. Trusting, however, that we each have some large or other-size role in correcting the course of our economy gives us a fighting chance to redefine the American Dream. Change for the better is long overdue. Commitment is required.

How many people do you know who routinely commit to 30-year mortgages and 36-month payment plans, for homes and cars respectively, and yet accept new jobs with no more commitment in-mind than one or two years? Yes, too many people commit to lenders for longer periods of their lives than they commit to employers. And employers grow less committed to employees. Have we Americans grown commitment-phobic?

"Unless commitment is made, there are only promises and hopes...but no plans."

—Peter Drucker

For many fear of success and fear of failure are hidden stumbling blocks in the path toward accepting responsibility for CHOOSING commitment. "Thinking through the blocks" while "thinking outside the box" are essential requirements for fully responsible leaders. Commitment is mission-critical.

Climbing a Hill is an Act of Will

Views from just-right HILL-height allow us to see people and things in-motion. Clarity from hills in our minds normally exceeds anything we see from flat plains, lofty mountaintops, or stale ivory towers. For a lifetime commit to climb hills.

Essential re-alignment of our daily thoughts and actions requires abundance of personal commitment to (1) pursue deeper wisdom, (2) maintain steadfast courage, and (3) practice abundant patience.

Imagination also fuels commitment. In the woods behind my former wife's family home, on Blackburn Road in Sewickley Heights, is a large marble-based pool that was built in the 1920s. I believe it remains one of many relics of when their Fair Acres estate was owned by the Jones family of Jones and Laughlin Steel Corporation (J&L). The cost to restore the fountains and pool, to again hold and handle water and modern-day filtration systems, was so exorbitant that the total would have been more than double the price of the large house they built, in 1964, on the highest peak in the borough.

Restoration, therefore, was not to happen. Although it was truly sad to see the sprawling masterpiece empty, overgrown, and otherwise unattended to, we were always amazed how our young minds would be able to turn on the many fountains and fill the pool. For long periods we would sit and easily imagine what it had been like, talk about it all, and discuss in-detail what it could be — if money and logic were not standing in the way of restoring the space to its former splendor. We imagined black-tie galas with guests dancing around the spacious periphery. I committed to someday earn enough money to restore these elitist symbols of Pittsburgh's faded Steeltown glory. Divine providence did not include such wealth or wedded bliss.

Interestingly, I never needed to see any images original splendor. Restoration happened in our minds and hearts. And I remember the thrill of those deep feelings of resolve and other commitment.

Let's all re-commit to imagine purpose and promise of commitment.

"The quality of a person's life is in direct proportion to their commitment to excellence, regardless of their chosen field of endeavor."
—Vincent T. Lombardi

"Please and thank you," as Grandmother Shearer would say in one quick breath and with steady eye contact — leaving her only grandson no room for escape. She knew how to secure my immediate and sometimes lasting commitment. She earned it.

Commitment. Expound.

Confluence

Chapter Inspired by and Dedicated to the
Reverend Carolyn Eaton Cranston

Insert or imagine seeing your first name: _____,

Seeing this chapter's title word, what immediately comes to your open mind? Do you already have a working relationship with this word? Somewhere inside of you does this word instantly appeal? As a response to a specific situation at-hand, will this word work to your and others' advantage? For this word to increase in real value, together we must dig, drill and think deeper, so we will reach, climb and soar higher.

Confluence defines and describes a fact or impression in which two or more things come together. Fully responsible leaders work to create, identify, nurture, protect, and otherwise establish value in confluence of people, money, ideas, crucibles, and other mission-critical resources. Especially in navigating a correction economy, committed leaders must seize opportunities for confluence in: (1) forging and fueling strategic alliances, (2) acquiring and merging organizations, (3) facilitating peer-to-peer support and success, (4) collapsing silos and silo mentality, (5) mentoring protégées to mentor their own protégées, (6) diversifying every leadership team to include more women, people of all colors and creeds, and those from walks of life different from outmoded norms.

Confluence in diversity in not only a worthy ethical issue for populist embrace, it is also the most promising vision and mission for long-term sustainable economic, intellectual, ethical, spiritual, and other growth. Leaders are wise to find richness in confluence of diversity and inclusion over poverty and paucity of exclusion.

Paraphrasing an earlier reference to hockey great Wayne Gretsky, in effect he said a good hockey player plays where the puck is, while a great hockey player plays where the puck is going to be. From your hill views at home, work, in your community, and from where you stand for your global perspective, where are people going to be? For those you must and can support, what are you doing to ensure for journeys underway their and your true-north direction?

The City of Pittsburgh's geographic confluence point is where the majestic Allegheny and Monongahela rivers form the mighty Ohio River. The Ohio River begins in Pennsylvania.

By declaration, Pennsylvania's confluence project of 1776 produced the United States of America. The U.S.A. began in Pennsylvania. Confluence of faiths, values, ethics, hunger, thirst, and resources became the American Free Enterprise Way-of-Life. At the confluence of faith and life, thinkers find wisdom, courage, patience — and purpose. During a related speech I used rhetorical flourish:

"In my idyllic mind's eye I live in a multiverse of the unknown, a galaxy of human stars, a world of possibilities, a continent of compassion, a nation of freedom, a region of justice, a state of appreciation, a county of accountability, a city of hope, a Mister Rogers-like neighborhood of make-believe — at the intersection of faith and life — in a home that's all heart." I mean and feel it all.

Before the Internet intensified cravings for instant gratification, brick-and-mortar lending libraries fueled this nation's imagination, and lubricated other internal engines of innovation and entrepreneurship. Pittsburgh's top Scot, industrialist Andrew Carnegie, forged alignment of his commitment to bettering the human condition with his obsession for books and detail. Long before the term was coined, Mr. Carnegie was a social entrepreneur, "...doing real and permanent good in this world." Carnegie's philosophic and financial endowment for libraries, museums, institutes, brain trusts, and other initiatives elevated our collective IQ.

Pittsburgh's WQED-TV was the first educational television company, later spawning public broadcasting as we know it today — including the original on-air values-based pulpit for kids and parents, "Mister Rogers Neighborhood." Steelers City's KDKA is the first commercial radio station in the world. The list of firsts from the City of Confluence fills volumes. Confluence is in Pittsburgh's DNA. Today The Burgh's breakthroughs in biotechnology, health care, and high-tech boggle minds. The sky's the limit when leaders intentionally align experience, education, money, resources, passion, drive, crucibles — and extra effort. Pittsburgh's confluence projects are shovel-ready and mind-ready for the Administration's injection of stimulus funds. Are we?

Confluence of purposeful and passionate people is the most powerful economic development engine for any city, county, state or nation. Beginning in the 1950s, Pittsburgh's Republican financier Richard King Mellon and Democratic-machine Mayor David L. Lawrence aligned their views from their respective hills. With often publicly and passionately stated intentionality and great on-camera respectfulness, they generated a cultural tipping point confluence that ignited Pittsburgh's ongoing renaissance.

Childhood lessons in power of collaboration came from my watching oil mix with water as vastly different Messrs. Mellon and Lawrence set for Pittsburgh a highly interactive culture of confluence; a city still well aware of the constant need for strategic alignment of people, plans and performance. Many staggering crucibles to come were forged into steel beams to build higher on this city's remarkable philosophic and spiritual foundation.

Consider for your organization forging a culture of confluence. Even proudest municipalities and leaders from around the world can learn from Pittsburgh, Cleveland, Baltimore, Atlanta, and a handful of other survive-to-thrive cities, great lessons in confluence and strategic alignment. Amazingly too few allow themselves humility, time, and openness to study or share available lessons.

In a 21 June 2011 piece in *The New York Times* about how the Internet is essentially creating confluence, this excerpt stands out: "Humans want nothing more than to connect, and the companies that are connecting us electronically want to know who's saying what, where," said Susan Crawford, a professor at the Benjamin N. Cardozo School of Law. "As a result, we're more known than ever before." So true.

From its start in 2005 Hillview practitioners and I encourage a clearer view of the term "social networking." As social networking toggles back-and-forth between creating "power" for direct connection for humans and data collection for organizations, "HC/DC" for Human Connection and Data Collection technology is a more representative name for the two AC/DC currents generated by Facebook, Twitter, LinkedIn *et al.*

Both Alternating Current (AC) and Direct Current (DC) were essential means to deliver to far-flung masses earliest radio broadcast signals. HC/DC seems to speak truth to power of social networking's duality in purpose, production and promise. Call it what it is, HC/DC networking. "Social networking" masks commercial interest in market-of-one data that erupts from the Internet in volcanic force.

For decades consumer credit reports from the three U.S. credit reporting agencies (each owned and operated by commercial enterprises such as Facebook, not owned and operated by government "agencies") have been whetting marketing's appetite for tracking buyer interest and behavior. For many years Equifax, Trans Union and Experian have been selling to marketers what could be called our individual "habits history" reports. To reverse risk and identify opportunity, credit reports are used as "character reports."

Soon we'll learn more and more about how credit bureaus and HC/DC-power companies are aligning their commercial interests. For the most part, this strategic alignment is happening below the radar screen of consumers, the media, the Federal Trade Commission (FTC), and probably U.S. Congress.

HC/DC power already electrifies and empowers the planet. Talk about imagery for confluence!

To lift our sights a bit higher than financial and electrical power, let's talk about power of confluence in labyrinths. In psychological, spiritual and religious contexts, I regard labyrinth walks as exercises in intentional confluence. Walking the path of a labyrinth, that's embedded in marble and other types of floors, is a way of getting with and staying with the mind, body and soul. Such meditative exercise allows for confluence of a practical and mystical nature.

Deeper breathing and higher thinking seem to meet to form a confluence of broader perspective about life and even higher thought. This type of intentional engagement in the upside potential within confluence invites to active conversation all senses and skills, and often includes hints of divine presence — and divine providence.

Thank you for your best-effort thoughts, words, and deeds toward honoring exceptional value in natural and supernatural confluence.

Confluence. Expound.

Courage

Chapter Inspired by and Dedicated to the
Reverend Dana Ferguson Myers (1966-2008)

Insert or imagine seeing your first name: _____,

Seeing this chapter's title word, what immediately comes to your open mind? Do you already have a working relationship with this word? Somewhere inside of you does this word instantly appeal? As a response to a specific situation at-hand, will this word work to your and others' advantage? For this word to increase in real value, together we must dig, drill and think deeper, so we will reach, climb and soar higher.

Definition highlights for courage: Quality of being brave, the ability to face danger, difficulty, uncertainty, or pain without being overcome by fear or being deflected from a chosen course of action (from onelook.com).

> *"Faced with what is right, to leave it undone shows a lack of courage."*
> — Confucius

HILL Word Applied: Courage is an innermost and essential understanding of self. Tried-and-true leaders know when, where, how, and by whom their courage has been tested. Although doubtful, somewhere there may be front-line leaders whose courageous feet have yet to land on hot coals of reality, risk or rapture. How do you think about, measure, and feel your courage?

From classic movies "Braveheart" and "Chariots of Fire" came lasting images, sounds and feelings of courage to fight, win, love and fail. These four courageous acts are only superseded in consequence by courage to believe. Fight. Win. Love. Fail. Believe.

For us servant leaders to do the right-and-proper things for the good-of-the-order, for ourselves, and for our highest authority, takes more than courage to succeed. Courage to fail not only sounds paradoxical, it is also functionally pivotal for fully responsible leaders.

Yes, upside-down reality in both failure and success causes even emotionally fit and otherwise mature brains to fear success as much or more than failure. Failure and success bring burdens and blessings. Misery, mystery, and miracles are found in both failure and success. Intentional courage before, during and after failure and success yields greatest clarity. Grasping and navigating this full spectrum of your mind requires wisdom, courage and patience. Fully responsible leaders courageously identify and rectify both fear of success and fear of failure.

Johann Wolfgang von Goethe (1742-1832) said, *"Whatever you can do or dream you can, begin it. Boldness has genius, power and magic in it. Begin it now."* Yet this courage Goethe espoused can intimidate, irritate, or even infuriate those less bold; individuals perhaps socially ascendant in ways other than high-risk. Unsung acts of courageousness include boldness to pro-actively follow trustworthy leaders. If following is intentional and thoughtful, this too is noteworthy courage.

There is timelessness about courage. Presence and lack thereof marks recorded and imagined human history. From all the transactions attributed to the Garden of Eden, to the courage required for you to assess your true levels of courageousness for tackling challenges today and tomorrow, fact and fiction pave the way for understanding the central role courage plays in how we think about and live our lives.

It takes courage to believe in any faith tradition that extends our thoughts beyond the Aristotelian five senses. Such courage emboldens us to have more faith in people and other factors about our lives.

Trusting scientific evidence should take less courage than believing in the unseen. For many good people this is simply not the case. Mystery is sometimes less demanding of courage than fact. Having courage to accept imperfection and doubt in imagined art, tested science, unfathomed mathematics, human condition, and incalculable higher power, can yield exceptionally promising thoughts and actions. It takes courage to think deeply about the validity of visible people and things we choose to take at face value.

"Friendship is the source of the greatest pleasures and without friends even the most agreeable pursuits become tedious." —Thomas Aquinas

Courage in our personal lives deserves more than a nod in this letter to courageous you from courageous me. Friendship of any significant variety requires levels of courage rarely discussed between friends in total candor. Relatively speaking, it is easy to like someone. It takes courage to accept and address difficult stages in truly loving. Courage to boldly go forth in a trusting friendship of any variety includes preparedness for polarity in feelings of both joy and fear.

"Overcome fear, behold wonder." —Richard Bach

It takes courage to put in these letters to you from me thoughts that should appeal as well as reveal. Significance of the word courage is incorporated into each courageous chapter of this book. Physically I sense in the pit of my stomach courage it takes for me to invite others to benefit from what I'm offering in my thinking, writing, speaking, or other acts. My brave heart actually races as I write.

Perhaps with each chapter any thoughtful book author's mind runs a marathon. Whether in my mind I am sprinting 100 meters or running 26.2 miles, I cross a finish line the moment I show any draft to someone. Do you also feel these illustrations of courage?

Rejection or criticism for what I write is not as much of a worry as the notion of risk that deeper meaning for others might be missed. I write to reverse risk of over-simplification of 52 high-impact words, knowing someone could accidentally conclude I am pharisaical; excessively or hypocritically pious in choosing and using certain words. Knowing my heart I underscore courage in trusting readers will be courageous in reaching with these words a higher plane.

"Cowards die many times before their deaths;
the valiant never taste of death but once." —William Shakespeare

Before the biopic masterpiece "Iron Lady" was released, staring courageous Meryl Streep as Baroness Margaret Thatcher — the most powerful British Prime Minister since Winston Churchill — biographer Charles Moore asked Lady Thatcher what her first choice might have been for her memoires The Downing Street Years. Quickly she said, "Undefeated," a one-word result of her unprecedented life of courageousness. Courageously she went where no woman had. Courage.

Elsewhere in this book and in nearly all public presentations, I honor the life-long and complex private psychology behind the public courage of

Apple's Steve Jobs. Wednesday 5 October 2011 he died at 56 years of age (only five years my junior). I saw the news with a text message ping on my iPhone from CBS News, which I found a tad ironic. The morning after his death, ABC-TV and NBC-TV Chicago stations asked for interviews related to my history with Apple and Steve Jobs. ABC's online transcript of the clip they used, "…'He opened the world of technology. He opened our minds, our hearts. And by taking a bite out of that Apple, we learned an awful lot about technology and ourselves,' said tech expert John Dallas." I said so much more.

In 1984 I was covering for my electronic publishing company a Gartner Group conference in Ft. Lauderdale, during which Steve Jobs introduced the Apple Macintosh computer. Returning to Manhattan, immediately I bought a Macintosh and placed it on my credenza next to my IBM PC. On many fronts that act was courageous. IBM was a high-profile client of mine. Apple was not.

Indeed my Wall Street and Park Avenue cronies thought I lost my perspective (*i.e.,* lost my marbles) as a lifetime early-adopter. "IBM was for serious business people and Apple was for kids and artists," they sniffed. The Street did not give the Apple Company a chance. Openly I disagreed. I felt Apple was making things easier and better. As I finish the editing of this book, I remain "a PC," yet I already own the next generation iPhone and iPad. Early adopters (and book authors) are courageous. You are courageous to continue to read this book's views, some of which may re-direct more than your attention. Be courageous. Being courageous is a state-of-being.

"The greater danger for most of us lies not in setting our aim too high and falling short; but in setting our aim too low, and achieving our mark."—Michelangelo

Dr. and Mrs. Peter Koestenbaum kindly forwarded the following quote to underscore the courage it takes to write books. Peter has written numerous excellent books that are available at bookstores, on Amazon, and elsewhere. Peter and I feel rather deeply words related to courage:

> Author Andre Dubus II said, "A first book is a treasure, and all these truths and quasi-truths I have written about publishing are finally ephemeral. An older writer knows what a younger one has not yet learned. What is demanding and fulfilling is writing a single word, trying to write *le mot juste*, as Flaubert said; writing several of them which becomes a sentence. When a writer does that, day

after day, working alone with little encouragement, often with discouragement flowing in the writer's own blood, and with the occasional rush of excitement that empties oneself, so that the self is for minutes or longer in harmony with eternal astonishments and visions of truth, right there on the page on the desk; and when a writer does this work steadily enough to complete a manuscript long enough to be a book, the treasure is on the desk.

If the manuscript itself, mailed out to the world where other truths prevail, is never published, the writer will suffer bitterness, sorrow, anger, and, more dangerously, despair, convinced that the work was not worthy, so not worth those days at the desk. But the writer who endures and keeps working will finally know that writing the book was something hard and glorious, for at the desk a writer must try to be free of prejudice, meanness of spirit, pettiness, and hatred; strive to be a better human being than the writer normally is, and to do this through concentration on a single word, and then another, and another.

This is splendid work, as worthy and demanding as any, and the will and resilience to do it are good for the writer's soul. If the work is not published, or is published for little money and less public attention, it remains a spiritual, mental, and physical achievement; and if, in public, it is the widow's mite, it is also, like the widow, more blessed."

Although I intend my words to trigger in you deep breaths full of increased wisdom, additional courage, and extended patience, I can also imagine you gasping for breath when your agile mind runs with or ahead of a chapter. With each word, together we get to a finish line that is always a new starting point. Every end in mind is a new beginning.

"Life expands or contracts in direct proportion to one's courage." —Anais Nin

From The HILL, would I see you courageously moving true north toward challenging, selfless and worthy destinations? Let's all choose wise, courageous and patient strategic alignment of people, money, and other mission-critical resources. Alternatives may be cowardly actions.

"Without courage, wisdom bears no fruit." —Baltasar Gracian

Courage. Expound.

Crucible

Chapter Inspired by and Dedicated to
Brian Jeffrey Nadeau (1972-2003)

Insert or imagine seeing your first name: _____,

Seeing this chapter's title word, what immediately comes to your open mind? Do you already have a working relationship with this word? Somewhere inside of you does this word instantly appeal? As a response to a specific situation at-hand, will this word work to your and others' advantage? For this word to increase in real value, together we must dig, drill and think deeper, so we will reach, climb and soar higher.

How do you view your life's crucibles; severe tests you encounter? From how high on a hill are you gaining perspective on your and others' crucibles — past, present or future? When death, loss, reversal, upheaval, catastrophe, crime, disaster, or other absence of obvious good strike, how do you feel, reel, deal, and heal? Do you claim, name and re-frame crucibles? Are you strengthened by your life's crucibles; inherently and ultimately stronger as you face each severe test? Do you view crucibles among the most reliable indicators and predictors of true leadership success; the ability to discern and learn value from the worst sets of circumstances?

Through your and others' fears and tears, do you see more clearly each crucible's impact? Firestorms can temper the steel of an individual's resolve to live a more fully conscious life; forging and aligning previously and newly identified strengths of purpose, will, character and selflessness.

The 2009 death of the best man in the May 1973 wedding with my former wife Cynthia, served to further intensify personal understanding of crucible, the word previously selected for this chapter. As I was not authorized by David (aged 63) to reveal his life's formidable crucibles, his untimely death emboldened me to boldly state, for lasting resonance and clarity, the depth from which I approach the value of this chapter's featured word. To avoid doing so would be inauthentic. In this candor I trust you'll find extra value for viewing, navigating and categorizing your and others' crucibles.

As I reveal elsewhere in this book to underscore other worthy perspective, just before turning 30 I was brought back by defibrillation from a flat-line cardiac arrest, caused by an infection that eventually lodged in the lining of my heart and stopped it — miraculously leaving zero damage to heart, brain or body. Yet immediately I was told by well-meaning physicians I might not survive more than three days. I was to update my Last Will and Testament. I did. After one month in hospital and another 30 or so days confined to bed in my temporary sleeping quarters at a private club, 11 months later our marital divorce was final. The end of approximately 18 months of back-breaking, spirit-draining, and faith-testing crucibles was marked by an uncontested divorce decree.

In 2003, following nearly 36 months of nearly unfathomable business difficulties that began with the unexpected acquisition of my employer, and in my personal life numerous debacles beyond my control, I survived a ruptured brain aneurysm and subsequent stroke. For 30 days following these two hits to my brain, statistics indicated I had a 60 percent chance of dying. I revised the Will, but never once did I expect to die. I would not die. I could not die. I have too much more work to do. Even though my eyesight was temporarily impaired by the stroke, I never lost my inner vision of the day I would eventually recover.

Forever I remain in debt to quick-thinking medical professionals and other dutiful caregivers. Daughter Jennifer and armies of family and friends gathered in faith and hopefulness. I still see faces and hear real voices of those ER angels, bedside hand-holders, and tireless home visitors. They and many others did not let me go. For prayers and greetings from nearby and around the globe, I pray each selfless soul stood a little taller and stronger when I acknowledged — then and now — their great and lasting value in my almost full recovery from three near-death experiences. One-breath-at-a-time, I live a healthy, rewarding, and otherwise abundant life.

Among my social circle there were two physicians I grew to value as close personal friends, both nationally recognized for their thought leadership and choices for high-profile visibility in their respective fields. Up-close and quite personally I was witness to crucibles they encountered in their private lives. With each M.D., over time I grew to worry about how both would perform while professionally tending to life-and-death crucibles of patients. Often stunned by their poor judgment, pettiness and immaturity, eventually I realized they too were probably often better in dealing head-on with crucibles of others than those they mishandle in their own lives. Many professionals do more good for others than they do for themselves. I can relate.

In her book Gift from the Sea, Anne Morrow Lindbergh asserts that security lies in the acceptance of the ebb and flow of life, of "intermittency." Rather than insisting on permanency and continuity in life, we do well to realize that "the only continuity possible, in life as in love, is in growth, in fluidity — in freedom." Crucibles have a way of creating feelings as if freedom is being denied. Ultimately crucibles seem to prove freedom to choose our attitude and altitude.

From the panoramic perspective of what I believe to be my mind's just-right hill-height, probably almost daily I point toward views for individuals to consider about themselves and other people and things in-motion. Not infrequently I sense I am more adept at seeing and sensing what others need to do, than I am able — or willing — to apply to myself. To guard against risk of overlaying on someone else's vision a rose-colored or opaque lens through which I may be seeing things for myself, I redouble my attentiveness to uniqueness of the human being in front of me. Yes, by instantly fighting back focus on my own needs, I believe I become more valuable to the person trusting me for guidance.

Among physicians and other caring professionals, great concern has been publically stated about increasing statistics pointing toward a rising trend toward alcoholism, drug-addiction, depression, suicide, divorce, physical abuse, reckless behavior, and myriad other loud warning signals. Several years ago I attended a world-famous medical school's graduation ceremony as the state's Secretary of Health, in her commencement address, blatantly scolded and warned the graduates about the medical community's growing reputation for abusing alcohol and other addictive substances. I was both alarmed and pleased to hear her bold words.

The highly regarded political appointee, also a physician, warned of dire consequences — essentially trying to avert, for physicians and patients alike, likely crucibles. Hours later at the medical school's lavish dinner for nearly 1,000 guests, each of us was handed shiny black gift bags containing, among other trinkets, two wine glasses etched with the medical school's coveted emblem. Indeed, just after being warned to cut back on drinking, all graduates, family, faculty, friends, and media representatives were given keepsakes to forever associate the medical school with drinking alcohol.

Boosters of this particular Midwest state's celebrated university claim their students are among the highest consumers of beer and other adult beverages. For too many binge drinking earns a badge of honor. They are quite proud of their alcohol-related crucibles past, present and in the future. Sadly I could fill two or more chapters with stories, with grim specifics, about this student body's celebrated abusiveness of people and substances. They are among the most proud students and *alumnae* I ever encounter. (See Chapter 38 for Pride.)

Knowing others certainly have more and worse memories or crucibles, I am nevertheless wise to remain mindful of my years of having endured two shocking suicides of friends, preventing a suicide attempt of a roommate, the protracted aftermath of the attempted murder of a close friend, direct and indirect experience with robbery, mugging, physical abuse, household fires, deadly traffic accidents, surgeries, divorces and deaths. Gone from this realm are my grandparents, Father, all aunts, all uncles, several cousins, the physician friend who managed my cardiac care in 1979, and two teachers I cherished as if blood family. Thankfully, my young-at-heart mother's crucibles yielded for her a renewed soul, now overflowing with love.

Certainly hardly alone in recalling mind-numbing childhood trauma, and innumerable business, career, financial, and relationship crucibles, my personal crucibles contribute to how clearly I view my remaining minutes and tasks on this earth. Indeed I am still 100 percent convinced in the transitional, transformative, and healing power of fervent prayer and positive thinking about crucibles.

"Our greatest glory is not in never falling,
but in rising every time we fall." —Confucius

Paradoxically, crucibles create in our minds reachable and teachable moments. Studies at Harvard Medical Center showed positive brain activity during most negative impact. Under pressure of life's crucibles, human brains quite literally open to change in ways about which neurologists, psychiatrists, psychologists, and scholarly theologians are still guessing. Yes, with 20/20 hindsight, even most horrific threat or loss can yield unexpected gain. In our darkest hours, mangled matters and their mysteries are waiting to be translated into hopefulness.

These emotionally, physically, and financially taxing economic times, and the steady flow of heart-tugging news headlines, make it extra important to define, describe and grasp power and potential in life's crucibles. Facing head-on life's crucibles, we must discipline ourselves to react — with intentionality — through Respect, Empathy, Authenticity, Clarity and Trust (R.E.A.C.T.). Especially when being tested to the max, not one of these words is to be taken lightly.

The day after Apple CEO Steve Jobs died, two Chicago TV reporters asked for my thoughts. Honoring his life's formidable overall achievements, I decided to avoid making reference to his many crucibles. Three or four days later I met with a journalist who said, "If Steve Jobs had started Apple in Chicago, he probably would not have been supported financially or otherwise encouraged." She was characterizing Chicago as a crucible for any entrepreneur who is trying to launch a business in the third largest city in the United States.

Walter Isaacson's best-selling exclusive biography of Steve Jobs takes a deep dive into the founder CEO's and Apple's crucibles. Understanding the ultimate value of failure is a core lesson that needs to be addressed head-on. It is far too easy to talk about Apple's successes. It is known that the best of the best entrepreneurs and their businesses often fail before, during and after succeeding.

In my head I still hear long-ago public statements of Sun Microsystems founder Scott McNeely agreeing, along with the late Ned Heiser, founder and CEO of Heizer Corporation, and many other entrepreneurs who eventually grew tired of Chicago's rejection and turned to investors from the coasts and elsewhere. Sun's founder wanted his company to flourish in his hometown Chicago. Effectively Chicago said no. So he and Sun's 40,000 jobs (at their peak) moved west.

Chicago's endemic (though lessening) resistance creates crucibles, over which many steadfast visionaries triumph — somewhere.

When you encounter crucibles in your own life and in lives of others, are you closer to, or further away from, your higher power? To a large degree, your response to any crucible's people, things, set of circumstances, or even to my bold question here, depends on the depth of your prior thinking about the unfathomable mystery and magnitude of life and faith.

> "*You only live twice. Once when you are born and once when you look death in the face.*" —Ian Fleming

Do you agree with the importance of working to discover value in crucibles? I stop just short of looking forward to crucibles.

In moments of deepest reflection I wonder if I feel more satisfaction while weathering storms than while basking in sunlight. Wanting more out of life for others and me began in my earliest years. Those premature yearnings for relief in plentitude of safety, peace, food, nourishment,

> "*Lord, grant that I may always desire more than I can accomplish.*"
>
> —Michelangelo

Crucibles are often tipping points. Your perspective on crucibles can tip your life one way or the other. Please choose a realistic and positive response to your crucibles, no matter how impossible such a reaction may seem at the moment of impact, or however long it may take you to get where you and others need you to be in order to survive and thrive.

> "*Memory Lane always seems to be under reconstruction.*" —JRDjr

With this deeper understanding of this one word, do you sense greater ability to reverse risk of crucibles ahead? Are you able to feel more promise within crucibles to come?

Crucible. Expound.

Delineate

Chapter Inspired by and Dedicated to Philip C. Calian

Insert or imagine seeing your first name: _____,

Seeing this chapter's title word, what immediately comes to your open mind? Do you already have a working relationship with this word? Somewhere inside of you does this word instantly appeal? As a response to a specific situation at-hand, will this word work to your and others' advantage? For this word to increase in real value, together we must dig, drill and think deeper, so we will reach, climb and soar higher.

The vital transitive verb de·lin·eate (*di-li-nē-āt*) gives this forever-in-training leader a burst of clarity – and even a little bit of a high-energy rush of adrenalin. This word lifts me when I'm unsure of what to do next. When in doubt, I delineate. When I'm sure, I delineate even more.

It is a leader's challenge, privilege, blessing and duty to delineate, delineate, delineate as we communicate, communicate, and communicate. Yes, this word deserves rhetorical flourish. Almost speaking in today's pop-culture language, the author of the U.S. Declaration of Independence and third U.S. President boldly put it to us this way:

> *"Do you want to know who you are? Don't ask.*
> *Act! Action will delineate and define you."*

Before his Presidential inauguration on 4 March 1801, Thomas Jefferson was the U.S. Delineator-in-Chief. Called "Man of the People" and "Sage of Monticello," his myriad gifts *by the people and for the people* included his masterful descriptions, portrayals, characterizations, illustrations, depictions, and other artistry with evocative and provocative thoughts and words. He was delineation personified. Indeed Thomas Jefferson is one of my all-time heroes of strategic alignment. From his breathtaking architecture to his brilliant writings, he was strategically aligned for all time.

Within Mr. Jefferson's long-ago turns of phrase and choice of words, We the People can still feel his and our collective majesty and might. His virtuoso violin playing may have helped him to think in organized and methodical ways that unleashed within him his best purpose, passion and prose.

Forever I remain in awe of Thomas Jefferson. Even though memory is fading about particulars of on-site lessons learned, my visits to Charlottesville, Virginia allowed me to bask in his delineation of life.

From the Latin word *delineare*, "to sketch out," delineate evolved from the root linea, "line." For a leader to delineate a subject or plan, connotes her or his intentionality in finding right words and ways to present essential detail. Yet delineating *ad nauseam* can be deemed loquacious, laborious, and sometimes outright ludicrous.

Inadequate or inept delineation may be among the greatest failures of leaders. Perhaps oral-retentive leaders believe they protect themselves from litigation by giving as little detail as possible to their employees, board members, investors, media, buyers, and other constituencies. Or they may be hiding an inadequate vocabulary, shyness, or some form of approach avoidance. Leaders of few words may be fearful of consequences should they overstate, understate, or somehow misstate something in such a way as to create instead of eliminate risk – rather than using oratory, writing, and other communication talents and skills to possibly create unforeseen opportunity.

To me "silence is golden" seems oxymoronic. A sonorous voice delineating purpose, passion and potential seems preferable to fear-based economy of words. Sadly fear-of-failure and fear-of-success put muzzles on many mouths.

When a California company acquired control of venerable Chicago Title Corporation, and eventually a majority of senior managers were released (including yours truly), during the prolonged buy-out process frequently I was struck by the paucity of the buyer's words offered to anyone. Wearing poker faces, anxiously we waited for smoke signals, skywriting, drumbeats, or even a funereal requiem for the masses. Lack of delineation for plans in-the-works ignited rumors and hearsay. Without delineation acquired parties often endure alienation.

As much as I tried, eventually I failed to calm my team. I sensed when I became in their minds a lame duck. They knew my absence of explanation and projection meant I was not being kept in the loop. I was known for over-delineation of facts and forecasts, and suddenly I was prattling instead of buttressing.

From the mid-1990s I was particularly attuned to this type of lack of delineation on the part of an acquiring company. When then $6-billion-in-sales TRW Inc., essentially a manufacturer of automotive supplemental restraint systems (SRS or "air bags") and other products, sold to Bain Capital and Thomas H. Lee Partners (Bain & Lee) its approximately $500-million-in-sales TRW credit bureau division for a mere $700 or so million (if memory serves me correctly), I was startled, to say the least. What logic in company valuation was I missing? As a brand name "TRW" and "credit bureau" were synonymous terms. Consumers would refer to their credit reports as "my TRW." A ubiquitous American brand name, TRW was in the credit world the *Kleenex* of tissues and the *Scotch* in cellophane tape. How could so much marketplace name recognition be reduced to so little cash value, a slight premium over a single year's gross sales?

Shortly after what I considered a ridiculously low-priced sale of this iconic business, I had dinner with TRW Credit's affable and star-quality CEO. Over a bottle of fine wine and an extended meal, we tried to guess what Bain & Lee was going to do. So far the buyer offered no delineation of their vision for owning the three initials some people feared perhaps just a little less so than IRS, FBI or CIA. "TRW" meant money flowing or not for consumers and lenders. To the selling parent company, the acronym appeared to be an albatross. The savvy acquirer apparently seized the opportunity for what I would call a fire-sale price. Other observers may disagree.

Soon thereafter *Experian* was born. A *portmanteau* replaced an iconic brand name. TRW was no longer the name of one of the three national credit bureaus. Former parent TRW was now able to shield itself from undue Congressional and media scrutiny that came with owning a credit bureau. The former parent's management team could get back to delineating for Wall Street and anyone else who needed to know detail of their massive business of precision manufacturing.

More than a credit bureau's name changed. The financial information industry shifted on its axis, or so it seemed to me. Suddenly Equifax and Trans Union were more recognizable names. At first Experian was thought difficult to spell and say. Experian caught-up fast, yet so far none of the three big bureaus enjoys the top-of-mind cachet of TRW Credit's days in the spotlight.

Not too long after the dinner, an Experian Executive Vice President and I met for an unsettling meal. One day after Bain's CEO addressed the senior management team of the credit bureau, my good friend was noticeably a bit depressed and distracted by the lack of delineation the Boston-based owners offered. Mr. EVP said something to the effect, "We all sat there in the audience, waiting to hear what Bain had up their sleeves for us. We expected to hear we would be merged with someone else, given a large amount of capital to grow our business, or hear good news about their vision for us. We heard nothing but empty words that sounded good but added-up to zip." Writing was on the wall, but we both failed to see it, or chose to ignore it: Zip meant flip.

Bain & Lee *flipped* the company (*i.e.,* quickly sold it after acquiring it) and earned from the eager U.K.-based acquirer hundreds of millions of dollars over what Bain & Lee had spent a few months earlier. Of course Bain had offered nothing to delineate their plans. How could they? They couldn't reveal the truth without compromising the deal in the works. The less said the better.

As an aside, shortly after this re-sale, the gentleman at parent TRW, the good guy who sold the bothersome division for so little, lost his job. Rumor promoted conjecture that board members of TRW did not like the fact that an asset was so grossly under-valued, which is what I said the moment I heard the price originally paid. No one I know is 100% sure why this fine gentleman was relieved of his duties, but the timing of his departure suggests a connection to the low price for which the division was sold to the Boston-based investors. Also he sold other related assets at low prices that defied logical delineation. I served as Executive Vice President of one of the credit units he sold, which I then tried and failed to acquire in a friendly management buy-out; eventually losing-out to Cendant, the world's largest marketing company. Cendant offered more than three times the millions I put forward.

Thinking back to the sale of the credit bureau, there is possibility parent TRW's CEO inadequately delineated marching orders when a decision was taken to streamline parent TRW's business. I can hear the frustrated leader saying, "Get rid of that darn credit division. It's causing us too much trouble on Capitol Hill and in the press. We have to get that monkey off our back." He may have neglected to delineate unspoken profit imperatives. Someone had to take the fall. No board of directors would see that much opportunity lost without delineating hindsight's need for assigning accountability.

Did my delineation of the above story about delineation illustrate the purpose and peril thereof? Did I delineate just enough or too much? To delineate or not to delineate, that is the question. Give as little as you can get away with giving seems to be the way of more and more CEOs. Not good. (In 2002 Northrop Grumman acquired TRW.)

For his witty prose and acuity in assessing the most threatening financial crisis in decades, JPMorgan Chase's CEO Jamie Dimon is the almost miraculous exception to the need-to-know delineation of information rule. His masterful Letter to Shareholders in the company's 2008 Annual Report is a work to behold. I commend to you for study his letter as a masterpiece of proactive delineation; a work of crafty leadership art and selective science. (An online Bing, Google or SEC search should produce a copy of the letter.)

Financial pundits dubbed Mr. Dimon "the next Warren Buffett." In addition to the Thomas Jefferson of banking, I think of Mr. Dimon as The Comeback Kid; having survived a very public ouster by Sanford Weill, a true titan whom I met after he himself was ousted by American Express when an infamous Co-CEO experiment failed miserably. Indeed Citicorp's famed Sandy Weill recovered from Amex's James D. Robinson III's untidy decision to kick-out Weill.

Similarly, ill-fated Manhattan Fund's Gerald Tsai, Jr. (1929–2008), and a handful of other titans I knew in my New York years, hit rock-bottom so hard they bounced higher than they were before their decent. Financier extraordinaire Tsai and I shared 26th floor offices in the Pan Am Building (now Met Life Building). During my highly impressionable 20-something years I listened to him delineate his and others' recovery and growth plans. Almost beyond comprehension, eventually Gerry would soar higher than even he could have imagined. I knew him well. Here I'll not delineate his journey to the top, but a Bing or Google search for Gerald Tsai will titillate any student of career renewal. You may not believe all you will find. It's true. I was there. His decade or so of recovery was a game-changer for Wall Street. As egocentric and unlikeable as some found him, he was even more unpredictable and unstoppable. Even giant Citicorp acquiesced to his brilliance as a master delineator of upside potential with hybrid and hijacked financial products and services. He built, broke and sold many molds.

When odd couple Warren Buffet and Bill Gates appeared together at Ivy League Columbia University's fall 2009 town hall meeting, they delineated for their enchanted New York audience their respective and shared views about economics and other matters of yesterday, today and tomorrow. Watching them on PBS, I was grateful for their willingness to speak up and out. Now no longer CEO of Microsoft, Mr. Gates seems considerably more comfortable with his role as delineator of digital discoveries, while Mr. Buffet now openly relishes his legacy as a disciplined delineator of value investing for the long-haul. I'm quite certain neither gentleman said a word that would put their respective companies' stock price in peril, yet they both seemed eager to delineate their views for a detail-hungry audience.

What Happened to the Term "Free Enterprise Way-of-Life?"

From my late teens into my early 20s as the very public modestly paid spokesperson for Junior Achievement, especially in 1969 when I was 19 years old and during JA's 50th Anniversary Celebration (the economics education organization was founded in 1919 by Ivy Hill), I knew I had to find ways to cleverly and compellingly communicate to hippies-in-the-making, and to others for whom "profit" was a four-letter word, some intrinsic benefits of capitalism and what we called The Free Enterprise Way-of-Life. When was the last time you heard this colorful term for the philosophic foundation for our economic system? Occasionally politicians use the term. Do you?

Give some extra thought to The American Free Enterprise Way-of-Life. For 10 or more years for me this phrase was a motivational mantra of sorts. In front of high school assemblies and lunch meetings of Rotary, Lions, Elks, Masons, and Veterans, and on radio and TV, I waxed poetic about an economics topic about which I knew very little. I had been fed words and lines — now called sound bites — that I took at face value. I never questioned any adult who took time with me to polish my prose and pronunciation thereof. I was a subject matter expert without much expertise, and yet I seemed able to at least adequately delineate what was needed to attract interest in JA and capital contributions to buy and refurbish an eight-story education center in downtown Pittsburgh. Photos of that building appear in the online photo album section for this book.

"Begin to imagine what the desirable outcome would be like. Go over these mental pictures and delineate details and refinements. Play them over and over to yourself." —Maxwell Maltz

For many years Pittsburgh's first lady of television was KDKA-TV's Marie Torre (1924-1997). I was thrilled to become a friend of hers and her entrepreneur husband Harold ("Hal") Friedman. Hal lived and breathed to see "his" Marie become the nation's next Barbara Walters, who was still co-hosting NBC's *Today* program. (At NBC I learned one was never to say *Today* "show." It is a news "program.")

Many hours Hal and I spent plotting Marie's migration from The Steel City to Manhattan. My views mattered to him because he wanted a younger audience demographic for his wife's ageless wisdom. While in Western Pennsylvania and she was still flying high, suddenly I was with Marie at Laughlin's Funeral Home in Mt. Lebanon mourning Hal's untimely death. As I stood speechless in front of his casket I remembered Hal telling me, "There are two ways to handle any word, define it or describe it, and do both clearly and creatively." Now I was tongue-tied. I could not define or describe my feelings about his dying before his dream for his wife would be tested. I wanted to see both of them succeed. I was invited to earn a long ride on their coattails.

A nationally syndicated *Marie Torre Show* was his life, Hal's *raison d'être*. He was gone. His otherwise always sturdy widow was quietly weeping. I was crushed. Speaking with Marie and Hal's children, Roma and Adam, both pre-teens, I almost choked as I expressed my regret and sympathy. I was 22. My unique loss was never discussed with anyone. I could neither define nor describe my complex feelings. Hal made big promises to me for a career in Manhattan, and now he and the vision were gone. Even Pittsburgh's Queen of Talk TV was speechless. We hugged in silence. For one year or more we exchanged handwritten notes, but I would never see her again. Perhaps I was too vivid a reminder of her Hal, the man who taught me to delineate thoughts by defining and describing words as clearly and creatively as I could, would, or dared.

At her own risk and expense Marie Torre left KDKA-TV, moved to New York City, and independently produced a national 20/20-like documentary program. For several episodes she earned critical acclaim but not a sizable enough national audience. Her appeal proved to be very local for Pittsburgh eyes and ears. Marie's TV career nearly came to a halt. In her Pittsburgh days as a news anchor, reporter, and talk show host, she was a master at delineating the journalist's "who, what, where, when, why, and how" for every story she told. Methodically and intentionally, her beloved Hal added the "Wow!"

A few years earlier, another master of delineation I respected committed suicide. No one had a clue why. He was on top of the world as the highly regarded General Manager of KDKA Radio, the nation's first commercial radio station. One year earlier a female mentor died when she fell asleep while smoking in bed, and she and her wing of an old family home burned to the ground. These fine people tutored me in what they both called my stentorian speaking style. At an early age I was being trained to delineate, in deep yet dulcet tones, my wet-behind-the-ears views. Several unrelated and consecutive deaths plucked from me shining examples from whom I yearned to learn more. Over four decades later, I remember them and their various lessons in delineation. Here I pay tribute by delineating their lasting value in my life.

More delineation occurs each time I return to hometown Pittsburgh. There I hear from family and other friends so many truly demanding stories. I try to support whomever I can. Too many of my own observations, memories, and unanswerable questions deplete more than inspire me. The drive back to Chicago allows me time to delineate, confront and correct facts and fantasies of my past, present and future. Deep prayer is required to rejuvenate my mind, body and soul.

In the business world, delineate is frequently used as a more powerful way of asking someone to "describe in detail" something or other. "To delineate" something suggests more *gravitas* than to merely describe whatever it is. And the word brings to mind a depiction of laying out the boundaries of something (such-and-such "delineates the problem").

This book is about having right words and ways to delineate fully responsible leadership thoughts to support each of us as we think and dig a little deeper while we reach and climb a lot higher. Words selected can turbo-boost both drilling down and flying high. Allowing yourself to ponder and practice these HILL Words can release in you an almost inexplicable energy to power-up for whatever life serves-up.

In Japanese "sokojikara" describes resiliency and ability to recover in new and often unexpected ways. Sokojikara for the U.S. rests on three pillars: (1) massive immigration, (2) an entrepreneurial open economy, and (3) vast natural resources, according to Japanese scholar Fuji Kamiya. In his book — The Next Hundred Million: America by 2050 — Fuji Kamiya uses sokojikara to illustrate "a reserve power that allows a nation to overcome both the inadequacies of its leaders and the foibles of its citizens." Sokojikara is a term of delineation.

> *"Do you want to know who you are? Don't ask.*
> *Act! Action will delineate and define you."* —Thomas Jefferson

For 25 years Dr. Carnegie Samuel ("Sam") Calian was quite literally the ground-breaking president of Pittsburgh Theological Seminary. He set records for delineating value his institution brought to both religious and secular constituencies. In addition to authoring 12 books and over 200 articles in professional journals and newspapers, Sam is the father of my close personal friend, Philip Calian, and grandfather to Phil and wonderful wife Jill's mighty foursome of future leaders: Luke, Sam, Christian and Julian, my high-energy adoptive nephews.

To others and me, Sam is a living legend in terms of devoting his professional lifetime to delineating definitions and descriptions of lessons in fully responsible leadership. Various extended conversations with Sam in social settings, were each a *tour de force* for his mastery of meaningfulness and mechanics of leadership. Sam's apparent approach to Spirit-driven mystery in leading brings to mind a favorite quote about humility, vision and creativity:

"The best artist has that thought alone, which is contained within the marble shell; the sculptor's hand can only break the spell to free the figures slumbering in the stone." —Michelangelo

Sam's wife Doris and he continue to exemplify values-based leadership for his fine family of three children and their spouses plus 10 grandchildren — all for the good-of-the-order. *The Spirit-Driven Leader* is Sam's 12th book about delineating leadership, which is especially eye-opening if you are in any type of leadership role within a community of faith.

Thank you for choosing to purposefully delineate and define value you bring to each other person. Others count on your definitions and descriptions of words that will free and motivate them and others to think, feel and be at their best.

For your acolytes (*i.e.,* followers) you may see procrastinating, meandering, or even slumbering on-the-job, with just-in-time and just-right words you can and must break the spell of their inertia. You may need to say, "We need to have a word." For me this not-too-subtle statement of fact worked wonders for setting the stage for a co-worker's rapt attention, and then boss-mandated remedial action.

> *"Everything should be made as simple as possible, but not simpler."*
>
> —Albert Einstein

In scripts for speeches, lectures, sermons, webcasts, instructional videos, movies, television, plays, and other means where an author's vocabulary is deployed to delineate and illustrate full pictures, photographs and other graphic arts often cover-up linguistic shortfalls. If leaders don't yet have sufficiently abundant vocabulary from which to choose words to express what they are seeing in front or inside of them, images they choose for web sites, Facebook posts, Instagrams, PowerPoint presentations, or other communication channels may be left to dangerously high levels of interpretation. Delineation requires deft alignment of words, images and audiences.

"A picture is worth 1,000 megapixels. High-definition (HD) TV images are used to camouflage some writers' low-definition (LD) vocabulary." —JRDjr

With their adroit choices for timing, words and delivery, fully responsible leaders free the bounty of delineation. Please work to entice, enrich and empower your followers, influencers, and yourself by discerning, tapping, and sharing — from within your accrued Language for Leading™ — words *for* wisdom, courage and patience.

Delineate. Expound.

Dignity

Chapter Inspired by and Dedicated to
The Reverend Canon John G.B. Andrew, OBE

Insert or imagine seeing your first name: _____,

Seeing this chapter's title word, what immediately comes to your open mind? Do you already have a working relationship with this word? Somewhere inside of you does this word instantly appeal? As a response to a specific situation at-hand, will this word work to your and others' advantage? For this word to increase in real value, together we must dig, drill and think deeper, so we will reach, climb and soar higher.

Our knowing, choosing and using just the right word and higher words are willful leadership actions. Right and higher words can lift others and us to new heights in thought and action. Dignity is just the right word.

Dignity is a higher word. Yet even for fully responsible leaders, dignity is a particularly difficult word to grasp for its practical applicability to personal and organizational development objectives. Dignity is a mighty and mysterious motivational word for leaders to genuinely embrace and adroitly use. Strategic team alignment thrives with shared deeper and higher perspective on dignity's purpose, passion, power, practicalities, and other promise.

When effectively defined, described, aligned and applied, dignity delivers extraordinary results for ROI — and Return-on-Leadership (ROL). Yes, dignity delivers. Absence of dignity divides and destroys.

How would applying this word serve to strategically align people, money, technology, and other resources? Thinking differently and creatively, for a few moments let's envision how "dignity" could be the middle name of many leadership thoughts, tasks or projects. As a prime illustration, healthcare dignity reform — as a project title in Washington, D.C. and insurance capital Hartford, Connecticut —

would probably move everyone closer to a viable plan of action. To name and frame debate and other deliberation "pursuit of healthcare dignity reform," ultimate accountability for such a higher goal would fuel any wise team's journey.

Without first digging deeper in this contemplative manner, We the People risk missing overdue opportunity to re-shape more than cash-flow projections for insured and out-of-pocket costs of medical care. Town Hall meeting leaders and made-for-TV and YouTube bullies seem hell-bent on narrowing focus mostly to exaggerated buyer frugality and victimization, and unbridled seller greed; mere dollars-and-cents *vs.* quality-of-care and dignity. What context would drive more of us to a bigger bargaining table? Dignity! Dignity in healthcare delivery and receipt.

Earning and discerning dignity in healthcare's long-in-coming renaissance is not only demonstratively ethical, it is also functionally mandatory for all duty-bound caregivers and their trusting recipients. As Americans talk about reworking basic economics and dignity of U.S. healthcare, we must arrest and sustain media focus and policy-making effort on (1) top-quality performance by providers, and (2) better-informed and fully engaged end-users of medical care, facilities, products, pharmaceuticals, technology, administration, and myriad other features and benefits of world-class medicine. Could intensified focus on dignity be a game-changer; a tipping point in this large battle for fairness in wellness?

Toward change for the better in healthcare, tax codes, education, politics, investing, law, regulatory compliance, corporate governance, economics, marriage, family, civil rights, equal rights, or other logic in a dynamic (*i.e.,* ever-changing) democracy, we are better served when each worthy cause is viewed, on a person-by-person basis, for acknowledging and strengthening human dignity. Yes, it's all about dignity; inherent nobility and worth of and for individuals. Please pause to feel dignity's empowerment.

In marketing parlance, a brand is defined as the *essence* of an organization or its product(s). Branding experts struggle with crafting just the right words and images to convey this essence. Dignity is the most exemplary essence of an individual's personal brand. Struggling with thoughts and words to characterize the significance of one's dignity is a worthwhile exercise in grounded self-awareness.

In 1967 a first sense of dignity came to me when I was transfixed, while seated in a high-school assembly. Junior Achievement (JA) membership recruiter Alan Kirkley read — in deep stentorian tone with added stage drama and *gravitas* — An American's Creed by statesman Dean Alfange. For me, it could have been called, An American's Dignity Creed. Please read slowly:

> "I do not choose to be a common man. It is my right to be uncommon if I can. I seek opportunity not security. I do not wish to be a kept citizen, humbled and dulled by having the state look after me. I want to take the calculated risk; to dream and to build, to fail and to succeed. I refuse to barter incentive for a dole. I prefer the challenges of life to the guaranteed existence; the thrill of fulfillment to the stale calm of utopia. I will not trade freedom for beneficence nor my dignity for a handout. I will never cower before any master nor bend to any threat. It is my heritage to stand erect, proud and unafraid; to think and act for myself; enjoy the benefits of my creations, and to face the world boldly and say, 'This I have done.' All this is what it means to be an American."

Seventeen-year-old I saw the light of dignity at the end of a dark tunnel of childhood insecurity. Suddenly I had reasonable words to illustrate positive feelings I could claim but heretofore couldn't name. Immediately I joined JA to see what this uncommon man stuff was all about. The speaker mentioned above, Alan Kirkley, and I became fast friends. He believed in An American's Creed, and so do I. Years later, and when appropriate, I still read to audiences this Creed. I continue to marvel at the way these words stir my soul.

Over four decades later, with this deeply felt sense of self, drive and duty, with my hopefully uncommon entrepreneurial pursuits, I still create for myself great joy and pain. I did not need to be an athlete to learn, "No pain, no gain." Instead I learned, "No pain, no gain, no dignity."

When inadvertently I step on someone else's sense of her or his dignity, instantly I am remorseful. Even when evidence is rather clear the other person is masking with indignation insecurity, ineptitude or immaturity, I am sad knowing the individual felt an unintentional affront to personal dignity. I do what I can and should to make amends. For sure I know my brain and heart are set (hard-wired) to

R.E.A.C.T. with Respect, Empathy, Authenticity, Clarity and Trust. To R.E.A.C.T. is to honor dignity. Yet there are those who insist on only seeing inherent shadows in even brightest light.

> *"Dignity does not consist in possessing honors, but in deserving them."* —Aristotle

It remains troubling for me to reflect on global inhumane indignities of over 61 years since the United Nations General Assembly adopted and proclaimed, on 10 December 1948, its admirable Universal Declaration of Human Rights, in which Article 1 reads: "All human beings are born free and equal in dignity and rights." What keeps certain parts of the world from climbing-up for dignity? Which countries come to mind? If today the 1776 framers were re-drafting the U.S. Declaration of Independence, would they replace "pursuit of happiness" with "pursuit of dignity?" Imagine:

"We hold these truths to be self-evident, that all men [and women] are created equal, that they are endowed by their Creator with certain unalienable Rights, that among these are Life, Liberty and *the pursuit of Dignity*." I rather like this formulation. Do you?

Even today, dignity denied individuals and large groups of American citizens — by governments, organizations, individuals and groups — may now be viewed by founding fathers as an unintentional consequence of their apparently intentionally fuzzy focus on happiness. As is the case with root myth about U.S. Constitutional entitlement to privacy, there never was a U.S. guarantee of happiness. From the beginnings of this country, for many even the pursuit of happiness was abridged (to say the very least). Yet how does any civilization guarantee dignity? Walking the fine talk of dignity gets us closer to the starting line for thoughts and actions required to reach the destination.

> *"I believe in human dignity as the source of national purpose, human liberty as the source of national action, the human heart as the source of national compassion, and in the human mind as the source of our invention and our ideas."* —John F. Kennedy

In Richard Wright's *Black Boy*, the loving mother does not tell her son about white oppression and crushed black dignity, yet we can tell his innocent eyes are seeing emerging truth of slavery in its rawest form. Today many of the world's children, of all races and creeds, are seeing and feeling oppression of crushed dignity. Dignity delayed is experienced as dignity denied.

Thinly veiled or blatant race-based attacks or undue focus on President Obama's skin color are sending mixed signals that could cripple further diversity of thought and action in future Administrations. The noble President is not leading with his multicultural heritage front-and-center in his mind. He can't allow himself such personal narrowness. As the world's most influential leader, one trying to arrest public attention toward his overflowing big-ticket-items agenda, he is exemplifying, more so than proving, his wisdom, courage and patience. Fine-tuning must continue for his and each other individual's entire lifetime in pursuit of dignity.

For creative visualization of psychological, societal and environmental risks to dignity, let's consider upside potential in formation of a Department of Homeland Dignity. To redefine and realign our minds and hearts, even for a moment imagine a Homeland Security-like warning signal color code for when dignity is being compromised and people and things are put at-risk in board rooms, on trading floors, in classrooms, during medical exams, over meals in each household's dining room, on playing fields, and even in bedrooms.

There are countless high-risk zones and venues, including e-mail, text messaging, Twitter bursts, Facebook postings, YouTube, mobile phones, digital cameras, chat rooms, water coolers, and locker rooms. Specifically in your home and workplace, what dignity-at-risk warning colors (if any) are flying today: Severe (red): severe risk, High (orange): high risk, Elevated (yellow): significant risk, Guarded (blue): general risk, Low (green): low risk? Let's work to never let down our guard to protect dignity against threats of ignorance, negligence, arrogance, insubordination, criminal intent, hate, maliciousness, carelessness, or other thoughts, behaviors and actions that threaten strength of our society found within dignity's foundation.

Fully responsible leaders overcome outmoded and undignified autocratic managerial standards that perhaps were first set in a pre-individualistic society. Machiavellian command-and-control mind-sets are yielding to collaborative strategic alignment sensibilities toward people, money, and other vital resources. With relationship-oriented leadership, dignity has more of a chance to take root in an organization's culture.

Organizations large and small — and their leaders of large and small minds — keep too many individuals unconscious of the dignity in individuality. Calling attention to perceived and generalized needs of the masses, concurrently we must identify with needs of fellow individuals therein. When ready — through faith, intellect and maturity — to measure against others our human condition, too many of us discover remarkably limited awareness of a richly diverse world of unique individuals.

Leaders and followers alike succeed only insofar as we can take care of ourselves. We hope and pray leaders lead us to potable water, and then we skillfully cup our own hands and trustingly drink from the deep well of dignity. An internal sense of any individual's dignity earned is more valuable than dignity conferred through heredity, ecclesiastical anointment, or organizational appointment. In other words, dignity we earn and feel within ourselves — based on true thoughts and feelings about our authentic (*i.e.*, imperfect) selves — is of overarching importance. Our sense of self-worth through dignity is tied to our self-confidence and personal-best performance.

Original dignity and worth are conferred by each woman and man's Creator. Perhaps not surprisingly, higher powers are credited with having a more clear sense of the dignity of us humans than we seem to have for ourselves. Without losing a sense of the paradox of father/mother god figures automatically conferring dignity to all children in their realm, mature and self-actualized seekers among us still aspire to earn earthly dignity in our thoughts and actions. A sixth sense seems to drive us to yearn for and earn more of what we were freely given at birth: dignity.

Economic disparity, racial diversity, political polarization, and genetic affectional-need differences prompt too many of us to rob our fellow human beings of the dignity of even acknowledging richness in distinctiveness and uniqueness. Right-wing, left-wing, or no-wing zealots are exceedingly unhappy with those in any opposing camp. Even those who always sit on life's fence seem to find disquieting those who speak up and out one way or the other. As so many malcontents drone on about what details or generalizations they "hate" or otherwise discount in or about other people, dignity is denied both decriers and the despised; the person venting and the victim. Neither is allowing time nor space for dignity.

"There is a healthful hardiness about real dignity that never dreads contact and communion with others however humble." —Washington Irving

Fortunately many of us find in ourselves and others sufficiency in our respective dignity. My two esteemed mentors exemplify dignity in almost all of they say and do. I am blessed and grateful for ever-steady demonstrations of deep-and-wide dignity from both world-class attorney Clyde O. Bowles, Jr. and business-world philosopher Dr. Peter Koestenbaum.

Several protégés I'm privileged to mentor say they sense dignity in the majority of what I say and do, yet not always. I am flawed. Occasionally with similarly inherently imperfect individuals, to whom I give limitless attention and value — and from whom I believe I am occasionally being denied respect and dignity — I allow truculent words and behavior to boil-up from deep inside of me. From accumulated stored heat of being denied dignity during childhood and later, several times each year I boil-over in anger. For as long as I can, I keep a lid on the pressure cooker. I'm getting better.

Not exactly out of the blue, my aggressively self-assertive and offensively belligerent gestures surprise others and me. Yet I remain surprised when I reach such boiling points. As I cool-down I realize I have again connected with past experiences the other individual's demonstrations of lack of respectfulness. My nagging sense of childhood dignity being denied still occasionally cripples me when I am sprinting toward a worthy goal. Tying the past with the present, I can grow remorseful while assessing and addressing root and current causes for inveighing with such undignified thoughts and actions.

From after 1993's ultimately destructive meltdowns with a remarkable yet frequently unyielding person to whom I committed a lifetime of alliance and allegiance, on the table next to my bed still sits Anger Kills by doctors Redford and Virginia Williams. This book is alongside John C. Maxwell's Leadership Bible and his The Right to Lead. John Baillie's A Diary of Private Prayer (from 1965 when I was age 15) and The Brand You by Tom Peters also sit there to remind me of psychological, spiritual, and even physical demands of dignity for all — especially for myself. Seeing books' spines aligns my spine.

Without claim of perfection or illusion of its attainability, I always strive to deepen the sense of dignity in my life's purpose — and thus

I affirm others' and my dignity. Even when I am at my least dignified, my higher calling remains clear. When I fail, I fall hard in the painful cinders and dirty ashes of previously burned bridges. As I pick myself up, dust myself off, and start all over again, I see behind me more collateral damage, and yet ahead I see brighter light of self-awareness.

Lessons in dignity are found in high and low places. In life's serious and lesser literature, seek reminders of practical thoughts and behaviors that lead you to choose dignity. Especially as indignities surround or engulf you, allow the word to lift you to a higher plane.

Your pursuit of dignity matters to the quality of your life, and to your positive and otherwise constructive influence in the lives of others. Facing head-on your grasp and acceptance of this word's purpose and potential, instantly you elevate your dignity. How far you allow this word to carry you depends on your level of engagement.

> *"Because unless someone like you*
> *cares a whole awful lot, nothing is*
> *going to get better. It's not."* —Dr. Seuss

How do you profess and assess your dignity? How attuned are you toward dignity accorded and earned by others? Having opened yourself to this brief excursion, surely you feel more of the intended passion, power, potential, and other promise in the U.N.'s declaration:

> *"All human beings are born free and equal in dignity and rights."*

Dignity is the right word. Let's deserve, develop and deliver dignity.

Choose dignity. It is a right and privilege for us to do so. Women and men die fighting for rights associated with dignity.

Dignity is a word that works. Dignity is a word to be.

> *"I am not what happened to me,*
> *I am what I choose to become."* —Carl Jung

Thank you for yearning for, earning, discerning, celebrating, and protecting dignity for all. Dignity is a higher HILL word. With this word in the front of your mind and emblazoned on your heart, already you and I are soaring higher.

Dignity. Expound.

Diligence

Chapter Inspired by and Dedicated to James H. Platt, Ph.D.

Insert or imagine seeing your first name: _____,

Seeing this chapter's title word, what immediately comes to your open mind? Do you already have a working relationship with this word? Somewhere inside of you does this word instantly appeal? As a response to a specific situation at-hand, will this word work to your and others' advantage? For this word to increase in real value, together we must dig, drill and think deeper, so we will reach, climb and soar higher.

Diligence is a mighty key word for today's correction economy. Leaders and others are being called upon to think and act differently than we did before, during and after the economic meltdown. Are we? What's new? Wage-earners, salaried workers, and commission seekers must tightly grasp, aggressively promote, and diligently practice: concentration, conscientiousness, determination, industriousness, innovativeness, alignment, and stick-to-it-iveness. Diligence determines most of life's favorable outcomes. Diligence pursued is value accrued.

> *"That which ordinary men are fit for, I am qualified in,*
> *and the best of me is diligence."* —William Shakespeare

The global economic free-fall reflects inadequacy of diligence. Specific periods for so-called due diligence are institutionalized in deal-making and other asset-based transactions. Yet, in the name of due diligence, wrong people are hired, bad investments are funded, weak teams are assembled, poor choices are made, and disastrous decisions are taken. Lack of diligence is perilous misalignment of principles, priorities and practices.

Ignorance, greed, and need-for-speed are among many enemies of diligence. Over-sized and over-priced mortgages, approved for families with high probability of defaulting, are testament to greed instead of due diligence. Certain lenders dishonestly signed their names attesting to diligence that never happened. Commission-only based compensation for sales professionals adds extra risk to due diligence. Especially in mortgage lending, real estate companies, car dealerships, insurance agencies, banks, brokerage services, and manufacturers representatives selling pharmaceuticals, weapons, ammunition, and other goods and services, taking shortcuts with diligence allows deals to close faster. In the name of expediency, some CEOs, attorneys, physicians, and auditors wrongly represent their diligence. Outcomes range from inconvenient to deadly.

Law requires due diligence. As a brief example, for the Chicago Board Options Exchange, Inc. (CBOE), 1998 Federal regulation 73(a) requires a floor broker "...to use due diligence to execute the order at the best price or prices..." Was this regulation stated as clearly as it could have been? Hardly. Are our own personal and organizational understandings of diligence deeply rooted, adequately defined, and richly described for real-world applicability in our busy day-to-day lives?

To regain and sustain economic stability, what do we individuals have to think and do differently to reverse this downward spiral? Let's dig deeper with diligence, the word and the deed.

"Diligence is the mother of good luck." —Benjamin Franklin

On a case-by-case and person-by-person basis, fully responsible leaders must clearly set, articulate, monitor, and otherwise ensure strategic alignment imperatives of diligence. More simply said, we must hear often from our leaders exactly what must be done, why, by whom, how, and when. Then all involved diligently stay-the-course until the job is done and done right. Diligence.

"Everything yields to diligence." —Antiphanes

Polarity in philosophic views about time, held by Isaac Newton and Immanuel Kant, intensifies my conviction to keep time top-of-mind as I think about framework around diligence. Sir Isaac subscribed to a realist view that time is part of the fundamental structure of the universe, a dimension in which events occur in chronological sequence. Dr. Kant decried time as a thing that cannot be explained, contained, nor sustained.

From my earliest years I knew timing was a big thing for life's tests of my diligence beyond classrooms. The moment a teacher would say "start" for a timed exam, I felt something *stop* in my mind. As those noisy wall clocks ticked, often my mind grew thick and my stomach sick. Diligently working under timing pressure is an acquired skill, art, science, and mindset. Finally I got it, this timing thing.

From 2009 until release dates, diligence yielded this book. Honoring stringent time requirements and methodology of Oxford's Essay, the so-called Hardest Exam in the World, over three consecutive hours the first draft for each chapter was written. I assessed what my mind could do in 120 minutes of tight focus. Then hours, days, months and years of diligent work began. Your and my diligence brought us both to this moment when you are reading and feeling these words.

Diligence is required to enjoy the chronographic psychology of this book's full-year journey with 52 high-impact single words. In conference rooms, war rooms, and family rooms, diligently remembering to call up and use these 52 HILL Words allows you and others to prioritize and invest more wisely, courageously and patiently time, thoughts, and other resources.

Lack of diligence creates risk. Over many years, collectively and individually, perhaps a vast majority of U.S. consumers played an unintentional part in weakening today's economy. From low classroom engagement and inadequate on-the-job performance, to knowingly living far beyond ones financial means, relevant culpability for today's economic malaise touches nearly all levels of our society.

Stories of diligence of leaders are being told on big screens and small monitors. The January 2012 release of "The Iron Lady," featuring Oscar-bound Meryl Streep, dramatizes Lady Margaret Thatcher's unprecedented diligence. With "J. Edgar" and other biopic films coming at a steady pace to big screens and our various monitors — especially during the 2012 Presidential election cycle — we are being reminded about fairly recent world history when bold, courageous and diligent leaders led on principle, with passion, and for higher and longer-term purpose.

With 20/20 hindsight of diligent historians, and diligence of tabloid diggers for dirt, all leaders are seen with some of their previously obscured or ignored human and other flaws. And yet each bigger-than-life leader must be seen in the context of the era within which she or he was in-command; ultimately judged for their diligence and impact on quality-of-life of those they led.

"Freedom of speech means setting words free.
Imprisoned and freed words have consequences.
Words are consequences.
Words have consequences."

—JRDjr

Reading-along with the transcript and footnotes while listening to all eight CDs of Jacqueline Kennedy's 1964 oral history about life with JFK's diligence, and almost immediately thereafter getting so wrapped-up watching on the big screen "J. Edgar," reminded me how President Richard M. Nixon inherited Hoover's obsessive diligence, and his blurred-world vision of right-and-wrong.

From the largest-ever corps of PhDs and MBAs, to those employees who valiantly struggled to earn their GED, individuals know if they are being truly diligent and productive on the job, always paying rapt attention and doing what they are paid to do. Attentive bosses know *if* workers are really working. And superiors know when they themselves are operating at less-than-optimal levels of diligence and productivity. There is a long list of likely infractions, including ignoring evidence of lack of diligence.

"Dignity does not float down from heaven; it cannot be purchased nor manufactured. It is a reward reserved for those who labor with diligence."
—Bill Hybels

Allow history's stories of diligence to inform your sense of rightness about diligently sticking with it. If it is worthy of higher thought, it is worthy of greater diligence. You are a higher thought worthy of greater diligence. Diligence will determine and delight your future.

"The leading rule for the lawyer, as for the man of every other calling, is diligence.
Leave nothing for to-morrow which can be done to-day." —Abraham Lincoln

Thank you for your diligence with this book, these key words, and whatever actions you choose to follow these moments of diligent focus, purpose and promise. With clear sight, an indefatigable spirit, and a smile in your heart, with diligence labor onward and upward.

Diligence. Expound.

Diversity

Chapter Inspired by and Dedicated to Tyronne Stoudemire

Insert or imagine seeing your first name: _____,

Seeing this chapter's title word, what immediately comes to your open mind? Do you already have a working relationship with this word? Somewhere inside of you does this word instantly appeal? As a response to a specific situation at-hand, will this word work to your and others' advantage? For this word to increase in real value, together we must dig, drill and think deeper, so we will reach, climb and soar higher.

Diversity is what we humans are about; what we have been, are, and always will be. We are diversity. Locally and globally we are a diverse people. Individually and collectively we are diversity personified. More than gender differences and similarities between Adam and Eve dramatically illustrate root definitions of diversity and ceaseless change. Creationist and evolution theory and fact drive home inescapable and often inexplicable wonders and worries about genes and their development. When emotionally and intellectually embraced, thoughts toward diversity ignite and stimulate mysterious and immeasurable wisdom, courage and patience for the mind, body and soul. Diversity is our mind, body and whole.

Denying diversity's divine and deductive-reasoning roles in sustainability of the species dooms destructive history to repeat itself. Philosophers and scientists shed their respective light on diversity's strengths, weaknesses, opportunities and threats. In perhaps equal measure diversity is about similarity and polarity. On balance, diversity is certainly not about perfection in any camp. In this realm perfection does not exist. For strategic alignment of interests of imperfect and diverse people, we're in this together.

"Diversity is the art of thinking independently together." —Malcolm Forbes

Combined we humans are proof-of-concept for diversity. When illogically separated from others, we disregard and diminish upside potential of our innate structural complexity. Philosophic and practical strength in numbers is borne of our grasp of diversity's unlimited potentialities. Billions of years of human existence prove this calculus. Yet historically humans deny ourselves the dignity and delight of these deeper truths about diversity. Ignoring any part of diversity's ubiquitousness compromises possibility of ongoing discoveries in laboratory Earth.

For purposes of economic, societal, personal, and spiritual renewal and development, in your thinking do you give diversity its rightful top-of-mind place? Do you? Really? This insistence is directed at all of us who think we do but don't. Many of us talk a lot about cosmetics and demands of diversity without giving much deeper thought to the word's overarching significance. Without due place and process in our thought order, diversity's importance and its renewing energy can't reach into all corners of our culturally restrictive consciousness and busy daily lives.

Well-meaning advocates for diversity often fall prey to cliché. Life-long students and practitioners of principles and practices of diversity choose never-ending pursuit of both questions and answers; a steady build-out of affirmation, addition, and adjustment to relevant thoughts. What are you doing about what you are seeing in both problems and potential within diversity? From where you are seated in today's audience, can you see where you'll stand on tomorrow's stage? Fully responsible leaders are mentally in both places at the same time. Are you reachable and teachable about possibly deeper dimensions of diversity? Have you inadvertently limited your view of diversity's limitless horizon?

Diversity, Wellness and Wholeness

Truth tellers admit diversity is too often reduced to a politically correct topic; more of a "should" than a "must." Behind-closed-doors private conversations and public facts reveal diversity's enemies of ignorance and duplicity are embedded in both majority and minority homes, organizations and communities. On the expected date when U.S. Census statistics may prove Hispanics or

African Americans mathematically overtake Caucasians to become the so-called majority, there will be further admissions of large-scale internal wounds within all factions. Without absolving in any way culprits on the outside, structural and spiritual damage caused from within minority communities will be named and claimed. External (*i.e.*, majority inflicted) and internal (*i.e.*, minority inflicted) damage is real. External and internal damage is deep. Inclusive diversity is the caregiver's prescribed healing salve, balm, potion, and medication for hurting individuals who yearn to heal. Healing people create, populate and sustain healthy organizations.

In expansive minds and hearts, inclusive diversity is considered a healing ministry. Inclusive diversity must be viewed and espoused as a long-term act of survival. Inclusive diversity as a cultural imperative, organizational policy, and ethical mandate, soothes, heals, strengthens and sustains households and whole nations. From kitchen tables to conference tables (ideally in this order), principles and practices of inclusive diversity address head-on corrosive and high-risk stupidity of racism, class warfare, hatred, homophobia, and other unnatural thoughts and acts that separate humankind from the universal whole of creation. Through wellness borne of wholeness, all humans and the organizations in which they choose to grow and prosper will benefit. The unified whole will be greater than the sum of its diversified parts.

Is this the Dawning of the Age of Diversity?

With diversity now exemplified so well in very top public and private leadership posts (albeit now only in quality, not yet in commensurate quantity), danger is more real for agents of change to inadvertently miss even louder calls for MORE personal and institutional clarity. Diversity is coming of age. The time is now. Is this to become the overdue dawn of the Age of Diversity? Are you fully engaged in this process? For personal perspective about diversity awareness, I remember when:

In seventh grade I heard how balconies were installed in some early U.S. churches as the place for parishioners' slaves and servants to sit for worship. Black, white, and servants of other races, without sufficient social or economic standing, were relegated in church (of all places) to back-of-the-bus second-class seating. In society and church, "lesser folk" among working-class souls must know and keep their place. It was 1963 when this lesson landed on my heart; I was 13. Accurate or apocryphal, encountering such despicable faith-based disparity about diversity, I was and remain both appalled and motivated.

So we fresh-scrubbed kids would never forget or repeat such stupidity from long-ago, I organized a silent and ongoing protest. As a founder of the Sunday evening youth group at First Presbyterian Church of Pittsburgh, a first thing I asked pastors was if we overactive teenagers could have the front part of the church's north balcony set-aside and roped-off for those of us who attend adult worship. Without a word to be spoken to those below, I told him what we would be saying by sitting up there. The youth pastor said yes. He liked our pluck. From where once thought-lesser folk may have secretly enjoyed looking down on their rather unenlightened masters and employers, I felt us kids could also get a better view of people quite literally beneath us.

Adolescent arrogance aside, we wanted everyone to see us "up there." Probably few got the message, but at least some did. On crowded Sunday evenings everyone below saw the bright future of our world seated where slaves and servants used to have to sit; where once deemed lesser adults and their youth were probably neither seen nor heard. We teens of the 60s were told we were servant leaders in-training, so sitting in servants' quarters seemed the right-and-proper thing to do.

Visualize, please, this stunning Gothic cathedral that was completed in 1905; still resplendent in the light shining through its 13 original and restored Louis Comfort Tiffany stained-glass windows, the priceless crown jewels among this church's 269 stained and leaded glass windows. With pen-and-ink sketched lineage to a log cabin consecrated in 1773 by a congregation of somewhat rebellious and independence-minded Scots, and as mentioned earlier, this church for leaders started its bold mission three years before the signing of the U.S. Declaration of Independence. Imagine pre-1776 sermons.

From 1905 onward, architecturally and environmentally all who entered, and allowed it to happen, were psychologically and spiritually lifted to places for higher thought. In these historic and hallowed halls, diversity in thought, race, age, gender, and sexual orientation seemed at least a bit easier for us inquiring Presbyterian kids to address. Emboldening some of us to ask questions we might not have dared elsewhere, it appeared we felt safe enough in our world of privilege of place. To support more levels of awareness of racial and other diversity, our adult leaders were sure we made our way beyond our stone walls to other churches, region-wide Youth for Christ rallies, Billy Graham Crusades, homes for the indigent, and other locations. In this quest for depth about diversity and life's other challenges, we thought we knew what we were doing. Our best intentions lead us.

A shadow appeared. Without any intention to do so, we fell into a common trap of thinking about diversity as intentionally embracing others' differences *from us* — instead of acknowledging diversity *among us*; their and our differences and commonality. "They" were in need of our beneficent views toward diversity, we were not. Wrong we were! No adult seemed to notice our in-good-faith accidental disconnect with the very equal people with whom we thought we were aligning ourselves. Eventually I got it. I'm still getting it.

> *"If we cannot end now our differences, at least we can help make the world safe for diversity."* —John F. Kennedy

Two months after First Church youth started symbolically sitting in the balcony, John F. Kennedy was killed. As the first and still only Roman Catholic President, JFK started many of us thinking differently about difference. That era's increasing racial tensions continued to cause daily headlines and broadcast news reports we teens hardly understood, and with which even teachers did not seem prepared to cope. The downward slide had only just begun. We all seemed to feel the rug being pulled out from under us.

From 1963 to the end of 1968, JFK, Malcolm X, Martin Luther King, Jr, Robert F. Kennedy, and many other luminaries of diversity's loud cry and some of their followers were murdered. Truth remains stranger than fiction. From 1963's shot heard 'round the world, through 1969's Stonewall Riots, the United States of America admitted to the world we were not that united after all; certainly not united *for* all.

> *"Ultimately, America's answer to the intolerant man is diversity, the very diversity which our heritage of religious freedom has inspired."*
> —Robert F. Kennedy

Only since 1956 Presbyterian women are allowed by the national ruling body to be ordained as Elders (elected lay leaders), Deacons (elected lay care-givers), and Ministers of Word and Sacrament (those highly educated, painstakingly accredited, duly elected, and democratically accorded full responsibility and privilege of callings to careers as professional pastors). I was six years old. By the time I was eight, we had on-duty in the chancel our first female pastor. We kids loved having her there, yet I recall some adults did not. Not too long after women first broke through the stained glass ceiling, public schools no longer permitted teachers and students to pray and read Scripture. To calm, focus and inspire fidgeting young minds and bodies, spiritual means and messages were judged un-Constitutional. I was stunned. When we stopped praying and reading, palpably I felt the loss. I did not know what to say or do.

Secretly, I had private need for the sense of belonging that came over us as we prayed; craving the safety I felt in prayer and reflection. Indeed I was very young, but formidable challenges at home made me grow-up fast. Denied prayer and Scripture, I was feeling singled-out, marginalized, and otherwise de-valued because of who and what I am. Little did I know how dealing with this set of raw feelings would serve me well for decades to come. These are my first memories of sensibilities toward inequality in diversity's value denied. Too simply I sure felt it and still do. Now I argue law cleared the way for diversity; making room for more than one way of viewing life's bigger pictures. There is so much more for us to see with this wide-angle lens.

In my junior year some faculty good-naturedly called me "speaker of the house." My 1968 yearbook is inscribed with reference to my deep-sounding voice in school matters. (From kindergarten, I had been a traveling boy-soprano soloist for schools, churches, and civic groups, so a change to baritone was a just-in-time downward shift.) I was the most frequent student reader of each morning's announcements over the school's blaring public address system.

For the few moments of required inspiration, occasionally I illegally read relevant passages from the then newly published modern-language Good News Bible. I simply did not state the source for the words. My heart was in my throat each time I dared. I am certain several teachers and our awesome principal knew exactly what I was up to. Many smiles, winks, and pats on the back sustained our code of silence. At least to a small degree, I felt I had overcome feelings of helplessness related to being silenced for in-school prayer and Scripture reading. Those thoughts were prayers.

"When Jesus Christ asked little children to come to him, he didn't say only rich children, or white children, or children with two-parent families, or children who didn't have a mental or physical handicap. He said, 'Let all children come unto me.'"
—Marian Wright Edelman

Perhaps removing prayer and Scripture from schools added more drag to the time line for diversity's ascent as a topic of more serious conversation and deliberation. Absence of education's built-in daily focus on higher values seemed to nearly erase a sense of communal right-and-wrong, at least at the student level. "Forgive us our trespasses, as we forgive those who trespass against us" seemed to set for each day a collaborative tone that dissipated when new law was invoked.

None of this centuries-old constriction and newfangled restriction on diversity made any sense to my yet unformed way of processing life's inherent polarity. As I youngster in my gut I knew holding back smart and otherwise capable women was flat-out wrong. Just as We the People started to come to our senses about women, it seemed we decided to hold back God. Paradoxically, it was a female atheist who successfully made her case against God in public schools. The feminist movement began to fight fire with fire. Not much I saw was adding up to any win-win outcomes.

Many deep-and-wide thinkers struggle with openly discussing race and diversity. Instead of digging deep before climbing high, some among all races and classes find it easier to assail than to hail diversity. In Richard Florida's best-selling Flight of the Creative Class, economic dependency on diversity was argued as mission-critical for the U.S. to survive and thrive. Closing our borders and minds after 9/11's atrocities cost us dearly in ways victims of that infamous date probably would not have wanted to see happen in their memory. A prior steady flow of immigrants to our shores brought from overseas unbridled entrepreneurial spirit, inventiveness, and other breakthroughs. It's not too soon to draw insight about adverse economic impact of this pipeline being shut-off. More than oil comes from other lands.

Middle-eastern and dark-skin racial profiling became more than an essential part of Homeland Security's defensive behavioral arsenal for protectors and the protected. In airports we still knowingly watch for unattended packages, and for sinister-looking, sweating, nervous, or other misfit human traits and behaviors. In subtle and direct ways, all are encouraged to be on the lookout for "the look." You know the drill. Perhaps we'll never be able to let down our guard.

Beyond justified concern for threats in transportation hubs, on Main Street we must assess the not-insignificant losses in segregating and vilifying large sectors of our population; unwisely missing strengths and win-win opportunities in their richness of diversity and other energizing difference.

> *"If we are to achieve a richer culture, rich in contrasting values, we must recognize the whole gamut of human potentialities, and so weave a less arbitrary social fabric, one in which each diverse human gift will find a fitting place."*
> —Margaret Mead

On-air and in-pulpit personalities — in many types of venues with various spotlighted influencer and/or leader roles — tie their popularity and paychecks to dramatically eliciting in others sometimes over-the-top negative responses. The ego satisfaction and childish glee they or anyone might feel while pulverizing a politician, political party, or a contrarian thought is hardly consistent with any God-fearing pursuit I know or can sanely imagine.

Too many big talkers and small walkers think they are praising and glorifying their God by constantly pulverizing some of his people, especially subordinating those of different colors, creeds, same-sex affectional genetics, or economic strata.

Despicable holier-than-thou exclusionary behavior is willfully misaligned response to any major faith's overarching spiritual imperatives. Apostles are named as people are blamed. In all of this stultifying self-righteousness, where is the God of compassion, love, mercy, inclusion — and diversity? The Christian triune God of diversity is himself diverse — all three forces of good in one: Father, Son and Holy Spirit. We are taught He is father *and* mother, brother *and* sister, friend *and* lover; once human *and* always holy. Other metaphors, similes, and analogies of God's diversity fill holy books and hymnals. We are created in God's widely diverse image. Imagine thoughtful believers thinking otherwise. Racism of any variety is a sin, I submit.

All Voices Must Be Heard.
All Voices Must Be Respected.

Fully responsible leaders R.E.A.C.T. to ALL people with Respect, Empathy, Authenticity, Clarity and Trust, even when beneficiaries of their maturity and sound judgment are anything but respectful, empathic, authentic, clear or trustworthy toward them. Having to turn the other cheek both hurts and helps. More simply put, for more than economic survival, we need to listen to the soft, mid-range, and loud voices of diversity's promise — our voices!

Diversity proponents need to be realistic about what has worked and not; what's good and not-so-good about their thoughts, attitudes, actions, and other behavior. In the high name of diversity, low standards are set. Hearing diversity's clarion call, some leaders and their followers hit a brick wall. Let's drill deep and climb high; deeper and higher than ever before toward diversity that's always a beginning instead of an end.

President Barack Hussein Obama's election brings out the best and worst of many. His every success or failure is reported somewhere within the context of the President's multiracial/multicultural personal heritage. Too many simpletons sending and receiving messages about The White House rush to race-based poor judgment. Respect for the office of President supersedes need for constant focus on the office-holder's complex genetics or skin color.

Scholars in sociology fear eight years of President Obama may involve more steps backward than forward for diversity; retrogression to public obsession only with differences instead of insistence on unlimited potential in also characterizing and synthesizing our commonality. It is wise for proponents of diversity to bring themselves and others MORE up-to-speed about lessons learned through the diversity movement's missteps in messaging, and pursue new mastery of the majesty in diversity's meaningfulness for all. Tears of joy and pain are the same color.

"The price of the democratic way of life is a growing appreciation of people's differences, not merely as tolerable, but as the essence of a rich and rewarding human experience." —Jerome Nathanson

For its overall significance and abundant beauty in words, music, sights and feelings, Sunday 11 September 2011 is an evening at Chicago's Fourth Presbyterian Church I'll never forget. From many faiths clergy and adherents joined political and other leaders for an ecumenical worship service to commemorate the global and local significance of atrocities on this date in 2001

From a seat in a front pew in the north balcony, I had a wide-angle view of all God's people — of many ethnicities and faith traditions — solemnly holding candles in the dimmed light of the large and high-ceilinged sanctuary. I could clearly see intense little faces of beautiful children singing from the high chancel, each wearing different symbolic colors of the same-style shirt. Combined choirs with various conductors demonstrated remarkable world-class agility with complicated time-honored and original scores. Accompanists played familiar and unfamiliar instruments. There were so many moving parts and hearts. It all came together in a seamless declaration of shared faith and trust in diversity and inclusion. So many words were used to underscore truth.

A sense of deep peace and high hope seemed to wash over all of us. Afterwards I had an opportunity to compare notes about the evening with Cook County President Toni Preckwinkle and others, and everyone with whom I spoke appeared to agree that this type of ecumenical worship should happen more often; perhaps at least every September 11th. I remain grateful to the many individuals in multiple organizations who collaborated so efficiently to allow such grand vision of diversity and inclusion to become so highly personal for each individual in attendance.

One week or so after the above experience, friend Tyronne Stoudemire invited me to hear The Chicago Symphony kick-off their 2011 Fall Season in the large sanctuary of Apostolic Church of God. Again I saw, heard, felt and otherwise sensed the promise of diversity and inclusion. For those of us who often hear the Symphony elsewhere, we knew this major and triumphant production was clearly a sign that a new era is dawning for diversity and inclusion.

After the memorable concert's final standing ovation, Tyronne was kind to include me in a small photo session with world-renowned maestro Riccardo Muti. I so enjoyed thanking Mr. Muti, commending his passionate statements to the audience regarding diversity and inclusion, and sharing with him a relevant personal story, that struck a harmonious chord for both of us, from my Pittsburgh days of association with The Pittsburgh Symphony Orchestra.

Please add to your life's milestones deeper, wider and higher definition, description and application of diversity and inclusion. For thoughts toward diversity's value, choose "the thrill of the HILL" — deep foundation-building satisfaction over the quicksand of shallow hubris or pride. Just-right HILL-height is the mental peak (1) upon which you need to keep watch, (2) from which you must lead people and manage things, and (3) toward which you guide others to set their sights. To see diversity's promise, lift others to higher ground.

Nudging others to climb to higher levels of awareness, sensibility and responsiveness about diversity serves individuals and organizations. Fully engage all types of buyers and sellers of internal and external messages related to diversity and other imperatives for success.

Embracing diversity we climb higher and see wider. From HILL **altitude** acumen accrues. With positive **attitude**, redirect any undue feelings of intimidation about diversity. Deep satisfaction is in each constructive thought, forward step, and arrival at worthy destinations.

> "*There is not one blade of grass, there is no color in this world that is not intended to make us rejoice.*" —John Calvin

Using as your night-vision goggles the High-Impact Leader Lens™ (HILL) will give you additional clarity toward seeing each diversity challenge, milestone and victory. Intentionally allow your 360-degree panoramic HILL vista to come into view. Welcome what you see.

Rose-colored glasses, however, must be removed. Diversity deserves a full spectrum of its light and promise to shine in all eyes and hearts.

What an enlightening, empowering and encouraging IMAX 3-D view you will see: Diversity Delivers Dividends — 3-D! Allow wide-angle views about diversity's purpose, power and promise to remain front-and-center in your wide-open mind and heart. Please.

Thank you.

Diversity. Expound.

Edification

Chapter Inspired by and Dedicated to the
Reverend Dr. Bryant Mays Kirkland (1914-2000)

Insert or imagine seeing your first name: _____,

Seeing this chapter's title word, what immediately comes to your open mind? Do you already have a working relationship with this word? Somewhere inside of you does this word instantly appeal? As a response to a specific situation at-hand, will this word work to your and others' advantage? For this word to increase in real value, together we must dig, drill and think deeper, so we will reach, climb and soar higher.

Your Personal Edification

The powerful noun ed·i·fi·ca·tion is more than a favorite HILL Word of fully responsible leaders. As servant leaders it is our duty to ed·i·fy (transitive verb) others and ourselves. From the 14th century, edify evolved from the French *édifier*, and the Latin word *aedificare* for "to build, construct, instruct, make;" further pinned to *aedis* of "building, temple" plus facere "make." To edify is to build. An edifice is a building, and an ed·i·fi·er is one who builds. Fully responsible leaders are in the business of edifying — building others and ourselves. Even if we did not have this set of words and meanings in the front of our minds, as leaders you and I choose to edify. Do you agree? In these chapters evidence is found of my lifelong commitment to edification. If you are leading from the perspective of full responsibility you are edifying those who follow you.

With inspired and thoughtful intentionality we leaders are to edify our peers and followers with intellectual, philosophic, moral, ethical, spiritual, and other functionally sophisticated (*i.e.*, inherently complex yet practical) points of illumination. Whether imparting a helpful practical best-practices suggestion or teaching a full-credit graduate course, someone who edifies others effectively enlightens, empowers, and otherwise supports her or his followers. Internal and external edification allows both leader and follower to dig a bit deeper so we all can reach a lot higher. To edify is to generate light for people about topics worthy of edificial effort. Essentially we are building strong human edifices set on sturdy foundations of responsible edification.

Edification is Elevation through Illumination

When you have an opportunity to lift someone to a new level of understanding or engagement, do you do it? Are you compelled (called) to edify others? During meetings, far too many people with value to offer rather selfishly keep their own counsel and say little or nothing. I know individuals who seem to get an ego boost from withholding their knowledge or perspective, rather than "paying it forward" for the good-of-the-order; avoiding edifying other individuals, the organization, community or household. I grow very uncomfortable when seated in meetings and note silence of those I know to have relevant subject matter expertise to offer. Often they don't. If I am moderating or otherwise in a leadership role for a meeting, edifyingly I'll draw out of others what I believe those at the table or in an audience need to hear.

Examination for Edification

You will want to pause for a few special moments of personal edification to deeply absorb the significance of this self-exam to test our intentions to edify others and ourselves with our thoughts, words and actions. Before I deliver a talk, chair a meeting, moderate a panel, write a letter, draft a book chapter, share a news article, post something on Twitter, add to the news feed on Facebook, or speak to a fellow life traveler who shares in my need for a continuous stream of edification, almost automatically I find within this roster sufficient encouragement to move ahead. If I cannot sense significant quantity and quality of potential edification in my responses to these questions, I'll go back and re-think my motivation. Sometimes I realize I moved all the way to the moment of implementation without giving sufficient thought to sustainable edification that would come from affirmative responses to the following and other questions. You too will benefit by asking yourself:

Betterment: Am I making people and things better?

Collaboration: Am I collaborating from a win-win perspective?

Constructive: Am I constructive in thoughts, words and deeds?

Courage: Am I exemplifying courageousness in thinking and action?

Elevation: Am I elevating others as I am elevating myself?

Enhancement: Am I enhancing whomever and whatever I touch?

Enlightenment: Am I enlightening?

Ethics: Am I committed to ethical leadership?

Guidance: Am I sensitive to guidance I am receiving?

Illumination: Am I shining light on people and things?

Information: Am I imparting and contemplating reliable information?

Instruction: Am I open as I am instructing; am I reachable and teachable?

Knowledge: Am I comfortable with validly of knowledge I impart?

Learning: Am I learning-by-doing and learning-by-accruing?

Morals: Am I morally bound to lead in the right way for the right reasons?

Nurture: Am I nurturing, with deference to human nature?

Patience: Am I patient with self, others, processes and procedures?

Teaching: Am I learning from teaching and teaching what I'm learning?

Truth: Am I aware of and imparting truth?

Uplifting: Am I viewed as an uplifting influence on others?

Values: Am I regarded as values-driven?

Wisdom: Am I discerning wisdom beneath knowledge?

Along these lines of examining your level of edification of others and self, there are countless other questions of this type. You will want to add to this roster what else came to your mind as you were reading my punch list.

FYI or FYE?

When you see scribbled on a Post-It note attached to a reading item "For Your Information" or FYI, the information may not be nearly as significant as if it had been marked, "For Your Edification" or

FYE. Many years ago, good naturedly I tried and failed to encourage my generous Manhattan clients, colleagues, and others to switch from FYI to FYE. Daily my mailbox was filled with stockholder reports, news clippings, articles, books, magazines, and other stackable materials marked "FYI." To start a trend, I had a FYE rubber stamp made. It did not catch-on. Perhaps I gave-up too soon with this clever campaign for a higher purpose in exchange of materials.

Decades before my e-mail boxes would overflow with unwanted spam and welcome-yet-unanswered messages, with a smile I would ask people to not send me something simply for my ever-increasing stacks of inbound information. As I write to you, still I can see the neat stacks on my credenzas and my secretary's desk. Yes, I maintained a clear-desktop policy, but that did not include the credenza or bookshelves. Still I prefer to believe generous senders are more interested in my edification than in filling my storehouse silos of information. Thoughtful souls I know send me things highly valuable, with occasional comic relief of a thought-provoking cartoon from *The New Yorker* or a timely up-to-the-minute news-based joke from the quick-on-the-draw and wound-up-tight traders on the floor of the New York Stock Exchange.

Edification *via* Social Networking Technology
LinkedIn, Facebook, Twitter, Blogs, Audio/Video Broadcasts, *etc.*

Sharing, forwarding, copying, Tweeting, texting, IMing, e-mailing, or snail-mailing information of value to others is edification by you and for them. "For your edification" is a term that implies (a) potential value to the recipient, and (b) an unspoken suggestion the edificatory item should be passed along in a viral marketing sense. Yes, if something sent to you is edifying for you, it is highly likely to be edifying for someone else. We fully responsible leaders pass it on; *pay it forward.*

Prior to publication of this book, for more than a solid year I sent for edification of many leaders, in three English-speaking countries, sample "HILL Words" excerpted from draft chapters of "We Need to Have a Word!" My head and heart were in the right place. I was determined to share — for their and my personal edification — these value-packed words that mean so much to our grasping upside potential in fully responsible leadership.

For 12 years I headed a company in New York City that was among the first (early 1980s) to use "X" in a company name. Several large companies we served as clients followed our lead. We changed the company name from National Business Intelligence Corporation (NBI) to ETX Corporation. With "ETX" my sales team and I were more able to edify our value proposition for prospects, clients and others. Eventually the obvious question would be asked in some way similar to "What in the world does ETX stand for?" With a practiced friendly and engaging glint in our eyes and a smile on our bright young faces, we would say rather boldly, while locking eyes with the highest-ranking decision maker at table:

> **E** for Editorial expertise (pause),
> **T** for Technological command (pause), and
> **X** for the "X Factor" — all the high value for which we'll be charging you. (Big smile.)

We were there to lead, solve — and SELL (*i.e.*, in this strategic order close the deal, and we did). To lighten the air after such a boldly ascendant statement, we would lead the laughter. Almost always the person(s) to whom we were selling would at least smile at our temerity, while some would burst out laughing and thanking us for being forthright. We would talk about how our editorial expertise would edify (*i.e.*, improve) CEO words we would process through our cutting-edge electronic publishing system, so the company's stock's value would be edified (*i.e.*, increased) by the institutional stockholders.

Big-ticket decision-makers would see our edited-for-clarity-and-accuracy reports within hours of any financially significant statements made by the CEO from anywhere in the world she or he happened to be — with one of my team in the room to transmit and report on what was happening in London, California, or any other venue where buy-side analysts and others would gather for edification related to featured companies.

We were careful to emphasize "edify" over "edit." CEOs of major companies are a bit skittish when someone suggests their words might need to be edited. Of course they always did. Always. And with nods and other affirmation, nearly every CEO we served eventually would acknowledge how good we made her or him look in the investor's eyes. The disclaimer printed on the cover page of nearly all our publications read:

"The following electronically expedited and professionally edited transcriptional record of the above-captioned dissemination event has been reviewed and adjusted for clarity. Although every effort has been made to ensure 100% accuracy, no representation can be made that such has been achieved. For your *edification* this publication is provided by the company featured herein."

"Edited for edification" might have been a succinct and more accurate tongue-twister way to state why our clients were paying us top-dollar to do what we did. In addition to subtly warning there may be errors (which, in fact, were few and far between), note that we avoided saying "for your information." In this case "edification" put the burden-of-proof on the receiver, not the sender; the document was to improve and build toward composite understanding. We were advised to avoid suggesting the documents could or should stand-alone while investment decisions were being made by Wall Street's largest (*i.e.*, institutional) and other investors.

A Hill View is for Identification and Edification

Hillview's High-Impact Leader Lens (HILL) Model for Viewing Strategic Alignment of People, Money, Technology, and other Mission-Critical Resources (The HILL Model) is based on four-part identification and edification of both peers and followers: (1) accentuating their strengths while (2) ameliorating their weaknesses; (3) facilitating pursuit of opportunities while (4) reversing risk of threats — all seen from a HILL view (*i.e.*, from just high enough to see where people and things are moving).

Abraham Lincoln's beloved stepmother, Sarah Bush Lincoln, recounted her guidance of the future President, re-living how Lincoln made rapid progress as an edifier. "He read all the books he could get his hands on," she recalled, and was already practicing writing and speaking at a young age, eager to get at the exact meaning of words. After hearing sermons by a local preacher, he would sometimes stand on a stump, gather the children around, and "almost repeat it word for word." Edification.

Much more could be said about ages, stages and pages of enlightenment. For now, when today or tomorrow you electronically send or physically hand to someone written information for their edification, please double-check your intention. Are you striving to enlighten the recipient with intellectual, moral, ethical, philosophic, spiritual, or other illumination? I hope so. I try.

We need to have a word for almost everything. Aglet is the word for the plastic part at the end of shoelaces. Do you feel edified, and a tad amused, with the faint comic relief of this little fact for edification?

> *"Knowledge speaks, but wisdom listens."* —Jimi Hendrix

In my consulting, coaching, speaking and writing work, I strive to discern and apply for each person — individually and collectively — words of character, words of strength, and words of performance. Words support edification for definition, description and application of the Language for Leading.™ For me such thoughts are edifying.

Reading We Need to Have a Word is to be edifying for you. Is it? These 52 featured key words are chosen, and expounded upon, to instruct and encourage readers in moral, intellectual, spiritual and other dimensions of awareness, engagement and improvement. Edification comes in many words and ways. Working together, you and I use this book toward edification regarding people and things.

Indeed, to know, grow and thrive, we each need a steady stream of edification. Let's aim for exemplary edification effort in most of what we say and do.

Thought and action toward envisioning and reengineering a global re-emergence economy must aim to do much more than support funding and sustainability for America's free enterprise way-of-life. Ever-increasing international interdependency commands of thought leaders and others deeper, broader and higher levels of edification and understanding of each psychoeconomic unit's strengths, weaknesses, opportunities and threats. Institutions and households depend on intentional and responsible edification by wise individuals.

Thank you for embracing the importance of this key word. High-purpose thought and effort toward edification will enlarge and enrich your sense-of-self and your interlocking relationships with others.

Edification. Expound.

Emergence

Chapter Inspired by and Dedicated to Douglas W. Pemberton

Insert or imagine seeing your first name: _____,

Seeing this chapter's title word, what immediately comes to your open mind? Do you already have a working relationship with this word? Somewhere inside of you does this word instantly appeal? As a response to a specific situation at-hand, will this word work to your and others' advantage? For this word to increase in real value, together we must dig, drill and think deeper, so we will reach, climb and soar higher.

Emergence is the act of emerging, a steady pace of *coming forth*. Emerging ideas, emerging ventures, and emerging leaders are views to behold as they unfold. Without overlooking value found within the untidiness of unavoidable trial-and-error stages in emergence, fully responsible leaders both participate in and facilitate presage of favorable outcomes for individuals and groups. In other words, seedlings of emergent solutions and ideas must be planted in fertile ground, and nurtured through various stages of emergence. A mind's emergence from a deep sleep or a coma — symbolic or real — is characterized as "coming to." Coming to what? One hopes the answer is "coming back to reality," and perhaps to a better-than-before perception of reality.

Especially while emerging from an era of global economic emergency, fully conscious, fully engaged, and fully responsible leaders must move toward more wisdom, courage and patience related to envisioning and empowering a sustainable "re-emergence economy." Do you allow yourself and others abundant space and time for sustainable emergence? Please be sure you are attuned to this strategic alignment imperative for surviving and thriving. Emergence.

In what aspects of your daily life does emergence manifest favorable results? What do you do to ensure sustainability of circumstances that enable you, others, and organizations to emerge to steadily increasing upside potential? Do you openly count the attributes of emergence? Do you strenuously avoid pitfalls of myopia toward emergence?

When hearing, seeing, or having an emerging idea — new or not — do you intentionally R.E.A.C.T. with Respect, Empathy, Authenticity, Clarity and Trust? Do you give emergent ideas room to breathe, or do you strangle and suffocate them with expressions of disrespect or disinterest? Are you known among colleagues and peers as one who thrives on sustainable emergence of ideas, or are you regarded as someone who is noticeably intimidated or threatened by new or renewed thinking? Through your intentional appreciation for the people and process of emergence, do your R.E.A.C.H. with Reality, Energy, Ascendancy, Commitment, and Humility? You and I must.

In your organization, are you a creator and curator of works of collaborative innovation? Or unintentionally are you a *thought-buster* determined to rid the world (or at least your sphere of influence) of emerging fresh and different thinking? Take a deep breath and whisper to yourself where you land when asked where you stand on a scale of a person who (1) respects or (2) rejects ideas, or are you somewhere in-between these essential and regrettable two extremes? What did you just tell yourself? Did you even pause for a nanosecond's worth of self-assessment about your views toward ideational development — your intentionality within emergence of solutions and ideas? Was the mere request for a pause of this type instantly welcomed or discounted? Did you waste or invest these brief moments of potential emergence? What just emerged in you and for you, something or nothing? Did you allow anything positive to emerge? Will you? Together let's emerge! We must.

Who said "perception is reality?"
Truth in-view is not always truth in fact.

In a New York City hospital a foreign-born father was assisting in birthing his first child. As the baby's head emerged, the attending physician encouraged the nervous daddy to gently put his index fingers under the child's armpits to ever-so-smoothly try to pull into light the emergent miracle. Suddenly the baby was out and being held high by the proud father. To the mother he announced with loud sports-stadium excitement, "It's a boy, honey, it's a boy! We have a son! We have a son!" Rather sternly the obstetrician said, "Young man, in this country we call *that* an umbilical cord. Your baby is a girl. You have a daughter."

With intended comic relief above, it's rather clear the exclamatory father's apparent need to see male-animal affirmation — of some almost misogynistic type — overwhelmed his ability to see reality in the beauty of his female offspring. One's very first view of any sight could be called a shadow of reality that will become clearer with continuously recalibrated focus. Through the lens of the viewer's wisdom, courage and patience regarding who or what is being seen, clearer and clearer perceptions emerge.

For the next few moments, together we'll allow to emerge highlights of three of 12 "points of emergence" seen through Hillview's High-Impact Leader Lens (HILL) Model for Viewing Strategic Alignment of People, Money, and other Mission-Critical Resources (The HILL Model); in alphabetical order: ambiguity, conflict, direction, ideas, leaders, opportunities, polarity, risk, strengths, threats, ventures and weaknesses. These are the Top 12 observations of strategic alignment best seen with HILL perspective; people, things, and matters in-motion that fully responsible leaders intentionally view from a hill — not from a flat plain, a lofty mountaintop, nor from a stale ivory tower.

This very moment, please press yourself a bit. With focus on the word emergence, are you already tuning-in or tuning-out; opening or closing to the possibility of experiencing a panoramic view of YOUR perils and possibilities? Are you ready to acknowledge likely new clarity about emergence, or are you more ready to kill the message and/or the messenger? For vastly different reasons, you and yours truly are wearing respective lifetimes of protective armor. Respectfully I suggest you'll want to remove your helmet and breastplate. We're aiming for your emergent head and your emergent heart. You are in good hands.

Along more personal lines of emergence, so-called "love at first sight" is never about the beloved, regardless of how long the perception of instantaneity remains for one, both, or others choosing such irrational assessment of connective emotional, physical, intellectual and spiritual experience. Wonderfully, any debate of this logic yields combustion toward new light of clarity, and sometimes even creates further bliss for the lover of the beloved whose good instinctive judgment is being more accurately reclassified. Appearance of cynicism aside, logic prevails. Instant attraction to another person is about the observer's accrued perspective and other experience. Since 1977 such immature attraction is called "limerence." From age five to 15 or so, "puppy love" was the term used to explain my limerent (and occasionally unreciprocated) attraction to neighbors and schoolmates. In my early 20s reading Eric Fromm's bestseller *The Art of Loving* rescued me from simplemindedness about emergent affectional relationships of many types.

For me emergence is a somewhat mysterious word. Great literature addresses emergence in evocative terms and turns of phrase far beyond the scope of this book's purpose. Your scribe finds himself emergent in the up-lifting nature of the word, and more aware of inherent perils of oversimplifying our human role in emergence of circumstances. From humankind's emergence in both evolution and creationism, to idea emergence in a group's brainstorming and one person's brainchild, emergence deserves its time and space in order to flourish — for the good of the order. There is no way to successfully implement a bad idea, so why worry about whatever emerges for consideration?

Emergence of Ideas. Emergence of Ventures. Emergence of Leaders.

For our shared focus on the powerful HILL Word "emergence," let's dig a little deeper so we can climb a lot higher regarding our thoughts and actions toward (1) emerging ideas, (2) emerging ventures, and (3) emerging leaders. Not unlike childbirth, emergence of ideas, ventures and leaders is untidy and full of surprises. In emergence one must look past early dishevelment toward eventual completeness. If in due course you allow emergence to happen, a more whole picture will come into view.

How a person responds to new ideas is a reliable barometer with which to measure aptitude for success with fully responsible leadership. People without traits of essential wisdom, courage, or patience to nurture and otherwise allow ideas to emerge are secretly or openly dismissed from most written or memorized rosters of leaders-in-training. Imagine choosing a leader who is shut-down to new ideas. It happens. Just when ideas are most needed, organizations in trouble often choose leaders for their mathematic analytical abilities. "Human calculators" are often prized over inherent innovators. Boards and investors accidentally preferentially reward metrics of math more so than they empower mastery of art and science of innovation.

In late 2010 I worked diligently *(pro-bono)* to respond to an organizational CEO who was unknowingly sounding loud warning alarms about his own effectiveness in trying to reinvigorate an institution founded nearly 250 years ago. I heard the loud alarms mostly as they related to this good man's lack of psychological or emotional readiness to learn deeper lessons about leading people, managing things, and strategically aligning people and things. I could not get through. I tried. I was unable to overcome his many years of military thinking about his having earned a "right to lead." His exclusionary actions spoke much louder than his inclusive words. We parted company. I was not the collaborative person to point him toward new views. He needs a duly commissioned command-and-control type of personality to call him to attention. I did my best.

The once thriving institution's ability to grow is directly related to the CEO's acceptance of the mission-critical need for him to become a fully responsible leader city-wide — far beyond the walls of his cloistered environment. He is a leader. In many ways he is a responsible leader. Yet he remains a far cry from being a fully responsible leader. I tried and failed to open his eyes, mind or heart.

Without using the terms, I knew I was being confronted with the personality and perspective of a "caretaker CEO" *vs.* a "groundbreaker CEO." As this book heads to the printer, evidence suggests this fine fellow remains more comfortable pointing fingers than pointing people (*i.e.,* blaming others instead of leading others). If he is emerging, I cannot see it, hear it, or feel it.

Cities are crying out for leadership from fully responsible leaders. Powerful local leaders are called by the Gallup Organization essential to economic breakthroughs. Powerful local leaders are not always fully responsible leaders. When fully responsible leaders emerge, all people and things that they touch benefit in more ways than any plan-of-action could or would predict.

Many leaders rose, in part, through their admirably deft handling of their own and others' ideas, yet eventually some became fearful of the very creativity and innovativeness that propelled their ascent to posts of authority. Why? Fear of failure? Fear of success? *Fear of emergence?* How did their and others' ideas become more threatening than elevating; fodder for risk-avoidance instead of risk-worthiness? There are as many answers as there are unemployment insurance checks being issued. Yes, risk is real for careers and whole organizations. Job terminations and bankruptcies are often traced back to endemic resistance toward ideas, and other avoidance of thoughts and acts that could yield solutions, opportunities, and other innovation.

Perhaps more intentionally than I realize, each year I reconnect with one or two key people from my emergent years in Pittsburgh and Manhattan. As finishing touches were added to this letter to you from me, an unexpected telephone call came from my barber from when I was 19 until 23. He is still Pittsburgh's "Barber to Bosses." This was the rarefied-air niche he decided to carve for himself. It worked. Back then and now I am fascinated by the CEO stories he tells. After nearly four decades since I left Pittsburgh (1973), and just before he recounted stories from my past, I asked him how he was doing. He said, "I'm still trying to figure out who I want to be when I grow up." Not "what" but "who." I told him this was positive. I celebrated his youthful spirit. Yet he sounded more sad than glad. I shared with him my joy in never-ending emergence.

"A boy's story is the best that's ever told." —Charles Dickens

Geographically speaking and in your mind's eye, exactly where do you allow your and other ideas to emerge? Do you know where your ideas more easily and fully blossom—away from home base, perhaps? Are you more open to thinking emergent thoughts when out in the countryside driving, or when you are aloft flying at 35,000 feet? Does an ocean view stimulate your creativity? How about sitting by a lake, surveying a mountain range, or when submerged in a bathtub of warm water and childhood's bubbles? For so many years I thought I am at my creative and emergent best in the above settings. Now I know I am at my emergent best when blessed to be in the trusting and comforting company of other emergent minds and souls.

High-Impact Leader Lens (HILL) views allow us to "get up and away" from the flat plains of boredom, constancy, and one-dimensional vision. Lives and ventures viewed from HILL-height are seen with perspective of yesterday, today and tomorrow; clear views of where people and things have been, where they are, and what's ahead. Allow yourself to FEEL the lift to a hill-level of your fine mind's perspective for observing your emergent past, present and future.

Fully responsible leaders never stop emerging. One of Stephen Covey's Seven Habits — Sharpening the Saw — is essentially about ensuring continuous emergence. Life-long learning allows emergence abundant time and space in our open minds and hearing hearts.

This moment what is emerging in and for you? Does hunger for emergence seem to be emerging in you? Are you feeling emergent?

"One way to find food for thought is to use the fork in the road, the bifurcation that marks the place of emergence in which a new line of development begins to branch off." —William Irwin Thompson

For me there's never enough emergence. I want and need more emergence in my life, personally and professionally. Let's continue to intentionally acknowledge and nurture the full nature of emergence.

"With the emergence of civilization, the rate of change shifted from hundreds of thousands of years to millennia. With the emergence of science as a way of knowing the universe, the rate of change shifted to centuries."
—William Irwin Thompson

Anywhere in this book that you see unused white space, allow your thoughts to fill-in the blanks with words, lyrics, sketches, doodles, geometric shapes, squiggly lines, or any other graphic representation of whatever is emerging in you. Even if you feel welling-up inside of you joy, fullness, frustration or emptiness, allow it — whatever *it* is — to emerge.

Examine whatever emergent you are bringing to light. Even darkest thoughts are better seen in the light of day. Whatever you choose to do about or with your emergence, choose a positive, productive, and otherwise constructive course of action. Change what you can. Accept what you cannot change. Invite from others input and support. Allow resurgence to reignite any stall in your emergence.

Thank you for allowing emergence to resonate for you in ways that release within you new views, ideas and actions. Allow thoughts toward emergence to electrify an ever-fresh vision of emerging you. Feel emergence. Honor it. Celebrate and sustain your emergence.

Emergence. Expound.

Empathy

Chapter Inspired by and Dedicated to Michelle Bardy Platt

Insert or imagine seeing your first name: _____,

Seeing this chapter's title word, what immediately comes to your open mind? Do you already have a working relationship with this word? Somewhere inside of you does this word instantly appeal? As a response to a specific situation at-hand, will this word work to your and others' advantage? For this word to increase in real value, together we must dig, drill and think deeper, so we will reach, climb and soar higher.

"Tea and Sympathy" is a classic movie from the 1950s. "Shoes and Empathy" is the unofficial sub title for this chapter's challenging message. From flip-flops and Nikes to wing-tips and high-heels, empathy is about putting yourself in someone else's shoes; understanding and entering into another person's authentic feelings. Empathy is mission-critical for fully responsible leadership.

Leaders wear many hats. Empathy is about shoes. How do your leader shoes fit you? Who do you expect to try to feel what it is like to stand in your shoes?

What does it feel like for you to stand in the shoes of your employees, buyers, customers, clients, vendors and peers? What about trying-on shoes of your boss, shareholders, lenders and investors? Try standing in shoes of small business owners, CEOs of multi-national corporations, heads of Wall Street firms, presidents of banks, mortgage lenders, civic leaders, elected officials, any former U.S. President, or the large shoes of our current Commander-in-Chief.

Imagine a laid-off U.S. auto worker slowly removing work boots in front of a very worried spouse. Consider thin soles of homeless individuals. How would an ex-offender feel walking out of prison wearing state-issued shoes, then trying to find honest work knowing he has served his time? Imagine the shoes of a grieving widow standing at graveside as her young husband's body is laid to rest following an unexpected and unexplained death. On Oscar night, could you stand in Meryl Streep's heels or *les chaussures de* Jean Dujardin? How difficult for you would it be to mentally stand in Whitney Houston's mourning family's shoes? Yes, good, bad and other circumstances influence the fit and feel of others' shoes.

Symbolically standing in someone else's shoes, can you really feel empathy for individuals who count on your top performance? Of course you can. Empathy is good. Empathy is mission-critical for fully responsible leadership.

Please also pause to squeeze into little shoes of our future leaders; foot gear of bewildered youngsters trying to piece together unworthy images and words assaulting their eyes and ears. From imagining joy of a toddler's shoeless feet on soft warm grass, to fear associated with steel-toes needed to endure pain of stomps from bullies endured during teenage and young-adult years, do you sense growing need within you to both protect and prepare younger generations? I do. Mentors should first teach definitions, descriptions and applications of high-impact empathy.

"The most valuable things in life are not measured in monetary terms. The really important things are not houses and lands, stocks and bonds, automobiles and real estate, but friendships, trust, confidence, empathy, mercy, love and faith."
—Bertrand Russell

Leaders must strive to put themselves in shoes of every individual they lead or otherwise serve. Too often the fit is painful, especially when difficult news is being delivered. Ah, but when joy is genuinely shared, the fit can be near-perfect.

"People will forget what you said, people will forget what you did, but people will never forget how you made them feel." —Bonnie Jean Wasmund

The above quote is mostly correct. With accrued sensibilities and skills, we allow ourselves to feel whatever way we feel. No one can make us feel one way or another. There is no doubt, however, about how others influence our choices. Yet the choice remains ours. Our level of emotional intelligence (EQ) supports or thwarts our ability to take unique ownership of our feelings. If we feel bad because someone has let us down or offended, we are choosing to feel bad.

For a period of constructive reflection, feeling bad is good. Although it would be cumbersome prose, Ms. Wasmund might have been more accurate had she said, "...people will never forget how you emboldened them to feel their true feelings, and then empathically stood by their sides as they learned what they could do with those feelings to move forward with new clarity and commitment." Feel those words. Put yourself in my shoes as I wrote them. This book demonstrates my empathy toward you. Do you feel my empathy coming your way? It's real.

Oddly each switchover to Daylight Savings Time reminds me of empathy once denied. In the late 1970s in Manhattan, I was Chairman of the Board for a modern dance company, The Greenhouse Dance Ensemble, headed by world-renowned maestro Gerard Schwarz's brilliant wife, Lilo Way. One Sunday of a switch to Daylight Savings, Gerard, Lilo and I had scheduled — at the Schwarz home in Montclair, New Jersey — a VIP reception for raising money for the dance company. It was a first-class affair complete with brass ensemble (under the maestro's baton), dancers, lavish buffet — and a painfully late-in-arriving main speaker. Yes, Chairman Dallas and his wife forgot to change our analog watches and clocks. Red faces!

Actually that morning we were traveling ahead of schedule. Thinking we were too early to arrive at the Schwarz doorstep, my former wife and I tarried and drove around for some neighborhood sightseeing. In that pre-mobile telephone era, the hosts worried themselves into anger with yours truly. To this second I remember the instant embarrassment when Cynthia and I erroneously thought we were arriving on-time. We were one painful hour late. Faces were red. Yet everyone had been in our shoes. Empathy! Yet I recall no empathy from the always on-time maestro.

As you can tell from this and other stories told so far, expressing and receiving empathy creates lasting memories. Expressing and receiving empathy are mission-critical factors of fully responsible leadership.

Speaking of shoes and empathy, Adam Daniels is a commercial photographer who worked on an advertising campaign showing U.S. football players standing in high heels. Pause. Imagine. I recall when my good friend Adam had to shop for the props. Listening over cocktails to his account of his whole journey was quite illuminating. He realized the experience could have boomeranged. His manhood was not threatened. He knows high heels do not make the man. It seemed to me his creativity was enhanced. He did not bother with feelings from simple and trite reactions. People who hear his story might superimpose their own skittishness about masculinity's inflexibility or even homophobia. I am pleased my Manhattan years among *Mad Men*-like advertising shoes of all types allowed me to freely share in his joy of discovery.

With his self-effacing sense of humor, Adam and the photogenic male athletes he photographed in-heels enjoyed the experience. It was all good for much more than a laugh or two. Adam and the football players will never again look at women in-heels without some extra empathy.

Only from 1956 (when I was six years old) are women "permitted" by the Presbyterian church to serve as elected Elders, Deacons, and called Ministers of Word and Sacrament — starting almost 250 years after Presbyterianism originated in Scotland; in 1707 when legally confirmed as The Church of Scotland. Well before 1956, an aunt, uncle, and Grandmother Margaret Long Dallas made certain I was already a never-miss-a-Sunday youngster at Pittsburgh's First Presbyterian Church; founded in 1773, only 66 years after legal ratification of The Church of Scotland — and three years before the 13 colonies declared their independence. Leadership is in our DNA.

Ascendant (*i.e.,* a somewhat disobedient tyke) I would not attend Sunday School. I insisted on only participating in 11:00 A.M. adult worship. Vividly I remember being thrilled to see our first female pastor in the First Church pulpit, Reverend Jean Kirkpatrick. Although I hardly recognized historical significance of her appearance in the formal black academic robes of Presbyterian ministry, from that moment I certainly noticed significant difference in how men and women lead in churches and other environments. I knew I was delighted to see and feel a kinder and gentler touch on my mind and heart. Of course I did not understand what was happening among less-enlightened adults around me. After only a few years with us, I was sorry when Reverend Jean moved on.

Sadly, rather quickly I learned how both men and women misinterpreted, mistreated and misused special gifts many women bring to leading people and managing things. Too recently I was witness to one of the all-time great travesties of misalignment in thoughts and deeds related to a woman in a senior-most leadership role. Effectively named co-CEO to quickly succeed a retiring male powerhouse, a cherished friend was obliged to throw in the towel after she realized her best thoughts and efforts could not conquer culturally endemic misogynistic misalignment in the significant organization she was to eventually serve alone in the top post. *Time Magazine* reported her story. Elsewhere she thrived, of course, and though now in far-too-early retirement, she still finds ways to lead from the head and the heart.

It is no secret that I wish more men would allow their empathic, compassionate, sensitive and other so-called feminine sensibilities to shine through in their thoughts and deeds while leading people and managing things — and strategically aligning people and things. I believe we modern men ARE getting better — though from my HILL vantage point, still far too slowly.

Unfortunately there are high-profile women in leadership posts who still think they need to be man-like (whatever that means) to get ahead. Misguided, they wrongly employ out-dated in-your-face male-style aggressiveness, instead of choosing to learn, embrace and practice strategically aligned thoughts and actions of what Hillview calls "win-win-*plus* assertiveness."

Remembering "Shoes and Empathy" — in addition to "Tea and Sympathy" — will keep a little smile in your heart as you think about your life's calling to be an empathic fully responsible leader. From envisioning fitting into a baby's first shoes though trying-on wares of a virtual shoe store in your mind, do whatever you can, wherever you can do it, to stand in the shoes of men, women and children who will benefit from your authentic empathy. I pray empathy also comes your way, but when it does not, be sure you are firmly standing in your own Sunday-best shoes.

Today identify more opportunities to empathize in ways that intensify your and others' human experience of life's ups, downs, and other-way movements toward success. With the next human you encounter, see if you can intensify your empathy toward the individual. Look down at her or his shoes. From smiling to crying, imagine standing, breathing, living and being in those shoes.

Empathy. Expound.

Engagement

Chapter Inspired by and Dedicated to
Margaret Nancy (Long) Dallas (1902-1978)

Insert or imagine seeing your first name: _____,

Seeing this chapter's title word, what immediately comes to your open mind? Do you already have a working relationship with this word? Somewhere inside of you does this word instantly appeal? As a response to a specific situation at-hand, will this word work to your and others' advantage? For this word to increase in real value, together we must dig, drill and think deeper, so we will reach, climb and soar higher.

What is your measurable and defensible level of consciousness (LOC) and level of engagement (LOE) as you navigate low and high seas of your leadership voyage? In thoughts, deliberations, negotiations, or other transactions, do certain developments and occurrences become temporary distractions or enhancements to lessen or increase respectively your LOC or LOE? While remaining on the lookout for icebergs, do you pay close attention to navigational demands of calm and smooth waters? At the helm, surely we all occasionally struggle to remain what emergency medical care providers refer to in triage code as "A&Ox4," Alert and Oriented to four measurements of basic patient consciousness: (1) your name, (2) exactly where you are when asked, (3) the date, month, year, and approximate time of day, and (4) the situation that brought you to this moment. In order to monitor and assess their own and others' levels of minute-by-minute consciousness and on-task engagement, in various ways fully responsible leaders need to ask these and more A&Ox4 types of diagnostic questions.

Hillview's High-Impact Leader Lens (HILL) Model for Viewing Strategic Alignment uses A&Ox4 logic to ask if a leader is at least adequately alert and oriented (A&O) to past, current and future (1)

Strengths, (2) Weaknesses, (3) Opportunities and (4) Threats related to alignment of people, money, marketplace conditions, and other areas for vigilant and sustained HILL focus — A.S.W.O.T. we call it; "A" for alignment. The HILL Score measures and calibrates for clients 36 vectors of vision for determining a leader's on-duty LOC and LOE. While standing at a HILL level to observe and influence imperative *true-north* direction in which individuals and teams must be moving toward stated destinations, how A&Ox4 are you toward A.S.W.O.T. criteria for your own and your team's top performance?

Imagine a neurosurgeon performing a craniotomy while unengaged due to undetected psychological burn-out, masked physical exhaustion, unspoken family distractions, hidden financial worries, obscured or obvious dependency on alcohol, drugs or some other addiction, or anyone or anything that takes the physician's mind and body away from the life-and-death leadership tasks quite literally at-hand. At the other extreme, I remember a situation when a sales representative selling a big-ticket item passed through procurement triage at Chicago Title Credit Services, Inc. and landed at the CEO's desk for final approval. At one point during the lackluster discussion I realized the robotic fellow was saying to me what he would say to anyone. Indeed I was offended. I scanned my intentionally clear desktop to see if the company's or my name were anywhere to be seen, and then asked the chap to close his notebook and look me straight in the eyes. When asked my name, he could not answer. When asked what company he was visiting, he hadn't a clue. Imagine the scene! My company and I were nameless.

In this bloke's disorderly and otherwise disengaged mind, Chicago Title and I appeared to be nothing more or less than sought-after commission dollar signs. Of course I stopped short of asking him other questions to test his A&Ox4, and firmly ushered him to the express elevator. For his long-range benefit more than mine, I let him know he had flunked A&Ox4 and was never going to get a second chance during my tenure in charge. I told him why he was never again to dare approach the 32nd or any other Chicago Title floor of 161 North Clark Street. He and I learned new lessons about lowest levels of on-duty consciousness and engagement in the business world. Since that oddball experience, I became extra sensitive to others' and my own LOC and LOE. In fact, he and I gave each other gifts of clarity about LOC and LOE. Trust I am A&Ox4 as I write to share with you these points of demarcation for consciousness and engagement of fully responsible leaders.

Over many years much has been written and said about exigency of full engagement at home and work. Front-page evidence of societal unrest and economic aftershocks more than suggests some women and men in leadership posts are not fully engaged and strategically aligned with people, money, and other mission-critical resources. Best-selling authors John Maxwell, Stephen Covey, Marcus Buckingham, Jack Welch, Jim Loehr, Tony Schwartz, and numerous other realists of leadership development agree that steady and accountable pursuit of full engagement is imperative for sustainable success.

Approximately at what percentage are you engaged in the work for which you earn salary, wages, fees, or other forms of monetary compensation? At roughly the same percentage point, would you and your immediate supervisor (or buyer) say you are fully or partially engaged; 95-100 percent, or perhaps as low as 40-50 percent? As U.S. and global economic pressures mount, wane, or remain a top-of-mind constant for your daily focus, how candid are you with yourself about the direct relationship between your percentage of engagement in your work and YOUR own economic impact on your employer, fellow employees, buyers of your goods or services, your community as a whole, family, your checkbook, and the wallets that depend on your top performance — your best-effort engagement? For at least the next year or so, has a daily reality check replaced your annual bonus check?

Approximately at what percentage are you engaged in your home life? At roughly the same percentage point, would you and your spouse or significant other say you are fully or partially engaged; 95-100 percent, or perhaps as low as 40-50 percent? If U.S. divorce rates and other mounting household pressures motivate you to measure your efforts in order to beat the odds (as they should), how candid are you with yourself about the relationship between your percentage of engagement in your home life and YOUR likelihood for sustainable long-term success as a mate or parent? To a greater degree than you may acknowledge, your home life's success depends on your top performance — your best-effort engagement. Do you agree?

Setting the stage for out-of-the-ordinary discussion about engagement, I assume you believe yourself to be fully engaged. For now, I believe you are. Psychiatrist R. D. Laing said, *"The range of what we think and do is limited by what we fail to notice. And because we fail to notice that we fail to notice, there is little we can do to change; until we notice how failing to notice shapes our thoughts and deeds."* (Dr. Laing's tongue-twisting profundity may require an extra read-through.) Yes, you and I may be failing to notice our true level of engagement in producing desired and measurable results at home, work and elsewhere. Are we at our best? Are we more engaged today than we were one or two years ago?

As for YOUR engagement in managing your organization's or household's finances, are you allowing yourself to drill deeper about your possible complicity, if any, in this era's economic meltdown? (Blame is too strong a word for this point of A&Ox4/A.S.W.O.T. assessment.) This somewhat invasive question requires pervasive thought. If you are 100% certain you've not contributed in any way whatsoever to the shaky economic conditions of any organization, perhaps you assess at the highest level possible your percentage of engagement at work. Do you? If this near perfection is the case (as I truly hope it is), you have my genuine respect and appreciation for your steadfastness and other strengths in your personal-best on-the-job performance. Fully responsible leaders must strive to become and remain extra conscious and engaged.

Among your many spheres of influence, are you more or less engaged in lives of: impressionable children, members of your collaborative worship community, residents of your interdependent neighborhood, voters in your vote-dependent political party, employees and beneficiaries of your favorite and probably struggling charities, or with trusting family, colleagues, co-workers, or friends? How engaged are you with strangers on the street; passers-by who are homeless, prosperous, or somewhere in-between? Do you at least occasionally nod and say hello to strangers riding with you in elevators or standing near you on-line at Starbucks? And how engaged are you in intentional pursuit of more knowledge, greater wisdom, exceptional courage, and unyielding patience?

Indeed, engagement is very personal. Sometimes a person's lack of engagement on-the-job comes from a personal life un-rooted by full engagement at home. Often I observe how full engagement at home allows full engagement at work, and *vice-versa*. Personal consciousness and engagement, therefore, require here a few lines of attention and deeper thought.

"Love does not consist of gazing at each other,
but in looking together in the same direction." —Antoine de Saint-Exupery

From the early 80s I recall a New Yorker Magazine cartoon showing a multi-tier wedding cake upon which was perched a small plastic man wearing a tuxedo. Seated alone at an executive desk, the spouse-less groom was shown married to his job. Everyone around the cake was toasting this man's choice of work over having a human mate. With nervous laughter I said to the prescient friend who clipped and gave me the classic cartoon (which I still have), "Hey! I am not married to my job. I am, however, fully engaged to my work, and will forever stay fully engaged. Besides, I decided I am not the marrying kind." We both roared that nervous laughter that comes from unspoken truth expressed through convoluted humor. A simple conversation with him would not have done justice to the complexity of my emerging sense of self, both personally and professionally. It seems I can master full engagement, but in marriage I fail. Connecting personal and professional concepts of full engagement allows us to experience polarity in our pop culture adaptation of the word "engagement."

Shortly after my December 1980 divorce, many of my fellow New Yorkers and others were waiting for me to become engaged and eventually marry again. The furtive guessing game was somewhat amusing. After 13 ensuing years of trial-and-error, including two full, robust, loving, and fully committed relationships, in 1993 by default I became what Grandmother Shearer frequently called a "confirmed bachelor." Indeed three times I was badly burned. My heat shield was gone. Emotionally beaten to the ground, I chose to redouble my engagement in my career. Among many gratifying career accomplishments to come there were many truly horrific backbreaking trials and tribulations, yet none was as taxing as the collapse of the true-love relationships I mourned losing. Yet I was not afraid to be alone. With the glowing exception of the blessing of being married to father my beloved daughter, perhaps thereafter I was meant to remain unattached. Still I am not the marrying kind (for now). I am, however, fully engaged in any worthy pursuit I undertake.

On those occasional lonely nights, I comfort myself with the wisdom of Alfred, Lord Tennyson, the chief poet in the Victorian age of poetry, *"Tis better to have loved and lost than never to have loved at all."* As for my business life, I paraphrased Tennyson, *"It is better to have served as CEO and failed at times, than to have never been a CEO and succeeded in all efforts."* Personal and professional pleasure and pain are found between every word in both turns of phrase.

As if yesterday, I recall the moment it dawned on me I may never again marry. I can't say I was thrilled with the inward revelation. Nearing 20 years as a free agent have allowed me to grow in ways I might not have pursued while in a committed relationship. Humbly I feel stronger than ever. Since the 1993 moment of clarity, I weathered six or so perfect storms in my career and health. I am both blessed and grateful to have survived. If I remain a single man, I'll continue to live an abundant and good life. I may never know if another wedding ring would make things better or worse for me or a mate. Truly I'm okay with this logic. Thanks to the good Lord above, I have a bigger picture in mind.

> *"Marriage requires four types of "rings:"*
> *engagement ring, wedding ring, suffeRING, and endurRING."*
> —Anonymous

Many thoughtful souls and I discuss how the traditional year or more of pre-marital engagement, prior to exchange of matrimonial vows, is sometimes the only extended time both parties are on their best behavior; perhaps more fully involved with each other than shortly after the two say "I do." In a large percentage of the 50 percent or more of U.S. marriages that end in divorce, the marriage itself often becomes taken for granted. In hindsight, months or more time of engagement are often remembered as periods of more passionate and otherwise more emotion-charged "best practices." Not always, of course, yet often one or both people remember being more alert to the other during the engagement phase of their relationship. During engagement they worked harder to put forward their best feet and feats. The stakes were high.

Wedding days can be instantaneous tipping points during which one or both parties STOP being "engaged," and thus begin an almost ritualistic decent into one or both taking the other person for granted. Dire as this may sound, too many married or once married folk "felt" something change once the engagement was off and the wedding rings were on. Within many 20/20 hindsight stories told, there seems to be intentionality in engagement that slips away. Even if a year or so of marital bliss follows the end of the formal engagement, more than half of marriages morph into something less than full engagement. Many suspect a considerable percentage of those who remain married are less than thrilled with their choice to stick it out, stick with it, and remain stuck. One wonders if at least 40% of married couples are enjoying as much or more connection as they enjoyed and valued while they were engaged prior to marriage.

If you grasp and embrace philosophic context for Sufficiency of One and Abundance of One, and choose pursuit of success in single life, nonetheless are you proactively pursuing higher quality for your life and lives of others? With psychological self-agency, emotional clarity, intentional acuity, and abiding grace in your attentiveness and patience toward self and others, how candid are you with yourself about the relationship between your percentage of engagement and your and their quality-of-life? How does the quality of your life enrich or encroach on lives of others? To a greater or lesser extent, are you mindful of the influence you surely have on the sufficiency and abundance of those near and far from you? Are you engaged at a high level of your ability and availability; applying adequate skill and time?

Draw from these human illustrations, please, relevant parallels with your career and organizational duties. How often have you felt alone out there on that limb? How often have you courted someone with whom you wanted to do business, only to ultimately be rejected? And when the would-be buyer finally said yes, and you jumped in bed together, how quickly did you discover incompatibility and regret consummating the deal if not the marriage?

As I begin public speaking assignments, I always acknowledge for the audience our shared likelihood of engaging in In-and-Out Listening; they will be with me for awhile then check-out for brief seconds or long minutes. I might say something that causes them to think about things related or not to what I am addressing. "We all do it," I assure each audience. To help each participant to focus on the message, I ask everyone to avoid grading my deportment or speaking ability, and instead grade their own attentiveness and engagement in what I am saying. If the organizer of the meeting plans to distribute evaluation forms for people to give me grades for my effort, I ask the audience to reverse the process and grade themselves for their performance.

Grading me is not as important as audience members evaluating their own receptivity and responsiveness — their levels of engagement.

This logic actually galvanizes their attention to what I am saying, instead of how I am saying it. I seem to have a very attentive audience whenever they hear the requirement that they only focus on what they are hearing, learning, and thinking. Instead of ranking me for my entertainment value or my grasp of my own subject material, by asking them to rank themselves I succeed in getting more engagement from each. It works. During your next meeting, try it.

So far only once did an audience member figure out the win-win ploy. When he announced his conclusion, in front of everyone and with a big smile he said to me, "Mr. Dallas, I think I know what you were saying when you asked us not to pay attention to you or rank your ability as a speaker or grade your material. Cleverly you got us to pay more attention to you than otherwise we might have. Did I catch you at your game? If so, you sure won us over. I think I held onto every single word you spoke. Thank you."

To avoid rushing to judgment about others, even those of us with best intentions occasionally need reminders and permission to focus on what is going on inside of ourselves. Pointing fingers outward can come more easily than pointing inward deeper thoughts and feelings.

Self-agency is defined as the conceptual understanding of self as an agent capable of shaping motives, behavior, and future possibilities (Damon & Hart, 1991). Respectfully, prayerfully and hopefully I encourage all fully responsible leaders to join me in tapping more of our newly found depths in self-agency — in order to increase our appreciable levels of consciousness and engagement at work, home, and in the communities we each humbly serve.

Thank you for stepping-up to engage others in shared commitment to personal and professional lives of full A&Ox4 consciousness and engagement — defining, designing, resigning, aligning and assigning our strengths, weaknesses, opportunities and threats:

A&Ox4 S.W.O.T.

Engagement. Expound.

Esteem

Chapter Inspired by and Dedicated to
Regina Elizabeth (Meals) Shearer (1900-1995)

Insert or imagine seeing your first name: _____,

Seeing this chapter's title word, what immediately comes to your open mind? Do you already have a working relationship with this word? Somewhere inside of you does this word instantly appeal? As a response to a specific situation at-hand, will this word work to your and others' advantage? For this word to increase in real value, together we must dig, drill and think deeper, so we will reach, climb and soar higher.

For my life it is blessing beyond earthly measure to value someone highly; to have high-to-highest regard for somebody. It is real joy for me to discern in someone else her or his quality thinking and commensurate actions. More deep pleasure comes when I am able to support in small or other ways those for whom I have respect and high regard. Since my earliest years I have been surrounded by certain women, men, girls and boys for whom I sustain exceptional admiration and sometimes reverence. Ten or so of these dozens of fine minds and hearts have already died, yet they live on in my vivid memory, and still walk side-by-side with my corps of caring and sharing family, colleagues, clients, caregivers, neighbors, and other friends.

Indeed esteem is the word that fits to express both the objective and subjective nature of my approval of someone else and myself. I use this word rather rarely and almost always carefully. Esteem stems from root Middle English and Ancient French words for acts of intentional assessment; appraisal of things believed to be of value. When I say I hold someone in high esteem, I mean it. I've thought about it. Sometimes I even prayed about it.

Choosing this rich word is not this book's first hint of self-esteem issues you and I might have in common, or close approximations thereof. For a few moments, let's study and use this evocative word to our personal and shared advantage.

"Esteem needs" are among the must-haves Dr. Abraham Maslow believed we humans require during our respective journeys toward higher psychological stability. As we replace with more mature substance our childish ways of thinking and feeling about life, we indicate to ourselves and other observers that our basic needs for survival have been met. Some of us adults are still struggling. In his seminal work known as "Maslow's Hierarchy of Needs," we learn (1) self-actualization is at the top, followed by: (2) esteem needs, (3) love and belongingness, (4) safety needs, and (5) physiological needs.

Too many leaders might think esteem is a soft word, perhaps even something that is too subjective to have defensible merit as a word for strategic use in an organizational setting. Once when a high-ranking meeting chair introduced me to an audience as an "esteemed colleague," for a nanosecond or two I floated on air. As I began my talk, I realized again it feels good to be esteemed. I put even more of my heart and soul into that presentation, and the speaker evaluation grades and comments were among my best. It feels extra good to surround yourself with people you hold in high esteem, and when they express their high esteem for you, I'm sure it feels extra special. It does for me.

Fully responsible leaders must remember to express their esteem for others. It is wise, however, to be extra careful with this word. Misplaced expressions of esteem can eventually haunt a leader. Taking a calculated risk in offering others a glimpse or more into how you esteem (*i.e.*, evaluate) others is a wise move. It must be real; an authentic expression of your true delight in someone else's excellence of some type.

Self-esteem requires a closer look. As children and older individuals become self-aware, we humans develop need for self-regard or self-esteem. At first self-esteem comes from esteem held by others for us. When parents display unconditional positive regard for their children, the kids develop self-esteem. When less enlightened parents show children conditional positive regard, there is high possibility the under-appreciated youngster will develop inaccurate conditions of worth, thinking they are worthwhile only if they think and behave in certain ways.

"You are what you do" is the pop-culture message heard by kids when parents withhold unconditional positive regard. This was my plight. Perhaps for the remaining years I am privileged to live as a fully responsible servant leader in-training, I'll find more healthy self-esteem that's not tied to views of others. I am getting there. For me hubris has no place in the equation. Person-by-person and project-by-project I want to be pleased with what I do. For the most part, I am. Overall I want to be well pleased with myself. It is a winding and scenic road to get from here to who I want to be. Can you relate?

In my late teens and early 20s, teachings of self theorist Dr. Carl Rogers added hope to my church's empowering lessons about my being able to do all things through unquestioned belief in the King James version of the Philippians 4:13 verse — *"I can do all things through Christ who strengtheneth me."* Dr. Rogers gave me a secular frame of reference regarding my unique pattern of perceptions, attitudes and behaviors, against which I evaluate events and other individuals. Blind faith was at the center. I just knew there was something good going on inside of me that time would reveal. Dr. Rogers called it congruence, a tight fit between one's thoughts, feelings, behaviors, and self-concept; a coming together, if you will. I call such congruence self alignment.

Highly esteemed jazz vocalist Morgana King — who played Mama Corleone in The Godfather movies — and I met. I made sure of it. I had to meet her. Several more times I made sure we would see each other and speak. This brilliant woman's inexplicable impact on my early life is still difficult for me to grasp. She verified the date of my first memory. In 1953 I was three years old. That's when I first heard Ms. King sing on black-and-white TV's *The Ed Sullivan Show*. I was mesmerized by Ms. King's highest-highs and lowest-lows voice. I never heard such a sound in my 36+ months of life; her moving from soprano to baritone in a single breath. My face was glued to the screen. It remains nearly impossible to believe I was three when something in me related to her high and low sound. I was mesmerized by Morgana King. I did everything I could to watch *The Ed Sullivan Show* just in case she would appear again, and occasionally she did. Age three's fragmented yet vivid memory remains.

In my pre-teens I recall yearning to get a deeper voice someday — perhaps like Morgana's? That's a low voice. It seemed she symbolized for me a full-range of life's high and low options. In the mid-70s my former wife Cynthia and I were standing with Ms. King after a set in an East Village cabaret. I confirmed with Morgana my childhood memories. For more than a musical grand pause (G.P.) she was speechless when she heard me recount what I captured in my three-year-old mind. My G.P came when I learned the 1953 TV show was not filmed, and no record exists, at least to Morgana's knowledge.

When I told Morgana what I recalled her wearing on that show, suddenly she had misty eyes. She remembered the exact outfit and "look" she admitted now slightly regretting. She wore a black gown with a large white boa on her ample shoulders. Morgana said the fur piece was a dramatic prop, more so than an article of clothing. It seemed I retained just enough memory to both startle and warm her. For her artistry and humanity, she felt my lifetime of high esteem. I needed and wanted her to know. I knew my esteem for her would give a much-needed lift. For a selfless reason I was driven to tell her. I had read her beloved husband died in a horrific auto crash. The pastoral side of me wanted to boost her in some way. After all, occasionally she boosted my spirits during my early life's trials.

During a 1971 Lincoln Center concert she sang Leon Russell's American classic, "A Song for You." The self-deprecating lyrics hit me hard, "I know your image of me is what I hope to be." Many have heard me repeat these lyrics. With Morgana's high and low voice and message, she got to me. I heard those words with poignancy that lasts to this day. I felt pain knowing people were seeing me as I would surely be, instead of who I most definitely was. I still work to live up to others' and my higher expectations.

It was important to me when Morgana King said she would never forget me. Even if she did forget, for those fleeting moments I felt esteemed by someone for whom I have high esteem. She was amazed by my vivid recall, and I was amazed by her music. She got to me again and again. In storage I believe I have most of her albums and re-mastered CDs, but it has been 10 or more years since I needed to hear "the voice." Someday I'll be sure to buy a turntable, dust-off the records, pray for the best, and sit back and think back.

This and other stories underscore my early need for external unconditional positive regard, or support for building self-esteem. Home life for me was anything but unconditional. Dad was 27 when I was born; seven years after the birth of my older sister. Until a month or so before my birth, my family lived in Seattle. Just before I was to be born, saintly Grandmother Margaret Long Dallas took ill in Pittsburgh, and she was not expected to live. The late-20s couple, John ("Johnnie") and Yvonne ("Muffy"), with seven-year-old daughter Judy (not Judith) Ann, drove east from Seattle to Pittsburgh to be at my dad's mom's bedside. I was born as my future Grandma Dallas was teetering. Mom and Dad never made it back to Seattle, the only city where it seemed they were happy. Seattle became synonymous with "missed opportunity." Pittsburgh, therefore, became a place for me to escape. I never eyed Seattle. Thankfully Grandmother Dallas lived for nearly 29 more years, doing as much good for others as she possibly could. I never blamed her for what was to be my life in Pittsburgh instead of Seattle. I love both cities.

In more ways than geographically, eventually somehow I felt responsible for my parents being stuck in Pittsburgh. To my young mind it seemed they blamed Grandma Dallas, but because I was born that year, I recall feeling at least somewhat responsible. Some kids have ways of accepting undue blame. She and I were not, of course.

Years later Grandmother Shearer explained what she recalled. She said I would sing soprano solos to get attention. Some would say I had to sing for my supper. Sister Judy and I both inherited from our songbird mother singing voices that earned us many solos in our city's schools, churches, senior citizen centers, homes for the indigent, and other places where we would be invited to perform for free. As often as I could, I followed in sister Judy's footsteps. At 18 we each moved away from home base. Neither of us sang again.

When I was eight, Mom began working part-time for Allegheny County Community Trust, which become The United Fund of Allegheny County, and then was eventually renamed The United Way of Allegheny County. When I was 10 she began working there full-time. She stayed there for over 35 years. By the time Mom made it home from work, my older sister and I did our best to have a simple dinner on the table. Mom was always grateful. Too often I made my specialty — creamed peas in toasted bread cups. Don't ask, please. For some reason I can't recall the elementary-school type of recipe.

Although I seem to have inherited a steel-trap memory, I have precious few memories of childhood. Early, trusting and absolute faith in a triune God allowed me to deal with life's mystery. I sensed I would survive and thrive, but it was not going to be a simple path to get me away from what I secretly felt as "the perils of Pittsburgh." Now I love and enjoy visiting the gleaming Renaissance City at the confluence of three mighty rivers. Still I regret too many of my earliest formative years spent there. Childhood pain still lingers alongside a lot of adult gain. This too shall pass — the pain.

Perhaps surprisingly, public figures I met lifted me to new levels of clarity about my life's potential. I was attracted by, and attractive to, a high-profile personality type and its hype. Unknowingly I was working to identify and feel esteem for others from which I could build esteem for myself. This formula mattered more than it should have. In bonding with public role models, I failed more than I succeeded. Too many one-on-one conversations with household names eventually left me with a sense of having been had.

Especially in Chicago, where many public figures appear to have been pulled from fiction more often than reality as I know it, having a good view of someone who is in the public eye is growing more difficult. Manufactured personalities, profiles and photographs create a nearly impossible set of credibility hurdles to overcome. These faces win elections, sign big contracts for books, earn major speaking fees, and continue to prove how quick we are to judge a book by its cover.

A disgraced golf champion was among public figures I held in high esteem. In short, I fell for his nonstop blue-smoke-and-mirrors public relations apparatus. His name and photo always made me smile from a sense of perceived goodness about him. I never expected perfection of him or anyone else, but I certainly did not anticipate the trash he put out on his curb (quite literally) for all to see. One can't help but to expect more revelations. Millions of fans felt a big kick in the gut when this reality check hit the airwaves, front pages, blogs, Facebook and Twitter. For redemption and restoration, he's making progress.

Mostly while in Manhattan and Washington, D.C., my early career brought me into close proximity with stars of entertainment, politics, business, academia, and broadcast news. In the 1970s and 80s, I met face-to-face every anchor of nightly network television news (*e.g.,* ABC, CBS and NBC). I enjoyed memorable special times with Walter Cronkite and Peter Jennings, two individuals for whom I hold high esteem, and for vastly different reasons of insight. In 2002 ABC's Charles Gibson and I finally shook hands, and I relished telling him how highly I think of him. As an observer I rode the roller-coaster of Charlie's career when he was unceremoniously released and then apologetically re-hired by "Good Morning America," and then subsequently he was by-passed then eventually named, apparently by default due to his predecessor's misfortune, anchor for *"ABC Evening News with Charles Gibson."* Again he's gone.

With grace, Charlie endured many crucibles. Charles Gibson is the real thing, and perhaps the last male of his era of baby boomer authenticity, responsibility and accountability in broadcast journalism. From my vantage point, he still sets and maintains relatively high standards. I hope to see him again. I expect to find a man at-peace. Similarly admired Diane Sawyer has taken over Charlie's post as anchor of ABC's nightly news "show." When I met her, instantly I realized she's all about business, even when it appears she is not. She has to be.

After two days of front-line participation in a forum to shoot high-impact TV footage for a two-hour NBC News broadcast about the inner-workings of the U.S. Presidency and the Electoral College, over two subsequent days John Chancellor and I spent 16 hours working together in a "30 Rock" editing suite. There may have been six of us in the busy room with a dozen or more TV monitors, lights, levers and buttons. These 30-plus years later, all I can remember now is John Chancellor's calm, brilliance, and innate goodness. When he died journalism lost a true champion. Brief cocktails with David Brinkley during a small party at Boston's Ritz-Carlton, had a different lasting impact on me, but I'll save for another time that news story.

Perhaps to my benefit, it has been years since I've been star-struck or uncomfortable with a celebrity. Too well I remember the days when my palms would sweat and my tongue would tie. Just when I wanted to say the right things, out of nervousness and intimidation I said wrong words. For some strange reason I wanted to be liked by the notables as much as I thought I liked them. When I concluded the majority of the stars I knew were considerably different when the microphones and camera lights were off, and for the most part they were remarkably approachable for me, I relaxed and found my true voice in such situations. Younger readers and others may not recognize by-name two classical music luminaries I enjoyed, Van Cliburn or Artur (not Arthur) Rubinstein. For detail-oriented readers, Google and Bing searches will yield copious background for every celebrity named in this book.

One spring Saturday morning, an NBC News executive called to ask if I would like to fly from New York to D.C. to meet and sit in the "Meet the Press" Green Room with Canada's Prime Minister Joseph Philippe Pierre Yves Elliott Trudeau (1919-2000). Of course I would! For some reason Prime Minister Trudeau was traveling without staff, only security guards. No NBC employees were going to be available that particularly busy Sunday morning. With a smile, wonderful friend and "Meet the Press" Executive Producer Betty Dukert said she knew I could handle it. The Prime Minister handled me more than I handled him. He was the master. I was his student. I loved it all.

Indeed the Prime Minister and I had a few deep laughs. I certainly avoided laughing at his red rose boutonnière in his brown corduroy suit. I had not yet heard a flower in his lapel was a political trademark for him. The wrinkled suit reminded me of one I bought in my teenage years. (None of the wrinkles in his suit or face showed on-camera.) He seemed genuinely intrigued by the electronic publishing business I ran to process words spoken by top business, political, and other leaders, especially our exclusive work with all the U.S. Presidential Debates and other high-profile events. Not surprisingly, I sensed the P.M. wanted me to like him perhaps even more than I wanted him to like me. He was, after all, a politician *par excellence*.

Yet my eventual esteem for a neighboring country's Prime Minister did not come easily. After a year or two of reading about him, and watching for his TV appearances, eventually I grew to respect his quirky blend of leadership skills, personality, and his boyish (almost impish) sense of wonderment about it all. At least that's the lastingly impressive way in which I experienced P.M. Trudeau. I enjoyed meeting him. And I am thrilled to see his legacy with Justin Trudeau, a steadily rising son on Canada's political horizon.

Richard M. Nixon was my highly esteemed and first political hero. I was young and impressionable. I am not fully convinced my enchantment was unfounded. Though deeply flawed, still I see him as raw political power personified. Perhaps his Watergate comeuppance (intentional understatement) changed for-the-better him and us. Quantitatively and qualitatively his and our worlds shifted on a power axis. Divine Providence saw to it that insecure and rather unlikable Nixon became the strategic scapegoat for sins of J. Edgar Hoover and others in-charge, including lingering legacies of some of Nixon's predecessors whose Presidential ghosts remain in The White House.

When Hoover died in 1972, Nixon *was* The White House. While Hoover was arguably the most power-hungry man in D.C., the Justice Department, FBI, and other law enforcement apparatus were widely known or suspected to routinely "bend the law" — mostly for higher and occasionally lower Cold War-related purposes. U.S. warriors for freedom are held in high esteem. Simply because a person is in-power or leading a charge, now you and I know better than to automatically envelop with our esteem anyone in authority. Demonstrating respect for an individual's position of authority differs from according esteem for the empowered person.

In contrast to known and greater infractions of the era, Watergate crimes of the Nixon campaign and Administration were less egregious than convenient blindness of lawmakers and others. The public had grown to expect, tolerate, and sometimes secretly or openly admire Hoover's Oedipal hand on the FBI's wheel. Someday I want to explore my theory that J. Edgar Hoover's over-the-top Machiavellian ways set a Dantesque stage for Watergate's inferno.

The Watergate travesty became D.C.'s long-overdue ethical tipping point. With the above reflection, now I am truly grateful for Watergate's relatively minor infractions. Suppose it would have taken another World War to realign our culture's priorities and our collective sense of right-and-wrong? Indeed Watergate's campaign HQ break-in, cover-up, and the ensuing tissue of lies were impeachable offenses. Yet today I remain grateful things did not need to become worse. Highly esteemed President Gerald R. Ford's pardon of soundly trounced and otherwise disgraced Richard M. Nixon took into account opportunity at-hand for the U.S. to immediately reach for higher ground. We did. Diligently we must continue to reach, climb, and soar higher.

As a related aside regarding our need to have and to hold esteem for leaders and others, Disney's ABC-TV set the highest-ever amount for advertising time for their 2012 annual Academy Awards broadcast (between $1.6 million and $1.7 million for a 30-second spot). With major movie and DVD releases for "J. Edgar" and "The Iron Lady," ABC's predictive modelers know all ages of Red States, Blue States, and other free-to-be rainbow colors will be watching. Is the current wave of retroactive awarding of esteem signaling another societal tipping point?

Often esteem for ourselves and from others is heavily influenced by limiting labels stuck on us by insecure bullies, jealous siblings, misguided parents, worried competitors, or even well-meaning souls. Incorrect labeling by well-intentioned yet inept priests, pastors, rabbis, teachers, professors, counselors, neighbors, strangers, physicians, therapists, dentists and others can burden our young and older minds and hearts. Labels belong on products, not on people.

Yet perhaps warning labels should be affixed to negative-minded people whose mouths spew toxic waste of ignorant narrow-mindedness, hate, racism, homophobia, and other psychological weaponry intended to harm any human's mind, body or soul. Indeed these pathetic perpetrators do real harm to others — and themselves.

An overweight food-loving child being called "fatty" or worse could delay learning best nutrition and exercise habits. An art-loving boy's interest in unbridled creativity being labeled "faggy" or worse could impede the youngster's acceptance of his special gifts. Risk is real.

Your reading and absorbing what's written between lines and words of this book's composite narrative allows me to hold you in high esteem. Your caring about your life's best-effort impact on others puts you at the top of my esteem list. Mister Rogers put it this way:

"When I say it's you I like, I'm talking about that part of you that knows that life is far more than anything you can ever see or hear or touch. That deep part of you that allows you to stand for those things without which humankind cannot survive. Love that conquers hate, peace that rises triumphant over war, and justice that proves more powerful than greed."

—Fred Rogers ("Mister Rogers Neighborhood")

Please carefully invest your esteem for other imperfect human beings. For the good-of-the-order, increase your own self-esteem based on your worthy thoughts, actions and results toward and with others.

"One great mistake is to try to extract from each person virtues which he does not possess, neglecting the cultivation of those which he does have." —Hadrian

Every word in this book can be a bridge, pathway, or superhighway for you to reach new destinations of esteem for others and yourself. Allow this word to work for you and with you.

Esteem. Expound.

Imperative

Chapter Inspired by and Dedicated to Michael G. Russell

Insert or imagine seeing your first name: _____,

Seeing this chapter's title word, what immediately comes to your open mind? Do you already have a working relationship with this word? Somewhere inside of you does this word instantly appeal? As a response to a specific situation at-hand, will this word work to your and others' advantage? For this word to increase in real value, together we must dig, drill and think deeper, so we will reach, climb and soar higher.

Why are so many CEOs and other team leaders hard-pressed when I ask them to list for their businesses/organizations measurable groupings of only 10 examples for each of these four basic leadership development and organizational development classifications for strategic alignment: (a) cultural imperatives, (b) regulatory and legal compliance imperatives, (c) performance and quality imperatives, or (d) financial imperatives; 40 hardly optional enterprise-wide foundational understandings? Pitching the word *imperative* throws a curve-ball at some otherwise hard-hitting CEOs known for home runs.

Quite to my surprise, behind closed doors top leaders reveal they have to think long and hard to succinctly list — in crisp, concise and clear verbiage — at least 10 entries for each of these four of various categories of top imperatives for the organization. With or without adroit language to use with others, of course they have top-of-mind at least some of their organization's more obviously pressing imperatives.

Department-by-department, product-by-product, market-by-market, and other types of compare-and-contrast imperatives require identification, definition, description and communication — prior to implementation and evaluation. Exacting organizational inculcation (*i.e.*, intentionality of impressing imperatives upon minds by frequent instruction or repetition/reminders), and routine evaluation of strategic alignment with imperatives of related work products, teaching/training, or internal and external messaging — all require specifically focused diligence and extra vigilance. Formulation and communication of highly specific and functionally memorable language are mission-critical requirements for imperatives to take root in minds and hearts.

"No one said fully responsible leadership rests easily on
any head so crowned or shoulders burdened." —JRDjr

When asked what differentiates a c-level mind from others I might say something like this, *"...the ability to see from a hill — not from a mountaintop or up in an ivory tower — the organization's whole chessboard of imperatives."* Mixed metaphors aside, top thinkers feel this see-the-whole-picture point. They know they must work hard to see where thoughts, people and things are moving. It is their job to set, see, affirm and correct course. To help today's unavoidably cluttered-minded leaders think more clearly, I respectfully yet methodically ask the following — in complete questions stated in an intentionally ascendant and somewhat urgent tone and fashion (skewing thought order for the respondent's benefit). "Do you believe it is imperative for you and at least your top-level fellow employees to know, to a measurable high degree of 80-100% certainty, your organization's: (1) vision, (2) mission, (3) history, (4) product/service definitions, (5) markets/buyers served, (6) markets/buyers identified for expansion/growth, (7) revenue/profit goals, (8) regulatory/legal compliance mandates, (9) best practices and S.W.O.T. assessments for top competitors, and (10) at least five examples each of major strengths, weaknesses, opportunities and threats (S.W.O.T.) the organization secretly and/or publicly identifies and addresses?"

CEOs almost always agree with relevance of all or at least eight of the 10; normally 80% or higher. Asking CEOs which of the above they themselves have clearly communicated to their top reports, and I discover significant trickle-down effect for organizational misalignment. Sometimes a CEO will admit she or he never really memorized (or took all that seriously) the Vision Statement, Mission Statement, or even a 30-second elevator pitch; the very "musts" expected of everyone else. Some excuses heard translate into discernible danger.

Imperatives Hell can break loose at one or more levels below any CEO. Here I'll spare you first-hand stories of COOs, CFOs, and other c-level folk who choose to keep the CEO in the dark about certain misalignment related to stated or un-stated imperatives. Perversely some executives glean illusions of power and strength in excluding their bosses from detail related to misalignment with imperatives. Even higher risk is found with bosses who secretly tolerate the blinders they pretend to wear. Courts are full of defendant CEOs claiming ignorance to misdeeds of subordinates. If I were a prosecuting attorney, I would ask an accountable CEO how and when certain imperatives of strategic organizational alignment were communicated and routinely measured for understanding, engagement and implementation.

Too frequently *imperative* is a word used imprecisely. Economic evidence more than suggests superficial grasp and application of the word. If imperative had been a key word for muddled masterminds at Drexel, Burnham and Lambert, Enron, Lehman Brothers, AIG, Circuit City, Linens and Things, and many dozens of other defunct or disabled businesses and organizations, there would be fewer horror stories of violation of common sense, public trust, and law.

In almost every case of organizational failure, some combination of arguably culpable institutional shareholders, regulatory authorities, boards of directors, executive committees, CEOs, and/or c-level officers failed to expect, articulate, legislate or instigate specific imperatives. To more adequately castigate perpetrators who violate stated imperatives for lawful and otherwise just performance, for publicly traded companies *The Sarbanes-Oxley Act* could be viewed as legislation for ensuring strategic lawful alignment of non-hypothetical imperatives.

> *"A categorical imperative would be one which represented an action as objectively necessary in itself, without reference to any other purpose."* —Immanuel Kant

For a moment, it helps to glance backward. These distinctions allow us to drill deeper before we climb higher. Originally introduced in philosophical writings of Immanuel Kant, a "hypothetical imperative" is a commandment of reason that applies only conditionally. In older language, Immanuel Kant divides hypothetical imperatives into two subcategories: (1) the rules of skill, and (2) the councils of prudence. The rules of skill are conditional and are specific to each and every individual to whom the specific skill is mandated. The councils of prudence (*i.e.*, set rules of prudence) are attained *a priori*, unlike the rules of skill which are attained *via* experience, or *a posteriori*.

Almost any moral rule about how to behave in certain situations is hypothetical, because the rule itself assumes ones goal is to be moral, to please God, *etc*. Non-hypothetical imperatives tell us to do something no matter who we are or what we want, because the thing to do is good unto itself; *for the good of the order*. Hillview's version of modern-day organizational imperatives are non-hypothetical.

Imperare is the Latin root of imperative; "to command." Your deeper understanding of the singular and plural use of imperative can mark you well as a knowledgeable, wise, experienced, ethical and moral fully responsible leader. A shallow grasp of this word, however, could destroy any leader's legacy by her or his inadvertently contributing to lost jobs, wasted dollars, and maybe destroyed lives. Yes, the word *imperative* deserves, demands, commands and rises to both intellectual and emotional high scrutiny.

Deep down we know and feel the make-it-or-break-it nature of imperative: someone or something absolutely necessary and perhaps unavoidably so; an attention-grabbing, commandeering and authoritarian person, deed or word. When on-the-job duty is deemed by your supervisor as urgent or at least essential, it is good practice to confirm details related to the imperative nature of the work — particularly any hidden or otherwise obscure points-of-impact your top performance will strengthen, or your poor performance would weaken.

"Adapt or perish, now as ever, is nature's inexorable imperative." —H.G. Wells

Indeed, imperatives are serious business. Today's next breath is all the time we each have for sure with which to seek to understand imperatives. This fragile inhalation/exhalation fact of mortality may be the one condition all humans and other living and breathing creatures share equally. *Here today, gone tomorrow* — a crass-but-true cliché. Even this moment may be cut short by an uninformed, misinformed or careless medical caregiver or transportation mechanic (including drunk drivers). While it is true that their grasp and engagement in their respective professional and personal imperatives may determine if you and I live beyond the next surgical procedure or trip to a vacation destination, this word — imperative — is presented as highly personal for your depth of understanding. Trust I am always working on this word's applicability in my public and private lives.

Imperatives in medical care and airplane maintenance are not dissimilar. From Hillview's vantage point of intentional strategic alignment of people and things, life-and-death imperatives are exactly the same — regardless of the definition of the person's role into whose hands we've placed our safe passage from this moment to the next. From a human body's pre-surgery physician to a human body's plane's pre-flight hydraulic systems inspector, life hangs in the balance of imperatives.

Standing during cocktails with great friend Patrick Chantelois in Willis Tower's (formerly Sears Tower) Metropolitan Club's 66th floor meeting suite, we chatted with a high-energy manager of a large fleet of leased corporate aircraft. In explaining Hillview's model for strategic alignment of organizational imperatives, the discussion turned toward how misalignment in aircraft maintenance standards costs lives. More than one passenger and freight airline folded, reorganized, or renamed itself because of shamefully poorly administered (to say the least) safety and maintenance imperatives.

A mere reference to 9/11, and all three of us were more painfully aware of the *gravitas* of across-the-board applicability of the concept of strategic alignment with imperatives. To raise a bit our somber thoughts and moods, I added the fact that every size and type of organization needs to identify likelihood of misalignment by first assessing presence of strength, not weakness; finding among teams secure strategic alignment with organizational and other imperatives — an ongoing strengths-based diagnostic and remedial effort. We moved on to thoughts toward how fragile U.S. and other economies are glaring testimony to more than financial risk associated with misalignment with imperatives.

Aligned by-default with our conversation, then we sat to hear "The Rise of the Skyscraper," a multi-slide photo history presentation by the proud president of the Chicago Architecture Foundation (CAF). With every photograph shown and word spoken, I'm sure we three were thinking similar thoughts about the justifiably stringent and unyielding alignment imperatives of architecture, engineering, construction, and other art and science in urban development — where lives are both greatly enriched and clearly at-risk.

> *"Disarmament, with mutual honor and confidence,*
> *is a continuing imperative."* —Dwight D. Eisenhower

Imagine inherent challenges in identifying, defining and describing myriad strategic alignment imperatives within each of these 10 of many U.S. areas of misalignment: (1) withdrawing in due course U.S. troops from Afghanistan and Iraq, (2) overhauling the U.S. health care delivery system, (3) re-evaluating, re-stabilizing, and re-engineering the core (*i.e.*, small business) U.S. economy, (4) expanding U.S. fair trade with other fair nations, (5) reconstructing the U.S. environmental footprint, (6) reversing to a responsible and respectable work ethic the growing trend in the U.S. toward unbridled blue-collar and white-collar entitlement, (7) demystifying, decoding and eliminating political rhetoric and practices that impede instead of empower the U.S. electorate, (8) adding true equality to the U.S. concept of equal rights for all, (9) protecting U.S. children and youngsters around the globe from on-line, on-air, in-home, and other threats to their innocence and safety, and (10) practicing right-and-proper good that is preached and prayed from U.S. pulpits, minarets and podia.

> *"Every man has his own destiny; the only imperative is to*
> *follow it, to accept it, no matter where it leads him."* —Henry Miller

Occasionally it is imperative for front-line leaders to navigate and otherwise tackle truly Herculean tasks. Herculean is a word to honor and embrace, yet one to use judiciously. Deciding how best to overcome a major human, political or financial obstacle is more likely to be served well by naming, claiming and framing the process as a Herculean task. Summoning the strengths, weaknesses, opportunities and threats of the life and legacy of Hercules focuses minds, channels endorphins, and grounds egos. Imperatives require intense focus. Adaptive imperative thinking allows leaders to intentionally consider relevant past, present and future factors related to challenges at-hand

In metaphorical terms, fire prevention and firefighting are imperative.

Please add to your leadership of self and others imperative thoughts and words. Express in defensible and ascendant imperatives your conviction to honor and sustain strategic alignment of people and things. With clearly formed and stated imperatives, always strive to (a) lead people and (b) manage things — toward worthy destinations.

Imperative. Expound.

Influence

Chapter Inspired by and Dedicated to
Estelle Wilson Baker (1914-2002)

Insert or imagine seeing your first name: _____,

Seeing this chapter's title word, what immediately comes to your open mind? Do you already have a working relationship with this word? Somewhere inside of you does this word instantly appeal? As a response to a specific situation at-hand, will this word work to your and others' advantage? For this word to increase in real value, together we must dig, drill and think deeper, so we will reach, climb and soar higher.

Influence Must Be Earned

With his choice and delivery of words, Martin Luther King, Jr. earned his influence over generations today and for centuries ahead. Although he was murdered in 1968, his influence can and will remain. Every child, street, church, school, park, bridge, or other resource named in his honor should at least cause us to pause a brief moment to consider one or more tenets of the strength and substance of his influence. Dr. King's Dream of a level playing field for all women and men of every race and creed follows in the letter and spirit of President Lincoln's *Emancipation Proclamation*. Dr. King's body of work takes us to higher levels of influence for Lincolnian thought.

Many claim to embrace Dr. King's teachings, yet too few have ever actually read or studied in-depth his voluminous works. I am committed to learn more about his life. Authentically human, mightily he struggled with his own demons and weaknesses. In God-fearing and God-hearing ways that produced incalculable value for any student of his journey, Dr. King pointed us toward a true-north destination of equality for all. He felt called to heed and lead. He believed right influencers shall overcome wrong influencers.

More than 40 years after his death, our questionable actions about ensuring equality for all speak louder than even our best politically correct words. Blatant, thinly veiled, or secret racism, often hypocritical and always revolting homophobia, demagoguery of emotive dictators of countries, companies, places of worship, households, or other bodies of followers, simplemindedness about a gigantic universe's higher power, and numerous other causes and symptoms of inequality still haunt this known world — where all are created equal (a key phrase not to be viewed in simple terms).

To achieve equality for all we must be more strategically aligned with Dr. King's and other thoughtful scholars' words and acts of right-mindedness. To overcome negative influence of societal disinterest in change for the better and other inertia, fully responsible leaders must keep alive Dr. King's Dream. Try to read whatever you can find online or elsewhere about Dr. King's *"I Have a Dream"* exhortation.

The following affirmation is based on words of Dr. King, and was read in unison during a 2010 Martin Luther King, Jr. worship service at Chicago's Fourth Presbyterian Church. I was deeply moved as we said with stentorian tone, deliberate tempo, and solid timber of true conviction:

> *"I refuse to believe we are unable to influence the events which surround us.*
>
> *I refuse to believe that we are so bound to racism and way that peace, brotherhood, and sisterhood are not possible.*
>
> *I believe there is an urgent need for people to overcome oppression and violence without resorting to violence and oppression.*
>
> *I believe we need to discover a way to live together in peace, a way which rejects revenge, aggression, and retaliation. The foundation of this way is love.*
>
> *I believe that unarmed truth and unconditional love will have the final word.*
>
> *I believe that right, temporarily defeated, is stronger than evil triumphant.*
>
> *I believe that peoples everywhere can have three meals a day for their bodies, education and culture for their minds, and dignity, equality and freedom for their spirits.*

I believe that what self-centered people have torn down, other-centered people can build up.

By the goodness of God at work within people, I believe brokenness can be healed. 'And the lion and the lamb shall lie down together, and everyone will sit under their own vine and fig tree, and none shall be afraid'."

Please consider using a highlighter or underscoring single words above that jump out at you as exceptionally influential words. There are many.

The three influential single-word cornerstones of Hillview's High Impact Leader Lens (HILL) Model for Viewing Where People and Things are Moving (The HILL Model) are: Wisdom. Courage. Patience.

Wisdom beyond knowledge. Wisdom beyond facts. Wisdom beyond years. Wisdom beyond fears.

Courage to think. Courage to act. Courage to fail. Courage to succeed.

Patience with self. Patience with others. Patience with process. Patience with divine providence.

Faith is behind Trust at the core of The HILL Model. Definitions and descriptions of faith are respectfully left to each individual's private thoughts, faith traditions, or other personal delineators of this influential word. In coaching with couples engaged together in a business or other type of venture, "love" is added to influential words that evoke emotion and provoke action. Love is one of the most influential words ever devised and exemplified. When used and practiced properly and meaningfully, love influences many outcomes.

Do these single words (wisdom, courage, patience, faith and love) influence you to *think and dig a little deeper as you reach and climb a lot higher?* Pause and think about what other words come to mind that you ponder, pray, chant, repeat, whisper, yell, or otherwise use to ignite your passion for top performance and other personal bests?

The Influence of "Yes"

Yes is one three-letter word that can change everything. So can "No." For better or other outcomes, choosing a single right word can positively influence listeners or readers. Poorly chosen or inadequately articulated words add more threat to success than we dare to admit. In marriage proposals, job interviews, sales meetings, negotiations, client communication, courtroom presentations, speeches, Presidential Debates, and in countless other settings, right words used, at right times, in right ways, work wonders. Wrong words can wreck havoc.

If you have heard me speak you know I almost always share with audiences the story of *The Wall Street Journal* reporter who asked President Mikhail Gorbachev for ONE WORD to characterize the state of Russia's economy. "Good," was President Gorbachev's one-word response. Puzzled, the WSJ reporter asked a follow-up, "How about TWO words, Mr. President?" Pause. "NOT good." When audience laughter dies down, I follow with how prospective clients for Hillview's consulting practice claim, when asked, that their teams are "aligned." In a large majority of cases I already know their teams are "not aligned." One key word. Audience members nod their understanding that certain good things on their minds are "not good." Many reactions convey that their people are not aligned.

In presentations I almost always talk about in-and-out listening; the risk of hearing from a speaker only what you hear when "in" and fully engaged and paying rapt attention, as opposed to "being out" for a few moments or minutes of distraction and missing substance still being delivered. "In" and "out" take on new meanings. Dramatically I influence outcomes with another short word "Yes!" Numerous other single words are used to set the stage for almost any message I am retained to deliver. I know it is my job to use the right words to open ears, eyes, minds and hearts — and sometimes even to open wallets for audiences to contribute to a cause, hire new employees, buy books, attend seminars, and other favorable responses to my words. Single words transport audience members where they and I need to be. Resistance can thwart my intentions.

As with adding drops of different colors into a can of paint being custom-mixed to achieve the exact shade, hue and texture you want for your living room walls, dropping into conversation just the right words can create a masterpiece in the mind of other people you are engaging with your words and delivery thereof. The art and science of influence is heavily weighted by word choice, timing, delivery, and related actions.

When snuggled with your beloved, mentioning a name of another love interest (past or present) can get you kicked out of more than the embrace. Talking with a prospective customer disparagingly about a competitor can have you categorized in ways that could cost you the sale. The other persons involved may not even tell you what you did with wrong words and why the door was closed on you. Many wrong words used at wrong times have undesirable influence.

Buyers listen for a seller's choice of words. As *"marketplace value is always ultimately determined by the buyer and never by the seller,"* a buyer's due diligence in assessing the seller's words is logical, expectable and unavoidable. When a seller of professional mind assets involving clear thinking and mastery of language or numbers, slaughters nomenclature and appears unclear about numerals, often she or he loses her or his place at the table. Sadly the person who closed the window of opportunity will rarely invest enough time and stomach acid to tell the offender it was poor choice, use, or delivery of words that scuttled the deal. It has been painful for me to interview writers who can't write to even basic standards. In resumes, misspellings, bad formatting, and poor choice of words keep from being hired possibly otherwise qualified job candidates. The list goes on and on. In terms of risk to influence associated with words, what comes to your mind?

Influence is the Measure of Leadership

Some leadership experts say influence is the only measure of leadership. Even beyond their careful choice and adroit use of words, fully responsible leaders know how by their mere presence they influence meetings with one or many. How they enter a meeting room where others are waiting for them can lift, lower, or have zero impact on the room. A wise leader breathes oxygen into every room she or he enters, while an inattentive leader sucks oxygen out of each room entered. You know leaders who do both. Pause to name in your mind one or more of each type. What type of leader are you? To influence favorable outcomes during meetings, do you breathe fresh oxygen into the room, or suck out so much oxygen that people are left gasping for breath?

President Richard Milhous Nixon knew very well how his influence could be used to command-and-control situations. He was very autocratic, exceptionally organized, a bit cool to the touch, and yet amazingly influential. Being in his presence was quite an influential experience. He left an impact on me, especially when I was 22. At this tender and ill-prepared age I was named Pennsylvania's Citizen Blocs Chairman for the Re-Elect the President Campaign. On TV and during rallies I watched his every move and hung on almost every word he said. Perhaps I was obsessed with his adroit use of key words. Without hesitation I admit I was blown-away by his commanding leadership presence. So was the rest of the world, especially China.

President Nixon had a "lifter" walking to his left who looked like a Secret Service agent (and may have been). As the President would enter the Cabinet Room or other space where people were watching the door for his arrival, and especially when the U.S. Marine Band (called *"The President's Own"*) were cued-up to play *"Hail to the Chief"* upon his entrance, out-of-sight of those within the door that was about to open, his "lifter" would quite literally firmly LIFT the President by his left forearm so the Commander-in-Chief would enter each room on an "up" step; yes literally appearing a little higher in physical stature for the first-impression moment that would subconsciously stick in peoples' minds and influence whatever was about to transpire under his imminent acts of leadership. Before he opened his mouth, Nixon was leading with his "up" entrance to the room. Try to visualize someone walking into a room on an up step, as opposed to appearing to casually stroll into a room with everyone at least somewhat anxiously awaiting the arrival. He knew what he was doing. Until he tuned-out warnings that his clumsy handling of the Watergate fiasco could be his undoing, he was firmly in control; some say too firmly in control.

Character drives determination for who earns the greatest amount of influence, followed by knowledge, wisdom, courage, patience, trust, faith, intuition, experience, and myriad other strengths and factors. There's a proverb that applies, *"He who thinks he leads, but has no followers, is only taking a walk."* As mentioned elsewhere, in my senior year of high school I was wordy and politically incorrect with this apparently then noteworthy quote from a speech that hung for years in the school's entrance:

"He who is a master of words is a master of men." —JRDjr

Today, for others and my sake, with a smile I might offer something politically correct — *albeit* probably unquotable — like this:

"Fully responsible leaders, with true influence over win-win-plus outcomes, are women and men worth respecting, honoring and following."

Who influences your life today? Starting with yourself, do you proactively work to have a positive influence on your life by focusing on your strengths more so than weaknesses, pursuing opportunities without overlooking threats to your potential? Are you alert and oriented to your influence on those around you? At work, home and elsewhere do you project, perfect, protect, monitor, and possibly even measure the influence you have on favorable or other outcomes?

Self-agency and self-efficacy influence your thought patterns, actions, and emotional engagement. At higher levels of self-agency and self-efficacy, your performance accomplishments increase.

The more aware you are of your own personal influence over your life and lives of others, your coping behavior will produce different levels and modes of influence, you will handle more effectively physiological stress reactions, and you will resist depression and despondency reactions to your failure experiences. You chalk-up everything to learning-by-doing, and thus increase your genuine influence. At many points in my career, I made a lot of noise disclosing my failures, and soft-peddled my successes. I felt it was important to reveal lessons I learned from both failure and success, but I was not one to toot my own horn. I did not, however, discourage others from doing so.

In preparing for drafting this chapter, I wrote a confidential personal list of key individuals who influence my life in specific and positive ways. Some are no longer living, but their influence continues. I was surprised by the number when the list exceeded 50. In the Acknowledgement section you'll see many of these names honored for their direct and favorable impact on the development of this book. Somehow I thought I had fewer true influencers. I had not identified how many people I intentionally allow to influence my focus, mood, and other reactions.

Today I am blessed beyond measure to surrender to the influence of my God, certain blood family, adoptive family, two Presbyterian pastors I count as personal friends, several closest personal pals, two mighty mentors, a trusted physician, several clients from whom I learn so much while teaching, and a host of other saints who care enough to offer me their input and other treasures. I am praying that my name makes it to 100% of their similar lists, should they too decide to take inventory of the influencers in their lives. You may want to make such a list, starting with the top 10 people who influence deeper conviction, broader perspective, and higher thought.

Indeed strangers you never meet can influence your quality-of-life. On 28 December 1975, my former wife and were both 25 when she, our dog Carrie, and I returned to New York City's LaGuardia Airport from Christmas in Pittsburgh. (Daughter Jennifer's birth was approximately two years hence.) Overly anxiously — as always — we waited for our adorable dog's puppy kennel to emerge from baggage claim doors adjacent to a large wall of coin lockers passengers used for storing luggage. The very next day, 29 December 1975, TV news reports showed us those same lockers and that area — in which we were standing fewer than 24 hours earlier — as a site of deadly terrorism. Eleven people died. Influence from this date remains alive.

Friends are somewhat shocked to hear my vivid memories of domestic terrorism we endured in the 1970s — while wife, close friends, and I were in our 20s. In years beyond the above atrocity, there were so many bombings of places I often had business meetings for our company. Terrorists in the U.S. influenced my early career. Detailed memories inform my judgment. That's influence.

Influence is a very personal word. What does it mean to you now? Meaningfulness of influence in your life depends on your discernment of meaningfulness in the word and its implementation in your life. Who influences you? What influences you? What events do you allow to influence you? How do you influence yourself and others? Are you earning influence with each thought and deed? Do you nurture and guard the privilege and blessing of having influence?

A line from an old film influences me. Cardinal Wolsey is portrayed advising courtiers to King Henry VIII, *"Always tell the King what he should do, never what he can do."* Thank you for using your influence to do what you should do — instead of whatever you can or could do.

Influence. Expound.

Innovation

Chapter Inspired by and Dedicated to James F. Sweeney

Insert or imagine seeing your first name: _____,

Seeing this chapter's title word, what immediately comes to your open mind? Do you already have a working relationship with this word? Somewhere inside of you does this word instantly appeal? As a response to a specific situation at-hand, will this word work to your and others' advantage? For this word to increase in real value, together we must dig, drill and think deeper, so we will reach, climb and soar higher.

As we jump into this promise-filled chapter, please pause to think about your last fresh idea, the last new idea you heard, or the last time you cared enough about an idea of yours or someone else's to follow it through to implementation, or through cycles of in·no·va·tion? Do you want to stop reading and make a list? Will it be long or short?

Innovation moves ideas to market and keeps them there. Without ideas energized and facilitated by innovation, a village or global economy can wither and die. Given yet undiscovered cures for disease, it's not too bold to say without ideas and innovation, more people, animals, and other precious living organisms suffer for-life or die prematurely. A never-ending supply of ideas and related innovation are essential to righting this global economic ship that was capsized by the first worldwide *perfect storm* I've witnessed. Innovation may not be a word that connotes smooth sailing, yet I'd rather be on high seas — with an innovative skipper at the helm — as we yeomen navigate choppy waters of commercialization for money-making ideas and other seaworthy concepts.

This is a book about what all just one word brings to our two minds — from my mind to your mind's response. With each word, how you engage or push-back is instructive for you and about you. Rarely am I in the room as someone reads what I offer, yet I am certain there are some souls who don't get it, don't want to get it, or won't get it. Thankfully a majority of readers will and does. Personal, organizational, societal, economic, political, spiritual, emotional, and other value in single words bubble up from one leader's life experience to date. Your heart and mind take it from here.

Readers are encouraged to embrace each word for its untapped potential to make things better for themselves, other individuals, and groups they influence. Each word is chosen by a humble yet bold author with over 40 years of front-line leadership experience; more than four decades of both formal and casual study of how leaders use and abuse words. Personally I have read and edited for clarity and correctness key parts of hundreds of documents containing words of top leaders of countries, states, cities, companies, law firms, media giants, auditing firms, non-profit organizations, and houses of worship.

For 12 years I ran a company in New York that was paid to do just that. Routinely I jumped-in to support my highly trained and exceptionally talented editorial staff — especially if the speaker was a CEO I personally knew, or candidates for The White House were debating. I've heard and studied best and worst words used by greatest seasoned leaders — from the very top all the way to promising leaders-in-training. I was in the room when leader-in-training Jack Welch was named CEO of General Electric, and forever I'll remember predecessor Reginald Jones' and Jack Welch's respective choices of words. To allow his words to flow unencumbered, with best speech therapists money could buy, Mr. Welch soon overcame a life-long serious stutter. In a recent book he finally addressed this personal reality many of us witnessed in-awe.

Perhaps not paradoxically, the noun innovation was the first of 52 featured words in this book to encounter writer's block. I surprised myself as I struggled with this particular word. Why? I was determined to approach innovation from a different angle or two, as the word seemed to command of me extra creativity. For you I could not write about the word at the same level of awareness I had before setting explanatory words to paper. Quite naturally this word called out for me to innovate. I became paralyzed at the thought of the word's daunting significance. I practiced what I preach about breaking through mental blocks to think outside the box, and yet for too long I was frozen in-time. I was stopped. I was stunned. Now I am grateful it happened. Determined to keep it real, I decided to let it flow.

"Ideas are a dime a dozen," I heard too often during my east coast years. Even when I was not offering an idea for consideration, deep inside I experienced this un-clever barb as a put-down from someone who probably has few if any original ideational thoughts. In retrospect, the meaning of the slam was correct. Ideas are plentiful in New York City, suburban D.C., and other hotbeds of creativity. In more than a decade living in Chicago, truly I can't recall if this cliché ever made it into a conversation. Chicago is a hotbed of creativity.

For fully responsible leaders who are accountable to higher and highest authority for organizational impact and growth, here in this chapter innovation is best understood as the term to define implementation or execution of ideas. Whether ideas are sold by the dozen for 10 cents, or borne of millions of dollars invested in top laboratories, ideas move *via* innovation from germination through implementation. Without ideas there is no call for innovation. Without innovation an idea is highly unlikely to become reality.

A top executive of a large company in Chicago told me the only ideas Chicagoans bring to his door are ways to get him to contribute more tax-deductible foundation money to schools, parks, fireworks displays, street furniture, concerts, festivals, parades, bullet-proof vests for law enforcement officers, gun control, and other worthy or not causes. To this redacted effect he said, "They are almost all good charitable ideas for the people of Chicago, yet I'm not sure if more than a dozen or so small businesses have knocked on our door with ideas to help us run our business better, serve our clients better, envision our future better, or better our bottom line. When we were headquartered where we were founded it seemed local small businesses were always lined-up with new ideas to help us fuel innovation for building our business stronger and stronger. Perhaps back then we took for granted that steady stream of ideas coming to our open door. Now I miss that line-up of creative people. Here we're not exactly languishing for the want of ideas, yet we find ourselves reaching outside of Chicago to discover small businesses interested in presenting their ideas to us. I wonder how long we'll last here if small business does not seem interested in our big business." I was more saddened than stunned. I said what I could to assure him we are trying to open floodgates of opportunity for small business, and someday his giant company will see at his doorstep a line of eager and hungry Chicago entrepreneurs.

Déjà vu brought me full circle to when I heard words of this type from other business leaders. Seven or more years earlier, Sun Microsystems' Scott McNeely, a proud Chicago native, said as much to a luncheon meeting of The Chicago Executives Club. He was focusing on his earlier and highly frustrating inability in his hometown to raise capital for Sun's innovations. He then had 40,000+ employees (if memory serves me), and he genuinely wished they were located and paying taxes in Chicago. Oh! A graduate of nearby New Trier High School, Scott was almost begging us Chicagoans to be more open, more responsive, more innovative, and more in-touch with the world around us — as opposed to waiting and expecting the world to reach out and touch us.

Then to calm any frayed nerves and soothe bruised egos of Sun customers and prospects in the large audience of perhaps 1,200, suddenly he had people enter the room (while he was speaking) to give us gifts from Sun of $400+ in free software. He said he knew he was stepping on some toes, and wanted the gifts to deaden the pain. Applause. His points live-on in my mind, and I suspect a few others in-attendance that day may have more complete memory than I about the passion with which he spoke about Chicago's need for creative, innovative, and risk-ready — *vs.* risk-averse — thinking. From a "Wake-up, Chicago!" admonition of Baxter's Dr. David Amrani, while speaking to a meeting of Chicago Technology Leadership Forum which I chaired, to a Yale professor of economics addressing a seminar at the Federal Reserve Bank of Chicago, some best brains are still sounding clarion calls for ideas and innovation to bring Chicago up to where it needs and perhaps deserves to be as a capital city for innovation and entrepreneurship.

For the want of a small business community that freely thinks and offers up for consideration a non-stop fireworks display of new ideas, compared with a community bragging of aging broad shoulders to support manufacturing and distribution of ideas coming from other locations around the nation or globe, Chicago is a fine laboratory to study what ignites and douses ideas and innovation. As a tireless evangelist for Chicago's unique readiness to ascend to the top of any list of cities for supporting and sustaining small business, I realize creativity and innovation need to be fueled by more than investors' and buyers' money. Chicago is undergoing a sea change in societal attitude toward small business economic development – and not one moment too soon.

Ideas are the lifeblood of any free-market economy. Even intentionally cockamamie ideas thrown out to whack us upside our heads might trigger someone at table to think more creatively. Brainstorming sessions I've facilitated in different cities and regions have distinctly different levels and types of tolerance for risk and readiness. Conversations in Madison, Wisconsin are radically different from discussions in Chicago. One of the two cities gets it — this innovation thing.

"Children should be seen and not heard." —A Wrong Adult

Always I encourage people — sometimes almost begging — to *"Break through your mental blocks while you work to think outside the box."* I do what I can, of course, asking with a smile: "What is holding you back? Was there an elementary school teacher, priest, pastor, parent, sibling, or other influencer in your young life who told you to shut-up when you offered first whiffs of ideas you smelled as buds in-bloom? Were you shot down each time your hand shot up? Did someone's destructive laugh greet your creative craft? Were you silenced more often than handed a bullhorn? Did someone tell you to keep your ideas to yourself? Were you encouraged to think your share and say nothing?" I try to remind everyone that there is no way to successfully implement a bad idea, so any idea is worth venting and vetting. Let it out! Let it out! *It's in there, so let it out!*

Men in particular seem reticent to venture forth with an idea that's not fully thought-out, or one that may sound somehow soft or even — *Heaven forbid!* — effeminate or somehow unmanly. People appear to be growing less fearful of bringing ideas and themselves out of claustrophobic closets of worrying about retribution for being authentic and imperfect works-in-progress. Are Americans becoming more aware and accepting of our world's energizing economic and other dependency on respecting, encouraging, embracing, affirming and sustaining diversity in ideas and people?

"Concerning all acts of initiative and creation, there is one elementary truth, the ignorance of which kills countless ideas and splendid plans: The moment one definitely commits oneself than Providence moves too. All sorts of things occur to help one that would never otherwise have occurred." —Johann Wolfgang von Goethe

Recently in Atlanta I witnessed results of five years of transformation of a grand Presbyterian church in the lovely in-town Morningside neighborhood, a stunning structure un-creatively yet lovingly consecrated in 1949 as Morningside Presbyterian Church. In fairness to all American descendants of *ye olde Kirk of Scotland*, from First, Second, Third, Fourth Presbyterian Churches and so on (including a few dozen or more churches named for Scot St. Andrew), few Presbyterian churches in the U.S. are creatively named. Creativity in nick-naming any church occurs in the hearts of parishioners. Perhaps most congregants choose "My Church" as the most frequently used name, which for me is all well and good. When in 2004 great pastor pal, the Reverend Dr. Joanna M. Adams, arrived at Morningside Church, she felt called to create, innervate, and innovate in the name of the Ever-Rising Lord of Non-Stop Innovation. And did she ever!

A few months after her arrival at Morningside, I traveled to Atlanta to joyously celebrate Joanna being named *Georgia's Woman of the Year*, following in predecessor footsteps of Mrs. Martin Luther King, Jr., First Lady Roslyn Carter, and other leading female luminaries of The Peachtree State. Early the morning after her grand black-tie event in Atlanta's nearby Buckhead enclave, without her I visited the Morningside church she was stewarding, shepherding, educating and innovating. Instantly I too felt the call, pull and tug of the place. The affable church secretary shared her unbridled joy at Joanna's arrival, and warmly welcomed my interest in seeing every nook-and-cranny of this sadly deteriorating edifice. I'm not sure if she saw my occasional tear. I was feeling it deeply. Joanna was needed here.

Over five decades earlier, the ideas for founding, designing and building this church were dared by people who may no longer be alive, yet evidence of innovation to sustain this great place was now difficult to discern. Innovation had slowed or stopped. With perhaps 100 members (if I recall correctly) the church was teetering. I felt in those halls past and present love of God and community, yet the musty odor of damp carpeting and walls was irritating to nostrils and higher sensibilities.

The building had fallen into a state of unsafe and unhealthy disrepair; the ceiling leaked, carpeting was soaked, walls were stained with rust marks, dirt was in corners, paint was peeling, and the kitchen probably could not pass white-glove or health department inspection. There were even some unwashed hand prints of children from early years who were now young or order adults. Although I enjoyed seeing, and probably incorrectly dating, the little hand prints, I kept to myself my conflicting thoughts and feelings. Yet toward each corner I turned, in my mind's eye I saw fresh paint, new carpeting, better furniture, and even heard a better sound system. Nothing that came to my mind, however, matched the grandeur I saw five years after Joanna's innovative response to her call to shore-up more than The Church's One Foundation.

Today Atlanta's Morningside Presbyterian Church is a sight of beauty to behold; a bold statement of the healing and feeling power of innovation. Now in the capable hands of Pastor Baron Mullis, everything about this place welcomes wanting, needing or pleading hearts and minds. When in Atlanta, visit Morningside to witness this work-in-progress. Pastors Adams and Mullis are forever aligned.

On the economic development side of innovation for my Chicago world, there is an unfunny joke about entrepreneurship's chances in the too-windy city. An entrepreneur attends a weekend barbecue with neighbors and happens to say she or he is starting a promising new venture. The other person says, "That's nice. Do you think the Cubs are going to win the World Series this year?" The *non-sequitur* suggests immediate endemic societal disinterest in embracing, trusting or supporting someone else's idea, and long-standing comfort — perhaps enjoyment — with nearly one century of a storied ball team's missing-the-mark.

Perhaps an entrepreneur in Chicago is secretly thought to have as much chance of winning the world series of commerce as the Cubbies appear to represent potential for taking it all in baseball. Whatever *pathos* the indecorous joke is supposed to be signaling, it seems disrespectful of old-as-mound-dirt notions: (1) whatever the idea happens to be to launch a potential job-creating, value-generating, and tax-paying business, and (2) the nearly 10 decades-old idea of the Chicago Cubs as World Champions. I am, however, a believer in the potential for both global-impact and meteoric growth for Chicago's entrepreneurial ventures, and I believe the Cubs could be next season's World Champions.

Some conspiracy theorists or citizens preoccupied with doomsday visions predict everything will soon be gone, unless we change our wayward criminal and pollutant ways. Apocalyptic vision becomes more pronounced with the absence of creativity and innovation. Paradoxically, envisioning the apocalypse actually fuels creativity and innovation. This is polarity, contradiction, and clarity achieved through creativity and innovation.

Fortunately for all of us, history is full of under-appreciated, appreciated, and over-appreciated idea people whose ideas become realty through cyclical stages of innovation. Quite often the person with the idea is someone different from the individual who implements innovation.

Ideas begin and take shape in a mind's eye. I have had startling ideas come to mind at most inopportune moments. Badly sunburned while driving on the Long Island Expressway, heading back toward Manhattan from an East Hampton escape from reality, I suddenly renamed my company and instantly saw the new logo flash across my mind. A glance at a license plate ahead of me triggered the ideas. I almost wrecked the car. Wisely I pulled over to the side, and on a soiled napkin sketched the logo before I wrote the name and said loudly, "That's it! That's it!" I was thrilled. I was grateful. I was sure. The next day our lawyers and graphics artists were called, and innovation began with the ideas on a crumpled napkin. We had a new name and logo to modernize our stodgy sounding business. We were not at all stodgy, but our name and branding were.

From National Business Intelligence Corporation (NBI), quite literally overnight, we became modern-sounding ETX Corporation. "**E**" for editorial expertise. "**T**" for technological command. "**X**" for "The X Factor" — to symbolize all the other types of value my company brought and sold to each client. All of this, including the stylized logo popped into mind in less than an instant. The whole thing just happened, exactly as stated above. I feel it again as I write this for you. Monday-morning innovation picked-up the idea ball and ran with it. Several clients we served followed our lead and embraced the powerful sound of "X" in their company name or NYSE ticker symbol. I was thanked, but never financially rewarded (of course) for setting or increasing the pace toward symbolism within the letter "X." With this book it seems that I have evolved to encouraging and embracing whole words instead of single letters. Indeed progress is a whole word.

In 2009 a trusted pal revealed he disliked Hillview's stylized "sterling silver H" logo. As I designed it and understood its symbolism for strategic alignment, I was quite unprepared for this level of disconnect from a young person whose assertiveness and creativity I value highly. My respect for the push-back from Tim Courtney's head almost instantly caused a synapse in my brain that allowed me to create the current true-north Hillview logo. Not unlike The Flying Lady hood ornament of Rolls Royce, Hillview had The Flying H.

For good reason I'm revealing my graphic arts interest and acquired skills. I admit I've created dozens of logos, brochures, ads, and even a few TV and radio commercials. Clients thought they were buying work product of a creative department, and since they never asked, I never told. Why am I bragging? Trust I am not. With a bit of a red face I'm confessing. Knowing how idea people such as graphic designers were ONCE thought of in a lesser way in the business community than were executives (now called "suits"), as a company president who ALSO wrote and designed collateral materials, I hid behind the impression of having outsiders delivering the goods I created. I did not lie, but I did not offer total truth. I was afraid of being thought of as a creative person *vs.* an innovative executive. Long ago I got over that mind muddle. I designed this book's jacket.

As so-called personal computing started to come into its own as an industry, many of us Baby Boomers concluded Apple's dearly missed Steve Jobs was all about ideas, and Bill Gates was all about innovation; illustrating a creator and innovator as differentiated for the purpose of this chapter's exercise about innovation. Rightly or wrongly, it appeared Gates was *stealing* from then vulnerable Steve Jobs the art of Apple's ideas, to which Microsoft would apply science of innovation. True or not, someone had seminal ideas to which someone else applied innovation. Occasionally the idea person is also an innovator, but by the time the innovation cycle is in full-motion, the idea person is on to the next idea. Thank goodness! Perhaps this is a natural order of things — from ignition of ideation to innovation for implementation. Does my "Four-I Formula" ring true for you?

As an idea begins to take shape, and plans to implement the idea begin to look viable, innovation takes the idea the extra miles needed to get to the starting line, innovation fires the pistol to start the race, then innovation keeps the idea running for the longest possible period of time. Innovation is the foundation of any form of sustainability.

If ever there was a factor about human nature I regret, it is the too frequent immediate dismissal by so many people when they hear from someone else a seedling of an idea. Four decades and counting into my career (since high school days PR-stumping for Junior

Achievement), I remain amazed that the people who push-back the hardest on my ideas are those from whom I rarely if ever hear an original thought. My heart hurts from these memories.

If ideas expressed in draft chapters of this book were expected to be fully developed, I would have heard negatives on top of a majority of positives. Drafts are drafts; work-in-progress. Mostly I heard encouragement. The excusable typo or two, and an occasional grammatical error, are part of the ideational process. Editing is innovation. I am grateful for this book's innovative effort. The editing process moved ideas from rough drafts to deliverables.

To unscientifically test for my own edification a half-baked theory, several months before first drafting this chapter I monitored only two weeks' worth of conversation in both my personal and business life. I went out of my way to say nothing to anyone that even hinted at an idea of mine related to something new. I listened. I waited. I yearned. I needed to hear someone, anyone utter even a hint of a fresh idea; actually, any idea would do, fresh or stale. Toward the end of the 10th day, former protégée Tim Courtney was abuzz with new ideas for making better the annual Social Networking Development Technology weekend "camp" for techies he directs, now held at DePaul University. I breathed a sigh of relief and jumped-in to support his thinking. I added two cents or more of my thoughts, and truly thanked the Creator someone said something new. I wouldn't interrupt Tim's flow of ideas to tell him he had just won an invisible and otherwise nonexistent prize. Since he was on such a roll I let him roam free and unencumbered by my comparatively boring points. I was relieved.

Until Tim reads this chapter, he will not have known he released a pressure-cooker valve — my burning desire to hear something new, instead of rehashed business stories, news reports, status briefings, political barbs, gossip, sports scores, or complaints about whatever and whoever was in the speaker's line-of-sight for recapitulation or annihilation.

In all conversation I went out of my way to avoid triggering discussion about fresh ideas. I needed to know if my sense was more right than wrong — knowing, of course, it could be neither without sufficient blind sampling in a measurable opinion poll. What I got was just enough to underscore in my mind some social issues associated with ideational development (*i.e.*, daring to think creatively and then speak openly about ones fresh thoughts that might lead toward sustainable innovation).

For a moment, please, forget the above rhetoric and think about today so far, this moment in time. So far today, did you hear or read about a fresh idea? Did you think about a fresh idea? Did someone trust you by sharing for your input an idea for a new business, product, ad campaign, book, article, software, smart phone app, movie script, breakthrough in health care, way to end wars, a solution to global warming, a drug to cure any disease, a formula to reverse aging, a theory to explain end limits on a limitless universe, an across-the-board way to eliminate hate, murder, racism, homophobia, and paralyzing fundamentalist views about inherently complex and virtually inexplicable faith in higher power found in every known category of humankind?

On a lighter note, some wordsmith at The Ritz-Carlton in Palm Beach had an innovative approach to responding to a note I sent to commend them. Reversing the logic in language one normally associates with staying "at" a hotel, they wrote, "Thank you for your comments and enthusiasm! Thank you for letting us stay with you!" I love this reversal. Indeed every best-quality hotel experience "stays with me" — after I stay with them. Then again, certain spicy foods stay with me far too long, but that's another type of reversal. Did I hear you groan? You needed a smile — and a deep breath or two.

The far-reaching roster above was designed to push your and my limits. Whew! Did you rebel at all to this author's creative flights of fancy? Did this litany of categories of ideas annoy, intimidate or bore you? Or were you suddenly aware how long it has been since you heard from someone in your circle any fresh ideas addressing or even related to any of the above; ideas and innovation, not reports or opinions about others' thoughts and efforts? Dare to take inventory.

Forbes Magazine offered this insight, "There is no correlation between R&D spending and innovation. Or spending on innovation and rates of return. Companies over-spend trying to defend old businesses with unnecessary extensions, while under-spending on new innovations that can drive organic growth." Innovation means much more than any R&D definition I know.

Post War II, Big Ideas kept us Baby Boomers alert and oriented to the great big world around us. Eyes were pried wide-open by big-thinking political leaders Ike, JFK, RN (yes, Nixon), and Reagan. Creating the illusion of smallness for our challenging world — *e.g.,* "A Global Village" — may have unintentionally narrowed our vision and constrained our minds. Let's think big and bigger; great-to-greater!

Twice-former U.S. Secretary of Defense Donald H. Rumsfeld was among the most technologically advanced deep thinkers ever to serve in a Cabinet post. Prior to his last return to public service, he and his checkbook were on the front line with forward-thinking and adventurous private investors in enabling breakthrough technology.

> *"Status quo, you know, that is Latin for*
> *'the mess we're in'."* —Ronald Reagan

Children need to be a part of the innovation plan. Surrounding yourself with children and other younger minds allows adults to generate thoughts toward innovation. At my request, *"With the innocence of little children..."* was inscribed into the wedding band of my former wife. We knew the difference between child-like and childish. When we honored child-like thoughts, creativity and innovation flowed, and our marriage, friendships, and business interests thrived.

> *"No great artist ever sees things as they are.*
> *If he did, he would cease to be an artist."* —Oscar Wilde

Truly I remain in awe regarding how rarely I hear someone approach me with, "Hey, I have a new idea I'd like to run by you for your input . . . run up the flag pole to see if you salute . . . try it on for size . . . see if you've heard of anything like this before, *etc."* I hear too many people talk about others' ideas, often only after ideas have been adequately funded, or after the idea breaks unspecified revenue milestones. What are we waiting for?

> *"Countries and individuals that don't reinvent*
> *themselves get left behind."* —John Chambers

Wherever you live on Laboratory Earth, today let's commit to more creativity and innovativeness in our thoughts and deeds, please. Thank you for your steadfast innovativeness in using thoughts, feelings, and 52 key words revealed in this rather innovative book.

Innovation. Expound.

Inquisitiveness

Chapter Inspired by and Dedicated to Clyde O. Bowles, Jr., Esq.

Insert or imagine seeing your first name: _____,

Seeing this chapter's title word, what immediately comes to your open mind? Do you already have a working relationship with this word? Somewhere inside of you does this word instantly appeal? As a response to a specific situation at-hand, will this word work to your and others' advantage? For this word to increase in real value, together we must dig, drill and think deeper, so we will reach, climb and soar higher.

"I have no particular talent. I am merely inquisitive." —Albert Einstein

Are you creating and sustaining an organizational culture of inquisitiveness at home, work, or elsewhere where you lead people and manage things? Where you lead, is inquisitiveness a cultural imperative? From all ages and levels is a steady stream of queries invited, welcomed and rewarded? Are you on the lookout for questions within questions (*i.e.,* wisdom); perhaps value and concerns found within words and between lines? Do you and others work to discover depth in questions that may have been unintended by the questioners?

Ultimately questions can be more significant than any immediate responses or answers. Fully responsible leaders ask many questions, and listen with a third ear to myriad types of responses and answers. As if sifting through water for rare gold nuggets, it's wise for leaders to ask and encourage questions. Quite often a totally unexpected response or answer has little, if anything, to do with the question asked. Indeed value of some variety can be found in any response.

Too many of us ask for immediate and pat answers. As an experiment, try allocating fifty percent of your next staff/team meeting to fielding and sifting for gems through questions — without insisting on instant or firm answers. I suspect you'll probably find treasure. If you allow responses to resonate in your mind, you'll find light! Give questions a chance to enlighten, enrich and empower you and the people counting on your leadership skills of discovery (*i.e.,* your inquisitiveness and responsiveness).

"I to the world am like a drop of water that in the ocean seeks another drop, who, falling there to find his fellow forth, unseen, inquisitive, confounds himself."
—William Shakespeare

Inquisitiveness by definition and description keeps us on our toes. When toddlers, teens and beyond, our parents and others probably heard us say, perhaps 1,001 times per day, "Why?" Have you stopped asking, "Why?" Your adult "why" may or may not have much more *gravitas* than when you were badgering parents and others for answers. Child-like curiosity has its place in healthy adult minds. Childish questions, however, waste time and energy. Indeed some adults are pretty childish about asking questions. Child-like and childish are very different terms and states of mind. If need be, ask how the terms differ. Inquire. Inquisitive minds ask and keep on asking.

In general terms, physicians might report highly inquisitive minds are attached to bodies that last longer, live longer, and produce societal value longer. It is wise to use inquisitiveness as one of many tools to keep our minds as active as possible. Recalling responses, of course, is the proof in the process.

Why for some of us are questions intimidating, even threatening? Do we have lingering bad memories from elementary school days? Were we told at an impressionable age, "Children should be seen and not heard?" For me Grandmother Shearer's "Think your share and say nothing," was akin to "Silence is golden." Many early-life lessons kept us quiet. I had too much to say.

What fears can keep us adult leaders from asking questions? And what might keep us from really listening to responses to questions we ask? Fear of being thought invasive, nosy, aggressive, intrusive, rude or stupid may keep some of us from asking questions. Others fear a question might be a show-stopping reality check, or trigger some irreversible failure. Some worry about appearing inept by asking a question for which surely everyone knows the exact answer. Or is *fear of success* again raising its ugly head? As a leader, if you are not routinely asking yourself and others random inquiries for gaining additional insight, or posing mission-critical key questions, something must be holding you back.

A boss or team leader asking someone, "Where do things stand?" has never been enough of an inquisitive question. Nothing stands still. Change is ceaseless. "Where are people and things moving?" is a more inquisitive approach to what a leader needs to know. Even projects or ventures that stop continue onward in minds, discussions, court proceedings, press coverage, water-cooler conversation among spectators, and in other forms of life. Again, change is ceaseless. Inquisitiveness, therefore, should be attuned to ceaseless change. Even if a question or response debunks or otherwise breaks apart an erroneous or inadequate assumption or fact, the outcome sought after should be viewed as productive. There are many reasons and ways to ask questions. Ask away — in the best possible way; trying not to get in anyone's way. For the right reasons, ask, listen and respond.

Think about the number of times each day you ask yourself and others questions — from poignant rhetorical questions left to hang in the air, questions thought at-the-moment urgent or somehow pressing, and in-between questions with every degree of importance. Daily how many times are you asked questions? How many times do you respond to a degree that sets an example for responsiveness? Do you dutifully listen with wisdom, courage and patience to questions and responses, theirs and yours?

Small Talk has its Place, but its Place is Small

In extended collegial conversation over meals, drinks, or other concentrated times together, I wish more people would ask substantive questions, and spin fewer wheels with relatively empty queries. Warm-hearted ice-breaker types of questions are a-okay (*e.g.,* following John Maxwell's "Law of Connection"). An hour or more of multiple empty questions would be difficult for me to endure. Almost always I want to explore with others alternative responses to good and worthy questions.

To illustrate, I offer this Top 10 list for engaging me one-on-one; questions and responses I would welcome related to: (1) real global urgency for fueling innovation and entrepreneurial economic development, (2) the comparative dearth of venture capital coming from the entire state of Illinois and elsewhere, (3) lasting socioeconomic lessons proud Chicagoans can learn from losing The Bid for the 2016 Olympics, (4) due diligence and dignity in health care delivery, (5) education revamped from both teaching and learning sides of the equation, (6) social networking technology and related economic realities projected five or so years out, (7) faith, values and ethics, (8) hard-knocks lessons from entrepreneurial career paths, (9) mid-life perspectives on parenting, friendship and love, and (10) personal quality-of-life applications of Hillview's breakthrough principles, practices and models of strategic alignment for people, money, technology, and other resources. For these conversational lines of thought, I have many questions and responses, and just a few answers.

Although I welcome a personal word or two, to get my attention, rote small talk is not necessary. I am simply never going to care enough to be up-to-date on sports scores, team players' lifetime records, Tiger's last championship cup, celebrity gossip, or one dozen or more other conversational "filler topics." No need for me. Since my earliest days in the business world (1967 onward), I am thrilled almost no one asks me about sports, weather, movies, popular music, or the points I shaved off of my mortgage rate by clever refinancing. By directly or subconsciously noting what are called my clinical *communication markers* (*e.g.*, eye contact, body language, smile, *etc.*) and upbeat turn-taking skills in conversation, others seem to sense I am almost instantly available for connection and substantive dialog. Often I am. Normally rather quickly I become engaged. Tricks are rarely required to get my attention. To some souls in conversation with me, I hear it seems I am so focused that it "feels" as if no one else matters, or nothing else is on my mind. Sometimes that's nearly true.

Candidly, often I wonder about how certain people can justify investing countless precious hours discussing and dissing accomplishments and failures of others, while leaving unspoken lurking concerns for their own relevancy, impact, and likely legacy. Discussion topics mean the most to me when they ignite the creativity, innovation, and problem-solving spark plugs in others' and my brains. I yearn to both learn from others and share what I know. With a robust circle of bright colleagues, clients, and other wise friends I'm truly blessed to know, I have very little time left over for idle chatter. If necessary, of course you can count on me for small talk, but thankfully only for a small amount of time, please. We'll both like it better that way.

As with all matters, there is a shadow side to being inquisitive and responsive. Unchecked it can be exhausting! Inquisitive and responsive brains need to shut-down or they might burn-out. Late in mid-life I learned to shift my inquisitiveness — during weekends — to topics that I could navigate with more calm and peace than my professional world allows Mondays through Fridays. For those of us with careers that are enhanced by our eagerness to acquire knowledge, pursue wisdom, increase patience — and then earn our professional compensation by putting these attributes to work for the benefit of others — our weekends must be designated for recreation, relaxation and reflection; yes, strategic alignment of mind, body and soul.

This is the Dawning of the Age of Inquisitiveness

Visionaries toward *The Age of Aquarius* probably never envisioned where we would be 40 years or so after the 1960s movement. (In the lore of astrology, we Aquarians are known to be 50 years or more ahead of our time.) Today's Internet-active, smart-phone attached, iPad-empowered, FourSquare-tracked, and Twitter-linked "inquiring minds want to know." Almost everyone seems more ready — yet perhaps not exactly willing or able — to respond to questions asked face-to-face, in e-mail, *via* text messages, blogs, IMs, surveys, polls, on-the-street interviews, Tweets, voting booths, and in other forms and forums of information gathering and exchange. So much information is moving so fast. Where are we heading on this information superskyway or *databahn*? Questions find you if you don't ask them first. Ask questions of Bing, Google, Ask, McKinsey, Accenture, Harvard Business Review, Ted, or other .com resources for responses and answers.

Quick-on-the-draw so-called 18-second elevator pitches are crafted and memorized to respond to the most frequently asked networking question and its derivatives, "What do you do for a living?" In 18 or fewer seconds, I have to entice an instantly qualified questioner to want to know more about a 40+ year career path that led me to this moment of inquiry. I have to treat as a blessing not a curse the other person's interest in me, knowing she or he may be feigning interest or really only interested in herself or himself. Boy Scouts are not the only leaders who need to "be prepared." We fully responsible leaders need to be prepared to respond to inquisitiveness of many types.

Lessons in inquisitiveness and responsiveness are learned at an early age. As my mother would tell you, frequently I would take things apart to discover how they work, then put the darn things back together. To family dismay, often I dissected the inner workings of the old-fashioned telephones of my youth. By asking myself questions a telephone repair technician would be asking about the dozens of little multi-colored wires, screws, springs, and other pre-digital-age parts, I figured it out. I spare you reports of remembered hubris following each triumph. From this specific inquisitiveness about old telephones, clunky audio equipment, and newfangled computers, at age 24 I created a small piece of equipment around which was built a breakthrough electronic publishing business I ran for 12 years (before selling it to a Wall Street investor).

Many of us have an insatiable appetite for more, more, more input from others. We want — and sometimes need — to know. Yet we don't always know what we don't know, so we may not be able to ask the very questions for which we need responses and answers. If we are sufficiently ascendant in our social boldness, we ask a lot of questions. In similarly assertive ways, others respond to us with truth, half-truth, or no truth at all. Wisdom, courage and patience are required with the people and process of inquisitiveness and responsiveness. Risks and rewards are real.

"The principles and modes of governments are too important to be disregarded by an inquisitive mind . . ." —James Madison

Certain questions are used as rhetorical psychological weapons during White House press briefings, and statutory annual meetings of shareholders for publicly traded companies. And if an angry spouse or significant other questions a beloved saying, "You were due home three hours ago. I smell alcohol on your breath. You said you were working late at the office. You did not call. Where were you and with whom?" At the moment of inquiry, probably no answer is going to suffice. True, disrespectfully put questions annoy me when coming from questioners who don't seem to give the question or me benefit of doubt. Every boss knows what it's like to have an employee ask an impertinent question. At times the poser is less interested in the response the boss might give, and instead is more invested in questioning a leader's judgment, authority, or perhaps base intellect. Such questions can test more than knowledge.

Questions asked and responses offered build or shake trust; strengthen or weaken relationships. You must ask questions, and you must respond to questions. Do you agree? Ask me what I think. This is a point of this exercise about inquisitiveness. Hearing your questions in my mind as I write, here is more response to your welcome inquisitiveness.

At a moment's notice upwardly and outwardly mobile leaders have to be prepared for probing questions about our place of employment, and the city, county, state, and country in which we live. At times we'll be asked if we are married, divorced, have kids or want kids. No longer off-limits are questions about where and how we worship, what we think of President Obama's time on-the-job, stimulus funds, Wall Street salaries and bonuses, Homeland Security, and prosecution of wars in Afghanistan, Iraq and Libya? From younger folk we may be asked about drugs, our affectional life, sexuality, views about same-sex marriage, racism, child abuse, and where we really stand on a woman's right to choose. Questions about our favorite cars, bars, drinks, food, clothing, vacation spots, and sports are bound to surface in extended social conversation.

In my personal privacy policy, what happens in bedrooms, in boardrooms, and in confidential meetings with clients, family and friends remains strictly confidential and resource-proprietary. Politely I'll redirect focus of someone asking an accidental or intentionally inappropriate question. Be firm. Still so many acceptable black-and-white questions are asked, normally with precious little time allowed for fully responsible leaders to offer Technicolor responses.

"There are innumerable questions to which the inquisitive mind can, in this state, receive no answer: Why do you and I exist? Why was this world created? Since it was to be created, why was it not created sooner?" —Samuel Johnson

Why indeed! Are you thought by others to be inquisitive and responsive to others' inquisitiveness? Do you ask a lot of questions? Do you listen, really listen? In all responses to your questions, do you expect immediate black-and-white absolute answers? Are you comfortable with ambiguity? Do you enjoy the exploration of responses more so than eventual answers? Are you comfortable with questions layered upon of questions? Does the period during which questions compound annoy or energize you? Think an extra beat about these probing questions, please.

At 19 I was inquisitive about what took us so long to land on the moon. Parents, peers and others were startled, and some were openly unimpressed with my misguided ho-hum — yet still inquisitive — attitude toward the news of the 1969 landing. I kept asking questions, and no one seemed to have satisfactory responses. I thought we were too far behind George Orwell's 1948 forecast in his "Nineteen Eighty-Four" masterpiece. And I am still waiting for all of his helicopters to unsnarl our highway traffic jams.

In my client work I use the term psychoeconomics to stimulate inquisitiveness and deeper discussion about aligning people and money. Putting people first, putting people second, and putting people third can reverse the risk of global misalignment caused by prioritizing profit over people. The upside-down profit-over-people equation has been with us for thousands of years. People first!

"Q&R" for Questions and Responses

In the early 1980s I was testing my company's telephonic connection technology while participating in a closed-door rehearsal for a quarterly financial talk by David Kearns, then CEO of Xerox Corporation. To his dismay he discovered a $35-million typographical error in a slide that could not be repaired in time for the morning briefing with the New York Society of Securities Analysts (NYSSA). Back then presentation slides were made of permanent Kodak film, not today's easily changed PowerPoint data files. Annoyed David wondered aloud if the slide should be removed or explained away. He rose to the CEO post through a triumphant career in sales and marketing for Xerox, so he wanted to put his best foot forward. He pulled the slide, then asked us in his mock audience how he could handle any questions related to those missing numbers. I took the opportunity to say he could change the title of the Questions and Answers (Q&A) section of the agenda to "Q&R" for Questions and Responses — as not all responses are answers and they needn't be.

David roared with laughter hearing "Q&R." He and we needed comic relief. The next morning, before a question would be asked, he truthfully addressed the missing slide's correct numbers, and he also used Q&R instead of Q&A. He shot me a smile and later said thanks.

For many years "Q&R" stuck as an entertaining title for the Q&A agenda step for many big companies. As our electronic publishing services company cornered the New York City market, many top CEOs began to use my Q&R term. It became theirs, and I was thrilled.

By the early 80s, our clients included 100% (!) of the *Fortune 500* companies based in Manhattan, and nationally top-most companies in virtually every major field and industry. (I have a yellowing copy of the company's client index, and still look at it in amazement.) Yet when three times I suggested using Q&R during our firm's contract work for the 1976, 1980 and 1984 U.S. Presidential Debates, the sponsoring National League of Women Voters remained un-amused.

Voters deserve answers from candidates for the Presidency, I was tutored. Yes, but we all know candidates provide clever responses when they can't produce answers. Today I still think the slight smile that would come with the announcement and explanation of Q&R would make future Presidential Debates and other big and small meetings more real; more authentic.

No one has all the answers, but a fully responsible leader has a thoughtful response to every question. Responses lead to answers.

"We shall not cease from exploration.
And the end of all our exploring will be to arrive where we started,
and know the place for the first time." —T.S. Eliot

Thank you for increasing your meaningful inquisitiveness and thoughtful responsiveness. With an ever-inquisitive and ever-responsive nature, please join me in always deepening conviction, broadening perspective, and elevating thought. Allow your inquisitive and responsive mind and soul to wonder about ways and words to support you as you deepen, broaden and heighten your awareness of people and things. Together let's redouble our inquisitiveness and responsiveness to each of 52 key words this book proclaims.

Inquisitiveness. Expound.

Intentionality

Chapter Inspired by and Dedicated to Jeffrey L. Russell

Insert or imagine seeing your first name: _____,

Seeing this chapter's title word, what immediately comes to your open mind? Do you already have a working relationship with this word? Somewhere inside of you does this word instantly appeal? As a response to a specific situation at-hand, will this word work to your and others' advantage? For this word to increase in real value, together we must dig, drill and think deeper, so we will reach, climb and soar higher.

"The road to hell is paved with good intentions," is more than a half-serious cynical cliché. Intentionality is an antidote to toxicity you might internalize when hearing "good intentions." Often you think about your and others' good or not-so-good intentions, correct? Yet how often do you think about, speak to others about, or write about intentionality — proactive strategic alignment of thoughts and actions?

> *"Ultimately, human intentionality is the most powerful evolutionary force on this planet."* —George B. Leonard

In open minds and capable hands of fully responsible leaders, good intentions become great intentionality. Yes, good intentions to great intentionality. Bestseller-book Good to Great's imagery of "a seat on the bus" suddenly becomes inadequate. With great intentionality, instantly you are in the pilot's seat of a supersonic transport. Your crew members are where they need to be in co-pilot, first-class, business-class, and coach seats. You make certain no one is stowed away in the baggage compartment (*i.e.*, unengaged or asleep on the job). For every project team's flight to new heights, intentionality creates required lift, thrust, weight and drag. Where are you this very moment, captain? Are you plotting your course, checking the weather, ready for take-off, in full flight, or triumphantly landing at your next destination of this multi-leg leadership journey?

Each day fully responsible leaders awake with an acute and positive-minded sense of intentionality for living their lives. Whether sleep-deprived by downside worry or upside excitement, an overarching sense of intentionality can give a maximum-strength energy boost to mind and body. With intentionality a fully responsible leader can leap out of bed, shake away cobwebs, and kick into high gear with 110% conscientiousness needed for the 16-plus hours ahead. Intentionality is accelerated movement of mind and matter. Intentionality allows us mortals in leadership roles to think, feel, and act with a sharp yet humble sense of our place and higher purpose. Often, therefore, we sleep rather soundly.

Allow the power of this one word to wash over you. Firmly and clearly say it out loud. "Intentionality." Do you feel intentionality's potential for you? For career callings or choices, intentionality is a hybrid fuel combining rational mind and mysterious spirit; polarities of left-brain and right-brain awareness. With just enough combustion, intentionality keeps a leader's pistons firing for high-torque performance.

With intentionality in applying wisdom, courage and patience, fully responsible leaders react with Respect, Empathy, Authenticity, Clarity and Trust (R.E.A.C.T.). In Being and Nothingness, French philosopher Jean-Paul Sartre aligned intentionality with such exceptional consciousness. Good to Great, The Seven Habits of Highly Effective People, The Maxwell Daily Reader, Blink, and countless other works of masters of words, impress us with expression of intentionality. A wise reader's intentionality enables good-to-greater outcomes.

Apple's Steve Jobs was a master of intentionality. Following his untimely death I was asked by a TV reporter how I reflect on Steve Jobs' legacy. I offered, "Steve Jobs was the embodiment of 'Different.' Intentionally he challenged us to see different, think different, *do different*. Steve Jobs knew at a deeper level how 'different' delivers what ceaseless change demands of us."

With authorial intentionality, each weekly word herein is boldly presented for your enjoyment and enrichment. Featured words command our respect, extra effort, attention to nuance, and other intentionality. Drilling deeper while reaching higher, allow these words to resonate with immediate and lasting significance. Ultimately you derive and determine value of these words. Intentionality within this book's development includes reversing risk related to trivializing dialogue we have within ourselves and with each other. Here are words and supportive thoughts to deepen, broaden and elevate all dialogue. From a mere utterance to a symphony of words, with great intentionality readers find themselves enjoying personal enrichment through forging strategic relationships with these 52 key words.

> *"An utterance can have intentionality, just as a belief has intentionality, but whereas the intentionality of the belief is intrinsic, the intentionality of the utterance is derived."* —John Searle

Humans are uniquely blessed with gifts of intellectual (IQ) and emotional (EQ) intelligence. Through perceptiveness and feelings we know intentionality is a key to our success. Perhaps intentionality is more influential in our success than inspiration.

> *"Inspiration is hogwash. My work comes directly out of my loves and hates. Muses don't whisper in my ear, and ideas don't flow over my body like a cool rain."* —James Victore

Perhaps to live life with extra measures of intentionality is a calling. Intentionality, I believe, is a choice.

> *"Everybody can be great because anybody can serve. You don't have to have a college degree to serve. You don't have to make your subject and verb agree to serve. You only need a heart full of grace. A soul generated by love."*
>
> —Martin Luther King, Jr.

Intentionality increases the resonance and other impact of a leader's voice. A leader's every word has consequences, intentional or otherwise.

> *"Words form the thread on which we string our experiences."*
>
> —Aldous Huxley

Thank you for fully grasping the essentiality in intentionality. Your intentionality with reading, considering and using each of this book's 52 key words proclaims your understanding of this basic premise.

Intentionality. Expound.

Mentor

Chapter Inspired by and Dedicated to
Byron J. Bardy, C.M.C. and Byron J. Bardy, Jr.

Insert or imagine seeing your first name: _____,

Seeing this chapter's title word, what immediately comes to your open mind? Do you already have a working relationship with this word? Somewhere inside of you does this word instantly appeal? As a response to a specific situation at-hand, will this word work to your and others' advantage? For this word to increase in real value, together we must dig, drill and think deeper, so we will reach, climb and soar higher.

Mentors matter. Mentoring matters more. Do you have mentors? Are you actively mentoring?

Noun: A knowledgeable, experienced, wise and trusted guide, counselor, advisor, or sounding board. Verb: Serve as a knowledgeable, experienced, wise and trusted guide, counselor, advisor, or sounding board.

How to these definitions empower and enrich you and others? As both a noun and a verb, having mentors and mentoring matter equally in the abundant lives of fully responsible leaders.

Thoughtful adults among us can trace to childhood our root attitudes toward mentors and mentoring. Grasping these nuanced factors can make a world of difference in mentoring's functionality for your grown-up career and home life.

Alert and dutiful parents are mentors. In their roles as progenitor, caregiver, police, warden, disciplinarian, ethicist, theologian, referee, interpreter, tutor, medic, psychologist, pastor, judge, cartographer, technologist, underwriter, chauffeur, cook, launderer, custodian, prayer partner, and other functions, parents mentor each other and their children.

"Do as I say, not as I do" was a confusing mentoring quote I recall from my dad. "Children should be seen and not heard" followed. "Don't salt your food before you taste it" is a less toxic tip. Yet the most painfully memorable mentoring came while I was being whipped, "This hurts me more than it hurts you." And his too-frequent-to-be-funny "Go play in traffic" still sends shivers up my spine. Someday I will more fully understand these first lessons in life's polarity.

Although parents are positioned to be each household's primary mentors, children often bring mentoring lessons back to parents from teachers, pastors, peers, parents of peers, and others. Have you thought of this household dynamic as win-win mentoring? Value from protégée to mentor is called "reverse mentoring." Parents and children should respect, listen, and respond more to each other's mentoring messages. In modern households already stretched-to-the-max for time to devote to meaningfulness of life lessons and their mastery, do you see potential for more collaborative parent-child/child-parent mentoring? As the child tutors parents in mastering i-Pods, surly more i-Phones are sold. Can you feel this Mac/PC logic? In practice, it will be untidy. Yes, adult-world mentoring delivered and received is often untidy.

As mentioned earlier, "Home Life" was the theme of a city-wide poster contest for which I won First Grand Prize. From the yellowing 1964 newspaper clipping, I can tell the blue ribbon was more for the H.O.M.E. L.I.F.E. acronym than the 14-year-old's modern artistry of a highly stylized mom, dad, son and daughter:

H = Happiness

O = Organization

M = Manners

E = Education

——

L = Love

I = Inspiration

F = Fun

E = Encouragement

These words were mentoring guidelines I was very publicly delivering to my parents. I needed my home life to add, not subtract; strengthen me, not weaken me. Somehow I realized Mom and Dad also needed home life to build and not destroy them. Unrealized expectations were exhausting for all of us. Forever I will leave judgment to a higher authority as to whose mentoring had the most positive impact on the family unit. I should not separate the value of lessons I learned from those I infused. I would not have been teaching if I were not learning so well what to not do. In the supercollider of my young brain, lessons I taught seemed to smash into and cancel out those I learned. What I was saying to my parents was negating their best-effort offerings. They tried. I heard something, I'm sure. Combustion caused by this convoluted set of family circumstances created a nuclear power plant for my later years.

Mother's high degree of respect for business executives surely formed the foundation of my comfort in business. In various capacities, "Muffy" Dallas worked for 35 years at The United Way of Allegheny County, at 200 Ross Street — an address I came to know as what is now called a safe haven. Mom was radically different in the office than she was at home. At business she was a model employee. Muffy was exceptionally deferential toward her bosses and startlingly familial with numerous co-workers. I was the indirect beneficiary of all the goodwill she allowed to develop at her place of employment. In my early teens I would drop-by to say hello, and it seemed everyone in the building knew my mother, and loved the stories she told them about her son. At first I was unprepared for the dichotomy between Mom's home and office life, but I grew to count it as a blessing. At 200 Ross Street my visits were celebrated. What I first learned and remember about my mother, mostly stems from my view of her at her workplace.

Thanks to Mom's professional persona, at 17 years of age I felt I was ready for my first business-world CEO mentor, Frederick Ernest ("F.E.") Schuchman. "F.E." for Free Enterprise, he would tell all. He was in his 70s, a long-time board member of Junior Achievement and numerous other community groups, and the combative President of the Allegheny County Civic Club. He was CEO of Homestead Industries, a Pittsburgh producer of precision valves for the U.S. Navy, and the pioneer in high-pressure mobile steam cleaning equipment (the Jenny® brand). At 23 I married his grand niece

Cynthia, whose father (my daughter's paternal grandfather), the late Scott A. Norris, Jr., had succeeded F.E. as Chairman of the ill-fated old family business. Company's demise was a result of misalignment.

F.E. chose me to mentor. I discovered it was very intentional on his part. Never would I have dared to visualize, suggest or expect such a commitment from him. For perhaps three years or more, on average he and I saw each other two or three times every month, and almost daily we spoke by telephone. Everyone around us and I seemed amazed by how close we grew. My parents said they were happy for me. F.E. did not have a son, and his only daughter moved to Manhattan to open "Nancy's Fancy," a Nantucket-style gift shop that made no serious money, but seemed nevertheless to somehow enrich her Upper East Side neighborhood. She was a local celebrity in her own right. At her funeral we heard how Nancy always had a mentoring word or two for every visitor to her quaint store, including me. Her deceased father was speaking through her. I knew it. I felt it.

F.E. was tireless and often unsmiling as he worked to rein-in my unbridled and premature zest for the entrepreneurial life. He was determined I would see the highs and lows of it all. Junior Achievement had only shown me the spotlight's glare. From tutoring me in the intricacies of a hidden world of the best private clubs for the then power elite — starting with the still world-famous Duquesne Club — to in-depth discussion of what he called terrorist acts of the late-60s blue-collar unions he fought, F.E. wanted me to know what to think and do in high and low situations. He was very direct in his lessons. I never incurred his wrath, but I knew it was at one remove.

With a glass eye, deaf ear, and rather frail health few people ever noticed, F.E. was nonetheless indefatigable. He would not slow down, and retirement was a forbidden four-letter word. I learned so much from F.E. To this day I recall his selfless beneficence. I'm not certain he ever knew how much I valued his tutelage, friendship, and other generosity. Perhaps I was too wrapped-up in my early-20s insecurities to pause to adequately express my heartfelt gratitude. I pray he sensed what I may have failed to say enough. Today I pay tribute to F.E.'s mighty mentoring. I try to follow in his footsteps.

As I turned 20, Bethel Park Borough Mayor Peter Paige appointed himself to me as a specialized political mentor. He decided I was too lop-sided with only having business leader pals. I needed a dose of political reality. Mayor Paige served as President of the Pennsylvania State Mayors Association. He named me statewide Communications Chairman for the group of 100+ mayors. I was 21. He supported Philadelphia Mayor Frank Rizzo's desire to run for Governor, and I was to help make it happen. Unbidden, most of the Pennsylvania mayors I would meet seemed to have at least some mentoring insight to offer this wet-behind-the-ears kid from Baldwin Borough. That's how I experienced their largess. Too late I learned they saw things differently. I did not realize they were expecting me to spend the rest of my life in service to the people of the Keystone State. I was being groomed.

For the 1972 Committee to Re-Elect President Richard M. Nixon, I was appointed Pennsylvania's Citizen Blocs Chairman. With a large promotional budget and pals of both parties in high places, I seemed to be the right guy to rally votes for President Nixon from ethnic and professional troops: Scots for Nixon, Lawyers for Nixon, Germans for Nixon, Physicians for Nixon, *etc.* This was my memorable introduction to target marketing. The politicos seemed to sense I was reachable and teachable, so all they had to do is point me in the right direction, and I sprinted forward. I wish I had thought to charge for my time and effort. The lessons freely offered me were my in-kind compensation.

After many busy people mentored me for an unspecified future in Pittsburgh and the Commonwealth, ultimately I failed to capitalize on the doors they swung wide for me. I left it all behind. After the Nixon White House failed to deliver on their promises of an Assistant Press Secretary post for me, boldly my new wife and I went where I learned my mentors hoped I would not go: New York City. I was smarting from the broken promises, and my new sense of politics as a netherworld of doom-and-gloom. The shock and shame of the Watergate scandal sealed the deal. No more politics for me! I was going to devote 110% of my attention to climbing ladders in business. For many years I did not look back.

Grateful as I was for many political mentors, I simply did not think highly enough of my value to realize they were investing in my future, assuming doing so would benefit the community (and probably eventually themselves). I had blinders on blocking my view of win-win motivation in early mentoring.

In New York Lyman C. Hamilton, Jr. took me under his wing. I was 26. Lyman rose to the CEO post at ITT, only to lose his job through clandestine board room machinations fiction writers would have trouble besting. Lyman and I chose each other. It happened so naturally. We just clicked. He was Executive Vice President and Chief Financial Officer of the world's largest conglomerate (owner of 340 companies operating in 104 countries). Until I reached age 40, Lyman and I were in touch, with countless 7:00 A.M. so-called power breakfasts from 1977 until 1990. Lyman's second marriage to truly delightful Beverly Lanquist rightly arrested his undivided attention. He was smitten. I was delighted. My badly managed move from Manhattan to Northern Virginia created insurmountable hurdles to keeping in-touch with Lyman. Within two months of leaving New York, I was flat on my back in D.C.'s George Washington Hospital suffering badly from burn-out's insurmountable stress. There I felt alone. In Virginia I never had a mentor. A reporter from *The New York Post* had frightened me into flying on my own.

As my relationship with F.E. was essentially unintentional, very intentional was my strong bond with Lyman. Almost immediately after being introduced by a mutual friend, Robert H. Savage, I sensed in LCHjr a perhaps unacknowledged need to download to a willing protégé his wealth of wisdom, courage and patience. For sure I knew I needed someone in my world of his brilliance and complexity; yes, the father figure lacking in my life. Lyman's wonderful sons were roughly my age, but none had my level of interest (or need) in the business world. In retrospect I realized we were both rounding-off some heretofore unidentified gaps in our respective lives. Moreover, we thrived on each other's ideas. I was unprepared for the downside.

A writer for *The New York Post*, Don Mazzella, threw a monkey wrench into my mind's gears. He was trying to be a mentor for me, I suppose, but I felt I did not need anyone other than Mr. Hamilton. After interviewing me for an article about my electronic publishing company's history as the only publisher of official edited transcripts of the U.S. Presidential Debates in 1976, 1980, and 1984, *The Post*'s reporter kept in touch. I did not initiate contact with him. I did not sense he was digging for dirt, so perhaps naively I responded to any of his calls or invitations for lunch; never expecting nor receiving further coverage in *The Post*. He was more than intrigued by my mentor/protégé relationship with Lyman. Eventually he dropped a bomb on my late-30s ego.

Over a too-heavy and wine-facilitated lunch in one of the reporter's favorite Italian restaurants near *The Post*, he said, "John, you mention

Lyman's name every single time you talk about anything to do with your business. Don't you think on your own? Does Mr. Hamilton make all your decisions for you? Do you ever stop talking about him?" Mr. Reporter was not being funny. He was actually more than a tad nasty in tone and delivery. He was angry. He was being very *Post*-like. Oddly he suddenly seemed jealous. I was stunned. I was hurt. Then he said, "Speak for yourself, John! Think for yourself. Be yourself. Without mentioning Mr. Hamilton, you already have anyone's attention. With your constant focus on him I'm sure others are also wondering what weaknesses you are trying to overcome by mentioning him all the time." I was blown-away. I felt hints of truth in what he said. I did not realize my relationship with my mentor had possibly turned into a crutch instead of a credit – a liability instead of a leg-up.

Indeed Lyman had become the central figure in my thinking life. I leaned on him for much, much more than perhaps I should have. He was so gracious, always kind. Chances are he had no clue how much I depended on his brain and heart to balance out what I might not be able to handle on my own. Without much of a smile, Lyman would remind me to tell him mostly "bad news" — things with which he could possibly help me. He was not a fan of any bragging or pride. He wanted to help me solve problems. Applause was to come from others. I knew better. Even when he was reprimanding me for a stupid move, I always felt each of his course corrections as pats on the back. He cared. He understood mentoring. In the early 90s, sadly we lost contact. Someday I hope to see him again. I see *via* Google he's doing well. I miss his counsel. Indeed I had grown to rely too heavily on his input in almost all matters. *The Post* reporter was partially correct.

In my 50s and 60s I enjoy access to mentoring on-call from three generous individuals, distinguished attorney Clyde O. Bowles, Jr., world-renowned business philosopher Dr. Peter Koestenbaum, and Atlanta's Presbyterian pastor extraordinaire, The Reverend Dr. Joanna M. Adams. In my mind and heart, all three are blessings beyond measure. Although each of these three saints is determined to freely acknowledge value I bring to their lives, forever I remain in their debt. I pray they know from my words and actions how deeply I feel each lesson they allow me. They are wise, courageous and patient souls. I am grateful for their friendship, collegiality, and mentorship. Although our busy lives keep us from frequent sightings or contact, I know they are there. In mind and heart, each will always be with me.

Eric Broughton, Ken Hicks, Jason Jacobsohn, Noreen Kelly, Gary Punzi, James Sweeney, Michael Werbowsky, and several other good souls permit me to mentor them, mostly in business matters. I am truly honored. They know I also learn much from their mentoring of me — appropriately called "reverse mentoring."

How were your parents in terms of mentoring you and any of your siblings? Did you experience their mentoring more as meddling; your parents as meddlers more so than mentors? As you age do your views change? One hopes.

With expectable push-back from a child to a mom's or dad's unbidden mentoring, I need to believe significant value accrues. Daughter Jennifer knows she has on-deposit a wealth of mentoring lessons from which to draw as-needed.

> *"Always be on time. Always know your words. Be bold and greater powers will come to your aid."* —Sir Anthony Hopkins offering mentoring views for Welsh actor Matthew Rhys

Mentoring and reverse-mentoring, when intentionally and carefully given and received, create inestimable value for individuals, the economy, and society overall. Do you recognize the importance in your life of mentors and mentoring?

Mentors matter in ways far beyond the obvious. The best mentors are certain to affirm in each individual her or his unique qualities.

"I never heard that it had been anybody's business to find out what his natural bent was, or where his failings lay, or to adapt any kind of knowledge to him. He had been adapted to the verses and had learnt the art of making them to such perfection. I did doubt whether Richard would not have profited by someone studying him a little, instead of his studying them quite so much."

—Charles Dickens

For many of us, mentoring is a high calling. Mentoring is a ministry.

Having considered this word during this rather personal letter to you from me, will you step-up and increase your engagement in mentoring, being mentored, and being reverse-mentored? Learn as much as you can, before, during, and after each giving or receiving act in mentoring. Allow all mentoring to resonate with more value.

Mentor. Expound.

Mission

Chapter Inspired by and Dedicated to Kathryn Wood Madden, Ph.D.

Insert or imagine seeing your first name: _____,

Seeing this chapter's title word, what immediately comes to your open mind? Do you already have a working relationship with this word? Somewhere inside of you does this word instantly appeal? As a response to a specific situation at-hand, will this word work to your and others' advantage? For this word to increase in real value, together we must dig, drill and think deeper, so we will reach, climb and soar higher.

Vision without mission is a promise without a plan.

As this past football season began, the incomparable Pittsburgh Steelers had a vision of becoming Super Bowl Champions for the sixth time, even though no other team had won this many Vince Lombardi trophies. Yes, until the very last seconds of their nail-biting win, the Steelers' game-by-game, play-by-play mission unfolded for all to see and feel. Now Pittsburgh has become the nation's most valuable sports franchise, adding even more global interest and economic vitality to America's unstoppable Renaissance City. From long-gone steel mills to gleaming towers of high-tech innovation, Pittsburgh leaders align vision with mission. Recently Pittsburgh celebrated 250+ years of pursuing ever-sharper vision and better-and-better mission.

Panoramic View from The HILL

Too few of us can recite from memory or even closely approximate our employer's organizational vision or mission. In practice, perhaps vision requires less team buy-in. Mission, however, demands all-team engagement; commitment to, and accountability for, actionable and measurable tasks. Vision can remain somewhat non-specific, while mission should be as specific as possible.

Vision statements clearly articulate a leader's sight toward the future; "what" is seen, "why" it is being seen, and by "when" what's seen will likely become reality. Vision is what we see ahead . . . where we'll be and by when.

Mission statements contain measurable detail for how vision will become reality; "who, what, when, where, why and how." Strategic team alignment adds energizing and empowering "Wow!" Mission is how we'll realize our vision . . . what we have to do to get there.

Vision aligns with mission. People align with purpose. Passion aligns with practicalities. Performance aligns with profits.

More than linguistic nuance between vision and mission supports fully responsible leaders in understanding the difference between right-brain and left-brain balance for strategic team alignment. Toward our personal and organizational true-north destinations, we must align innovative visualization with practical implementation.

"When you discover your mission, you will feel its demand. It will fill you with enthusiasm and a burning desire to get to work on it." —W. Clement Stone

Questions for Leaders: What applicable lessons are you learning from observing The White House add practical "mission statements" to President Obama's captivating "vision statements?" Can you see, hear and feel the front-line reality check underway? Do you expect the Obama Administration's vision to change? Have you changed your personal and organizational vision for this protracted correction economy? How far out are you looking and planning? Have you changed your mission?

Are you applying to today's thoughts and deliberations exceptional amounts of wisdom, courage and patience? One must.

*"Every person above the ordinary has a certain mission
that they are called to fulfill."* —Johann Wolfgang von Goethe

The United States of America is a name that expresses the mission of founding mothers and fathers. The Aligned States of America (ASA) might have been a better name to articulate the long-range and ever-changing vision for what we have to do to get there: Align people, money, technology and other mission-critical resources.

"Aligned we succeed" is a call to action, and quite different from "United we stand." Aligned we succeed. Divided we re-align. Inactive we fail.

Nothing stands still. **Change is ceaseless**.

Elsewhere in this book we discuss how asking "where do things stand?" has never been the right question. Instead, "Where are people/things moving?" allows minds to engage with the reality of ceaseless change. As the question is asked and response is offered, people and things are changing. Missions change. Vision changes.

Hillview's concept and context for True-North Strategic Alignment is about constant forward movement toward worthy destinations that are new beginnings. Alignment does not necessarily mean 100% agreement, yet it does mean full-speed-ahead toward established goals, milestones, objectives, and other "ends in mind" that are each starting points — a mission of momentum.

> *"Each journey's end is a new beginning. Along the way every stop is a start.*
> *Every destination is the next point of departure.*
> *Any ETA on your schedule is also Time for Departure (TFD)." —* JRDjr

On a lighter note, I recall a mission from my early teens that served me well for the lifetime ahead. In 1964 I was 14 and a bit too young to know about how big companies financially and otherwise support charities. That summer WTAE-TV Pittsburgh was encouraging kids to have backyard carnivals to raise money to support research for Muscular Dystrophy. It was the same year of New York's World's Fair, so I felt my Baldwin Borough neighborhood needed its own World's Fair. Yep, I was thinking big. (I tried and failed to build a New York-like small-scale Unisphere, but that's another story.)

Without hesitation I called Ma Bell's operator for the telephone number to H.J. Heinz Company. My young voice was transferred to a woman whom I asked if she could "spare," for my carnival's Hot Dog Stand, any extra bottles she might have of Heinz Ketchup. I was on a mission.

Not only did she spare a large box of several hundred little packets of Heinz Ketchup, but I also found in the package (without my asking) Heinz Mustard, and Heinz Relish — plus hundreds of little green Heinz 57 Pickle lapel pins and paper napkins. Wow!

The nice lady voluntarily gave me names of people at a bakery and a meat packing company who might be able to spare some "extra" buns and wieners. I called and asked, and the other companies also spared more than we were able to sell to the 105 people who paid the five-cent price we set for a carnival entrance fee. All I had to say was the nice lady's name from Heinz, and spare food came our way. Double Wow!

In addition to remembering a painful week recovering after bad sunburn from that long sunny day managing our carnival, I recall learning how Heinz Ketchup put a smile on a lot of faces. To anyone who would listen, for a long time I told my innocent story about all the genuine helpfulness of the Heinz lady (whose good name I wish I could remember). Because of her and her great company, I decided I would never touch Hunt's Catsup. And since Hunt's did not even know how to spell the word Ketchup, Hunt's watery red stuff can't be any good anyway. Yes, I was a highly opinionated teenager. Suddenly I was on a mission to protect Heinz Ketchup's brand.

Occasionally I think and talk about the above early lessons in corporate support for worthy charities. Several years later, my first real mission-based job was as a teenage fund raiser for Junior Achievement (JA). H.J. Heinz was one of our largest cash contributors, and they provided a steady stream of executive-level mentors to work with students running the mock JA corporations formed to teach real-world entrepreneurship and Economics 101 to a percentage of over 5,000 high school kids in our Southwestern Pennsylvania JA program. Search online to learn more about JA.

If you have time to do so, please go back and scan this book's Table of Contents, and perhaps read again a prior chapter you recall having special resonance for reminding you about an early mission, or enlarging or otherwise enriching your life's up-to-date vision and mission.

Thank you for including in any vision and mission all or some of the significance you discern in key words explored within these pages. It takes abundant wisdom, courage and patience to align your past, present and future statements of vision and mission.

Mission. Expound.

Momentum

Chapter Inspired by and Dedicated to Andrew Mason

Insert or imagine seeing your first name: _____,

Seeing this chapter's title word, what immediately comes to your open mind? Do you already have a working relationship with this word? Somewhere inside of you does this word instantly appeal? As a response to a specific situation at-hand, will this word work to your and others' advantage? For this word to increase in real value, together we must dig, drill and think deeper, so we will reach, climb and soar higher.

Momentum is an impelling force or strength creating velocity. Fully responsible leaders live, breathe and thrive with this mighty word. Momentum deeply understood is enlightening, energizing, and otherwise uniquely empowering. Goethe also said, "The moment one definitely commits oneself, then Providence moves too. All sorts of things occur to help one that would never otherwise have occurred." Observing momentum, one sees Providence move in mysterious ways.

In physics, momentum refers to the quantity of motion an object has attained. An object in motion has momentum. There is mathematical power in momentum. A quadrupling in velocity crates a quadrupling of momentum. As a plan for high-impact performance, I like this algebraic equation. A person or team on the move has momentum. A leader's mastery of increasing and decreasing momentum creates light and might.

How do you masterfully gain and sustain momentum in your life? With intentionality, what do you do to accelerate your mind's velocity? How do you measure and value such speed? How do you react when you or someone else puts up a roadblock or sends you in a wrong direction? To keep up mission-critical momentum, how facile are you in reading signals, mapping detours, charting alternate routes, building bridges, paving pathways, or walking on slippery tightropes or hot coals? How and when do you slam on the emergency brakes? Obstacles navigated exceptionally well can markedly accelerate momentum.

Yet speed only for the sake of increasing momentum is not always in your or anyone else's best interest. Standing still in your thoughts is in no one's best interest. For the lift, thrust, drag and weight of flight to new heights, fully responsible leaders never stop learning how to build, calibrate, and regulate momentum. Lift requires power; the power of momentum.

Do you learn at the speed of instruction? Life's lessons in momentum management can come in hard and unexpected ways.

Ten or so years ago, while flying low on an Interstate in southern-most Virginia, I was accelerating to pass what I considered a slow-moving vehicle. The intervening police officer asked me if I knew I was traveling well over 100 miles per hour. In this situation, I did not.

Strategically, if not exactly ethically, I appeared in court in hopes of negotiating a lesser punishment than the ill-tempered trooper chose for my infraction. A kindly judge looked at my then perfect driving record, asked me what happened, and I told him truth, "German cars have minds of their own, and I was not using mine." In a few ways the judge smiled.

Justice declared, "Equipment failure. Case dismissed," thus dropping charges. Gratefully and sheepishly I whispered, "Thank you, your honor." With chilling *gravitas* he covered the microphone and whispered, "Be careful with that fancy car, Mr. Dallas." I got his point.

The downstate judge realized a lasting lesson in managing this city slicker's momentum was not going to be delivered by dollars fined or points assigned. Although I was both relived and suffused with shame, for the court's record Stuttgart's engineers took the blame. I knew the culprit was my life's normal full-speed-ahead momentum, my "Top Gun" need for speed.

All the way to Washington, D.C., feeling more than a bit unworthy, I drove only five miles over the speed limit (while being passed by 80 percent of vehicles traveling north). Those four hours seemed like four days. I had a lot of time to think about roles of momentum in my life. Since then I apply restraint to pressing anyone or anything — "simply to press." When I must, I will pull — pulling to not push.

Getting started with a thought or deed is ignition of momentum. Moving forward with thoughts and related actions is momentum. Even stopping for the right reasons to take measurements or correct course is momentum.

In medicine, momentum for a particular type of therapy or diagnostic modality gains nearly mysterious providential momentum through a phenomenon called, "Enthusiasm Hypothesis." This is a posit that attempts to explain the tendency of physicians — mostly in a geographic region — to become openly enamored with something of considerable value thought worthy of recognition and rapid general acceptance.

Unbridled enthusiasm of influencers and practitioners accelerates momentum. For studying technology adoption cycles, Silicon Valley would be an ideal site for a case study for how medicine's Enthusiasm Hypothesis builds and decreases momentum.

Accepting the axiom "change is ceaseless," fully responsible leaders know how to build and sustain momentum in contemplation and implementation. Do you enthusiastically and passionately build your and others' momentum by increasing wisdom, courage and patience?

Fellow Pittsburgh native Andrew Mason is a cofounder and CEO of Chicago-based Groupon. Shortly after launch, his online coupons-everyday business was dubbed by *Forbes* the fastest growing company in history. Three days later I interviewed Andrew. That's momentum.

Within three years of launch, Groupon's 4 November 2011 Initial Public Offering (IPO) exceeded expectations — by the close of its first day of trading. Expectably, many critics come out of the woodwork to find and assign fault. I remain bullish about Groupon.

Writing and dedicating this chapter, I wholeheartedly celebrate Andrew Mason and his ever-clever team's momentum. I always look forward to seeing Andrew in-motion. He *is* momentum personified.

Accelerating your momentum, however, is this chapter's worthy goal.

"Begin it now." —Goethe

Momentum. Expound.

Passion

Chapter Inspired by and Dedicated to the
Reverend Dr. Joanna M. Adams

Insert or imagine seeing your first name: _____,

Seeing this chapter's title word, what immediately comes to your open mind? Do you already have a working relationship with this word? Somewhere inside of you does this word instantly appeal? As a response to a specific situation at-hand, will this word work to your and others' advantage? For this word to increase in real value, together we must dig, drill and think deeper, so we will reach, climb and soar higher.

Passion? During a 1999 make-it-or-break-it meeting in Manhattan, eventually I asked a troublesome client of Chicago Title Credit where he found passion in his work. He was so dull I was driven to ask. Paradoxically my question elicited a type of passion I was not expecting to witness. In front of one of my vice presidents of sales, he barked, "Passion? Passion? What a whacked thing for one man to ask another man. I have passion for my wife. I have passion for the Yankees. My work? Passion? What kind of question is that for any man to ask another man?" I was unprepared. I saw in the word no threat to his manhood.

The passionphobic client was owner/manager of many multi-unit residential rental properties in Queens and Brooklyn. This rough-around-the-edges landlord (slumlord?) was suspected of violating FTC permissible purpose (*i.e.,* need-to-know) rules related to protecting privacy of consumer credit data. As CEO of Chicago Title Credit, then the nation's leading aggregator and reseller to lenders of credit data from the Big Three bureaus, in-person I was sitting at his desk to decide if I would allow him to continue to do business with my highly ethical company. He knew why I was there. Over one decade later, I remember his face contorting at the sound of the word "passion." I was startled. He also said it was the most stupid question he had ever been asked in any meeting. He soon discovered the sting of my passion for protecting the privacy of U.S. consumers' data.

Evidence of his obviously low EQ (for emotional intelligence) tracked with earlier reports of his many infractions with people and things. In conversationally asking about passion for his work I was genuinely trying to discern character strength. To reverse my predisposition we needed to have grounded discussion about his trustworthiness and related FTC regulatory compliance. Eventually I accepted this odd fellow had no intention of playing by strict rules.

Handing him a prepared letter, formally I notified him we immediately stopped serving his sizable account. He told me to go straight to hell. Instead, I alerted the FTC and all our competitors about my decision. It was the ethical thing for me to do. I thought it would be impossible for him to find anyone willing to do business his way. I marveled at the identity of the one greed-over-creed supplier that looked the other way; a company I would grow to know very well in months to come. There's always hope for redemption. He may have learned a lesson or two in corporate ethics. I told him passion is not a four-letter word. "STOP" is. We stopped serving his account.

Passion identified is value qualified. From *Hebrews 12:1-3*, best-selling author John Maxwell interprets Biblical imperatives for leaders to "Run with passion, purpose and perspective." Faiths and philosophies call forth passion for what we think and do. Fully responsible leaders engage others in passion they have for their true-north destinations. Proclaimed passion paves bridges and pathways. Unclaimed passion increases risk of misalignment.

Take passion out of spectator sports, and even the great Pittsburgh Steelers would suffer. Take passion out of medicine, education, law, governance, art, leadership, personal relationships, parenting, or other pursuits and what remains would not be enough. Any passionless pursuit may be worth reconsidering. I am blessed to be surrounded by passionate pals aging in every decade from teens to their 80s. Yes, a passionate life is abundant, and age-agnostic. I note with interest the intensity of passion for work in earlier and later years of careers, while middle years seem to be subject to less intensity. My suspicions about reasons are beyond the purpose of this chapter.

As this book goes to press, accomplished actor Doug Pemberton is at The University of Syracuse, New York. He'll also study in London. When he was 14, I was assigned to Doug as his one-*with*-one Elder Mentor for the Confirmation Class at Fourth Presbyterian Church. He, his family, and I became friends. Because of his passion for living an authentic and highly productive life, I hope to support Doug's emergence in any mentoring way I possibly can. Even without a spotlight shining on him, he's a star.

Doug's passion for living drives him to succeed. His is wildly popular with peers and adults. More than anyone else among over 700 individuals on Facebook, people I know personally from face-to-face meetings, Doug's Facebook wall posts contain the most words of affirmation and other online applause. With his over 1,000 Facebook pals, he's a star – because of his authenticity and passion for people.

Doug's youthful passion touches my soul. We agreed to be pals for life. I know Doug's parents, siblings, maternal grandmother, uncles and other family. We all connect through Doug's passion of living.

*"Put people first, put people second, put people third.
Profit of many types follows focus on people, people, people."* —JRDjr

Peter Koestenbaum, Ph.D. lives a life fueled by his passion for today's people and their descendants, set against the backdrop of Peter's studies of 4,000-plus years of leadership philosophy. His books, lectures, leadership models, and "Weekly Leadership Thoughts" reflect the life's work of a scholar with a brilliant brain and a warm heart. Any student, colleague or friend of Peter's would point toward purposeful passion in all that he thinks, says and does.

Wife Patty Koestenbaum shares in the passion of Peter's calling to imbue each person he touches with new depth about every significant topic he reveals for investigation and discussion. I am grateful beyond measure for his steady stream of expression of passion for me as a person, and for my life's humble work. He is not one to withhold from another human his genuinely affirming and passionate thoughts and words. Peter's forever-young passion touches my being.

In the Acknowledgment section of this book, you see names of revered individuals I hold in high esteem. Each person is passionate in ways that I admire. And I also thrive on each person's compassion.

Passion and Anger are Strange Bedfellows

Anger unleashed from someone who deeply cares about or craves performance, usually comes after prolonged periods of gut-wrenching patience and silence. Too often fearing anger of passionate leaders stymies personal and organizational growth. Anger, therefore, should be redirected toward less toxic responses to others' egocentricity, ineptitude, immaturity, disrespect, or ignorance. Risks are real when causes and effects are ignored related to on-the-job or at-home anger.

Watching unbridled expressions of anger, in the stands of stadia and at sports bars, is an amazing study in how people re-direct anger that actually relates to someone or something else altogether. Long ago a few times I asked, "Are you really that worked-up and angry about this player's fumble, *etc.*?" As I asked, occasionally I actually feared for my immediate safety. Wisely, I no longer ask why someone is fuming with anger and rage about a lost ballgame. Now I can guess about what's really going on. Only occasionally my guess will be correct.

For better or worse, in post-World War II days I was trained for leadership roles among command-and-control types of autocratic — yet passionate — leaders who would release their anger mostly when the other person was "worth it." More or less I learned how to translate such drill-sergeant anger. I did not like it at all when a boss or client would "explode." Too often, in more ways than one, I got it.

Yet lack of anger often signaled the leader had written-off the other person as unworthy. My dad convinced me he was angry because he loved me, and he expected more from me than he ever expected of himself. When I was being physically punished, Dad would say, "This hurts me more than it hurts you." He was hurting himself. In my mid-30s I concluded Dad's anger was mostly directed toward himself.

Eventually the great success of Apple's passionate *l'enfant terrible* Steve Jobs allowed others to weather the internal storms caused by his outbursts of creative fury. Among too many CEOs of companies I served I saw this syndrome. Now I am certain anger management classes should be offered to all team leaders. And understanding anger's upside is essential for fully responsible leaders. There is value in navigating anger felt within you, and some anger unleashed by others. I am enrolled in a program to study childhood roots of anger.

For whom and for what do you feel passion? Make a list of the top five or 10 most passionate people in your circle, and see if you can arrange to spend more win-win time with them. Do you have passion for your work? If your answer is no, dare I suggest you reconsider your choice of jobs? Passion and performance walk hand-in-hand.

Mel Gibson's *Passion of the Christ* is a 2004 award-winning film I've not yet seen. Did you? At a last minute on a busy day, I was invited by a friend to meet Mel Gibson and participate with him and three others in a private screening of *Passion*, I was already retained to speak to a group of executives I could not and would not offend with a change in plans. I so wanted to be with Mel Gibson to hear from the artist's mouth what else he could possibly say about a movie that was believed by some to be nearly indescribable. I had read pro and con reviews, heard my pastors talk from our pulpit about the conflict they felt related to the film, and generally sensed enough in the buzz to realize I would be overwhelmed, and possibly physically sickened, by the characterizations and illustrations of passion run amuck.

Months earlier I survived a hemorrhaging cerebral aneurysm and subsequent stroke. Still recovering in 2012 and perhaps for a long lifetime ahead, I remain wise to protect myself against likely stress. Privately (until now), I decided I need not see on-screen the gore of Christ's blood to affirm or intensify my faith. The empty-cross symbols of my Church of Scotland-based tradition emphasize "Christ risen," not "Christ crucified." Some churches and schools are filled with countless crosses with a tortured, bleeding, and nearly naked broken body — *i.e.,* death almost always in full view of worshipers and other students. Deeply rooted is my alive-and-well view of faith.

Now nearly fully recovered from the 2003 ordeal, someday I may rent the DVD. I will probably regret the years I waited to encounter Mr. Gibson's literary license with depicting passion. Until then I need not imagine the literally gut-wrenching exhibition of passion.

With these few vignettes about my encounters with passion, your passionate author hopes to elicit within you passion for the HILL Word itself — passion. Think it. Feel it. Use it. Perfect it. Project it.

In ways far beyond expectation, for the rest of your life you will profit from your deeper, wider and higher relationship with passion. From deep within your authentic self, let purposeful passion flow.

"Only as well as you know yourself can your brain serve you as a sharp and efficient tool. Know your own failings, passions, and prejudices so you can separate them from what you see." —Bernard M. Baruch

Fully responsible leaders identify, cultivate, protect and project their passion for people. Enthusiastically preserve your purposeful passion. Your passion ignites and fuels strategic alignment of fired-up people.

Perhaps new-found passion for featured words and overall value in this book brought you to this page. Passion may be motivating you to read straight through Exhibits. Passion drives me to care about your immediate and sustainable benefits derived from this reading journey.

"A memory of passion that refuses to give in, a vision not eroded by present tense satiation, these are the stuff of faith. Do you know what happens to people who remember in resistance and who vision uneroded? They live differently in the present. They do not accept the dominant values and the daily bribe of the rulers of this age. They enter the present with a different identity, a different purpose, a different calling, determined to love a different loyalty, even when that puts us at risk. Faith is not for conformists. Faith is for those who received life and who say "no" to the terrible power of fear. Faith is flinging the memory against satiation in the present. Faith is flinging the vision against present tense eschatology too much realized." —Walter Brueggemann

Passion is faith: faith in self, faith in others, faith in process, and faith in higher power called by any name that takes us beyond this realm. Perceive, project, profess and protect your heart's purposeful passion.

Seize, translate, and maximize value from your feelings of passion. In your personal and professional activities, do what you can and should to allow your passion to produce favorable results for others and yourself. Use the word. Use the feelings. Use new understanding that will be derived from examining roots of your passion. Be passionate.

You may want to use white space in this book to list a random sampling of people and things you value, and for whom and which you express passion. Passion for your beloved deserves extra effort. From altruistic passion for helping unknown souls of faraway lands who are suffering from malnutrition, to escapist passion for The Pittsburgh Steelers *et al*, monitor the full range of feelings you have that you would characterize as passion. Honor and feed your passion.

Passion. Expound.

Patience

Chapter Inspired by and Dedicated to Ernest U. Buckman (1926-2002)

Insert or imagine seeing your first name: _____,

Seeing this chapter's title word, what immediately comes to your open mind? Do you already have a working relationship with this word? Somewhere inside of you does this word instantly appeal? As a response to a specific situation at-hand, will this word work to your and others' advantage? For this word to increase in real value, together we must dig, drill and think deeper, so we will reach, climb and soar higher.

> *"Patience is the companion of wisdom."* —Saint Augustine

Dictionary snapshot for definitions: Capacity for waiting: the ability to endure waiting, delay, or provocation without becoming annoyed or upset, or to persevere calmly when faced with difficulties. Thesaurus snapshot for synonyms: Endurance, staying power, stamina, persistence, perseverance, tolerance, forbearance, imperturbability, fortitude, unflappability, serenity, placidity.

Panoramic view from The HILL: Abundant patience was required for President Obama to navigate the choppy waters of his high-seas voyage to The White House. Many icebergs failed to dent or sink his ship. At the helm it took masterful precision, perseverance and patience. For presidents and other leaders of nations, companies, or any type of organization, patience is essential for fully responsible leadership.

As the Obama Administration is already strategically aligning information, interests and resources for a rhetoric-wary world, this date may begin what someday may be called "The Age of Alignment." Yes, for such a sweeping grand view from The HILL to become reality, patience is required. Let's give every new President the gift of patience.

The overdue correction economy ahead of us requires perhaps unprecedented types of independent and collaborative patience with people, property and process. When we are alone in our thoughts or at table with colleagues, it takes patience to think differently about people, money and other mission-critical resources. Fully responsible leaders must intentionally pursue, achieve and measure strategic alignment of thinking and action. It takes patience.

"How poor are they who have not patience!
What wound did ever heal but by degrees?" —William Shakespeare

President Obama is asking each of us to think outside the box — and Hillview encourages fully responsible leaders to "think through the blocks." Patience is required. Patience with self comes first. Patience with others follows. Patience with process is next. Yet patience with inherent mystery of faith seems to test us most. Faith and patience do not come easily. Does your faith yield greater patience with self, other people, process, things, and other matters? Patience with self. Patience with others. Patience with process. Patience with providence.

Patience with Technology

Technology tries our patience. Mere seconds waiting for Internet pages to load on our monitors push our patience buttons. Patience is stretched when better parts of allocated hours are consumed for defragmenting our tens of thousands of computer files and related data. Even by the fourth ring before a telephone answering system asks for a message, we grow impatient.

Expectation of technological instantaneity seems to increase our predilection for psychological impatience. How impatient are you when seated at a monitor compared to when holding a book? The mere tactile sense of having a firm grasp on a hardback book may actually allow you to develop and sustain more patience. We don't worry about a book crashing or its batteries failing.

Twitter and blogs remind me of my youth when telephones were connected to single "party lines" with multiple homes (with different phone numbers). Neighbors were able to eavesdrop on each others' conversations (and we kids did). Unscrupulous AT&T ("Ma Bell") operators were known to secretly "check" connections for their personal amusement or other purposes. Politicians and policing authorities found ways to "telesnoop."

Unleashed impatience with neighbors who "hogged" party lines was dealt with in rather unpleasant ways. When a telephone was in-use by a neighbor for too long, choices included "banging down the receiver" back into its cradle, yelling expletives and threats, complaining to Ma Bell's operator, and sometimes even calling the police. Telephony and other new technology increased impatience.

In early years of telephones there were many who would not use their home phones for anything but emergencies. Cost and fear of "spies" were stated as reasons to avoid picking-up the "receiver" (*i.e.*, handset). Early-adopter I had no such reservations, of course. Recently I realized I stopped talking on the telephone as much as I "text." I confess to being too impatient with most telephone conversations. Customer service representatives usually work my last nerve. Now to address a need from a vendor, instead of talk on the telephone I would rather send an e-mail or "chat" with text. Impatient I am. I'm considering starting an online 12-step program for Humans Impatient with Technology (HIT).

With Twitter, Facebook posts, blogs, and Foursquare-like apps, almost everyone is invited to "listen-in" on today's global party line. Privacy of many types is going to grow very difficult to protect. Erosion of any sense of privacy is contributing to our growing impatience.

Many U.S. citizens believe privacy is a Constitutional right. It is not. The U.S. Constitution does not guarantee our right to privacy. Years ago JFK's daughter Caroline Kennedy wrote a book exposing the myth of privacy's importance to our Founding Fathers and Mothers. Our "Founding Parents" did not trust themselves -- or U.S. and "foreigner" kids for generations to come. Facebook's founder probably has a copy of Caroline's book. His lawyers must.

Patience, however, is found embedded between each word in the Constitution and other such documents. Imagine the patience of the earlier scribes for the Bible and other holy constitutions. Imagine the patience those original drafters applied to trying to write *le mot juste*. Shamefully too many of us busy readers are impatient with words borne of abundant patience of authors.

In years gone by I would allocate one hour or so each day to apply patience as I used my hard-earned Peterson System cursive handwriting skills, and U.S. postage stamps, to keep in touch with others. Now Facebook, Twitter, LinkedIn, FourSquare, and other cyber-writing tools for messages are my choice by default. If only one other person finds value in whatever I share *via* cyberspace, I'm okay with that fact. I no longer have the luxury of patience with what is required for handwritten communication. Yet patience is a necessity with my daily avalanche of e-mail, and with inadequate spam filters.

Patience by the People, for the People

You may be able to protect your patience more easily than you'll be able to protect your privacy. Don't think of these terms as unrelated or mutually exclusive. The more impatient we are with technology I suspect we compromise more of our privacy. This theory deserves its own book.

"Adopt the pace of nature: her secret is patience." —Ralph Waldo Emerson

As extended patience produces results, some passages in this volume are crafted to try your patience a tad. No words were written to offend or irritate, of course. In reading and otherwise experiencing this narrative, there are moments that are likely to require overcoming impatience. Ongoing effort to build and occasionally test your patience should pay dividends.

If you discover you have little patience with this very chapter about patience, I commend to you an A&Ox4 type of challenge. Go back to Content, and try to recall earlier chapters with which you may not have had much patience.

Words, thoughts and feelings compete for your attention. Perhaps test new levels of patience by re-reading chapters with which you may have had little or no patience. Allow patience specific blocks of time.

As you are reading, perhaps try experimenting with setting an automatic timer on your computer, tablet, smart phone, wristwatch, kitchen timer, or other device. See when impatience rears its head.

With extra commitment, please strive to be more patient. It will not be difficult to accept the need for adding to your life more patience.

"You must first have a lot of patience to
learn to have patience." —Stanislaw J. Lec

Patience. Expound.

Peace

Chapter Inspired by and Dedicated to John R. Dallas (1921-2001)

Insert or imagine seeing your first name: _____,

Seeing this chapter's title word, what immediately comes to your open mind? Do you already have a working relationship with this word? Somewhere inside of you does this word instantly appeal? As a response to a specific situation at-hand, will this word work to your and others' advantage? For this word to increase in real value, together we must dig, drill and think deeper, so we will reach, climb and soar higher.

"Go in Peace."

At age 29 my heart stopped. To arrest your attention to the life-defining, life-giving, and life-saving importance of peace, dramatically I reveal my 1979 cardiac arrest. As my body's blood flow was cut-off by a stopped heart, the 1950 model brain's electrical system started to short-circuit, sputter, and shut down. Final cerebral synapses allowed me to leave my body behind. I was very aware I was instantly one with something other than whatever I knew to that point or since. I was at peace with whatever it was. Precisely where I was, exactly with whom, and concluding why, were not yet concerns I registered in the instantaneity of this electronically altered state. To say otherwise would be fiction and conjecture. What I experienced was real. A startling sense of peace is what I recall the most — deep peace.

Rarely do I disclose these facts. Until drafting this chapter, I don't recall doing so in public writing or speaking. Why now? Enough time has passed for me to have sufficient and selfless distance and perspective. I'm sure of applicability of my story in underscoring key roles of peace in your life. Understanding more about peace was one of many favorable outcomes of my near-death experience.

In the Vatican, The White House, 10 Downing Street, and other symbolic homes of the powerful — and in dorm rooms, first apartments, mansions, and other types of residences — servant leaders of organizations and households must find for themselves real peace, and never stop trying for more. Today I'm certain the absence of deeper understanding about inner peace is a glaring and clamoring void in our global culture that contributes to meltdowns of meaningfulness, marriages, money and more. Worthy and vital relationships of all types suffer when one or more of the persons involved can't adequately define, describe or exemplify attributes of choosing a lifetime in constant pursuit of peace for and in their minds, bodies and souls. In-house, local and world leaders must work to strategically align with other people their pursuit of inner peace.

Through fully responsible leadership's clear thinking, choice of words, and other intentionality, we each can see — and treat in new and peaceful ways — the whole world and its people. Lead in peace.

With ever-emerging clarity I see value for all who pause to listen with a third ear to quite specific highlights of my humble-servant journey's major milestones toward peace. From teen years onward I chose specific words as my life's milestones; understanding and applying, to the best of my ability, meanings, majesty, mystery and miracle of words. Quite literal physical discomfort for me accompanies today's thinking and final drafting process for exploring peace. Here I push through it to share several illuminating insights that may allow you and yours to avoid certain pain and achieve extra gain.

Fully responsible leaders must always pursue deep levels of internal peace. The pursuit alone is a stabilizing force when faced with stormy seas. Doing something — anything — to "keep the peace" is not enough unto itself. "For the sake of family peace" was for many of us a childhood home-life reminder to remember to walk on eggshells, keep our mouths shut, hide truth, fake-it, or otherwise keep someone from overreacting to uncertain perception or certain reality. Phony peace is just that. Peace for the sake of peace is likely to be temporary absence of conflict. Absence of conflict in certain countries hardly heralds peace. The higher purpose for pursuing peace is bigger than the word's dictionary definition.

"Never, 'for the sake of peace and quiet,'
deny your own experience or convictions." —Dag Hammarskjold

The moment I endured the cardiac arrest, suddenly I was looking down on the whole world with an optical perspective I never before thought of or dreamed about; surprised by seeing the world below me as a concave saucer — of all things. Imagine that view. Can you imagine the magnitude of seeing in this way the whole globe? Looking down I was very clear on what I was seeing, yet slightly disbelieving. Looking in front of me, swiftly swirling and sparkling white masses — not cloud-like; more like fiberglass angel hair used for decorating Christmas trees — were framing friendly yet faceless persons who were clearly reaching out to me. In this state of my brain's electrical struggle for a dying-wish explanation for what I was seeing and feeling, quite matter-of-factly I whispered to my inner-self, rather calmly, peacefully, and without a sniffle or tear of regret,

"Oh. Wow. I died."

That was that. I felt deep peace, but curiously so. Next came, "Well, look at that! Earth is a concave saucer. A surprise. Who are those people? They know me. Why can't I see their faces? I wonder…"

BAM! My eyes popped open and I was back on Earth. Milliseconds before, perhaps I was about to look up, or directly ask myself if I had yet landed at Heaven's Gates. I sensed I was *en route* somewhere that I never imagined quite this way.

The second-chance at life started with my noticing expressions on the attending strangers' faces. I saw them appearing both relieved and terrified; a twisted combination of expressions I would not see again until October 2003. They and I sensed my calm. I had seen what I now thought was the other side, and it was intoxicatingly peaceful. This Code Blue hospital room scene wasn't. I may not have been immediately grateful for their interruption of my discovery of deep peace, at least not right away. Fortunately for all, I did not share my mind's muddle. I was still in a state of re-entry into Earth's atmosphere. I did not say, "Let me go back to peace."

The peacefulness of the so-called out-of-body experience was in sharp relief to the prior 10 or more months of staggering career and personal demands on my young mind, body and soul. Among many sad happenings that watershed year, on 11 July my cherished friend and mentor, Lyman C. Hamilton, Jr., was unfairly and very publicly fired from a CEO post in one of the Top 10 companies in the world, now defunct International Telephone and Telegraph Company (ITT). Lyman was my rock. Psychologically I did not bounce-back as quickly as he did from his unwarranted fall from highest power. Today I think of his being fired as a tipping point in my life. I started to fight harder. I made many mistakes because of mind-numbing fear of falling prey to sharks and vultures, as Lyman did. I did too. Witnessing his positive approach to it all, I learned lessons I hoped never to need. In downward spirals, I need and heed Lyman's many and varied lessons about "not letting the turkeys get you down."

Just under three months after receiving the telegram about Lyman's undue departure from our all-consuming ITT, on 2 October I walked out of what would become known in divorce papers as "the marital residence." Then November was another make-it-or-break-it cash flow deficiency month threatening my incurably seasonal company's survival. After a difficult Thanksgiving, I was stricken with a silencing strep throat infection. The company survives to this day. I almost did not.

Clearly not a poet, it is still rather eerie for me to see a poem I wrote within a month or so of moving for eight months into my temporary bachelor quarters; nightly coming home alone to one of 180 sleeping rooms at The New York Athletic Club on Central Park South:

"This is the end of my beginning. Clearly the stop of my start. Just as I thought I was winning, the pounding stopped in my heart. The pounding stopped in my heart. Start!"

The 29-year-old's eerily prescient words still haunt me. Within a day or so of writing them, I set the simple prose to a funereal tune I concocted to sing to myself (thankfully). I would end with a dramatic spoken and not sung, "Start!" Sharing this with you I reclassify this secret as one of my life's most unsettling experiences with my inner journey toward peace. I can still sing the exact tune, and feel the pain and promise of the lyrics I wrote. I doubt I'll share with anyone the stately music behind this message. When I die I would not be surprised if the tune plays in my head. And with "Start!" I suppose I will still be trying to beat the odds of mortality. It worked before.

Around 10:30 A.M. 13 December 1979 I got out of a taxi and walked into a New York City emergency room claiming I was having a heart attack. "No doubt about it," said I. Pain in the left arm, chest, shoulder, and back all felt for me like warning signs for which we were taught to watch. At 2:00 P.M. or so, the ER doctors told me to take the rest of the day off from work, go home, and relax. All my blood work and EKG showed the specialists a strong heart inside of me. I was not having heart problems, said they. Healthy I was at 29. Over-the-counter Di-Gel was prescribed for what they patronizingly called "heartburn." I knew better. This pain was 8, 9, and maybe occasionally even a 10 on today's pain rating scale. With typical resolve, I hunkered-down and nearly fought to stay there in the ER for more tests. The pain escalated and my agitation increased. I became delusional with pain, I later learned. A sympathetic triage nurse continued to try to reach my super-busy personal physician, a top Park Avenue internist on the hospital's teaching staff, the late Leonard E. Ancona, M.D., who was also a personal friend. Finally she found Lenny enjoying a rare weekday off. He was out-of-state and could not get back to New York until early the next morning. Later I learned instantly he dropped everything and was on his way.

Pain increased at an alarming rate. Nothing changed in my subsequent tests. On paper my heart and I looked healthy. Until *via* telephone the ER learned from my personal physician that I was to be treated with utmost VIP care, mostly because of my access to Manhattan's top legal counsel, they were going to send me home. I still shudder at the thought. Six months after the fact, I learned about Dr. Lenny's regrettable yet essential ploy to get ER to focus more. As they waited for a cardiac care unit bed to become available, a full-house kept me on a rolling cart in the hallway for 10 or more grueling hours. I had grown delirious with pain, and pain killers were not working. Now (finally) everyone was worried. My estranged wife would not come to the ER. I said no when many staff members showed up. I was better off alone. I was a mess, inside and out. I was unaware my office had summoned from Pittsburgh Mom, Dad, Grandmother Shearer, Sister Judy, and Sister Shirlee. They were on the Pennsylvania Turnpike, nervously on their way to New York City.

Only four or so hours after the cardiac arrest, a hospital stenographer asked if she could collect my recollections while I was "out," if any. The hospital was gathering so-called data about all near-death experiences. Of course I would tell what I could recall. She appeared transfixed by the report of deep colors I recalled of deep peace. The unexpected optical dimensions of the concave (*i.e.*, deeply indented) sphere intrigued her as well. The hospital's transcript I later approved reflects I saw vivid sights, and reported having been transported to an unknown and then unnamed paranormal dimension. Several times I mentioned to the transcriptionist the deep peace I experienced while "above it all," deep peace I still can feel — over three decades later.

What I experienced while my heart was stopped did not track with anything I had read or heard. There was no light at the end of any tunnel. Long-dead relatives and friends were not yet rushing to welcome me. God and his entourage were not yet in view, at least I did not think so. In size it was all so much bigger than that. Imagine. I always expect safe passage to a higher realm, but this diorama was better than what I saw earlier that same year while flying Mach II, at 57,000 feet, while enjoying a supersonic transport Concorde flight on earthly British Airways. With slight darkness of space in view outside my small window, to my delight I saw the curvature of the earth. It was not concave. Two years later, a Concorde flight on Air France rekindled both indelible memories of convex and concave Earth.

How could I ever forget what my brain experienced while the heart and I were flat-lined? Peace came to me, undeniable deep peace. For sure I knew I was warmly enveloped in explicable, ethereal, spiritual, and metaphysical peace. Yes, I wanted more of it, and certainly not less. Forever I have a benchmark against which to measure peace.

When my heart was re-started by courageous first-responder Lynn Glickman, R.N., on what I would learn was her very first night on-duty in the Coronary Intensive Care Unit of Park Avenue's Lenox Hill Hospital, I was not exactly thrilled. Eventually I was grateful, to be sure, but not really happy about it all. The peace in my near-death moments was replaced with organized chaos around my bed. For many minutes I was frozen in-time, only somewhat satisfied I was alert and alive, but wholly dissatisfied the deep peace was gone.

Deep peace for me was not destined to last. Within seconds of my heart starting to beat again, and upon opening my eyes, a physician barked, "Sir, do you know where you are?" I knew I was "at 77th and Park," and said so. He told me he only needed to know I was aware of being in hospital, not the Manhattan-style street address. Probably I laughed a little. I'm certain he did not. My New York sense of humor was intact. Thankfully his was on-hold. He then followed A&Ox4 (pronounced A and O times four) ER triage protocol, asking if I was Alert and Oriented to my (1) name, (2) date, (3) place and (4) why I was where I was. A&Ox4. I knew and said all four answers. "Probably no brain damage," out-loud they rightly and thankfully surmised. Surely I preferred hearing a more delicate proclamation.

Suddenly I realized the suffocating number of people crammed in my very small room. I had just returned from a peaceful psychological and physical sense of no boundaries whatsoever, to a room that was closing-in on me. "Mr. Dallas, you suffered complete cardiac arrest. Your heart stopped. We have no idea what happened. We'll not take our eyes off you until we figure this out." I surmised this attentiveness was a good thing. A temporary pacemaker was installed.

Early the next day two staff doctors told me I may not have more than 36 hours to live, as I suffered what they called massive coronary failure. I was advised to "get my affairs in order." Three attorneys from Skadden, Arps, Slate, Meagher & Flom were summoned to revise my Last Will and Testament. Hours later they returned with a hot-wax red seal to memorialize my signed gift of all I owned to precious daughter Jennifer Gray Dallas, age two. Where was peace?

Two nurses came in to kick-out the "Brooks Brothers Brigade" of attorneys, as later they would be called. The monitors said my heart was racing. Suddenly I thought I did not want my Jennifer to see me this way. So it seemed I knew soon I'd hold her again. I was already on a positive-minded trail to recovery from whatever this was.

Shortly thereafter, my personal physician pal arrived to stop all this nonsense. Without my knowledge, for hours he had been downstairs studying every word and every test, and had very different views of what happened and what would. He was correct. The Chief of Cardiology was wrong. A turf war began in a teaching hospital where my doctor was a professor, and the Chief was his boss. Through a third party I learned Lenny's job was at stake. My life was more important. I was the beneficiary of this stepped-up intellectual medical debate about how all of this could have happened to me.

The very next day two attending doctors in the Coronary Care Unit announced "they" were wrong again. The heart stopped, yes, but fortunately not because of any heart damage before, during or after the cardiac arrest. Thankfully it was not a heart attack. An undetected infection was filling with fluid the pericardial sac around the heart, and eventually the heart was squeezed and stopped. Myopericarditis is inflammation of the muscular wall of the heart and of the enveloping pericardium. They now agreed with my Dr. Ancona. Thanks to angel nurse Glickman, I sustained zero damage to the heart or brain; physically as if it never happened. I am eternally thankful. Even medical insurance companies would discount any significance whatsoever to this set of cardiac circumstances. Peace.

As I write this chapter, I have sitting to my side a photocopy of the paper tape from the machine that shows the flat line. With an elitist cartoon from The New Yorker depicting a CEO patient in hospital too busy with business matters to allow his physician to examine him, my internist gave me the flat line image to frame and hang on my office wall as a reminder of life's preciousness. Lenny autographed the cartoon, not the flat-line. Until now I chose to tuck them away. Someday I may make my way to a framing store.

"If I have been of service, if I have glimpsed more of the nature and essence of ultimate good, if I am inspired to reach wider horizons of thought and action, if I am at peace with myself, it has been a successful day." —Alex Nobel

Now you know I believe fully responsible leaders must grasp a much as possible about the deeper nature of this awe-inspiring word. Peace. And we must acknowledge how many opposing forces are working against deep peace. Without more understanding of deep peace, why would we leaders strive for whatever levels of peace we can facilitate in our organizations, relationships, families, communities, and the world at-large? Perhaps the absence of deeper thought and feelings about deep peace *vs.* relatively shallow peace keeps too many of us from knowing just what it is we're after; why peace is worth pursuing at all. From experience I know it is ahead. Something miraculous happens to the mind, body and soul when *the peace that passeth understanding* flows in. More peace flows out to others. Can you feel it coming your way? Stay at peace. Lead with peace. Go in peace.

On Chicago Marathon Sunday of 2003, I was not planning to be out there running 26.2 miles. That date sudden hemorrhaging from a ruptured cerebral aneurysm was eventually stopped by a then somewhat new platinum coiling surgical procedure within my brain. Against considerable odds, I survived. Then 72 hours later I succumbed to a related stroke. This time damage was more evident. Vision, speech, mobility, hearing, taste, and numerous other functions were impaired. I was down, but most definitely not out.

With physicians warning of a 60 percent statistical probability of dying over the next 30 days, fortunately I had my 1979 sense of deep peace to sustain me through rehabilitation therapy, psychotherapy, speech therapy, positive thinking, and almost nonstop prayers of adoration, confession, thanksgiving and supplication. I would survive and thrive.

By some medical history standards I have yet to question or measure, I was told I would probably only recover 80 percent of prior functionality. Over the year or so to come, I reached what I calculate to be 97 percent recovery. I was aiming for 110 percent. My highly valued internist, Steven K. Rothschild, M.D., remains amazed at my positive attitude's impact on my recovery, and he is still kind to say so. I thank him. He thanks me. We both thank God. Others involved in my ongoing care exclaim when they totally forget I am still experiencing constant pain on the entire right half of my body, and all of the skin on that side has no sense whatsoever of any external temperature. Nearly ten years later, this remaining nonstop discomfort is hidden from view. I use the discomfort as a constant reminder of others' and my blessings, but I confess it can become almost unbearable at times. I am at peace.

The Year the World was Yearning for Any Sustainable Signs of Peace: 1968

As peace is in the eye of the beholder, peace is also defined related to the *Zeitgeist* (*i.e.*, spirit of the era) in which it is defined, described and pursued. The 1960s are known for peace signs. From JFK's 1963 murder, for myself and millions of others I recall no signs of peace.

To this day I believe 1968 was arguably the worst year in modern U.S. history. In February of 1968 I turned 18. In June I would graduate Baldwin High School. The whole summer I'd work at Ligonier Camp and Conference Center. In September I would matriculate at Pittsburgh's Duquesne University. A U.S. military lottery system added risk to my grand plan. Since age four, I am handicapped by total neural deafness in my left ear. My 50 percent hearing loss would eventually disqualify me from serving. I did not want to fight in Viet Nam or in any war. No one I knew could convincingly explain what it was we were doing over there and why. Eventually the Viet Nam conflict proved nearly inexplicable.

That year's Launch of Apollo 8's first U.S. mission to orbit the Moon signaled more than another achievement in the Cold War's Race for Space. Our eyes, minds and hearts quite literally turned upward. We needed to shoot for the Moon to try to jettison our communal feelings of tearful grief, embarrassment, despondency, sadness, helplessness and hopelessness. We were ready for any good news.

On 19 February 1968, for the first time WQED TV's "Mister Rogers Neighborhood" was broadcast nationally. Yet nightly Walter Cronkite brought CBS News reports of mind-numbing accounts of assassinations of leaders, carnage, terrorism, debauchery, drug overdoses of celebrities, riots, civil disobedience, arrests, crime, economic turmoil, and other unrest. No peace. Young and other ages among us were left gasping for breath. Not only believers pleaded with higher powers for explanations and relief. Far away the Viet Nam War raged on. From 1600 Pennsylvania Avenue to Main Street, war on peace was waged within scarred and hurting minds and hearts.

Indeed the year 1968 is U.S. history's *annus mirabilis* and *annus horribilis*. Still it remains difficult for me to acknowledge any of the bright-light wonders of that year, when set against the pitch-darkness of its non-stop horrors. We thought JFK's 1963 assassination was as low as we could go. We were very wrong. The worst was yet to come.

World Peace was, therefore, the nearly paralyzing assigned title of the commencement address I was awarded to give to my Baldwin High School class of 649 distracted teens, juniors, parents, family, faculty and others. Principal Dr. James Weaver decided to put me to yet another thinking and oratorical test. Even today my mother would tell you how one spring day I came home from school, and hurriedly passed through the living room while casually announcing to my parents the day's news of my World Peace speech to come.

Mom says I disappeared into my bedroom, closed the door, and started pounding away on my Royal standard-size (*i.e.*, large and noisy) typewriter. Ten minutes later (parents would say) I emerged with a fleshed-out outline of key points I would use for the talk.

For years Mom and Dad talked about their only son's quick grasp of what had to be said to the 2,000+ people assembled in our football stadium. Yes, I too thought I knew. The Kodak 8-mm film of that speech shows a very determined and unsmiling young man. Forty some years later, I find some peace in writing and speaking about it. While reading this exploration, I trust you are experiencing peace.

In 1968, Viet Nam was heavy on our minds and hearts, and on some boys' induction calendars. So I surprised many when, in my 4 June commencement talk, intentionally I side-stepped the hot topic of war and said, "World peace must first come from within." Boldly I told everyone global peace begins with inner-world peace. Individually (1) knowing at a deeper level who we really are, (2) what we are called to do on planet Earth, (3) when we have to do whatever it is that we are supposed to be doing, (4) where we are likely to be heading, and (5) why all of these questions must matter to us — individually and collectively — would allow deep personal peace a fighting chance.

If we could achieve peace deep within ourselves, peace for the world was possible, preached I. With too many words to this effect, I intoned, "If we create peace within ourselves and in our homes, schools, churches, and local communities, world peace becomes more feasible." I knew I was not alone in needing these and other venues and factors for peace, yet some surely heard my conclusions as evidence of ageless naiveté. Truly I felt I knew what I was doing. Announcing my views about World Peace, I was commencing my adult journey toward inner peace. To underscore for the audience my higher points, I invoked these pithy words of The Bard of Avon:

> *"This above all: to thine own self be true, and it must follow,*
> *as the night the day, thou canst not then be false to any man."*
> —William Shakespeare

The years ahead would not allow me to be as true to myself as I am becoming. I am always getting there. I have regret about not always being able to practice what I preached that 1968 night. Born into Presbyterian tradition of respect for the good-of-the-order, my need for authenticity is occasionally subordinated in priority; bowing to precedence of higher demands. Pastors, teachers, mentors and others taught me why and how they navigate personal truth and public duty.

From teen years onward, knowing, respecting and serving influential c-suite minds, hearts and checkbooks, I learned how *discretion is the better part of valor*. Essentially there is private complexity in each leader's life I am privileged to witness up-close and personally — including my own. Telling full truth carries undue risk. I concluded if personal truth is for the good-of-the-order, I'll tell it. If any personal disclosure risks causing disorder, I honor and protect my privacy.

The world's soul is fused with truths, stories, faiths, politics, economics, affectional desires, physiological needs, yearning for love, doubts, regrets, dreams, and myriad realities of its entire people. Is peace to be found within chaos? The interdependency of *anima mundi* commands of us deeper and higher thinking, feeling and acceptance.

Peace on Earth was denied my father. During formative childhood years, inexplicably his physically healthy parents placed him and three siblings in an orphanage insensitively called The Home for the Friendless. He never recovered. Only on his deathbed did I see, in his startling blue-gray eyes, a glimmer of heavenly peace. After Senior's funeral, I fit together big pieces of the father-and-son peace puzzle.

Reaching through his philosophy of freedom and "bad faith" (*i.e.*, self-deception), Jean-Paul Sartre (1905-1980) taught us how we have unavoidable responsibility to choose our life's course, thus exposing ambiguity we perpetrate on ourselves in order to avoid accepting change. Change is ceaseless. Forever I am a work-in-progress. I'm always getting there. I am developing and adapting to my self-agency, a psychoanalytic term akin to Sartre's point about honoring each individual's unique role in her or his life's course. For ourselves, are we choosing ways and means to envision, achieve and sustain peace?

The Dominion of Dreams Under a Dark Star

A Gaelic Poem by Fiona MacLeod

"Deep peace I breathe into you,
O weariness, here:
O ache, here!
Deep peace, a soft white dove to You;
Deep peace, a quiet rain to you;
Deep peace, an ebbing wave to you!
Deep peace, red wind of the east from you;
Deep peace, grey wind of the west to You;
Deep peace, dark wind of the north from you;
Deep peace, blue wind of the south to you!
Deep peace, pure red of the flame to you;

> Deep peace, pure white of the moon to you;
> Deep peace, pure green of the grass to you;
> Deep peace, pure brown of the earth to you;
> Deep peace, pure grey of the dew to you,
> Deep peace, pure blue of the sky to you!
> Deep peace of the running wave to you,
> Deep peace of the flowing air to you,
> Deep peace of the quiet earth to you,
> Deep peace of the sleeping stones to you!
> Deep peace of the Yellow Shepherd to you,
> Deep peace of the Wandering Shepherdess to you,
> Deep peace of the Flock of Stars to you,
> Deep peace from the Son of Peace to you..."

Christian lyricists further tailored this hauntingly provocative poetry:

> "Deep peace of the running wave to you.
> Deep peace of the flowing air to you.
>
> Deep peace of the quiet earth to you.
> Deep peace of the shining stars to you.
>
> Deep peace of the gentle night to you.
> Moon and stars pour their healing light on you.
>
> Deep peace of Christ, the light of the world to you.
> Deep peace of Christ to you."

Quite interestingly, particularly for students of gender identification issues, Fiona MacLeod was believed to be a Celtic visionary and romantic of the late 19th century. Readers of her time were enchanted by the weaving of myth, vision, folklore, and personal observation she brought forth in prose and poetry. Fiona MacLeod was, in fact, Mr. William Sharp. Mr. Sharp feared publically expressing an inner female nature, and so he chose to use a feminine *nom de plume*. Perhaps his apparent lack of inner-peace yielded depth about the deep peace for which he so privately, painfully and eloquently yearned. Imagine his navigating such day-to-day polarity.

Tom Morgan was the assumed name my late father would occasionally use when he feared using his real name would rob his Junior or himself of peace and quiet. I was amused to note when he would switch over to Tom, especially when registering complaints.

Occasionally someone reveals suspecting John Dallas as a trumped-up stage name. When the 1980s TV hit series *Dallas* featured "J.R.," many people — including actor Larry ("J.R.") Hagman, whom I met in Beverly Hills during a shoot for the TV show — enjoyed noting my 1950 initials and suffix are both "J.R." It was as if I had been branded with a Southfork Ranch branding iron. I love it. With *Dallas* returning to TNT, I guess there will be no peace for the J.R. in me. Great fun ahead!

As a youngster I would use the full name John R. Dallas, Jr. to differentiate myself from my dad. Then, at a tender age, I realized the full name allowed me to be taken more seriously. The formal church of my childhood insisted on using our full names, regardless of age.

What peace is in your name word? Do you seek and find peace in your name? See if you already align your name with peaceful feelings.

Over the three-plus years this book was drafted and painstakingly prepared to go to press, I counted at least 16 deaths among family and friends. Some younger friends lost parents, including startling deaths of a devoted mother of two who died at 48, and a delightful daughter's doting dad who died just before his 50th birthday. Many grandparents were laid to rest. When we celebrate such abundant lives, these souls remain with those who mourn. Peace will come.

Shortly before I started the book, three friends each lost children at 21, 25 and 26 years of age. Daily I pray for an angelic child I love who has a rare genetic disorder that may cut short his precious life. Not a day passes without concern for the well-being of my daughter Jennifer, for whom I pray she always seeks *deep peace of the infinite peace*.

The above adaptation of "Dominion of Dreams" or "Deep Peace" (as the work is often called) soothes many grieving and giving souls. I encourage you to mark these pages for future reference — and just-in-time distribution. With these soothing, soaring, and otherwise salient words, you too may need to comfort someone or yourself. For unsettled people and unsettling events, peace is the word we need.

Thank you pursuing with me *deep peace of the infinite peace*. Fully responsible leaders must never tire *or* retire as they pursue deep peace with and about their past, present and future thoughts or actions.

Peace. Expound.

Perspective

Chapter Inspired by and Dedicated to
Judy Ann (Dallas) Bardy and Shirlee Lyn (Dallas) Heiber

Insert or imagine seeing your first name: _____,

Seeing this chapter's title word, what immediately comes to your open mind? Do you already have a working relationship with this word? Somewhere inside of you does this word instantly appeal? As a response to a specific situation at-hand, will this word work to your and others' advantage? For this word to increase in real value, together we must dig, drill and think deeper, so we will reach, climb and soar higher.

To see what you need to observe in your leadership roles, from what vantage point do you monitor movement of people and things? How far up do you climb in your mind? From intellectual (IQ) and emotional (EQ) heights, you observe movement of resources. How high you climb in your thinking will influence your perspective on who and what you see, and when. The accuracy of your vision — and timeliness of your responsiveness to what you see — depend on the depth of awareness from which you perceive yourself and others. Are you known for drilling deep in order to reach high?

From an intentionally elevated state of mind, you can more efficiently focus all your leader senses. Choosing to stay above it all, so in-peace they can think things through, too many leaders accidentally escape to detached ivory towers of theoretical construct or to mountaintops where they develop a delusional sense of invincibility. Fully responsible leaders know climbing to just-right height — on *hills* in their minds —allows sharper real-world focus and perspective.

More than a few times I say to gracious and patient audiences, "My mind has a wide world of its own. I think with an English accent, experience beauty in French, eat in Italian, analyze in German, laugh with Aussie gusto, tell time with Swiss precision, monitor my pride in both of the languages of Canada, speak Manhattan American, experience the four letters of pain and gain in similar-size Anglo-Saxon terminology, exclaim amazement in Yiddish, dissent with a Scottish brogue, and fervently pray in the language of King James." I enjoy my life's complexity, yet sometimes I yearn for some simplicity.

This symphony of voices in my head, and the cacophony from the pounding in my heart, influence my complex and positive perspective on people and things. These internal signals and I cannot be silenced. How big and broad is the world you allow your mind to travel? Are you hyper-local or generally global? Do you feel a need to expand and improve your perspective?

Strategic alignment is about true-north forward movement toward your or a leader's clearly set destination. Change is ceaseless. Movement, therefore, must be accurately observed, and variances adroitly corrected. Standing on hills, fully responsible leaders recalibrate — with wisdom, courage and patience — their internal and external viewfinders.

"For those who have seen the Earth from space, and for the hundreds and perhaps thousands more who will, the experience most certainly changes your perspective." —Donald Williams

In *Doubt*, the widely acclaimed movie about perspective, a Catholic school principal saw hellish things from a nun's heavenly perch. This film underscores society's growing tendency toward instant and excessive advocacy, confrontation, judgment and verdict. Ignorance and fear intensify human-ego drive to be right.

With need-for-speed in decision-making toward posting profit, Wall Street's quarterly earnings goals contribute to too many regrettable outcomes. From flat plains or up in the clouds, there is great danger in misinformed and greedy leaders rushing to snap judgments about people, money, and other mission-critical resources.

Hill imagery is exceptionally efficient for illustrating height for ideal perspective. A big picture painted from a hill allows the artist to see and include much detail. Mentally, fully responsible leaders must always be where they can see, hear and feel the most.

What is your considered perspective on today's movement you detect in Washington, New York, Iraq, Afghanistan, North Korea, China, or in your own backyard? From where are you looking? If you are following only scholarly journals, you may be looking from an ivory tower and missing street-wise reality. Try seeing people and things from a hill in your mind.

If you restrict your news intake to Wall Street's business and financial press, you could be standing on a mountaintop and ignoring Main Street's journalism. If, however, you align scholarly, real-world, and visceral (*i.e.*, Blink-like gut instinct) experience and observation, you would be standing just high enough on a hill. With hill views fully responsible leaders take-in enough detail. They work to R.E.A.C.T. with Respect, Empathy, Authenticity, Clarity, Trust.

In 1972 it was a distinct honor to meet pianist Artur Rubinstein. I learned dramatic lessons in artistic perspective. Mr. Rubinstein was rehearsing for a performance with The Pittsburgh Symphony Orchestra, where I served at the first independent Executive Producer (*i.e.*, outside investor) for the then new Heinz Hall for the Performing Arts.

When his hands first touched the Steinway concert grand's keyboard, he jumped up and screamed in anger his perspective, "This is not tuned!" He walked off the stage. Music Director Maestro William Steinberg, Manager Sy Rosen, the entire orchestra, and I were stunned. Being new to this rarefied air breathed by classical music's geniuses, I was just short of shocked.

A very red-faced piano tuner appeared out of nowhere, and tweaked what may have been a very minor infraction. No one else could hear it. We tried. Several people "tested" the sound. A still very frustrated Mr. Rubinstein was escorted back onto the stage. Once he started to play, all was forgiven. He seemed totally lost in the beauty of his own playing, and was very effusive with his praise for the orchestra. His perspective shifted. Piano, he and they performed to his standards.

As we were discussing Mr. Rubinstein's perspective — and his perfectionism — his PR person was sure to tell me Mr. Rubinstein's first name is to be spelled without the "h," and the pronunciation is quite different. Pop culture keeps alive the misspelling. Now Google, Bing, Amazon and others simply show both spellings. Artur Rubenstein is the correct name to remember.

This was one of numerous startling experiences when working with or near true world-class greatness. It is safe to say each person offered me new perspective in every conversation. I confess the appeal of some of their passion and fury became part of my early career. I am still shedding a final layer or so of unrealistic impatience with others and myself. Even as my passion for a person or a project grows, I aim for less fury and more forgiveness.

Pop culture also produces many new words to support us in updating our perspective about ceaseless change. The more outrageous of these words find their way to the semi-serious online annuls of urbandictionary.com, while the more resplendent and otherwise illuminating new words are etched into Oxford Dictionary of English, New American Oxford Dictionary, Oxford English Dictionary, Merriam-Webster's Collegiate Dictionary, and other mainline repositories of definition and description. Daily at least once I use onelook.com to check spelling or a definition, and I subscribe to and use daily visualthesauraus.com powered by Thinkmap, Inc., a truly remarkable resource for animated graphic representations of words and their relatives.

Enjoy using any of the above resources to try to find definitions for these examples of new words to enlarge your perception about modern-day life and other emerging truth: automagically, bargainous; big media, bromance; carbon credit, carbon offsetting; catastrophize (*v.*), cheeseball; cool hunter, cougar; eggcorn, flash mob; flyover states, frenemy; friend (*v.*), green audit; green-collar, hater; heart (*v.*), home-shoring; hypermilling, locavore; matchy-matchy, or megachurch.

What do you do when you detect apparent inadequacy, ignorance, excessive timidity, or unwarranted impatience? What is your perspective about these questions and your responses?

Enduring life's challenges damages your perspective. Expecting and embracing life's challenges improves and broadens your perspective. When others sow seeds of discontent, they cannot take root in your realistic mind or grateful heart.

Seeing people and things from just-right HILL-height improves your perspective on your view of people, things — and yourself. You know from my writing how much I value the perspective of mentors. I am particularly delighted when experienced souls share their views.

Perhaps seven or so years ago, valued mentor and close friend Clyde Bowles was kind to introduce me to his long-time thinking partner, former U.S. Senator Adlai Stevenson III. Twice the Senator's father, Adlai Stevenson II (1900–1965), ran for the Presidency against Dwight D. Eisenhower.

In addition to his own perspective from many years as a distinguished public servant, Senator Stevenson has a steel-trap memory for telling riveting stories about various members of his family once in-service to our country. Several times I heard him hold forth in group settings, and I simply did not want him to stop sharing his perspective. He is a noteworthy historian, and a master storyteller.

During a three-way telephone call with Adlai and Clyde, we discussed importance of Presidential Debates. We were preparing me for an upcoming appearance on WGN Radio's "Extension 720" program, hosted since 1973 by Milton Rosenberg, Ph.D., formerly Director of the Doctoral Program in Social and Organizational Psychology at The University of Chicago, where he is now Professor Emeritus.

After the valuable conversation among us, Clyde and I sent Senator Stevenson an earlier version of this book. Within days, gentlemanly Adlai sent me a stately letter of thanks, with a copy to Clyde. Immediately he read certain chapters and scanned others, and did not delay taking the time to write to offer his seasoned perspective. He wrote: "Indeed, the entire book is most timely and perceptive, characteristically sensitive." I remain grateful for this and his numerous other affirming comments about the book and its author.

Offering perspective is in the senator's DNA, of course. I was reminded of a memorable and otherwise powerful quote from his father related to higher and broader perspective about what it means to be a citizen of The United States:

> "*As citizens of this democracy, you are the rulers
> and the ruled, the lawgivers and the law-abiding,
> the beginning and the end.*" —Adlai Stevenson II

Thank you for allowing me to raise the bar on the importance of knowing and enhancing your perspective. Please never stop trying to see things from your fertile mind's rolling hills. Honor perspective.

Perspective. Expound.

Persuasiveness

Chapter Inspired by and Dedicated to Robert H. Savage (1917-1986)

Insert or imagine seeing your first name: _____,

Seeing this chapter's title word, what immediately comes to your open mind? Do you already have a working relationship with this word? Somewhere inside of you does this word instantly appeal? As a response to a specific situation at-hand, will this word work to your and others' advantage? For this word to increase in real value, together we must dig, drill and think deeper, so we will reach, climb and soar higher.

The powerful noun per·sua·sive·ness is a double-edge sword. As a fully responsible leader forever in-training, I experience this word as both smooth and rough. Wooing a beloved should be smooth persuasiveness. "Arguing" a case is perhaps rough persuasiveness. Win-win ethical selling is persuasiveness (*i.e.*, smooth). An obsessive haggler's buying at the lowest possible dollar amount is also persuasiveness (*i.e.*, rough). For a lifetime of pursuing this HILL Word's fullness, persuasiveness is a term to grasp more fully. With meaningful persuasiveness life is more abundant.

Today's top big-ticket sales professionals are front-line thought leaders for whom I have highest respect. They are masters of win-win thinking and collaborative persuasiveness. Sadly you and I know too many other types of people who sell (*i.e.*, persuade) for only one reason. Money. Persuasiveness deserves best efforts, best practices, and full engagement of good, better and best people. Fully responsible leaders must be adept at win-win persuasiveness. Persuasiveness is a prerequisite for success.

In first-hand conversation with many attorneys, physicians, educators, CEOs, and those from a host of other careers, openly they deny they "sell" anything; thus instantly failing in their persuasiveness and truthfulness of the moment. Is it fair to say virtually everyone is selling something to someone, and some who sell do it more openly and ethically than others? Internally or externally, if you and others are using thoughts, strategies, tactics, and other acts of persuasiveness to encourage a course of action, a point-of-view, or an economic value-exchange acquisition (*i.e.*, a purchase) of a thought, product or service, you are selling. You are persuading. By choice, you are either a master or a mangler of the higher sensibilities and skills of persuasiveness. There is science and art in persuasiveness, and both types of components are respected and learned by fully responsible leaders. For those who take seriously and derive great pleasure from their persuasiveness, my sincere congratulations and thanks. You are to be celebrated and appreciated.

On the shadow side, without persuasiveness a society languishes and could wither away. Dramatic as that imagery may seem, pause to think of the people sitting on their hands waiting for The White House or Capitol Hill to persuade the world and the nation to have new hope and jump-start our stalled economic engines. Are you? I think not. You would not be reading a book of this *genre* without intention to be part of the proactive solution instead of the problem of inaction. Entrepreneurs and others are persuading anyone who will listen to give innovative new businesses a fighting chance. Many entrepreneurs believe they are fighting for their lives and ours. They may not reveal their battle cries, but in-private their real tears release the flood of emotional commitment an entrepreneur must sustain in order to succeed against formidable odds. Entrepreneurial persuasiveness is among the most energizing fuel a society can use to fire-up people and production lines.

Does the word "salesman" make you think of the President of the United States? The Honorable Barack Hussein Obama is this country's Salesman-in-Chief. With a smile, and not a smidgen of disrespectfulness, take a moment and imagine how much President Obama has learned about persuasiveness, especially since his earliest post-win top-secret briefings about the real whys-and-wherefores behind unpopular wars and policies that were launched by his predecessors (yes, plural). This is not an illustration about politics, any President, or a single party. Our Presidents are the world's most influential persuaders and crusaders. Even for when it may be best to remain silent about topics the world is wondering about, Presidents are tutored in using heightened sensibilities and skills of persuasiveness. I remain in awe of most of any President's powers of persuasiveness.

Ronald Reagan was known as "The Great Communicator," which essentially meant "The Great Persuader." When Persuader Reagan demanded, "Tear down that wall," he was demonstrating his mastery of persuasiveness. Even when I disagree with what I am hearing, seeing or otherwise sensing, often I am startled, spellbound, and occasionally dumbstruck by words, tone, tempo, timing and complexity of intentionality in Presidential (or CEO) persuasiveness.

Any student of the timber of U.S. Presidents or U.K. Prime Ministers knows only a fraction of the tightropes over great chasms these chief persuaders must walk. We suspect fiery hot coals under their feet while they stand in-service persuading to the greater global good. Overstatement? Quite the opposite. Think and feel deeper, please.

In 1976, 1980 and 1984 my New York-based electronic publishing, editing, and document expediting company served as the official documentarian for all Presidential Debates. We published the only official transcriptional records of all Presidential and Vice-Presidential debates in those election years. I was privileged to deliver our work to the U.S. Library of Congress. Reviewing my file copies, I still marvel at our boldness to try to align all the technology and people we assembled for such an unprecedented task. When in 1986 I sold the business to a Wall Street absentee owner, the company lost the Presidential Debates contract. The company never again touched such history-making words.

In mid-1976 somehow I persuaded the D.C.-based National League of Women Voters (then the only sponsors of Presidential and Vice-Presidential Debates), The White House, Library of Congress, Congress, ABC News, CBS News, NBC News, *The New York Times*, *The Washington Post*, and dozens of other influencers that they could and should trust my transcriptionists, editors, proofreaders, project managers, technicians, my former wife Cynthia (effectively our co-founder, COO and CFO), and me. The morning after one of the startling Ford-Carter debates, on *Today* NBC's Tom Brokaw held up on-camera the hard copy my team and I produced within 90-minutes of each debate's adjournment (breaking document editing and other turnaround records long before today's voice recognition and PC technology). Through bleary eyes I saw on the back cover my company's logo and my personal signature attesting to the authenticity of the document. Almost everyone in-authority referred to our publications while analyzing and commenting on the highest-profile Presidential debates since the Nixon-Kennedy showdowns.

At my company's expense, every Ivy League and state university library received *via* next-day delivery hard copies of each debate. For many months I enjoyed seeing CEOs of *Fortune 500* corporations proudly display their copies on their coffee tables, desks and bookshelves. During at least one meeting I recall with a Top 10 CEO, he had no clue my company had produced the four booklets he proudly had on display. After I showed him my signature and company logo on the back cover of every edition, he agreed to sign the Letter of Agreement I had ready for him. All smiles. In this case our stellar work product was more persuasive than any of my words, and I like it when that happens.

The New York Post ran a feature article headlined: *ETX Corporation Cashes-In on Debates*, and my photo is side-by-side with candidates Reagan and Mondale. Foolishly I did not like the crass and sensationalistic headline, so I did not reproduce and distribute copies of the coverage. That was a snobbish PR mistake on my part.

Although in gift-giving to libraries and our carefully timed promotional activities, my company spent nearly every penny we made producing and selling hard-copy versions of the debates, eventually we enjoyed having as clients 100% of the *Fortune 500* companies based in the New York area, and the No. 1 U.S. leader in virtually every field. Our only marketing plan, rightly or not, was based on going for the top. All three Detroit auto makers, all the top aerospace companies, largest law and accounting firms, and dozens of others top-ranked buyers were persuaded to trust and buy. Online documents and photo galleries for this book include a list of these companies, photos of our work with Presidential and Vice-Presidential Debates, and other illustrations of the power of persuasiveness — all backed-up with peak performance.

In these early years, was I always persuading? Was I making my living by always selling? Was I almost always losing sleep worrying if we could live-up to the high expectations I set in-motion? Yes, yes, and yes. For 12 years as head of that pace-setting entrepreneurial venture, I persuaded, I sold, and I worried. Now I look back and realize how I loved it all. Elsewhere in this book I reveal how I somewhat regret selling the company to a greedy Wall Street firm. After one dozen years at the helm, it was a good time (I was 36) for me to try new fields for my persuasiveness. Above all else, my next employers put my persuasiveness to the test. Upon reflection, they wanted the world-class client roster my colleagues and I achieved, perhaps more so than they wanted me. Back then I confused myself with my work product. The Presbyterian work ethic that was drilled-in from childhood days in The Steel City left me with little sense of any difference between myself and my work; for me "You are what do" preceded the cliché, "You are what you eat."

Skipping over a decade of sometimes rewarding entrepreneurial trial-and-error in the consumer credit data arena, in the mid-90s my persuasiveness was tested to the max when I was introduced by *The Wall Street Journal*'s Washington Bureau Chief to The Honorable Lawrence B. Lindsey, then one of the seven governors of The Federal Reserve Bank, and later President George W. Bush's Chief Economic Adviser. Governor Lindsey and I met for nearly two hours. During similar demanding meetings with a top attorney at the Federal Trade Commission (FTC), the Washington Bureau Chief for *The Wall Street Journal, Money Magazine*'s almost daily face on ABC's *Good Morning America* Tyler Mathisen, and a handful of other regulatory and media influencers in the financial markets, my persuasiveness was judged by the favorable outcome.

Strategically I needed their buy-in before daring to approach with a Big Idea the heads of the Big Three national credit bureaus. I had to be sure powers-that-be saw what good I would do in terms of unprecedented real-world benefits to American consumers nationwide — if all three competing national credit bureaus allowed my fully funded new venture to gain paid access to and merge their competitive consumer credit data. We then would sell through American Express and other "endorsers" and "sponsors" three-bureau credit reporting monitoring services. No one had yet dared.

We closed various deals, and soon American Express was thrilled with almost immediate favorable consumer response. With 156 varied mailing *test cells* and a large-scale roll-out, we broke many direct-marketing response records. American Express was pleased to be our revenue-sharing endorsing partner, and so were the three fee-collecting national credit bureaus, Equifax, Experian, and Trans Union. Many millions of dollars were involved. I lost touch with my former employer, yet I hear and read they continue to prosper.

To get to this success, our executive team's collaborative persuasiveness to do such a big deal included discreetly presenting reference to billions of dollars of net worth of our company's primary stockholder. Adroitly we referenced his Wall Street-powerful family name. Learned skills of persuasiveness involve *"lowering names gently"* into mission-critical conversations. Never once did I "drop the name" of our principal stockholder, or abuse (*i.e.*, drop) names of any of the above referenced major influencers who wisely embraced the concept I presented. One doesn't. We gently *lowered their names* when and where needed. The bureaus knew my team and I did our homework, I made the rounds with mission-critical V.I.P.s, and I was not going to take no for an answer. Four revenue-sharing deals were cut, and then an industry shifted toward more collaboration among three competing credit data collectors and packagers. Everyone continues to win.

Does it take a lot of unbridled ego to dare to try to persuade someone else — or millions of would-be buyers and satisfied customers — to follow your lead? Do the above true stories I recount for your edification appear to you to be ego-driven reflections? With both questions, you are partially correct. Superego is the response that best characterizes my engagement in so candidly sharing these words. You'll recall form *Psychology 101* superego is called the third psychic structure. Ego is in second place, behind Id, meaning the unconscious physiological drives embedded within us. Ego is self-awareness, and paradoxically ego is often evidenced when one delays gratification.

Superego is your and my moral guardian. Superego is the built-in standard bearer in my life for setting sights high, living through constantly escalating ascendancy, and paying rapt attention to others through remarkably full engagement. Superego is a key to understanding the structure of your and my personality. Pop culture parlance has bastardized almost any use of the word "ego." Properly used, ego is not a four-letter word.

Superego drives me to live a life of win-win persuasiveness. The more I want to learn, the more I want to share. When I stop learning I'll stop sharing. If an accident, disease, another stroke, another cardiac arrest, or other illness robs me of my mental faculties, my living will has strict provisions for family, friends and lawyers to stop me from speaking, writing or leading. If by circumstances beyond my control I am forced to stop learning, I want to be stopped in my tracks, regardless of how fast I may be physically running. Someday I'll ask whoever looks after me in any infirm years that might come, if and when I should dare to say I have all the answers instead of some caring responses, to find me a quiet corner and keep me there. If, however, I ask for an Internet connection or books, I'll welcome the accommodation. Note my psychic structure allows no plans or time for mental weakness or thoughts toward retirement. Self-agency will keep me busy. I pray to remain useful to others until 100 or so. Yet I'll settle for reaching 95, the age at which my fully alert maternal grandmother's body gave up. Her mind never did.

At 90 and on birthdays thereafter I'll start celebrating my 100th birthday, perhaps by leading old-style salon discussions about why mighty organizations, institutions, governments and leaders failed while others flourished. Perhaps by then today's G-20 countries will be among the G-100 or greater. Perhaps these economic powerhouses will still meet together in hometown Pittsburgh, and maybe by then my Chicago will have won an Olympic bid. Is anything possible through win-win persuasiveness? Surely you know my response.

Thinking of life-cycle adjustment and growth, indeed a hint of built-in sales resistance and buyer's remorse comes to mind with the word persuasiveness; more precisely, resistance to the mere hint of a stereotypical used-car salesman's disingenuousness, dishonesty or lack of ethics or authenticity in the process of her or his persuasiveness. Among 10 or so sales positions I can recall, at least three times John, Sr. sold used cars, including owning in the mid-60s his own business; "Johnnie Dallas Used Cars" was the overhead banner sign my junior-high classmates would attribute to me. I was thrilled for him. He seemed to have found himself. The most time I ever spent with my dad was on his "car lot." When I was age 12 and later, he allowed me to move cars around his property.

Once a prospective customer pulled in, saw me behind the wheel, and waved me to drive out onto the highway. Dad came out of his office screaming, "No, no, no! He's only 12 years old! He can't go out on the street!" The disapproving would-be customer made a U-turn and drove off. Dad roared with laughter. I cried because I caused Dad to lose money. No family story about my dad and me was repeated as often as this one. He was proud (yes, proud) of his son's interest in cars. Actually, I was more interested in attracting and sustaining his favorable attention than caring about his cars.

As an entrepreneur Dad tried to earn an honest dollar, yet Grandfather William McKinley Dallas told his youngest son, "No Dallas ever makes it running a business. We're not built that way." I saw Dad was crushed. I was, however, oddly motivated to prove wrong that twice-married, mean-spirited, ne'er-do-well, and crotchety old man (whom I was taught to not like and didn't). Whatever Grandfather Dallas meant, he obviously may have regretted not following ancestors' persuasiveness in their considerable entrepreneurial footsteps. Soon Dad gave up because his dad gave-up on him. I was too young to know to run interference on this family playing field.

Perhaps partly to prove my grandfather wrong, almost immediately I jumped-in to my own entrepreneurial fantasies. In 1967 Junior Achievement (JA) set me on the entrepreneurial path on which I still travel. A JA recruiter's compelling persuasiveness directed me away from youthful career plans to teach English or save souls as a pastor.

Knowing I was running an exciting business in Manhattan, from Pittsburgh my ailing Grandfather Dallas called me to his hospital bedside. I hardly knew him, having seen him no more than six or fewer times in my life. (Until I was 18 I did not Grandfather Shearer, but that's a story for another book.) Grandpa Dallas was dying. I was the last family member to see him alive. Before and after he died, not much was adding-up for me. Other than my now deceased dad, I was (and am) the last male Dallas of a grand old Pennsylvania family. As of the writing, the male line ends with me. So, without a hint of love for anyone in Grandfather's failing voice (and certainly none for me; respect, yes), he felt compelled to tell me untold Dallas family marital, business and political history he had not bothered to share with anyone.

Oddly I find I'm still mildly annoyed by it all. I may never bother to verify a thing he said. His and Dallas ancestors' past is just that. I'm not bitter, I'm realistic. I'm too busy with today's and tomorrow's challenges, allowing only an occasional glance back at my own fading memories. Grandfather Dallas failed to persuade me to act. As I write, I cannot recall attending his funeral, yet I'm told I did. I must have been in a state of disbelief about it all. After seeing Grandfather Dallas in hospital, and my plane landed back at LaGuardia, I remember deciding to leave Pittsburgh where it is — at the confluence of three rivers of truth, lies and consequences.

Grandparents, parents, teachers, pastors, priests, rabbis, therapists, physicians, bosses, spouses, significant others, and any influencer with advanced sensibilities and skills of selfless persuasiveness must be held accountable for the guidance they sell or give. If someone you meet represents full knowledge of perfect truth, run the other way. If perchance you profess at your local coffee shop or elsewhere your full knowledge of faith or any of all else life has to offer, you would not be reading this book. A book you might write from the perspective of being all-knowing would be laughed off of modern-day bookshelves. Or would it?

For a little smile, a TV-famous all-knowing self-proclaimed real estate mogul comes to mind. (I once met for conversation his first wife, and still admire her pluck.) I'll not fill-in "The _____" blank. You already guessed correctly, so go ahead, laugh out loud. University students have asked me if he is a typical CEO. No! Thank heavens he's not even close to the real thing. He's mostly a D List entertainer, but no one can argue with his rock-star career of persuasiveness — surviving against odds of his multiple bankruptcy filings, law suits, foreclosures, horrific press coverage, and enduring innumerable public and private battering rams — from which he learned how to beat others to a pulp.

In your local and world views, both personally and professionally, what does the above definitions and descriptions of persuasiveness mean to you? As you think about your persuasiveness, in your fine mind, are you climbing ivory towers, mountaintops, or hills? Are you where you need to be to see and ensure forward movement through persuasiveness?

Your well-meaning servant author of this book is hardly all-knowing — I'm all-asking. I am still eager to be persuaded and to persuade; willing to learn and share what might be of value to you and others. Each HILL Word in this book is about two-way persuasiveness. Your views matter to me. I trust these words persuade you to think and dig a little deeper before you act and reach a lot higher. Together let's never stop digging and climbing. How are we doing?

Persuasiveness. Expound.

Pride

Chapter Inspired by and Dedicated to
Christian Paul Joppa (1955-2001)

Insert or imagine seeing your first name: _____,

Pride is this book's only counter-productive and otherwise negative featured word for your consideration. It has to be here. Pride is so embedded in our collective consciousness it needs to be called-out. For good reason this is among the more intense chapters. Instinctively you will pause to acknowledge each Aha! You may need to re-read an unavoidably difficult sentence, paragraph, page, or the whole chapter. This is complicated psychology. I write from a layman's point-of-view.

For many solid reasons, pride is one of the Roman church's ancient Seven Deadly Sins — considered the deadliest. Along with lust, gluttony, greed, sloth, wrath and envy, pride is punishable. Wise pastors, priests, rabbis, CEOs, consultants, coaches, parents, mentors, and other leaders and teachers of creed, philosophy, or practicality must seek to dislodge pride within whomever it is suspected or confirmed. Perhaps some sharpshooters aim for all seven on the hit list of seven sins of egocentrism. Pride is the hardest-to-hit moving target.

Over 20 years since I first delivered a lay leader's talk about the corrosive impact of pride on individuals and organizations, I remain intentionally provocative and bold to assert my layman's thesis:

Pride Equals Shame

Did you *feel* that statement? Immediately you may agree, disagree, or agree in-part. For now, please at least agree in-part. On the next page, starting at the top (the 12-o'clock point), allow the flow of the words on this simplified diagram to speak truth to you. Monitor what comes to your mind. See if you immediately see how shame can yield pride.

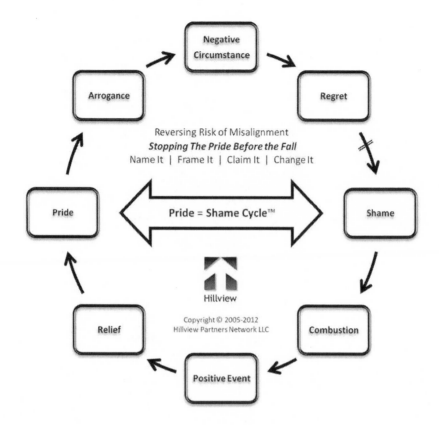

Scratch the surface of pride and just under the veneer you are likely to find shame. Tackle this layman's theory in both your brain and heart. If, however, these thoughts and feelings set you on a particularly difficult journey, please seek counsel of a professional caregiver who knows how to support you to reverse risk of peril of both pride and shame. Linking and then breaking through these two states of mind takes extended time, hard work, and divine intervention. With shame and/or pride, we have to *face it to erase it*.

Be Pleased, Not Proud

"Being pleased" is the good news alternative to "being proud." With great and true respect for all faith traditions and expressions, here I offer how Christendom's literature and teachings underscore alternatives to pride. In 12 of 15 translations of the Christian Bible I checked, *Matthew 3:17* is essentially identical: "Behold," a voice out of the heavens said,

"This is my beloved Son, with whom I am well pleased." Three versions replaced likeness to "…with whom I am well pleased" with approximations of "…in whom I delight." For mental health and organizational development strengths, being pleased and declaring delight far exceed in value being proud. With forgivable irreverence, I suggest God's SUV chariot could have a bumper sticker, "Pleased Parent of Best Son." God would not, however, focus attention on pride. "Perfect Son On-Board" is more likely to be God's modern-day message. Such logic is likely to appear in ancient texts of nearly all faiths.

Continuing with my requesting and appreciating literary license granted by readers of alternative faiths and other approaches to higher power, it appears the Hebrew God did not choose to communicate pride in his son. I observe throughout Scripture he chose to focus attention on our human deep-thought process that leads to grounded pleasure (*i.e.*, true delight) of demonstrating discernment; the joy that comes from thinking through — with feeling — life's features, benefits, attributes, and other worthiness. God's scribes shared preferable thinking and feeling alternatives to inherently perilous pride: being well pleased, well satisfied, deeply delighted, secure in knowledge, sensing wisdom, and in other ways garnering and sustaining the human brain's and heart's joys of discernment and sound judgment. Deep thought yields high reward.

Responses more productive than pride can become learned reactions to life's inflection points. Inflection points are the abrupt elbows in a mind's graph of personal or organizational growth — when a new thought, set of circumstances, or paradigm kicks into play, and suddenly there is no turning back. From inflection points, what's new takes off and the old goes into decline, whether it is a new standard of thinking or behavior, or a new idea filling a known or hidden void.

Before each U.S. economic meltdown we remember Wall Street's wretched excess of hubris and pride. How soon thereafter did Wall Street return to its delusional sense of imperviousness? On Wall Street or Main Street, shameful and painful lessons from pride's peril are often eventually replaced with more pride. The Pride Equals Shame Cycle can be never-ending. Watch what happens when momentarily ashamed global markets rebound. Pride? Highly likely. Ratings-worried news media will show proud stock traders jumping for joy, and CEOs in luxurious settings toasting their success. Then we can count the days until the next fall. Note the vicious cycle of shame leading to pride, pride leading to shame, and various wobbly steps in-between.

In order to redefine, realign and protect economic stability, should we abolish pride in our mass communication about business and financial matters? Yes. Could we eliminate in advertising and selling intentionally instilling pride in home ownership, vehicle ownership, and ownership of luxuries; thus re-define The American Dream to exclude pride? Would ad agencies succeed in selling without pride, and only with words and images of discernment, good judgment, sustainable delight — and fun? Promotion of pride moves products, sells stadium and concert hall seats, and causes other prideful buying decisions that perhaps could be solely based on good thinking. Pride even plays a key role in attracting, motivating and keeping our enlisted troops ready for combat and other service. Things could be different.

Pride projected is superficiality that seeks to overpower emotional intelligence (EQ). Fully responsible thought leaders on Madison Avenues around the world must model for others ever-increasing perceptiveness, sound judgment, discernment, and enjoyment. In order to imbue in children and adults their unique accountability for sensing the depths within themselves from which each of their noteworthy achievements emanates, let's steadily discourage pride and increasingly encourage honest assessment and challenges of human strengths, weaknesses, opportunities and threats (S.W.O.T.). Pride has no place in this equation. Being pleased is the alternative we consider in this chapter. Being deeply pleased with solid rhyme or reason behind ones accomplishments allows personal and professional achievements to take root for fostering and supporting further growth.

The stunning and raw 2011 award-winning British film "Shame" (NC-17) could have been called "Pride Equals Shame." Director Steve McQueen floods our senses with words and images about how shame is poorly masked with pride, and how such choices impede our adult development.

So-called "writer's block" and "stage fright" of overtly proud creative artists can often be traced to unchecked prior shame that yielded to unstoppable pride in earlier achievement. In other words, with pride in ongoing accomplishment, feelings of shame about prior failure can deepen. In too many lives unchecked shame remains a threat. When pride is used to bolster self-esteem and self-confidence, shame is nearby. My bold layman's views are subject to clinical interpretation, of course.

The Pride Before the Fall

You've heard it many times, "the pride before the fall." Did you take this seriously? It is serious. Pronouncements of pride are "in your face" and thus out of place. For motivational or other reasons, inject pride into a team's or a whole organization's vision, mission, plans, slogan, motto, promotions, ad campaign, brand positioning, or PR strategy, and you've introduced potentially fatal exclusionary emotional superficiality. Do you expect your buyers to have so much pride in dealing with you that they will say for years, "I'm so proud to be signing this check...this contract...this letter of recommendation, *etc.*?" Can buyers share in your organization's pride? Instead, choose for your messaging diverse and inclusive relationship-building words. Focus attention on your organization's strengths of higher thinking toward win-win outcomes about which everyone can be justifiably pleased.

Sometimes too late swashbuckler free marketeers learn the axiom, *"Marketplace value is ultimately determined by the buyer, and not by the seller."* With her or his promotion of pride, a proud seller inadvertently creates objections and obstacles to overcome in order to close the sale. Already there's plenty enough to tackle in any selling process, so adding pride to the sales cycle is asking for trouble. Don't do it. Encouraging sales executives or others to convey pride in themselves, their employer, their products, or their services is off-the-mark in terms of what buyers truly value. How can your buyers put a dollar value on your organization's pride?

Where does this pride thing come from? What is its function in our daily lives? What level of a wise mind's perceptiveness chooses to stop at pride when deeper value is at one remove? May I ask if you are a proud person? If so, do you pronounce your pride with empathy toward listeners? How? Why? What value does your pride bring to others, especially buyers? You may have facts to prove me wrong. I'm open to learning. For now, consider the high probability that pride may mask shame from years past, current or future. This is not a topic for easy self-exploration. I'm choosing a lifetime of introspection about roles pride played in certain failures in my life, especially in personal relationships I muddled, mangled, and otherwise mismanaged.

Over 16 of my 40-plus years as a servant leader — a humble layman, and certainly not a professional psychologist — among audiences I have provoked thoughts toward leadership solutions by bluntly stating Pride Equals Shame. Knowing how out-of-the-blue this sounds for most of us, for comic relief I invite good-natured jeers from avid sports fans of perennially losing teams, and from long-tethered university alums who probably can't recall much of what they learned at their oft-mentioned *alma maters*. Later in some talks, early nervous laughter can yield to a sorrowful sob, or a tear or two, from shame-filled proud parents of under-achievers, adult children of abusers, spouses of displaced workers, physically or otherwise challenged individuals, persons with great regret from their poor choices in life, and others who harbor deep shamefulness. Hearing perhaps for the first time the disruptive yet constructive Pride Equals Shame message, individuals may have realized they use in-your-face pride to camouflage their in-the-heart shame. For deeply inquiring minds, this bold assertion can require a cognitive therapist's ear and shoulder. Especially for fully responsible leaders, the following true story will illustrate key points about the perils of pride and the promise of being pleased.

The Story of Billy and His "B"

After a 1999 presentation to a noticeably proud New York audience of a company's top sales executives, a statement more than a question came from a participant. Until the message hit him hard where it mattered, he revealed he thought I was full of hot air. Seeing the many mind-bending slides and listening to the Pride Equals Shame message (which I originally wrote five or so years earlier), suddenly he reached a tipping point. Later I learned he truly changed his family's life for the better. Today I remain humbled, grateful and pleased.

The proudly dressed and somewhat unsteady stranger firmly holding the microphone brought the room to an almost palpable hush as he spoke with *gravitas* along these lines; paraphrasing: "Mr. Dallas, when you started out, I thought you were way off-the-mark. You lost me when you opened your mouth with this pride-equals-shame stuff. I wanted to get up and walk out. Instead I stayed and hoped you would soon stop talking and sit down. While you were talking 'at us,' suddenly, almost magically, I felt you were speaking directly *with* my wife and me — and she's not even here. My stomach sank. Deep inside I felt your topic's purpose. It hurt like a sucker-punch to the gut. You got to me.

At last I admitted to myself my wife Mary and I had been very ashamed of our under-achieving 12-year-old son Billy, but we did not identify it or call it by its name, 'shame.' With Billy's bad school work we were inconvenienced, annoyed, angry, frustrated, downright mad, embarrassed — shamed. When Billy brought home his first-ever B instead of his normal C, D and F grades, my wife and I showered him with OUR pride. For days we were beaming. Billy was not.

Two weeks later, a sad Billy asked us if we were so proud of his B because we were so ashamed of everything else he ever did. He said it just like that. Like you did today, Mr. Dallas, Billy caught us off-guard. We said, 'No, no, no…' Yet now I know he and we knew better, but we simply did not have the words or the guts to express what was happening. Now, hearing you say all these things, I'm sure we were and are ashamed of being parents of a kid making terrible grades — fearing we were being called, by teachers or other parents, stupid, negligent, abusive, unloving or worse. When I get home tonight, my wife and I are going to talk, and together we'll find some way to apologize to Billy for our unwarranted shame and our selfish pride. Thank you, Mr. Dallas. I'm sorry I was too proud to give you the benefit of the doubt."

Slow-to-steady then thunderous applause erupted in the room. When the room calmed, eyes turned toward me. Handkerchiefs and tissues appearing had distracted me. During the applause I mopped my brow. Without forethought, quite naturally I allowed an extra beat of silence in the room before disciplining myself to R.E.A.C.T. to Billy's dad with Respect, Empathy, Authenticity, Clarity and Trust. He was a wreck, and suddenly I was not exactly at my best. He needed me to R.E.A.C.T., and I needed to choke back my own tears. I felt his pain and gain.

Gently I congratulated him on this giant step forward, and told him he was blessed to have new clarity with which to view his son, wife, and himself. Fresh-air perspective of this type can leave one gasping for breath, I told him. With a comforting big smile, I asked him to breathe deeply to allow this new oxygen to fill his spirit. It was clear to all of us that he had more than enough to breathe-in and think about, so I decided to not elaborate any more. With polite reference to this robust overload, and this group's and my affirmation, I offered to keep in touch. Applause. Responses I gave to next questioners allowed me to indirectly give Billy's dad a few more supportive thoughts. I knew this crucible made him more reachable and teachable.

Weeks later from Billy's dad, I learned that he, Mary and Billy were very PLEASED with their new perspective. I learned more than I could report here about the endemic nature of corrosive shame in this family's life. Pride was their tonic, their pain medication of choice. Those days appeared to be gone. Billy's grades remained at the C+ or B-level. From me The Story of Billy and His B earns his parents an A+ for the teenage semester of fully responsible parenting.

"Proud Parent of a Honor Roll Student" bumper stickers on SUVs call attention to the parents, not the scholar. If the bumper sticker reads, "Straight-A Honor Roll Student in Here, Honk if You Value Excellence," the obliging horn's message is about the achiever — and also about those passers-by for whom the student's shining example might be a positive influence.

Stating your pride in a child, spouse, employee, or anyone else risks taking something away from the achiever, even when you intend to be giving. During their reachable and teachable moments, please allow achievers to own their own accomplishments. Empower them to think and feel good about themselves. "Taking pride" in or from someone is not exactly in the best interests of the person with whom you hope to celebrate a lifetime of many, many achievements — including your own.

Billy knew his B was not about his parents. It was about Billy. Because his parents were so proud, totally accidentally and unintentionally they took away more than they added to Billy's essential sense of self-agency; the conceptual understanding of self as an agent capable of shaping motives, behavior, and future possibilities (Damon & Hart, 1991). In other words, Billy needed to know he alone could choose and pursue achievement of a lifetime of Bs or better. Time spent discussing pride of parents robs children of home-learning modules in self-agency, self-efficacy, self-actualization, self-confidence, self-esteem, and ultimate lifetime satisfaction with self. Elsewhere in We Need to Have a Word, all of these inflection points and others appear.

To avoid another "pride before the fall" era in the U.S., please pause here to sense future economic potential for averting eventual additional catastrophe after GM, Chrysler, and countless other corporate titans emerged from shameful bankruptcy and other embarrassment for their decades of misalignment of people, money, and other mission-critical resources. Encourage successful operatives involved in our economy's re-engineering to be well-pleased, and let's try to discourage their pride wherever we can and should. We must.

Toyota's prideful need to overpower General Motors as the largest vehicle manufacturer in the world led them to blindness to life-and-death safety technology for acceleration in even their very proud Lexus luxury cars. Forced by public scrutiny to save lives, millions of Toyotas were recalled. Buyer trust was shattered. Yet shame was slow to show its face. It did. History will show how the Pride Equals Shame Cycle plays out in Toyota's future. With the aftershocks of Daimler-Benz divesting itself of moribund Chrysler, GM cutting its losses with Hummer, and all the other lackluster brands in-flux between and among vehicle manufactures, perceptive economists, analysts, sociologists, psychologists, and other alignment specialists should watch for pride to rear its ugly head.

> *"Language shows a man; speak that I may see thee."*
> —Ben Jonson

Monitoring what CEOs say to securities analysts on Wall Streets around the world creates an early-detection system for pride. Especially in how company leaders react to questions from the floor or during webcasts, seedlings or mighty oaks of perilous pride can be detected. Analyst calls, meetings and reports are laboratory petri dishes with nutrient agar within which to study growth of pride's bacteria. If pride is dominant when testing a company's DNA, run the other way. Before setting aside mixed metaphors and biological imagery, think of pride as a virus that can strike any society's immune system. Being justifiably and analytically pleased is more than the antidote to pride, it is the cure.

Is it over-the-top to say pride kills? From worst outcomes of road rage to deaths by suicide of once-proud masters of the universe, pride kills. Pride kills whole societies. Many nations fell on their swords of self-inflicted pride. Even a moment of reflection brings to mind faces of many proud dictators. This second you may be seeing replays in your memory of their statues, busts or portraits being pulled down from pedestals of pride.

> *"A proud man is always looking down on*
> *things and people; and, of course,*
> *as long as you're looking down,*
> *you can't see something that's above you."*
> —C.S. Lewis

Just say no. Pride is a drug. For high-impact and sustainable illustrative purpose, and with any contrary clinical or linguistic definitions set aside, let's consider pride a drug. Without checking facts, this lay thinker believes excitement of pride produces endorphins; natural pain relievers resembling opiates in their ability to generate in humans a sense of well-being and analgesia. Can you feel this provocative point? For alleviating the pain of unchecked shame, pride may be America's number one hallucinogen of choice. Pride addicts drown their shame in an altered state of mind that makes the world seem somehow brighter, even if only until darkness of their shame returns.

Pride enables addicts *under-the-influence* to say and do things they otherwise might not. When high on pride, nearly all of what they do is potentially harmful. When a pride addict is on a binge, lives can be destroyed, people harmed, marriages ruined, children abused, employees harassed, jobs lost, money wasted, companies bankrupted, reputations trashed, spirits crushed, public trust squandered, and other horrific things happen that often can be traced back to the perpetrator's original shame. Shame happens.

Sports figures should be tested for pride the way they are tested for steroids and other banned substances. Imagine how this logic would play out in any team's locker room, or at a national conference of top coaches: Ban shame! Ban pride! Choose being thrilled over being killed. Be pleased, not proud. Even the introduction of this approach to pleasure *vs.* pride in winning adds value to each human who allows the message to pierce through thick skulls and mending bones.

Fully responsible leaders must creatively promote being deeply pleased with oneself through sustainable awareness of true inner strength. The U.S. Army's "Be all you can be" campaign came close to this line of thinking toward self-agency. What's wrong with a soccer coach telling David Beckham, "Get out there and be all you can be," without saying "Go out there and make yourself and us proud?" Encourage others and yourself to be all they and you can be, knowing each accomplishment is a hint of great things they and you are likely to do next. Where does pride fit in this thinking calculus about future greater accomplishment? It does not fit.

Add Pride to Any Team's Motivational Message and You Risk Fueling and Fanning Flames of Shame

Surely Madison Avenue's mind masters tap into shame, pride, guilt, and other pain when they calibrate messages in advertising campaigns and other types of sales promotion. Consider roots of Gray Pride for naturally aging Americans, Gay Pride for those of same-sex relational genetics, Black Pride for respectful Martin Luther King, Jr. Dream-driven African-Americans, All-American Pride for Constitutionally empowered U.S. citizens, ol' school alumni pride from pre-school through university, or unbridled fan pride in football, baseball, basketball, hockey, soccer, rugby, or other sport teams. Whew! That's a lot of pride.

Is a percentage of any group's communal pride collective shame? For years it would be wise to keep a watchful eye on Penn State's complex layers of shame. Pride is likely to be used to dull community pain, rekindle the team's fame, and ensure financial gain. Being deeply pleased with overall highest personal-best performance is a Joe Paterno legacy-based alternative to pride, a people-first/profit-later message that could be worked-up into a promotional froth.

Is promoting pride a sure-fire mass marketing ploy to make money from each of these groupings; capitalizing on obvious or subtle observations of collective shame yielding to their shared pride? During a Wrigleyville rooftop party or in Wrigley Field's Bleachers, it is better to not ask a Chicago Cubs fan any such dangerous question about pride in the Cubbies.

In terms of ethnic national pride, there are annual parades to offset 364 days during which some actually down-play their nationalities, beliefs, interests and religions. The awe-inspiring unto itself Olympics movement comes to mind as a global grab for currency in prideful pockets; from proud prospective host cities almost begging, to proud contenders from the smallest countries pinning their national identity on winning at least one medal of any of three. The pride-overcoming-shame campaign premise has sold billions of dollars or more worth of goods and services during parades, conferences, exhibitions, games, matches, and in other agora.

Pride-based spending during countless buying decisions brought proud Americans to our economic knees. For many buyers, their homes, cars, boats, planes, travel, and other pride-driven purchases yielded to shame of bankruptcy. This author argues, however, some shame of bankruptcy began much earlier with unchecked shamefulness that eventually prompted the ego's grab for delusional pride in owning products, achieving status, or pursuing other forms of escape.

Take away pride in promotional messaging, and what's left to promote? Lots! Promoting broader and higher awareness of any group's historical accomplishments, current worthy initiatives, and future win-win societal goals is much better. Pride is empty. Promise is full. Performance proves it all. Passion about performance is more valuable than passion about pride.

In consulting and coaching conversations I will say to clients bold words along these lines, "Speak your pride and you risk revealing unchecked shame. Although we leaders may choose to swim with wise and willing dolphins, nearby there are dangerous sharks who smell in pride the blood of shame." Without these extra measures of rhetorical flourish, it is very difficult to arrest attention and reverse risk related to pride. Often pride is deeply embedded in shame stone.

In the early 1980s a close friend asked me what I was so ashamed about. I was stunned by his impertinence. Why did he ask? He claimed I was unnecessarily using too often the words "proud" and "pride" to describe obviously formidable career accomplishments; "I am proud of my...whatever." I was. Until that tipping point, I was totally unaware of the connection between shame and pride. I was using pride to overcome shame.

Shame *in* me caused me to put pride *on* me. In my talks on this topic, I say to parents in an audience, "Saying to a child 'Shame *on* you!'

puts shame *in* the youngster. Avoid this reprimand." Thanks to my wise friend's observation and prescient question, over time I arrested most of this dead-end prideful behavior, and devoted my inner life to discovering alternatives to shameful pride — for others and myself. From time to time, a kernel of pride still slips into my thinking. If I identify it in-time, I examine it with an emergency triage procedure to mentally arrest it before it cardiac arrests me. Shame and pride are harmful to your and my health.

You too may want to pause and think back to times when you were particularly ashamed of something or many things. Perhaps do what I did and list 10 things for which you felt shame. Then try to recall or create 10 statements or examples of your pride that were or are directly or indirectly associated with helping you overcome the specific or generalized shame. Be prepared. This journey may startle you. Clients and others I know who followed this 10-and-10 path truly amazed themselves with the obviousness of (1) things about which they felt shame, and (2) examples of their feelings or expressions of pride apparently directly tied to the shame they identified. Quickly they agreed — Pride Equals Shame.

As this book goes to press, I have not yet heard of anyone who tried this exercise who was unable to link with 10 examples of pride 10 possibly causative or contributory examples of shame. Weight, height, looks, intelligence, family history, ethnicity, religion, social standing, schooling, neighborhoods, sexuality, indiscretions, health issues, handicaps, shoplifting, cheating on taxes, lies, and trumped-up resumes are among the easiest to identify causes of shame that could be quickly linked to specific expressions of pride. If you are unwilling to delve this deeply into your own life, take an imaginary walk in shoes of anyone with shame about the above, and think about how pride could be used to mask "the issue(s)."

How many proud people have you met who have been far too quick to let you know they "are" a Ph.D., graduated from Harvard, Princeton, Yale, or another Ivy League school, or grew-up in a community's neighborhood known for exceptional privilege?

Conversely, count those who came from nothing who rose to become doctors, Ivy League grads, and now live on the green side of the tracks. With both extremes, apply abundant empathy and extra understanding to try to reveal and deal with likely shame-filled roots of certain pride.

Yes, even middle-age and older adults who are eager for you to know they were born with silver spoons in their mouths, must have reasons to be prideful in boasting about their early years. For the exercise in compassion, assume the roots are connected to some degree of unresolved shame.

Encourage the proud to be **deeply pleased** about what they are doing today, what they envision doing tomorrow, and how the good they do touches others beyond themselves. No one may have empowered them to really feel good about themselves — for right-and-proper reasons.

It is right-and-proper to avoid forcing on others your pride. Let's all make a concerted effort to be deeply pleased, not proud. Deeply pleased. Feeling deep satisfaction rejuvenates the mind, body and soul.

Let go of shame. Let go of pride. To thrive we must learn and teach all children and adults lasting value in identifying and assessing their own inner goodness and strengths. Aim for deeply felt satisfaction.

Patience is essential with pride you encounter. Releasing ourselves from the bonds of pride requires exceptional amounts of patience with ourselves, others, process, and providence. Ancient words work:

"For everyone who exalts himself will be humbled,
and he who humbles himself will be exalted." —Luke 14:11

Or, for the purpose of this chapter, "*Too many with unresolved shame will grow proud, and their eventual fall will bring more shame.*" Let us stop it all.

Empower yourself and others to feel uniquely and deeply pleased with skills and other blessings of perceptiveness, discernment, and sound judgment. Then, with genuine excitement about your impact on yourself and others, selflessly share specifics of the humble and hubris-free wonder of you — the self-actualized and high-EQ you whom you are deeply pleased and highly satisfied (not proud) to be.

"Give pride a rest. Put deeply felt satisfaction to the test.
Be thrilled — not proud — to be functioning at your best." —JRDjr

With a deep breath or three, please pause to imagine feeling deeply pleased. Feel deep, deep satisfaction. Feel relief from releasing shame. Lift thoughts and actions toward ever-greater greatness. Feel it all.

Pride. Expound.

Randomness

Chapter Inspired by and Dedicated to Steven K. Rothschild, M.D.

Insert or imagine seeing your first name: _____,

Seeing this chapter's title word, what immediately comes to your open mind? Do you already have a working relationship with this word? Somewhere inside of you does this word instantly appeal? As a response to a specific situation at-hand, will this word work to your and others' advantage? For this word to increase in real value, together we must dig, drill and think deeper, so we will reach, climb and soar higher.

Randomness may not seem a likely word for illustrating for fully responsible leaders true-north strategic alignment. Indeed it is. Random thoughts reap great rewards for strategic alignment of people, money, time, technology, and other mission-critical resources.

Brilliant, perceptive and empathic Steven K. Rothschild, M.D. suggests, in effect, randomness is really about mindfulness (hence the above salutation next to which you wrote your name), allowing our brains to roam unencumbered; giving ourselves deeply internalized permission to free-associate with a specific or an unspecified purpose. Identifying with the nuanced meaning of this HILL Word's value, Dr. Rothschild wrote, "Randomness is about the importance of not getting stuck in our work, in our relationships, and in our lives. There are many times that I allow myself to feel frustration about a problem, then when I open myself up — through meditation, running, or creative play — I discover random experiences that point to an unexpected solution." In effect Dr. Steve said randomness is mindfulness about randomness. I like that a lot. We must give our good minds and hearts time and space to land in uncharted places.

In 1966 we started hearing on television, "Space, the final frontier. These are the voyages of the starship *Enterprise*. Its five-year mission: to explore strange new worlds, to seek out new life and new civilizations, to boldly go where no man has gone before." This sounds a lot like randomness — unfettered exploration of wide-open space called The Universe; essentially spotlighting the human mind's limitless multiverse for random thinking.

In the early 1980s a Hollywood friend at Paramount arranged for daughter Jennifer and me to take a private tour of Star Trek's amazingly fragile, very dusty, and closed-to-the-public original television set. After an excited workman struggled to remember how to power-up all the little lights and motors so Miss Dallas could sit in Captain Kirk's chair and feel what it was like to push lighted buttons to command the *Enterprise*, suddenly I realized the TV program's melodramatic introduction was prime-time dramatization for visualizing my electronic publishing company's five-year mission; its five-year business plan, "...to boldly go where no *company* had gone before." I was so distracted by this leadership thought, I neglected to follow Jennifer's footsteps so I too could say I sat in William Shatner's famous CEO hot seat. When I returned to New York armed with this clever *Aha!* moment to motivate my teams during one too many staff meetings to come, I was demonstrating the real-world applicability of randomness. To my face I was spared being called a *Trekkie* (and I am not), yet surely some good souls "under my command" wished I had never visited the Bridge of the Enterprise. Randomness has its risks.

Now Detroit's Science Center invites children of all ages to its life-size replica of Star Trek's bridge. I hope companies take their leadership teams to sit in the captain's chair and stand at the control panels and monitors so they can try to feel the thrill of stretching their minds to be paradoxically ready for the unexpected. Going where no man had gone before, on 20 July 1969 *Apollo 11* Commander Neil Alden Armstrong and Lunar Module Pilot Edwin Eugene 'Buzz' Aldrin, Jr. became the first humans to walk on the Moon. The bar was raised. Even today's best video games probably fail to expand the mind's reach the way fantasy and reality of the 1960s era worked randomness into the minds and hearts of us teenage leaders-in-training. Now called by Tom Brokaw "The Greatest Generation," bold baby boomers we are.

Engraved in gold wedding bands my former wife Cynthia and I exchanged on 26 May 1973, were reminders of the importance of randomness to keep our relationship fresh: *"With innocence of little children we approach…"* Intentional nurturing of child-like wonderment in one's adult life is very good psychology. Childish thoughts and behaviors are different, and not to be encouraged. At times child-like thoughts and actions may feel childish, yet the profound difference grows more obvious with passing years.

Too many of us grown-ups don't allow ourselves or others (of any age) time or space for random thinking. Too few of us allow our brains to wander non-judgmentally. By training our mind's eye to focus on any and all, and attuning our third ear to hear sounds perhaps imperceptible to others, we enable mysterious dynamics of fresh-air thinking — thus increasing upside potential for true innovation to emerge from our thoughts and actions.

Inherent and inescapable polarity in natural order permits our minds to start-off in one direction and end-up elsewhere. When plotting a true-north destination for strategic alignment, it is good practice for fully responsible leaders to encourage flexibility for all the minds at-work on a set journey. Intentionally we must dismantle road blocks within our innovative thinking patterns and processes. Hillview clients are asked to *"Break through the mental blocks while trying to think outside the metal box."* By permitting instead of fighting randomness in our thinking, we create a better-than-even chance to "get there" and beyond. Eventually one must check a compass and streamline the course, but not too soon.

To chart a new thinking path for your roles in our country's economic strength ahead, what random thoughts come to your mind when you or someone else asks how in the world We the People periodically get to each loud and annoying economic wake-up call? Do you start by blaming others for recklessness with their fiduciary responsibility, and assailing others' fiscal imprudence? Or do you begin with connecting dots — from before each fiscal meltdown — with your own accrued credit scores, size of mortgage(s) and their rate(s), luxuries purchased beyond your means, household budgets ignored, charitable contributions delayed, savings plans forgotten, any sense of entitlement (even from unfulfilled childhood days), or even a hint in your mind of "getting as much as you can before someone else gets it?" Have you any view, behavior, or factor that could implicate you and yours with at least small parts in the big drama playing itself out on the world's economic stage? Is it time to craft and follow a new script? In quick-time and at a high level, let's think this through with both random and linear thinking below.

"We might be able to stimulate our way back to stability,
but we can only invent our way back to prosperity.
We need everyone at every level to get smarter."
—Thomas L. Friedman in *The New York Times*, 27 June 2009

In one-with-one conversation and meetings of many, give time and space for thoughts to roam — at least for awhile. For robust collaborative thinking, enjoin others in intentional randomness. Expect yourself and others to be startled by unexpected thoughts. You will be. With a deep breath, a smile, and a secret pat on your own back, reward yourself for allowing things into your purview you might have otherwise left out. Encourage others to note and feel good about their own breakthroughs when they move away from strictly linear thinking.

Random thinking should be enjoyable, not frightening; strengthening, not weakening. There is no way to successfully implement a bad idea, so there is no reason to fear contemplating a full range of ideational options. The very pursuit of any good, bad, or other thought or idea will yield more thoughts and possibly other ideas — particularly if we allow our gray matter time for the fullness of randomness, instead of the comparative inflexibility of a set-in-stone mind.

Victor Hugo wrote in *Les Misérables*, "The quantity of any civilization is measured by the quality of imagination." True. It's also helpful, I believe, to reverse two key words, "The quality of any civilization is measured by the quantity of imagination." Random thinking powers great quantities of quality imagination. Innovation requires imagination.

Do you learn at the speed of instruction? Classes taught in schools and on street corners teach restrictive and constrictive thinking. Black-and-white answers to life's Technicolor questions come from professors of letters and schools of hard knocks. Before or when a problem cries out for solution, or a sought-after opportunity remains elusive, cross-check in the equation applicable lessons learned, findings, and any so-called absolutes. Without these routine mental gymnastics, we may allow incorrect input to stop our innovative output.

Quantum mathematics and zero-tolerance sciences require rigidity. Yet mature mathematicians and scientists are quick to reveal how great discoveries in their fields were triggered by relatively random thoughts. Professor Einstein might have said there is relativity in randomness.

Was a mathematical truth discovered or invented? Was the truth there before someone thought a different way to reveal the truth that was there all along and waiting for discovery? Do you sense in discovery the key role of randomness? For leaders to build cultures of creativity and innovation, randomness needs to be defined, described, illustrated, encouraged, empowered, allowed and funded.

All random thoughts are connected to a greater force. Predestination is at one extreme of this assumption, and on the other is the scientific view of progressive neuropathic electrical impulses and synaptic processes of nature, nurture, and stored-up experience. In the spiritual realm or in neuroscience, random thinking produces noteworthy results. Random thoughts happen when we give our brains permission to fire at-will.

Giving random thoughts room in your mind to wander is not high-risk behavior. Random happens. Random works. Respect and nurture randomness in the ways you *think, think, think*. Un-think. Out-think. Re-think. THINK. Think and thank your random thoughts.

A 1978 pre-Internet visit to The New York Public Library, the majestic Beaux-Arts building on the southwest corner of Fifth Avenue and 42nd Street — guarded by the single-word-named lions *Patience* (to the south) and *Fortitude* (to the north) — allowed me to learn a bit more than I knew about the prestigious school chosen to give our native New Yorker a leg-up in her early education. On Manhattan's Upper East Side, former wife Cynthia and I would enroll our precocious 18-month-old Jennifer Gray Dallas in All Souls School.

While engaged in fatherly fact-finding, I was distracted by unrelated reference to Oxford's All Souls College. This is when and how I first uncovered Oxford's "Essay" to which I refer in the Preface. This random encounter with an unexpected fact stimulated a wealth of thoughts and ideas about what I could do with my love for words. I shall forever remain intrigued by the randomness of such findings, and also with polarity of a sixth sense acknowledging Providence at-work.

> *"If the doors of perception were cleansed, everything*
> *would appear to man as it is, infinite."* —William Blake

This moment, please allow yourself a few moments of random thinking about any evocative points above that arrested your attention. See how quickly you either find fault with what was just offered, or you give yourself a chance to think freely and randomly about whatever the above elaboration might have unleashed in you. Even initially negative thoughts can yield positive outcomes.

> *"Practice random kindness and senseless*
> *acts of beauty."* —Anne Herbert

How are you doing? Are you fighting this friendly appeal for at least a few moments each day of free-wheeling thought? Let it happen. See where your mind takes you. I suspect you will be pleasantly surprised.

> *"I would rather have a mind opened by wonder*
> *than one closed by belief."* —Gerry Spence

For mental, emotional, physical and societal health, let's always work to avoid the trap of feeling more powerful in darkness of negative thinking than in the bright light of positive thought. Instead of expecting or fearing destructiveness in your randomness, aim for and anticipate constructiveness. Instead of a victim's choice of constriction of myopia, choose the victor's conviction to always open the mind and heart to think things through—with both random and structured thinking.

In this life change is ceaseless. Randomness seems to walk hand-in-hand with change. In random order, together we're all in-step.

Thank you for allowing these not-so-random thoughts about random thinking to resonate yet untold lasting value in your life. The deeper we dig, drill and think about the meaning of life, randomness in our observations can yield surprises. Perhaps by fully embracing the notion of hidden potential in randomness, we have higher probability of finding otherwise undiscoverable meaningfulness in our lives.

> *"The meaning of life is to make life meaningful."* —A.C. Grayling

Randomness. Expound.

Reach

Chapter Inspired by and Dedicated to Karl Flemke (1931-1994)

Insert or imagine seeing your first name: _____,

Seeing this chapter's title word, what immediately comes to your open mind? Do you already have a working relationship with this word? Somewhere inside of you does this word instantly appeal? As a response to a specific situation at-hand, will this word work to your and others' advantage? For this word to increase in real value, together we must dig, drill and think deeper, so we will reach, climb and soar higher.

Being reachable and teachable about reach is more than a turn of phrase. For fully responsible leaders, reaching — and teaching reach — are mission-critical daily responsibilities.

Why do so many of us grown-ups stop reaching for brass rings on life's merry-go-round rides? In fearing failure or success, or worrying too much about being burned by hot stoves of many types, were too many of us overly warned of unspecified risk of reaching too high?

Real risk is taking no risk at all. Greater risk is in not reaching deep enough before reaching high enough. On your team, who appears to be afraid to reach deep before reaching high? Ask yourself, her, or him why? Why?

> *"Do not fear mistakes. You will know failure. Continue to reach out."*
> —Benjamin Franklin

A way up and out of today's global economic quagmire begins with fully responsible leaders reaching deep for wisdom, courage and patience about OUR ways of thinking and OUR actions — individually and collectively — that might have contributed to this multi-tier meltdown. Only then can we ethically and intellectually dare to reach high for solutions never attempted, or perhaps revisit remedies tried before their time. Professor Einstein taught us to use different thinking than the thought patterns that caused (or tolerated) the problem we are attempting to solve. Perhaps in ways we have never thought about or dared, we each have to reach deep, over, under, around, through, wide, out, and up. Yes, reach!

"By three methods we may learn wisdom:
First, by reflection, which is noblest;
Second, by imitation, which is easiest; and
third by experience, which is the bitterest." —Confucius

How soon will U.S. politicians and marketers again say exactly the same misleading words about reaching for "The American Dream?" Among replacements for The American Dream Wish List of big homes, luxury cars, fast boats, exotic trips, and the like should be (1) starting, investing in, or otherwise supporting any viable business that creates and sustains jobs, (2) giving back to communities through trustworthy not-for-profit organizations, (3) respecting and protecting God's blue-and-green earth, and (4) otherwise reallocating discretionary or sacrificed time and other resources to benefit more than oneself. How in the land of freedom for all did The American Dream become so selfish? Let's all reach deep and high to shift this paradigm toward equitability. We must never stop reaching for equality in opportunity for all persons to live life to the fullest.

"To reach a port, we must sail. Sail, not tie at anchor. Sail, not drift."
—Franklin D. Roosevelt

When daughter Jennifer was a toddler, former wife Cynthia and I would often encourage the reach of our cherub by demonstrating the popular early-play game called, "SO BIG!" Can you hear, see and feel this developmental psychology in play? Do you recall, "Bend and stretch! Reach for the sky?" Did you, or do you, do simple reach-building and strength-building empowerment exercises with children and adults counting on you to set standards for reach? In "SO BIG!" the parents' and the child's hands stretch and reach high. Reaching exercises are much more than physical. All children (and adults) are being taught to stretch and reach high — with thoughts, smiles, laughter, joy, and a sense of being "in this together;" collaborating on a mysterious win-win psychological developmental experience of hearing and feeling that it is possible to "reach for the stars."

"I hear and I forget. I see and I remember. I do and I understand."
—Confucius

Children taught by-example love and faith in their homes, schools, places of worship, and other safe havens feel the reach into their hearts of trusted adults. When untrustworthy sellers of goods, services, myths or myopia start to reach into their young minds and wallets, one prays the potential victim's earliest lessons in discernment took root.

Standards of Reach

Attacks on a high-reach individual's ego, intelligence, judgment, and other easy emotional targets are almost instantly launched by those who rarely reach beyond their self-imposed or societally dictated comfort levels. Reaching high in business or other ventures often brings animosity, envy, subterfuge, or worse. Innumerable successful multi-million-dollar business concepts first met with dismissive, pejorative, insulting, and otherwise damaging disinterest. Scowls, frowns, raised eyebrows, deep sighs, and rolled eyes can dampen spirits of high-reach leaders. Conversely, push-back by those who fight the childhood joy of "SO BIG!" can strengthen the reaching person's resolve to reach higher and higher. Pondering polarity (*i.e.,* identifying downside risk in shadows) is part of smart reaching. If only more of the many naysayers were unquestionable in assumed selfless motivation for instantly challenging others' ideas, plans and actions.

"You need to overcome the tug of people against you as you reach for high goals." —George S. Patton

With your vision and mission in mind, will you reach today's set (1) goals, (2) objectives, (3) standards, and (4) other predetermined performance criteria of fully responsible leadership? Will you (a) forgive yourself for unavoidably missing marks, (b) learn available lessons, and (c) consciously strive in your reaching to aim better or more realistically?

"When you reach the end of your rope, tie a knot in it and hang on." —Thomas Jefferson

Reaching through your mind's blocks is more significant for success than "thinking outside the box." If certain blocks remain, a box does not allow you to go outside. You would be trapped inside the box.

"Have no fear of perfection — you'll never reach it." —Salvador Dali

Reach deep before reaching high. Know for sure your heart and your mind are strategically aligned. Trust these simple-sounding words are anything but trite or mundane.

Allow trial-and-error to inform your reach for the next brass rings on your life's exciting merry-go-round. Reaching does not guarantee you will reach your goal or destination. Often you will exceed your reach and neglect to acknowledge the extra mile you traveled, almost as if you had planned to outperform your set goal. When you reach and fall short, perhaps fear of failure — or fear of success — interrupted your journey. Whomever or whatever extended or curtailed your reach, learn deeper, wider and higher lessons from the experience of successful or not-so-successful reaching. Lessons work in your favor.

"Would you like me to give you a formula for success? It's quite simple, really. Double your rate of failure. You are thinking of failure as the enemy of success. But it isn't at all. You can be discouraged by failure or you can learn from it. So go ahead and make mistakes. Make all you can. Because remember that's where you will find success." —Thomas J. Watson

Pause to allow your fine mind and heart to thoughtfully fill-in blanks for excerpts drawn from a strategic alignment assessment worksheet, selected from Hillview's Executive Coaching Toolkit for Reach:

"Today I am going to first reach deeper, wider and higher:

     for _____(a reachable goal)?

     to overcome _____ (a thinking hurdle)?

     to support _____ (a person in-need)?

     to strengthen _____ (an organization in-need)?

     to start _____ (a worthy venture or initiative)?

     to stop _____ (a bad practice, habit or policy)?"

What reach-worthy thoughts, people and plans came to your mind? Keep thinking. Keep reaching. It is Job No. 1 — to keep reaching.

"Choose a job you love, and you will never have to work a day in your life." —Confucius

Thank you for these few moments of being reachable about reaching.

Reach. Expound.

Rejuvenation

Chapter Inspired by and Dedicated to Susan Bardy Porter

Insert or imagine seeing your first name: _____,

Seeing this chapter's title word, what immediately comes to your open mind? Do you already have a working relationship with this word? Somewhere inside of you does this word instantly appeal? As a response to a specific situation at-hand, will this word work to your and others' advantage? For this word to increase in real value, together we must dig, drill and think deeper, so we will reach, climb and soar higher.

Take a deep rejuvenating breath, and slowly let it out. Again, please take a deep rejuvenating breath, and slowly let it out. For three, take one more deep breath. Below in this chapter I know what's coming-up for you, and we both need to keep breathing as your good mind and heart process these thoughts toward living and loving in rejuvenating ways. As I am burnishing this text for you, I am mindfully breathing more deeply, and exhaling more slowly. Join me, please.

Do you allow yourself ample time for rejuvenation through deep breathing and other rejuvenating exercises? It takes extra effort for me to think to slow down long enough to practice what I preach about making time for oneself for rejuvenating, recharging, regrouping, or re-energizing mind, body and soul. Thanks to caring souls mentioned later in this chapter, I am getting better.

With a constructive and otherwise positive mindset, practiced body language, and abundant ascendancy toward win-win outcomes, fully responsible leaders breathe oxygen into each room they enter. (Less responsible leaders seem to suck oxygen out of rooms they enter.) It is essential, therefore, for fully responsible leaders to breathe deeply and exhale slowly. Wisdom, courage and patience are the three rejuvenating HILL Words I encourage saying three times to yourself or out loud as a deep-breathing, deep-thinking, deep-feeling exercise.

The third set is whispered then followed by the deepest breath and relaxing exhalation of celebration for the peace of rejuvenation that comes with these three words used as a prayer, mantra, plea, chant, or statement of conviction and intention. Yes, three words can allow rejuvenation through *thinking and digging a little deeper while we reach and climb a lot higher.*

You know HILL Words in this collection of 52 weekly words allow us to focus on personal, organizational, economic, societal, political, spiritual, and other significance of individual words; single words than can make all the difference in the world in terms of success, failure, or finding ourselves feeling stuck somewhere in-between. Rejuvenation is a word that can allow us to break through blocks to think outside the box. This word is worthy of an extra moment or two of reflection for a lifetime of edification.

Economic growth is sometimes called economic rejuvenation. U.S. Gross Domestic Product (GDP) is the total market value of all final goods and services produced in a given year within our country, equal to total consumer spending, investment allocation, and government spending – plus the value of exports, minus the value of imports. Got it? Read it again, as this is an acronym that many use but few understand. As GDP increases at a speed notably faster than up-to-the-minute macroeconomics models predict, rejuvenation is heralded as a harbinger of more good to come. If the U.S. economy surges at a three to four percent rate, perhaps most economists would agree with rejuvenation as a sufficient definitive term. Unless there is an adverse environmental side-effect of fast growth, such as an increase in pollution or the creation by default of some other threat, economic rejuvenation is a good thing.

New products or services from entrepreneurs in hot pursuit of promise and profits can rejuvenate at least their local economies. Perhaps most economic rejuvenation stems from entrepreneurship. And if per chance the entrepreneurs' products or services promise and deliver rejuvenation or life-extension to humans, organizations, or other "living organisms," so much the better for all.

Nearly every part of my 20 years living in Manhattan was rejuvenating. There is an energy coursing through the veins of New York City that picked me up on some of my most down days there. There were many dark and dismal days. While there I lived through and survived two national economic meltdowns, divorce, cardiac arrest, suicide of a young friend, and high-profile front-page firings from *Fortune 500* top posts of two of my best pals, plus 101 or more other back-breaking tests of my mettle.

Thankfully bad memories of New York days are outnumbered by the good-to-great days. For readers, audiences and myself, I am trying to remember deeper lessons learned from career and personal crucibles there. Fairly quickly I always seem to get back to having a smile welling up from deep inside. New York survives and so do I. New York is rejuvenating. I hope and pray I am at least somewhat rejuvenating for family, colleagues, clients, readers, audience members, and other friends who honor themselves and me with the rejuvenating pause each HILL Word is intended to facilitate.

In our abundant imperfection there is authenticity in Manhattan and me. On that small island I saw the best of its quality-of-life, and I don't regret also seeing some of its worst. NYC is polarity. As the capital of the world, New York offers good and other lessons for every major city to heed. Even beloved Chicago can learn a thing or two from a city only 793.87 miles from my Gold Coast location to Wall Street's west entrance — but who's measuring? Chicago and New York are well within the eastern third of the U.S., and yet sometimes it seems as if both metropolises are in different countries. One of the two cities triumphantly plays on the global stage, while the other expects the world to come play on its proud stage. Take a guess which is which.

During a particularly formative era in my 1980s career, my office was upstairs of the New York Stock Exchange (NYSE). On rare occasion I would visit pals on the Exchange floor, usually to impress a VIP visitor in-tow who just "had to" see The Floor. Once would have been enough for me. I knew where the big decisions were being made. On the NYSE Floor the high-wire tension would get to sturdy me. Down there many were speaking a foreign language in other-borough accents. Back then too many exhaled deep breaths smelled of cigarettes, cigars, marijuana, and beer, and illegal drugs were not difficult to detect in bloodshot eyes, erratic behavior, and unjustified rudeness and impatience.

After either terribly trying or high-flying days of work, at least weekly a handful of us would gather at Michael's Pub 71 Broadway. For his senior folk our employer kept there an open tab. We counted on his generosity in underwriting those after-hours deep breaths of rejuvenation. The bartender was particularly fond of our owner's unchallenged deep pockets and our extra tips, so he lavishly poured what became known as a "Dallas pour." Lincoln town cars with drivers were always waiting to take us each to our next rejuvenating locale for the evening, so normally we knew when to quit drinking, sign, and move-on to the next of several stops ahead. Evenings in New York required a steady diet of rejuvenation. Sometimes we even stopped to eat food.

Our parent organization had empty executive offices on the 16th floor of 71 Broadway (formerly known as United States Steel Building), and eventually the subsidiary I ran moved there (roughly one wide block west of the Exchange). Outside my corner office was a clear view of the gleaming World Trade Center, and historic Trinity Cathedral and its storied cemetery were right below my window. During quiet evenings of spring, summer, and fall months I would open wide those giant old windows and take deep rejuvenating breaths before jumping back into whatever task was keeping me on the 16th floor instead of downstairs at Michael's Pub or elsewhere in "my city." During evening hours the Wall Street area of downtown Manhattan became a ghost town, relatively speaking. It was peaceful, and occasionally a bit eerie. Everything is relative.

When in 1999 I arrived to live and work in Chicago, I found rejuvenation of a different kind. Frankly, I was not welcomed with open arms. The widely distributed press release announcing my CEO post at Chicago Title Credit did not merit mention in any Chicago paper. The befuddled PR people stopped trying. An east coast business leader coming to giant old Chicago Title was not going to make news in Chicago. No one wrote a note or letter to welcome me to Chicago.

Even the church I soon joined never sent a note to thank me for visiting those many consecutive Sundays. Feeling somewhat rebuffed, yet hardly preoccupied with the notion, I decided mythical so-called Midwest Values did not include automatic hospitality to new leaders in town, and so I would have to earn my welcome to Chicago. Trust I was far too busy to be obsessed, yet I was aware of an undercurrent of disconnection in my life. I was being left alone. Perhaps because I was a divorced and unattached man, I did not fit in Chicago's couple-driven social set, or so I wondered. I knew in Manhattan I loved my unofficial role as "the extra man." Savvy hosts and hostesses invited and expected me to stir-up conversation and movement at parties, especially when couples might cling only to each other for social safety. At gatherings most upwardly mobile New York couples seem to know to strategically separate and circulate! It works.

During my first year or so in Chicago, every black-tie charity event I attended I learned about through my church or in the news media. After writing large checks and contributing to silent auctions, I marveled at the lack of thank you notes or inclusion on mailing lists for future events. In Chicago it seemed I was invisible. Even my political party seemed inept in their fund-raising follow-up apparatus.

Paradoxically I found it all rejuvenating. I was relaxing in Chicago in ways I could not relax on the east coast. In Grant Park, quite literally I was stopping to smell the roses. In New York's Central Park or the District's Rock Creek Park (for years I lived and worked in both New York and the DC area), I was almost oblivious to rejuvenating power of drinking-in natural beauty. Normally I was on my bicycle peddling away pretending I was getting a good work-out. In Grant Park I would get off the bike and enjoy the beauty. Sometimes the beauty actually hurt. I decided what I was feeling were holes in my heart being filled with unconditional access to a city's beauty.

Unlike New York and Washington, in Chicago back then I knew almost no one. Things have changed. Within one year after arriving to live full-time in Chicago, without a moment's hesitation I threw myself into servant leadership at Fourth Presbyterian Church, the neo-gothic architectural splendor across Michigan Avenue from The John Hancock Tower. Sainted Larry Nicholson, the Church's Director of Volunteer Ministry, asked me to be an usher. I totally surprised myself when I said yes. Years earlier at Manhattan's Fifth Avenue Presbyterian Church and Alexandria's Old Presbyterian Meeting House I would not add ushering to my Deacon duties.

Thinking back to those first steps at Chicago's Fourth Church, I had not yet identified how lonely I was. Now I know. Within one year of joining the large church, I was blessed to be nominated, elected and ordained as an Elder, and finally I started to feel welcome in Chicago. As a servant leader I worked hard, tried my best, and otherwise took seriously the centuries-old Church of Scotland tradition of lay leaders contributing time, talent, and other gifts to the church. Perhaps to the dismay of a truly stellar and large professional staff of clergy and other professionals, I needed little support for my committee work and other volunteer activities. Called to love and serve, I was loving and serving. My rejuvenation continued. Was I rejuvenating others?

When in 2001 Chicago Title Corporation was purchased by a California company, suddenly I was out of a dream job I thought I'd have for many years. Then mostly because of Fourth Church I remained living in Chicago. My Chicago Title severance package allowed me several years of flexibility. Friends were calling me back east, but I felt something rejuvenating in Chicago I did not feel quite the same way in New York or Northern Virginia. Yes, rejuvenation.

Hypothetically rejuvenation is the term used to categorize scientific and marketplace interest in at least cosmetic reversal of the aging process. Many skin products and other potions name or claim rejuvenation. The mere thought of rejuvenation may extend our lives. I plan to retire at 100 years of age, so quite often I think about rejuvenation. Rejuvenation is not the same as life extension. In order to slow the unstoppable human aging process, life extension strategies oppose causes of aging. Rejuvenation is intentional reversal of damage caused by aging, replacement or repair of damage associated with aging, or replacement with new tissue of damaged tissue. Rejuvenation can be a method of life extension. Rejuvenation keeps our minds sharp, I believe.

While I was rejuvenating myself in Chicago, Dad John, Sr. died in Pittsburgh. Grandparents, aunts and uncles all met their reward. Only Mother survives from her generation, and she'll out-live her mother who died at 95, my grandmother Regina Elizabeth Shearer. As for me, I am the last male Dallas of an old Pennsylvania family, so my mortality seems a bit more pronounced, though not imposingly. My rejuvenation continues.

In 1979, when I was 29, a flat-line full cardiac arrest was misinterpreted as a heart attack. So I was told to "get my affairs in order" (*e.g.,* say my good-byes and be certain my Last Will and Testament was signed, sealed and delivered to my estranged wife and precious toddler daughter Jennifer). As I might not live longer than 36 hours (based on the severity of the symptoms and result), I got my affairs in order. Well, sort of. I knew I would live. Three days later an unspecified viral infection was blamed — not heart failure from Type-A stress, as was immediately suspected by squadrons of teary-eyed well-wishers. Acute pericarditis and myocarditis occurring together stopped my heart, and yet there was zero cardiac damage. My heart just stopped. Period. Thank God that was not the end of the sentence.

On her very first night on-duty in Lenox Hill Hospital's Coronary Care Unit, young (27) Lynn Glickman, R.N. re-started my heart. Thank heavens for fast-thinking and fast-acting Lynn Glickman. Without much moral support from the physicians who jumped to wrong conclusions, almost immediately I knew my rejuvenation began. I had seen *the light*, so I was at-peace with any outcome of the next 36 hours or so. Vivid memory of my out-of-body experience has been explained away by scientists as my brain's electrical system shutting down, yet this moment I recall every peaceful and spiritual nanosecond. I returned to Earth. As I was sorting through what happened, immediately I knew I had my two-year-old precious daughter Jennifer to live for, and I did. I do.

In 2003 a hemorrhaging brain aneurysm and sub-arachnoid coiling procedure preceded a subsequent stroke, 72 hours after what they called "the bleed." Eventually I was bluntly told survival statistics for my combination of developments indicated within 30 days I had a 60 percent chance of dying. Seven days into the 30-day countdown, I was released from hospital and not to be left alone. I knew I was not going to die. From the smiles on faces when they saw me alive against formidable odds, I was already sure rejuvenation had begun. Adult daughter Jennifer was front-and-center in my mind as I struggled to regain mobility, mental acuity, normal eyesight, and regular speech patterns. Even after she returned to New York, she was with me every tentative and painful step of the way. At bedside, Fourth Church Co-Pastor Joanna Adams (now back in her hometown Atlanta) willed and prayed me back to a higher level of consciousness. Feelings and words she used helped to put me on the professional path I follow this day.

Sadly I remember almost no one from the squadrons of visitors I'm told came to hospital, yet daughter Jennifer, Michael Russell, David Turner, and pastor Joanna Adams each succeeded in parting the thick clouds. Through their eyes I liked what I saw, even if I could not yet express very well what I was seeing.

Talk about rejuvenation! As I was struggling for my life, boldly the Reverend Joanna encouraged me to enter seminary ASAP and become a Presbyterian minister. What in the world was she thinking? She knew what she was doing. Instead of seminary I chose a somewhat stealth faith-based ministry of sorts. As a strategic alignment consultant, coach and speaker — for my trusting clients and others rolling on parallel tracks heading true-north toward their personal and organizational success — I am driven by a cradle-to-grave calling to serve as a non-denominational rejuvenator. From time to time I still hear a faint call to traditional ministry. I'm listening.

During those post-stroke days a communion of saints at my side added to my rapid rejuvenation. My esteemed personal physician, Rush University internist Stephen K. Rothschild, M.D. suggested I would probably recover 80% of my former strengths. Then he and all other medical and rehabilitation pros were astounded when I appeared to break records. I am guessing, if somehow I were tested for a rate of recovery, long ago I probably passed a 95% milestone.

The left brain controls the right side of the body, and damage done in that portion of my tried-and-tested brain still seems resistant to re-wiring to reverse the head-to-toe infirmities on my right side. I still sustain faith someday my entire right side will be chronic pain-free, and perhaps someday I will regain lost temperature sensitivity on that side. Maybe a few other nettlesome nits will be history. The sooner the better, but I am not complaining. I am exceedingly grateful for what I have recovered, so I don't even pray for further rejuvenation. I have a sense it will happen in due course. Providence is at work. Rejuvenation of any type can take a long time.

Every Christmastide I think of New York City philanthropist extraordinaire Mrs. Brooke Astor, a woman who rejuvenated an entire city by her tireless philanthropic efforts for the arts, and especially for Andrew Carnegie's incomparable New York Public Library system. She died at 105 years of age. In the early 1980s it was a distinct honor for me to meet Mrs. Astor through a personal friend, The Reverend Canon John G. B. Andrew OBE, Rector of her beloved church, St. Thomas on Fifth Avenue at 53rd Street. For several Christmas Eve worship services, Mrs. Astor and I were seated together in special needlepoint-art cushioned-seats in the high chancel of the grand Anglican church, seating I was told architects dutifully designed for visiting royalty, high-ranking visiting clergy, and other VIPs. Humble and simple I was just thrilled to be singing carols alongside Mrs. Astor. I will always remember her good spirit and joy. Her generosity to The New York Public Library is legendary. Privately I was very aware of "small" kindnesses she would pass through "The Rector's Discretionary Fund" (*i.e.*, a constant-balance bottomless checkbook in his center desk drawer) for helping those in need. Many Mrs. Astor stories challenged my mind and warmed my heart regarding her magnanimousness, beneficence, and other generosity of spirit and funds. Mrs. Astor lived to rejuvenate others.

News reports of Mrs. Astor's sad final years in mind-wary seclusion weighed heavily on me. When in late 2009 her son was jailed for stealing millions from his ailing mother, after willfully neglecting her as if to wish her dead, a new lesson from Mrs. Astor hit me in a most poignant way. With all her millions she could not buy immortality, of course, or even secure humane treatment from her privileged son.

She rejuvenated millions of people with millions of dollars wisely bequeathed, and yet ultimately withered, died, and surely is sitting at the left hand of her Father seeing if she can influence Him to give more to His people. I purchased the best-selling book about her final years, read one or two chapters, and had to put it down. I have yet to get up more nerve to read additional detail about her undeserved trials and tribulations in her 80s, 90s, and 100s. She deserved better final days.

To think and dig a little deeper as we reach and climb a lot higher, physical rejuvenation and organizational rejuvenation deserve strategic alignment. The inter-connectivity of the physical self reminds us of interdependencies within organizations of nearly any type or size. Large, small, and other size organizations must be mindful of needs to align strengths at all levels; from bottom-to-top, top-to-bottom. Rejuvenation is strategic alignment of strengths.

Rejuvenation and innovation may not be synonymous, yet fusing in our good minds meanings of these words creates alchemy; at once a philosophy and a practice aiming for additional wisdom and sustainability. Too often fat-and-happy organizations need a swift kick in their assets to rekindle innovation to lead to rejuvenation. If the kick comes too late, even the next example of innovation will remain unseen, unheard, untested, unaccepted, and ultimately unprofitable. Timing is almost everything. Eras of protracted economic downturn accelerate discovery of organizational examples of Darwinian survival of the fittest.

Rejuvenation for organizations begins with people. All thoughts and matters associated with organizations begin with people, so one would hope ample resources are being budgeted for meaningfully developing and strategically aligning people. Although the people who make up an organization today may be gone tomorrow, other people continue to rejuvenate the organization until it simulates immortality (sustainability) or withers and dies. I remain disbelieving of the number of name-brand organizations I admired that once thrived on constant rejuvenation, only to meet the Grim Reaper. In Jim Collins' *How the Mighty Fall and Why Some Companies Never Give In*, there are major indications greed and need-for-speed succeeded in arresting attention away from mission-critical focus on non-stop rejuvenation and innovation.

Sometimes I lay awake as conflicting thoughts gnaw away regarding how superficial we remain about learning deeper lessons available to us during times of economic meltdown. Just as each crucible makes us more reachable and teachable, any economic recession should open floodgates of innovation and other creativity. When political expediency of government largess is quick to promise to take the place of self-reliance in a free enterprise capitalist system, innovation surely declines.

Waiting for money to flow from Washington, D.C. or Olympic sponsors in the wings tripped-up many of my fellow Chicagoans. As this book is published, the bulk of expected government bail-out money never made its way to stimulate or rejuvenate Main Street, USA. Chicago's Olympic dreams were dashed by false starts, false hopes, and false claims. Are deeper lessons being learned? I fear not.

When asked by meeting sponsors who retain me to address small or large audiences, I will go as far as I am asked to go in demonstrating misalignment The HILL Model identified in both D.C.'s recovery bail-out promises and pronouncements, and Chicago's Olympic bid announcements. When discreetly I questioned Washington's ways in shoring-up big business while leaving small business to fend for itself (relatively speaking), and how almost instantly I forecast Chicago should not and would not win the Olympic bid for 2016, a few fair-weather acquaintances dismissed me and stopped communicating.

At my stage of age and career, I do not need to hear anyone say, "Well, John, you were right and I was wrong. You win." This is not the point. There was never a personal contest to win. My self-worth is not tied to being right. My self-esteem is aligned with my penchant for intentionally thinking things through to the best of my current ability. New ways of thinking about old problems and issues give me a rejuvenating bolt of energy that carries me through many rough-and-tumble days.

For the good of our economy and society as a whole, I would welcome, however, hearing someone say, "John, patiently you tried to explain to me how you think things through from the perspective of strategic alignment of meaning and message, and maybe now I'll be more open to hearing what you have to say. I may not immediately or ever fully agree with 100% of what you say, of course, yet I could always use some rejuvenation for my thinking." Indeed I pray everyone stops, looks and listens before crossing into believing any economic recovery fantasy that looks too good to be true. If it looks too good to be true, it probably isn't true. There are rare exceptions.

In PBS TV's "Downton Abbey," Violet Crawley, Dowager Countess of Grantham, exquisitely and memorably played by Dame Maggie Smith, asks, "What is a weekend?" For your and my own long-term good, I hope I learn and share more weekend-like ways to rejuvenate mind, body and soul. Esteemed advisor Mike Russell wants me to practice Yoga, former protégées suggested audio books, returning to live, work and *relax* in Manhattan, and other wise tips and taboos.

James Sweeney encourages me to allow more time for relaxation. Ken Hicks underscores my built-in CEO need to lead another large team. Clyde Bowles and Peter Koestenbaum say, in their own Churchillian ways, "never, never, never give up — *persist, persist, persist* — and stay the course." Their rejuvenating thoughts refresh me.

Certain individuals have a milestone impact on our lives. This book honors certain people in my life who have left indelible marks on my mind, body and soul. When occasionally someone from my younger years reminds me of pivotal direction I boldly gave her or him, either directly stated or by example, I am humbled by their exact memory of what transpired. Often I was unaware something I did or said redirected someone's course. These are rejuvenating remembrances.

Words in this book are offered for their potential rejuvenating impact on your life at home, work and everywhere. Acknowledging a single word's deeper meaning can propel you to higher planes for viewing yourself, others, and what could be a limitless multiverse of possibilities. The American Dream is about yearning for rejuvenation.

Seventeen years after its 1886 formal dedication, in 1903 words of rejuvenation were engraved on a bronze plaque and mounted inside the pedestal of The Statue of Liberty. "The New Colossus," a sonnet by poet Emma Lazarus, added lyrics to the music immigrants hear in their hearts when witness to the rejuvenating sight of Lady Liberty:

> Not like the brazen giant of Greek fame,
> With conquering limbs astride from land to land;
> Here at our sea-washed, sunset gates shall stand
> A mighty woman with a torch, whose flame
> Is the imprisoned lightning, and her name
> Mother of Exiles. From her beacon-hand
> Glows world-wide welcome; her mild eyes command
> The air-bridged harbor that twin cities frame.
> "Keep, ancient lands, your storied pomp!" cries she
> With silent lips. "Give me your tired, your poor,
> Your huddled masses yearning to breathe free,
> The wretched refuse of your teeming shore.
> Send these, the homeless, tempest-tost to me,
> I lift my lamp beside the golden door!"

From elementary school until today, I memorize and recite "her cry with silent lips." Between each line and word above, feel the deeply rejuvenating and empowering breaths you allow yourself. Often following gasps caused by new vision and awareness, deep breaths and wide thoughts take us to higher places. Experience rejuvenation in the words: liberty, freedom, independence, equal, justice and all.

Rejuvenation. Expound.

Resistance

Chapter Inspired by and Dedicated to Jennifer Gray Dallas

Insert or imagine seeing your first name: _____,

Seeing this chapter's title word, what immediately comes to your open mind? Do you already have a working relationship with this word? Somewhere inside of you does this word instantly appeal? As a response to a specific situation at-hand, will this word work to your and others' advantage? For this word to increase in real value, together we must dig, drill and think deeper, so we will reach, climb and soar higher.

For fully responsible leaders who are determined to delineate and differentiate real-world factors involved in leading people and managing things, there's extra horsepower in this chapter's HILL Word. In physics, psychology, principles, and practices of fully responsible leadership, the noun re·sist·ance (*ri zis'təns*) plays a pivotal role. Forward, upward, backward, downward, sideways, and no-motion encounters physics of resistance. Physics is the science of measuring. Resistance must be acknowledged and measured. Leaders and machines accept the value of measuring resistance and responding accordingly; mastering methodology and mechanics of igniting, harnessing, releasing, moderating, and otherwise leading people and managing other propellants of *true-north* journeys toward stated destinations.

True-north strategic alignment of people, money, technology, and other mission-critical resources is a study in resistance that would measure up to Newton's Three Laws of Motion. Resistance in flight, car racing, bicycle riding, drilling for oil, and other acts of mobilization reminds us how resistance has benefits beyond obvious.

Imagine more logical reasons to anticipate and perhaps welcome resistance from would-be buyers (*i.e.*, sales objections), employees (*i.e.*, push-back to change), funding resources (*i.e.*, delays or rejection), or journalists (*i.e.*, incredulity or outright negative reporting on the quality of your products or services)? Can you imagine how anticipating, identifying and overcoming resistance can actually cause a favorable end-result to be more lasting and valuable for all parties? Did someone resist you only to eventually accept you or your proposition, and did it not feel better than had she or he immediately acquiesced? Sometimes your having to work harder to overcome resistance makes the reward taste at least a tad sweeter.

If you seize the experience of resistance as a particularly reachable and teachable moment for your understanding of what just happened, deep lessons can be learned. As you were reading this partial list, what other examples come to mind you would characterize as resistance to your leadership or your organization's marketplace competitiveness?

With each chapter of this book, how much resistance do you experience as we think and dig a bit deeper together about such carefully selected words? As you climb with me to higher functional understandings of organizational and personal applicability for each HILL Word, do you feel resistance of wanting to challenge definitions, descriptions, illustrations, stories, or this intentionally nuanced style of engaging you, your mind, and your heart in a collaborative journey? More than once do you have to read some sentences to get from them the meaning you need at the moment? Sometimes do you push-back until you have an "Aha!" moment? Resistance can yield to acceptance, and yet even acceptance contains degrees of resistance.

In one-with-one executive alignment coaching huddles, in awe I watch certain clients resist even the most rudimentary re-calibrations of their HILL views. Until clarity is attained, steadily and patiently I continue to adjust the lens through which each client is struggling to see who and what needs to be seen in new light. Occasionally I see demonstrations of resistance to my craft as a lens cutter. More often we celebrate break-throughs in new vision toward future victory. Resistance can give alert coaches, mentors, therapists, pastors, physicians, educators, attorneys, parents, leaders, bosses, and other supportive people rich insights into more of what needs to be addressed. Reachable and teachable moments can follow what appear to be un-reachable and un-teachable flashes of sometimes inexplicable resistance. There is always a reason for resistance.

Resistance in a National Opinion Poll

Eighteen or so years ago I retained a globally respected opinion polling company to test a number of high-risk assumptions I was making about forecasting national consumer responsiveness to a suite of products I created. As my team and I were eagerly and anxiously awaiting results, to my surprise I learned indications of resistance in such a poll mean the individual respondent is likely to have given a moment or more extra thought before answering. A "highly likely to purchase" response was believed to be more valuable — to my type of predictive behavior queries — than a consumer's choice of "definitely will purchase." This nuance about resistance in polling was news to me, yet instantly it made sense. I heard and felt the logic.

Then when 76% of respondents chose either "highly likely to purchase" or "definitely will purchase," we knew we had a likely winner on our hands. We won. Numerous types of direct-response records were broken. To conduct and analyze the poll cost us over $100,000 (a special discount price through a friendly CEO). Soon we knew the pollster's research was worth every penny and more. To say thanks I took to lunch the polling company's CEO, and he enjoyed basking in the sunlight of a happy customer for his wares. While eating, laughing and gossiping, he opened my eyes further. Although marketing scientists continued to test other elements of the high-profile offer we were about to launch, this poll's evidence of nationwide consumer interest overcame a large percentage of mostly nettlesome resistance from my company's largest stockholder.

Psychodynamic theory calls resistance "the blocking of thoughts whose awareness might cause anxiety," essentially reflecting the human defense mechanism of repression. Imagine all the things we think, say and do that cause or facilitate anxiety for others and ourselves. In your choice of words, speaking voice, tone, tempo, clarity, timing, body language, appearance, clothing, and a host of other factors over which you have control, do you do your best to limit potential for producing anxiety in others and yourself? Of course in most cases you are not ultimately responsible for anxiety developing in someone else, yet your awareness of this characterization of resistance may support you in having less anxiety-producing interactions with others, and eventually more favorable buy-in and win-win results.

Overcoming Resistance

"Think through Mental Blocks before Trying to Think Outside the Box"

New ideas meet resistance. Many worthy ideas are then never heard again or ever see the light of day. Are you resistant to ideas, or are others resistant to yours? You may have to pause an additional moment and re-read these questions and re-think your responses. You could be resisting responding in a forthcoming and otherwise authentic manner. Note, please, if you are resisting your truth. Resistance involves the tendency to block free expression of primitive impulses and ideas. Even in exercises in free-association and brainstorming, the ego works hard to repress threatening impulses and conflict. Again, this is quite possibly a defense mechanism of repression instead of progression. During solo or collaborative thinking, a heightened process of self-discovery and self-insight can yield exceptionally robust views, ideas and solutions.

Alternatively your thinking and feeling systems might shut down and you'll "draw a blank." It's known that just before major insights or ideas emerge, the brain's slate can clear to make room for "new." An empty canvass might soon be painted in bright colors of newness. The most viable and valuable ideas to come from a session of ideational development may be met with the greatest amount of resistance. Hillview's seasoned group facilitators know what to do.

In supporting my consulting work for strategic alignment of people and things, happily I'll add as-needed The HILL Model's executive alignment coaching curriculum. To discover, diagnose and overcome resistance to logical efforts to define, describe and pursue strategic alignment of people and things, one-with-one work is needed. Especially when I notice someone's disrespectfulness, disingenuousness, disengagement, or outright disgust with someone else's thoughts, I'll coach the offender toward more respectful and collegial behavior.

Frankly, with nearly four decades of leadership lessons so far, still I am startled by occasional snickers, sneers, laughter, guffaws, and wholesale disrespectfulness when I offer for consideration an idea, alternative view, or question. Sometimes months or longer later, I'll discover the very contribution I offered, the one that was immediately rejected, eventually became the other person's idea or solution of-choice. How very sad.

Sharp-Seekers, Sharp-Seers, Sharp-Thinkers, Sharp-Shooters

Resistance gives fully responsible leaders clues about topics, issues or facts that need to be pursued in greater depth, and sometimes urgently so. Identifying and responding to exigencies and other importance of resistance would have been a core competency of a consulting group formed by Aristotle, Copernicus, Galileo, God, and Newton (in alphabetical order). Mostly to bring a smile to the faces of would-be clients, Hillview once considered naming itself to honor history's true grand masters of strategic alignment — The ACG2N Group LLC was the tongue-in-cheek working title for Hillview. As a company name "Hillview Partners Network" also means to me a memory thread of my past, present and future thinking partners, including today's associates and Aristotle, Copernicus, Galileo, God, Newton *et al.*

"Hillview" met with little resistance from anyone to whom I explained its origin. For a panoramic hill view of where, how and why people and things are moving, even today each of these examples of history's principal sharp-seekers, sharp-seers, sharp-thinkers, and sharp-shooters guide our attention back to their discoveries and conundrums about matter and motion. They were masters of the physics of strategic alignment of people and things.

You and I must always challenge base assumptions about what we're seeing in our small, middling and massive observations made on the ground and from a hill. What we see is not always what we'll get. One or more degrees variance to plan could send a fast-moving project careening into a brick wall. As chief lens cutter for Hillview's High-Impact Leader Lens (HILL) Model for Viewing Strategic Alignment of People and Things (The HILL Model), thematically I underscore real risk to careers and organizations of inaccurate measurement vectors. There is risk in anyone carelessly oversimplifying misalignment detected or suspected in individual, team and organizational movement. Choosing to ignore misalignment is inviting unclassified forces to scuttle success. Seeing baby steps as insignificant progress is a common mistake we make. Too often we only pay attention to a front runner's last personal-best time.

Paradoxical Built-In Resistance to Inescapable Ceaseless Change

Change is ceaseless. Long ago I replaced "change management" with "change navigation." Somehow we leaders of people and managers of things talked ourselves into believing we can manage all change. I argue that the most one can hope to do is navigate change as if at the helm of a sea-worthy vessel of some type and size. Changing course to arrive at a new destination or to avoid an iceberg is change navigation. Effectively communicating navigation decisions is a requirement of strategic alignment of people and things.

Organizations expect people to sense risk when change is announced or rumored. Leaders anticipate resistance. To me absence of resistance to change would be worrisome. Fully responsible leaders use this expectable resistance to the advantage of individuals, teams, organizations, and other constituencies. Knowing a sense of risk will migrate to uncertainty then worry creates need for navigating change in such a way that brings more of a sense of security and comfort than insecurity and discomfort. Unpardonably hard-charging leaders often fail to anticipate resistance and the need to navigate fluid thoughts and feelings of those positively or otherwise affected by change.

Indeed resistance to change is almost automatic and completely expectable. Varying levels of severity of resistance to change have different types of impact on people and organizations. Collectively speaking, change is not *per se* an event, it is a state of being; ceaseless change is a fact of human and organizational life. Leaders who demonstrate with words and actions their grasp of this inherent reality more easily can calm waters stirred-up by rumors or announcements.

In no way am I suggesting change is felt uniformly enterprise-wide, nor should any leader ignore words or signs of duress or stress during periods of navigational adjustments toward change. Sustained push-back and unyielding persistence in resistance creates threats that must be dealt with head-on — for the harbinger's possible value in flagging good, bad and other possibilities.

Leaders may have to navigate decreased team morale, engagement, productivity and results. Buyer satisfaction can decline when those delivering products and services allow fear and other anxiety related to change to interfere with their duty to be at their best. Valued employees may start to look elsewhere for employment. Excessive resistance can delay or stop change. In such situations where worthy and needed change is totally arrested, I'm bold to say leaders are to blame. Chances are they were trying to manage instead of navigate change. Almost always resistance to ideas and solutions must be viewed as a positive, not as a negative. At least for the time such resistance allows the purveyor of ideas and solutions to re-check her or his assumptions and representations, and possibly re-double passion, confidence and conviction to see the idea produce desired or better results, resistance must be embraced.

Built-In Resistance to Being Right *vs.* Money's Might

A man I asked to serve as Chairman of a company I co-founded was a master of providing resistance. He was the principal shareholder's occasionally on-site and always hyper-critical ombudsman-like observer; the official representative of the billionaire's deep pockets into which we were reaching for mere millions. In one of too many heated arguments he I endured until we could no longer do so, I asked (in effect), "Why do you always push-back on anything I raise for discussion, anything at all for which I submit a justified request you disagree with me so instantly; react so dismissively, or give me so much resistance — and so often disrespectfully, insultingly, and sometimes directly in front of the people who report to me?" At a moment of such conversational volatility he would offer more resistance. He seemed to love sensing I was "asking for it." No relief. He loved watching me squirm. I rebelled. My inner-child was being abused. Until too late, foolishly I did not catch-on to his head game. Seeing or hearing from others about my mastery of anything brought out in this fellow counter-productive resistance. I was not amused.

Eventually I told him he was a bully and nearly begged him to stop. He declared me a brat, and then reminded me who controlled the company's purse strings. Daily I was filling-in the winning team's score book, while he was controlling the checkbook. I was the team's manager on the field, and he was the absent team owner's representative sitting in the sky box. Grossly I underestimated his power over my destiny. I was too busy winning games to cover my own assets. Erroneously I had written him off as a necessary evil, a gnarly nuisance surely the billionaire investor knew was expendable if push came to shove. I would win. I was wrong. I was very wrong.

To sharpen the swords he used as he lunged at me, he would invoke the investor's name and threaten shutting-off the cash. Blindly I refused to believe our benefactor could fall for such baloney. Always the bully was determined to press me up against any wall he could, and he did. When one of the walls against which Mr. Mean banged my head could collapse and threaten the largest deal I ever navigated, and I sensed legal and worse risk for the company, I unsheathed my claws and found they had already been clipped, and the stubs worn down. (Mixed metaphors flow.) I knew I was in deep trouble. My depth finder was way off. My ship was about to sink.

Mr. Mean was bragging to the billionaire about a stupid cash-conserving move regarding withholding (*i.e.,* denying me) investment in core technology that would allow us to fulfill serious contractual obligations underway with tens of thousands of unsuspecting buyers of our not-yet-fully functioning service. On his own he decided to wait and use the trusting buyers' incoming money to finish building what the customers thought they had purchased, in good-faith, as an up-and-running machine to deliver peace-of-mind security that was promised under my personal signature. While they thought they were being served 24/7, the machinery was not yet fully operational. I was furious. The master of resistance beamed with pride that he was getting away with the deception. I was warned into silence. Later I learned his investor friend was probably aware and amused by the ploy. I was crestfallen. I was threatened. I became belligerent. I became unemployed. My resistance to the bully's resistance cost me my job.

Fool me Once, Shame on You.
Fool me Twice, Shame on Me.

Six years earlier I had witnessed similar chicanery at another business a billionaire controlled for which I worked, and I thought for sure those ethical infractions were anomalies. After finding myself back where I started when he acquired my business, and after he graciously returned to me all the stock in my company, I asked a key person from those earlier days what really happened. Effectively I learned "money talks and *some* entrepreneurs walk." The bold strokes of creative genius to visualize and launch businesses were not as impressive to the money source as smoke-and-mirrors accounting and slippery representations thereof. Money allocated that was unspent was rewarded over fulfillment of obligations to trusting buyers. Law suits I feared occurring on-my-watch were viewed elsewhere as possible pesky annoyances. I was told the biggest law firms succeed in exonerating the wealthiest perpetrators. A directly related eight-figure fraud matter collapsed a business, yet before the Federal regulators moved-in to bolt the doors, enough money had been funneled away into an unrelated business with market value still in the billions. The funnel-fillers scurried to their personal banks. Over two years of unwinding the offending business, nearly 1,000 people lost their jobs, eventually including yours truly. What a blessing! Although the above old recollections are incomplete and may be imperfect, they relate directly to the way resistance both builds and destroys businesses and people. Polarity.

Years later when the resistance I had encountered long ago was explained to me in this earlier context; at age 48 my obvious naïveté astounded others — and me. "You should have seen this coming," was among the milder reprimands, at least when compared, to, "You knew what you were getting yourself into." Yes, I was and remain ashamed of my rose-colored glasses worn from those earlier dark-as-night years. Sure, I had seen battle with earlier unworthy opponents, but I never expected this swashbuckler swordsman's lunge at my core values, ethics, beliefs, common decency, and business logic. With my final parry I lost my balance and my heart met his blade's resistance. I fell. I fell hard. Occasional nightmares about this era rob me of sleep.

Eventually I accepted how my childhood's trials drive me to "save" others. Relatively speaking, I forgot to learn different thoughts and ways to save myself. Believing I am a master of always pursuing wisdom, courage and patience, I endured what I could, but now confess to having reached my limit long before he and I parted company. I was beaten to a pulp. Later through others I discovered this is precisely what Bully wanted to happen. He wanted me out of his way. My resistance to him was insurmountable for both of us, at least that's what the then $500-per-hour psychiatrist — who claims to work only with CEOs —

concluded after Bully and I sat with the doctor through several real-life reenactments of what I considered arbitrary and harmful resistance. The famed doctor was seen weekly by billionaire investors and several other CEOs I knew, so my views could never prevail. I was not paying the allegedly unerring doctor's large fees. Indeed I was growing bitter. Sadly the above prose contains remnants of my unvarnished bitterness.

Months earlier, now as if yesterday, I recall sitting one evening in the 11th floor dining room of the New York Atlantic Club, overlooking the lights of Central Park, eating dinner with my nemesis and another co-founder. Suddenly one of Mr. Chairman's and my many confrontations flared about what I believed to be resistance for the sake of resistance, and said so. Cocktails and fine wine were involved. He scowled back at me snarky words to the effect, "Don't you always get from me exactly what you want? Don't I eventually give you anything you ask for? When have I ever ultimately said no to you? I give you want you need, and you ask for what you need. It's my job to push-back until I'm comfortable with every request. You ask, and eventually I get from New York whatever you need, don't I? What's wrong with that?" His job? Job? Injecting resistance was his job.

You bet I was stunned, yet not assuaged. I said, "If my requests are reasonable and modest, and well thought-out, why do you always push me so hard." He retorted, "Someone has to. You always get what you want. You need someone to push back on you." He was jealous, concluded the third co-founder at table. Resistance comes in many forms. Character weakness was revealed. I was beaten down.

Within a month or so, dramatically I was off the payroll, and my pledged stock evaporated. Attorney friends told me to move on. They knew I could not afford to fight super-rich Mr. Deep Pockets. Any resistance I might offer would be lost time and energy. I was down but not out. There were tears shed on a bench in Battery Park. In a convoluted way, his steady drumbeat of resistance energized me.

This is a story about my failed resistance to malfeasance. They won. Or did they? I lost. Or did I? In my safe-deposit box I hold records of all these hard-knocks lessons. Here I only hope to dramatically whet your appetite for deeper understanding of the human side of resistance, instead of inviting attention to more B-movie melodrama of misguided hoarders of millions or more. Compared to stories of Enron, AIG, and dozens of bigger examples of great-to-greed and need-for-speed, I doubt many would care about my piddling war stories. Within a month or so of being a free agent, I was recruited for a dream position as CEO of a company I knew well for many years. Leadership lessons from the next post emboldened me to set this book in-motion. There were so many.

Resistance is a HILL Word about which we could write and discuss with almost unlimited facets related to strategic alignment strengths, weaknesses, opportunities and threats (A.S.W.O.T.). Resistance can come out of nowhere, or you might expect it always from the same corner of your world. It took me years, and now I am almost willing to see more good than evil in the word.

Admittedly I still bridle at anyone's instantaneous resistance to any idea, thought or topic I raise — especially when speaking with smart people I know, and who know me well. Almost always I discover once again I unintentionally intimidated the resistant individual, and so her or his guard went up out of self-defense perhaps borne of earlier references to repression.

Fear of failure and *fear of success* cause resistance. Resistance to failure and success actually has similar dynamics. Overcoming resistance for each category allows fully responsible leaders to think and dig a little deeper before they act and reach a lot higher.

> "*L'avenir, tu n'as point à le prévoir mais à le permettre.*"
> ("As for the future, your task is not to see it, but to enable it.")
> —Antoine de-Saint Exupery

Thank you for giving resistance more latitude to work for you — yes, while whomever or whatever is contemporaneously clearly working against you. Perhaps more frequently than not, there is richness, promise and other value to be found in this polarity called resistance. *Résistance!*

Experience any levels of resistance you may be experiencing to this chapter's views. Resistance is found within the physics, psychology, principles, and practices of fully responsible leadership. Investigate who, what, when, where, why and how you resist. Always expect a "Wow!"

In the above nuanced recollections, I overcame tug-and-pull resistance to revealing for you so much of my true pain and gain. This chapter ends to arrest any pain caused by reading it, yet we continue our quest for sustainable gain. Let's remain mindful of roles played by resistance.

Resistance. Expound.

Respect

Chapter Inspired by and Dedicated to Geoffrey Dallas Snyder

Insert or imagine seeing your first name: _____,

Seeing this chapter's title word, what immediately comes to your open mind? Do you already have a working relationship with this word? Somewhere inside of you does this word instantly appeal? As a response to a specific situation at-hand, will this word work to your and others' advantage? For this word to increase in real value, together we must dig, drill and think deeper, so we will reach, climb and soar higher.

R.E.S.P.E.C.T. Did you just hum or sing-out Aretha Franklin's 1967 hit? I was 17 when this classic was released, and 40+ years later I can still feel the deep impact from when Aretha spelled-out R.E.S.P.E.C.T. Few bothered to study the context of her overall message. Yet by itself the word hit the heart of our homes. At any age and stage of character development, thoughts and feelings about respect are foundational. It is never too late to learn respect.

"Respect your elders!" may have been the first parental admonition we recall involving respectfulness. Then followed authoritarian insistence on respect for: God, family, teachers, pastors, bosses, elected officials, law enforcement officers, fire fighters, community organizers, artists, musicians, athletes, and others. For you was respect adequately defined, described or explained? For me it wasn't.

Earning and paying respect are mission-critical fiduciary duties of fully responsible leaders. Especially for his strong and steady focus on entrepreneurship — for job creation and to re-energize this country's free enterprise way-of-life — President Obama continues to sustain my respect. In an extended correction economy, the D.C. regime needs our respect, constructive input, and patience. All leaders re-envisioning The American Dream must strive to ensure respect for all. With respect "The 1%" and "The 99%" can add-up to 110%.

Respect for all people, and their views, does not mandate agreement. Why, therefore, do thoughtful individuals bother with misdirected emotion of disrespectfulness? If a Republican says something with which a Democrat expectably disagrees, what value does it add to our check-and-balance political process to inject disrespectfulness into discussion or debate? Disrespectfulness is wholly counterproductive.

"I must respect the opinions of others even
if I disagree with them." —Herbert Henry Lehman

Anticipating future cheap shots, engaged citizens must re-double demonstration of our respect for the U.S. Presidency and its determined 44th office-holder. With respectful thoughts, words, prayers and actions, we contribute to this Administration's success. Our collective wisdom, courage, patience, commitment, appreciation, empathy and respect will add more promise to the President's vision and mission. Yes, we can. Yes, we will. We must. Respect is essential.

In large part, I write to speak to my respect for the embedded leader within my brilliant and otherwise multi-talented daughter. If Jennifer should come into her own as a leader before or after I am called skyward, these words from her father's mind and heart should serve to guide at least some percentage of her views toward respect, empathy, authenticity, clarity and trust. From her first memories of specific words I offered my only child, surely she felt my respect for her and for our shared pledge to better-and-better use of language. For years we expanded our vocabulary for respecting each other.

During hundreds of relaxing candle-lit evening meals, with gentle classical music accompanying our conversation, high-spirited Jennifer and I found connection through carefully learned and launched words. Long drives from Manhattan to and from Pittsburgh, Cape Cod, the Hamptons, or Jones Beach were fueled by extended discussion. Surely she knew I was working to build her adroit use of vocabulary, pronunciation, enunciation, emphasis, and boldness in choosing words.

Bibliophilia or bibliophilism is the love of books. Not unlike her mother, Jennifer became a bibliophile, and her daddy remains thrilled. She took it from there. Her truly remarkable writing skills emerged in the elementary and middle-school years. Jennifer has her own way with words. When I first heard of Oxford's one-word-based "Hardest Exam in the World," instantly I imagined my toddler taking and acing the test. She would have.

Jennifer was 10 when her half-brother Geoffrey Snyder was born, the biological son of my former wife's second of three husbands. Related circumstances thrust Jennifer into experiences and roles pre-teens are unprepared to encounter. As she rose to each challenge, my respect for her grew. Love was already limitless for my respected only child.

Knowingly Jennifer would transfer to her beloved half-brother respect and other quality-of-life lessons her adoring yet imperfect father worked to demarcate, articulate, and otherwise demonstrate for her. In this unusual way her Geoffrey and I bonded. Jennifer's respect allowed Geoffrey to connect with her father. In his college years we unofficially and respectfully replaced with Dallas his two middle names. This was a symbolic gesture of our mutual respect.

"The best thing to give to your enemy is forgiveness; to an opponent, tolerance; to a friend, your heart; to your child, a good example; to a father, deference; to your mother, conduct that will make her proud of you; to yourself, respect; to all men, charity." —Benjamin Franklin

Respect for oneself influences the degree to which respect for others is demonstrated. Fully responsible leaders faithfully earn, pay and give respect. Lesser leaders disrespectfully mock and belittle others in order to appear superior. Too often I witness among mangers this example of weakness of their character. I believe disrespectfulness is a character flaw that begs for a remedy. Forgiveness of self and others can work wonders to cure disrespectfulness.

"Above all, don't lie to yourself. The man who lies to himself and listens to his own lie comes to a point that he cannot distinguish the truth within him, or around him, and so loses all respect for himself and for others. And having no respect he ceases to love." —Fyodor Dostoyevsky

Respectfully I request your respect for all words offered in this book, and for this word-wielding author. I am certain mutual respect between and among us will serve us well. We need to have a word: Respect. It addresses our immediate and long-term requirements.

With **R**espect, **E**mpathy, **A**uthenticity, **C**larity and **T**rust, please **R.E.A.C.T.** to any and all people you lead, and things you manage. Lead and manage with respect, and all should reach rewarding destinations. Thank you for your respect. Feel how you have mine.

Respect. Expound.

Response

Chapter Inspired by and Dedicated to John J. Dallas

Insert or imagine seeing your first name: _____,

Seeing this chapter's title word, what immediately comes to your open mind? Do you already have a working relationship with this word? Somewhere inside of you does this word instantly appeal? As a response to a specific situation at-hand, will this word work to your and others' advantage? For this word to increase in real value, together we must dig, drill and think deeper, so we will reach, climb and soar higher.

Response + Ability = Ability to Respond

Life is response. Intentionality, frequency, and quality of your response determine how fully you are living. Steadily increasing ability to respond to life's ups, downs, and other demands influences the ultimate value of choices we will make to benefit ourselves, family, friends, co-workers, employers, our community, and other beneficiaries of our acceptance of accountability. Timely and otherwise accurate response to our unique personal views of strengths, weaknesses, opportunities and threats will influence choices we'll each make. How do you grade or rank your "response ability?"

In both parlance and practice, responsibility — response ability — emerged in pop culture as a frequently negatively weighted word. Ability to respond is hardly a burden, a blame-worthy skill, or a cross to bear. Responsibility, therefore, should not have become a word used to punish instead of praise children and grown-ups alike. "You must take responsibility for your actions, young man!" is heard as a reprimand without an offer of a remedial path or solution. It would be better to say something to the effect, "Young man, learn how to increase your ability to respond appropriately to such a situation. Let's review the set of circumstances in front of us and talk about clearly preferable and more productive responses you could use in the future." Agree?

Can you imagine applying adaptations of this "response ability" leadership development theme in your dealings with family, fellow employees, elected officials, and others? I can. I practice what I preach. Often I ask individuals to reconsider their initial or ongoing response to specific circumstances being brought into sharper focus — while standing on a hill instead of on a mountaintop or up in an ivory tower. As a HILL consultant, coach, and public speaker, I am paid to do precisely that. Some, of course, resist the panoramic view and often paradigm-shifting implications. Others almost instantly clear away hurdles and sprint forward. Perhaps most of us need the above clarification about the importance of always (!) working to develop better and better ability to respond.

An increase in response ability does not mean added burden. Instead it means added readiness to respond in ways more likely to solve, succeed, or lead to imminent or later achievement. So, please don't ignore, deny or shirk responsibility. Refine the word's two-part (*i.e.,* response and ability combined) significance in your mind and life. For the rest of your days, intentionally seek to increase your ability to respond in better and better ways.

More so than assigning to any person of any age a blanket, unspecified, and possibly onerous sense of "responsibility," let's think together about how to imbue in each of us more of a life-long craving to always improve our ability to respond with: wisdom instead of only knowledge, courage instead of only bravado, patience instead of pursuing instant gratification of rather arrogantly coming to premature conclusions.

> *"Between stimulus and response there is a space.*
> *In that space is our power to choose our response.*
> *In our response lies our growth and our freedom."*
> —Viktor Emil Frankl, M.D., Ph.D.

Do you believe today's economic meltdown was ignited and fueled more by inadequate or irrational response of leaders we trust to safeguard our finances? I contend inadequate response (wholly regrettable) caused the most trouble, and irrational (probably actionable) response ranks a distant second.

Are you on the emergency response team to resuscitate our economy? Have you tried to suggest to anyone else with influence something new; anything bold and promising for our own households, communities, state, nation, or the world at-large? Any constructive response is better than no response. Sitting on our heels (to be polite) waiting for others to respond is an ill-advised response. As I speak with many good people about my own response in offering for consideration viable and large-scale ideas to re-envision and re-ignite our all-important entrepreneurial economy, I confess to growing accustomed to their response of blank stares, sometimes feigned enthusiasm, eventually broken promises, some slight disinterest, and occasionally a rather rapid change in conversation topic. Thankfully there are notable high-response exceptions of fine minds with whom I am closely working to define and refine several of many needed solutions in the works. We will persist in our response to today's loud and alarming call-to-action.

FedEx founder Fred Smith is wise to forever continue telling about a Yale University management professor's response to Fred's paper proposing reliable overnight delivery service, saying, "The concept is interesting and well-formed, but in order to earn better than a 'C', the idea must be feasible." Sadly there are hundreds of thousands of response stories like this one, some of which form my own repertoire of occasionally nagging regrets. Relatively few of us have Fred Smith's resolve to overcome an inadequate response of someone else whose opinion matters to us. Thank goodness Mr. Smith persisted. FedEx revolutionized more than overnight delivery of letters and packages.

As a fully responsible leader, always work to hone your response ability and you'll continue to rise to your personal best. Each of us learned some or many inadequate or inappropriate response mechanisms from childhood years, some of which carry way into our adulthood, sadly perhaps even until our death. I choose to believe even worst childhood lessons in selfishness, passivity, narrow-mindedness, black-and-white responses to life's Technicolor questions, simple-mindedness in the face of complicated and sometimes urgent demands, and other conscious or subconscious coping mechanisms from toddler years or later can be intentionally transformed into grounded and mature response ability. Consulting, coaching, pastoral care, therapy, or other remedial support is likely to empower and expedite your true-north journey. You are not alone.

Strategic alignment of past, present, and anticipated future responses creates best-effort ability to respond most effectively. Ability to respond is part of what IQ tests measure, what interviewers looking to hire new employees evaluate, what prospective spouses look for in the intended, how parents monitor performance of their children, and how bosses experience, rate, and pay their employees.

Response is natural. Response is a blessing. Ten consecutive weekly visits to a state-of-the-art Biofeedback laboratory, at Washington, D.C.'s Georgetown University Medical Center, convinced me our human physiological reactions to both stress and pleasure cause automatic response in our bodies, quite literally from head to toe. I was and remain in awe of how the body and mind are scientifically shown to measurably work in tandem; particularly astounded by how stress instantly registers on meters attached to various parts of the body. If we acknowledge and manage natural, spiritual, and other mysterious messages our bodies are sending to our brains and hearts, we can benefit from our learned and innate response to almost any type or level of external or internal stimuli. I was taught to respond to mission-critical relaxation techniques.

As a tool for dealing with stress, I need to remember how the Biofeedback team taught me to keep the bold, all-caps, word "RELAX" in the front of my mind. The body responds to just hearing "relax." Response to big issues and small issues require of us different investments of ourselves and our requests of others. Author Og Mandino wrote to these evocative options for influencing our response:

> "If I feel depressed I will sing.
> If I feel sad I will laugh.
> If I feel ill I will double my labour.
> If I feel fear I will plunge ahead.
> If I feel inferior I will wear new garments.
> If I feel uncertain I will raise my voice.
> If I feel poverty I will think of wealth to come.
> If I feel incompetent I will think of past success.
> If I feel insignificant I will remember my goals.
> Today I will be the master of my emotions."

Winston Churchill delivered to his *alma mater* the now famous three-word commencement address about preferable response, "Persist. Persist. Persist." After uttering only three words, he sat down as a thunderous standing ovation signaled appreciative response to his brilliant succinctness. Your author would deliver, "Respond. Respond. Respond." If I sat down before explaining myself, I fear dead silence would greet my assumed impertinence. Yes, your response to this chapter's message may range from "That's exactly what I needed to hear" to "This was a waste of time." Either polar opposite response demands of you and me at least a moment's pause for introspection. Trust much good will come from improving your response ability when reading, hearing or seeing insight into a seasoned servant leader's mind and heart.

Increase your response ability, please, by always working toward developing your skills to respond authentically, appropriately, humbly, constructively, creatively and productively. In your bold-to-subtle response in collaborative situations, dutifully empathize (*i.e.*, be empathic) with the other people involved; putting yourself in his, her, or their shoes. In your response, be sure to feel your and their pain and gain.

> *"The soft stuff in trust is the hard stuff in trust: accountability, authenticity, credibility, honesty, integrity, respect and transparency."* —Noreen J. Kelly

Response keeps an economy strong, a society's resources properly allocated, a company's ideas hatching, an organization's cash flowing, a family's values loving (not hating), a home's financial value in realistic perspective, a child's wisdom growing, an older person's mind sharp, a Supreme Court's ideology in-check with majority rule, a White House in-touch with populist reality, a legislative body at all levels of government focusing on the peoples' business, and untold other numbers of outcomes of voices and votes expressed through response instead of repose; action instead of inaction. "Wake-up America and Smell the World's Coffee" is not too trite as a plea for response.

To double your response is one of life's timpani two notes to beat forever in our brains and hearts. The other is double-up on your caring. "The timpani's two notes are always the same notes:" CARE and RESPOND, RESPOND and CARE. Your ear's tympanic response to how you hear your heart demonstrates what you care about, and what you care about should influence your response — muffled or thunderous. In allegiance to their higher power, fully responsible leaders care first about people. People first. In your priorities and practice, put people first. The rest falls into place in varying order of precedence.

People first. Are you known for putting people first? It takes purpose, passion and patience to put people first.

What is Your Likely Response to "No Response?"

Thirteen years ago a sadly misanthropic colleague told me, "No response is their 'no' response." Mr. Grumpy did not mean this in any constructive philosophic way whatsoever. Not for the first time in my oil-and-water relationship with this then unreachable curmudgeon, again he was encouraging me to give up on something big. I wouldn't. I was negotiating the largest multi-million-dollar contract I ever attempted in the financial services field. Having envisioned and pursued a groundbreaking deal, for many long months I lived and breathed myriad details, including: ceaseless change, disappearing dollars, forgotten words, unbridled egos, and growing greed — on both sides of the table. "T'was ever thus" I would mutter to myself, so I must persist, persist, persist. I must guard against negative words becoming strongholds.

To put money where our mouths were, we sweetened the deal with an up-front good-faith check for $750,000; a money-talks demonstration of our supreme confidence in the upside win-win potential of the proposed collaborative initiative. Secretly we were fully prepared to increase to $1 million our advance on revenue-sharing funds to come. The other company was pleased with our bold gesture. Later we learned other companies had offered them more for projects with less potential, so $750,000 was sufficient for our unique and highly promising vision.

How Do You Know When You and They are Strategically Aligned and Ready to Sign?

Dozens of little and big steps forward eventually told me we were strategically aligned and ready to sign. I was confident this was a win-win. In my head I was already hearing buyers express their appreciation of our unique value, and instead of counting sheep to sleep, I was counting millions in shared profits. I was authentically unrestrained in my upbeat response to the favorable writing I saw on the wall. It was all good. I was, however, guilty of ignoring an old Wall Street investment banking adage, "Never fall in love with any deal." I did. It was ours to lose.

Suddenly, no response — only truly deafening silence.

After four upbeat, friendly, and positive-minded voice mail messages from me, our affable principal contact was not calling back. E-mailed notes were being ignored. A personal hand-written invitation to lunch received no response. Calls to her normally dutiful administrative assistant went unanswered. For me two weeks of silence were all nine circles of suffering in Dante's Inferno.

The billionaire lead investor's assigned representative to our company already gave-up on the deal. Sir Know-It-All said two weeks of silence meant they were saying "no" without yet actually saying it. "It's over with. We lost it. Move on." He would not even look at me as he spoke these toxic words. He kept his head buried in *The Wall Street Journal.* Peripherally he saw see me pivot and head to my office. I closed my door, took a deep breath, tried to calm my nerves, shook-off my disgust with his arrogance and negativity, offered up a prayer of supplication, and made the fifth and perhaps final call to the silent wonder. This time the previously M.I.A. executive answered her phone!

"Judy! I am so thrilled to hear your voice," said I. "Oh, John. (Pause.) I am so, so sorry." Pause. Sorry? My heart skipped more than one beat during a nanosecond-long pregnant pause. Sorry?

She continued, "John, I totally forgot to tell you for two weeks I was called away from the city on an urgent family matter, and I accidentally left you hanging. I just heard your messages, read your nice notes, and yes indeed we are ready to take next steps with you. We want to get this thing signed. I am so sorry to leave you in suspense. Please forgive me. Thanks for understanding. We're ready on our end to get moving. Are you?" Was I? Ever-ready! My crusty neighbor down the hall was not. When immediately I reported the successful contact, he only snarled, "We'll see." Still I work to forget his arrogant rebuff of my exaltation.

Three weeks later attorneys and we were finished tweaking legal text. This complicated contract became a widely circulated model for excellence in fields of co-branded and clearly endorsed marketing of third-party financial services. The other party and I signed the contract. Literally my name was on the line. I felt every stroke of that pen. I felt new personal pressure greater than the curmudgeon's. Shortly thereafter a lavish celebratory luncheon was given by the other company in honor of our now formally ratified collaboration. Response made it happen.

Each Destination in View is
Always another Beginning

Quickly the project succeeded beyond the grand plan's forecast and best-case expectations; breaking testing, timing and revenue records for similar types of co-branding marketing arrangements. In the credit card marketplace, the deal itself became and probably remains an exemplary benchmark for co-branding affinity marketing initiatives. A digital copy of the signed contract was somehow posted online by someone, and even now remains available *via* a Google search.

In this up-close-and-personal quick study of response, the "no response" example was response delayed. Even now too many times I still view silence as negative response. Do you? Normally silence means the other person is: (1) in over her or his head with a tidal wave of inflexible demands, (2) negligent in practices of steady and smooth executive-level communication, or (3) perhaps passive-aggressive in terms of maintaining the illusion of influence by withholding instead of advancing information and willful collaboration.

Pause, please, and think of reasons you do not respond when doing so would be to your and others' advantage? Do you trust yourself to respond adequately, appropriately, empathically, constructively, professionally, ethically, and in other desirable leader-like ways? Do you fear responding in ways that might make you look less competent than "no response" might render? In private thoughts, have a little chat with yourself about how and when you respond. You may surprise yourself with your answers and other responses.

Shortly before this book went to the printer, I was engrossed reading along with listening to the CDs of the late Jacqueline Kennedy's responses during an oral history project — recorded only four months after the Kennedy assassination. I was 13 when JFK was murdered. Vividly I recall his inauguration (I was age nine). I was mesmerized and terrified during the White House era now known as "The Camelot Years." In Jacqueline's responses — more so than her answers — I am finding clarity. She addressed some of the internal and external conflict I felt back then and beyond; questions I could not articulate, let alone try or know how to understand or respond. These were tipping point-years for the nation and the world, and much more so than I realized before hearing Jacqueline's youthful responses regarding these times — in her own unedited voice.

Q&R instead of Q&A

For fully responsible leaders, there is no reason to wait until one has a definitive answer to respond to a question. An answer offered MAY be an answer. A response is always a response. Here nuance is profound. In the late 1970s I began to advise CEOs of top-tier *Fortune 500* companies to re-think the Question-and-Answer segment of any annual meeting of shareholders, press conference, or session with the New York Society or other body of securities analysts. I would say, "Instead of calling it Q&A, call it Q&R — Questions-and-Response. Why? Not all responses can be answers." Relief! Too many unsure answers we hear are better characterized as responses.

In Q&R sessions a speaker would always have a response, even if only to say, "That's a question my team and I had not anticipated. Allow us to dig a bit and work to find a more thorough response, and quite possibly an answer." That is a response; hardly an answer. Q&R. Many clients and friends have adopted this practice and some even print Q&R in the formal agenda for meetings. I always enjoy being in an audience when ethics are followed and the chair acknowledges the humble author of the emancipating Q&R lesson.

Why not give Q&R a try for your meetings? With or without attribution to this author, allow Q&R to take some pressure off by releasing floodgates — in you and your respondent listeners. With responses you will have more in common than with pat answers. Allow yourself to discern miracles in when, why and how your brain suddenly has more answers. Words in this book trigger response. Some of your responses may become just the answers you seek.

Life is about response. Let's respond more quickly and thoroughly to worthy notes and e-mail messages. Let's respond more thoughtfully to significant voice mail messages. Let's each work harder to respond. Thank you for always persisting in improving your response-ability.

Response. Expound.

Restoration

Chapter Inspired by and Dedicated to
Hubert Franklin Shearer (1900-1987)

Insert or imagine seeing your first name: _____,

Seeing this chapter's title word, what immediately comes to your open mind? Do you already have a working relationship with this word? Somewhere inside of you does this word instantly appeal? As a response to a specific situation at-hand, will this word work to your and others' advantage? For this word to increase in real value, together we must dig, drill and think deeper, so we will reach, climb and soar higher.

Restoration for Relationships, Organizations, Families, Societies, Portfolios, Buildings, Automobiles, Clocks and Ourselves

For fully responsible leaders who are leading people and managing things, the call-to-action noun res·to·ra·tion captures the act of restoring someone or something to his, her, or its former good condition; getting back again someone or something good. As a strong HILL Word for leaders to use to characterize a planning or working model for visualizing a person, thing, or an entire organization returning to thoughts, foundational strengths, best practices, and admirable behaviors that have fallen short, restoration means: fix (an imperative), fixing (the implementation), mend (also an imperative), mending (another act of implementation), repair (stated imperative), repairing (illustrated implementation), reparation (imagery of top performance), restitution (more action), and other clear restorative words to illustrate and mark the journey from where someone or something is, and what she, he or it must do to arrive at the worthy destination called restoration. Can you feel the enormity, challenge and promise of this word?

With less trepidation, approach-avoidance, fear of failure, or fear of success, somehow our busy minds more easily wrap-around restoration than innovation, creativity, or re-engineering. For igniting group action, restoration allows Steven Covey's "end in mind" to more fully form. A leader's call for brainstorming for ideas for unspecified improvement is felt as if a starting gun was fired for a race that the known-to-be best creative minds are likely to win. Strategically, restoration can get a person or organization to a better starting place, before essential innovation is scheduled to begin. Is this a first time for you to think about restoration as a staging platform for moving things to good before great? Think about this logic. Talk about it. Try it out. You'll surprise everyone and yourself with exceptional positive results.

For fully responsible leaders, restoration is a mission-critical focus and function. As a prime example, restoring self-confidence is essential before tackling complex undertakings. Fully responsible leaders have a sixth-sense about their team members who need a boost. Leaders must also be on the lookout for need to repair or recalibrate their own sense of capacity and readiness to win. In almost all situations, restoration of some type should precede research, development, creativity, and innovation of any variety. Restoring vision toward personal and organizational mission is a good starting point for restoration prior to innovation.

This chapter about restoration will take us on parallel tracks for personal and organizational journeys; close to home and global. Allowing this HILL Word to resonate with exceptional value may take a bit of extra effort. Apply to each illustration provided herein examples from your life and the worlds directly around you. If, however, you are one to pride yourself on "never looking back," restoration may already seem irrelevant to your current and future thinking. Think again. Review logic highlighted above.

"Getting something back again" was the compelling definition of restoration that resonated with me as an aspiring fully responsible leader. Many finished and unfinished things from my past eras of living and working in Pittsburgh, Manhattan, Northern Virginia (DC area), and Chicago may deserve a second chance on my overflowing

To Do list. Desperately I seem to want to restore many fractured business and personal relationships, and take a second chance with business undertakings that were either ahead of their time or damaged by singular or mutual errors in judgment, circumstances beyond control, or flat-out stupidity or myopia of some key person(s) involved. I admit to having many regrets. Without obsessing, I learn many lessons by thinking about possible and impossible restoration.

> *"Being ahead of your time is the*
> *same as being wrong."* —A cynic

Some good and well-meaning people want our U.S. economy to be restored to the good old days. I do not. Well, not if the good old days are narrowly defined by and pegged to the rather recent Reagan Era of trickle-down economics. Visualization of defensible global economic stability must involve never-ending public debate about innovative solutions to unprecedented challenges, and maybe including restoring strategic alignment of ethics and values upon which this country was said to have been founded.

Note I am not 100% certain that globally restoring founding free-enterprise economic principles would be a right way to proceed, but I'm surmising considering doing so will be among the best capitalism-based free-market economy options the G-20 and other countries could consider. Time and currency exchange rates will tell.

Truthfully or not, whatever Americans were told and believed in 1776 was enough substance and meaningfulness for which to fight and die. Logic, fear, faith, loathing, regret, hunger, thirst, and hope were divinely aligned. So a new country was born. Word-of-mouth's fallibility filters and flavors messages spreading among and through pub patrons, Town Hall observers, and church-connected townsfolk. Ultimately it worked.

Rather disconnected farmers on the sprawling countryside of early America were probably last to learn about current events. They heard news when coming to town after each harvest to sell their fields' yield.

Arguably, it all worked. We the People made it work. Spilled blood and lesser high prices were paid. Over time we aligned our thoughts, prayers, efforts and resources. Divine providence moved in our favor, or so it seemed. Since then, what happened? What is happening today?

Creed of Greed and Need for Speed

As we move our society from Greed-to-Great *via* Green or other worthy thinking and societal shifts, public and private conversation about health care reform, foreign conflict, and corrupt politics must not overshadow meaningful attention to Main Street's and Wall Street's needs for top-to-bottom reform toward restoration of founding principles and practices. Perhaps restoring the peoples' knowledge, wisdom, and confidence in *circa* 1776 purported values of full equality would be a major step.

Wall Street seems to be getting back to its slight-of-hand chicanery for greed-over-growth. Quarterly earnings are still valued over long-term growth. Instant riches are sought by online traders sitting at home spinning their laptop roulette wheels for short-term gains.

Without core societal and Wall Street reforms related to greed and need for speed, health care cannot be restored to any founding father's or founding mother's level of ethical or economic sense of fairness or equality.

In many circles we devote more time to discussing building green buildings for earth's sustainability (which I strongly endorse), than we engage in thoughtful discourse for viable ways to allocate green dollars for equitable and uniform highest quality health care for all humans to survive and thrive.

For good reason LEED is becoming a welcome four-letter household word for many of us. The Leadership in Energy and Environmental Design ("LEED") Green Building Rating System™ encourages and accelerates global adoption of sustainable green building and development practices. Through the visualization, creation and implementation of universally understood, accepted, and applied tools and performance criteria, fortunate people enjoy benefits of LEED certification's reach into our workplaces and homes so we will live better lives — and then may not have to worry as much about hospitalization costs after exposure to asbestos, accidentally drinking non-potable water, suffering lead poisoning, or enduring other perils of environmentally careless builders and owners of buildings, vehicles, outdoor spaces, and commodities we must trust in order to live free.

The Restoration (1616-1789)

The Restoration, as you'll recall from lessons in middle-school years, has great historical significance. In the 1640s England suffered civil war; essentially a contest of power between Parliament and King Charles I. In December 1649, King Charles I was executed, following a trial by "the Rump," the unflattering name Parliament was called after the UK army excluded my fellow Presbyterians and other less anti-Royalist members. Generally dated to 1660, the beginning of the Restoration was the *annus mirabilis* when UK's Charles II returned to England, rather than attributed to 1661, when he was restored to the throne. The Restoration era probably ended in 1685, when Charles II died, or perhaps 1688, when his younger brother and successor, James II, was overthrown in what was called the Glorious Revolution. This year marked the Stuart's *annus horribilis* when their rule in Britain ended. Restoration means many things to different people. Timelines for restoration may not be accurately measured or marked. Restoration is serious business.

Is this the combustible restorative era in world history, can collaborative strategic alignment of best principles and practices of restoration, reparation, rejuvenation, repatriation, restitution, redemption, and other reconstitution of thoughts and deeds flourish for the common good of all? Can a global vision of shared peace and prosperity ever emerge as viable? Well, the vision has emerged, but short- or long-term viability has its detractors.

Restoration of Family and other Love Relationships

For most of us, I surmise, restoration of relationships is a very personal matter. Like many parents and their children who are estranged for reasons that defy mature logic or wisdom related to our blink-of-an-eye and here-today-gone-tomorrow mortality, I would love to restore with my cherished daughter Jennifer Gray Dallas the limitless joy we found in each other's company. From 6:01 P.M. 3 October 1977 when she was born at New York Hospital, greatest joy and deepest peace came to my life. She was and is all I could have wanted in a daughter. With Miss Dallas as my only child, she and I thrived as if I had six or more kids. Yes, she and I are that complex in our serious and silly interactions.

For each one of us single folk. and perhaps unhappily married souls, recurring thoughts toward restoring dissolved love affairs have deep transferable lessons related to restoring business connections or any other types of relationships. Four times in my adult years I was blessed to be deeply and totally in love, including the ill-fated eight-year marriage with my daughter's mother, Cynthia Gray Norris, with whom I remain friendly and for whom I'll always be a sounding board or strong shoulder. Cynthia's second of three former husbands fathered a towhead son, my daughter's half-brother, awesome Geoffrey Snyder. Now contemplating a Ph.D., at 25 Master Geoffrey still looks as if he is my son. In spirit, he is. We hold for each other real father-son love and respect. He is his own man, truly a free soul.

For years our family and friends celebrate the odd coincidence of Geoffrey's and my physical resemblance. In appearance Geoffrey's absentee biological father is polar opposite from Geoffrey and me; different coloring, character, and demeanor. As Cynthia and I were divorced seven years before Geoffrey was born, many jokes were made about Geoffrey being the product of the longest human gestation period in history. Indeed Geoffrey and I share a special love for each other, and he knows I'll always be here for him. His mother has encouraged her son and me to remain close, and we will. His unofficial name is Geoffrey Dallas Snyder — GDS for short. GDS and I both look forward to someday seeing our brilliant star Jennifer back to center-stage, where again she'll perform to standing ovations.

Restoration often requires deconstruction. Since my former wife and I never wanted Jennifer to lose sight of her daddy's total allegiance to her, Geoffrey learned to call me J.D. — for Jennifer's Daddy. Yet perhaps he never knew the root reason for the nickname. I was so fearful of offending my precious daughter by possibly appearing to take something away from her by giving something to Geoffrey, so painfully I walked a fine line. Every time I held him or saw him, I felt I was putting at some risk my relationship with our Miss Dallas.

Geoffrey knew I was always with him. All he has to do is look in a mirror. Someday I'll ask him if he wants to formally change his last name to Dallas, knowing he'll decline, while relishing the authenticity and legitimacy of the genuine gesture for us to bond by a shared surname. I would adopt him, if I could. I'm guessing it's too late. Jennifer, I believe, would be thrilled. For better or other outcome, we are family — someday to be restored to enjoy a wide world of possibilities. We have Frostian miles to go before I sleep.

Have you been happily married then divorced, or in a committed monogamous relationship that could not or would not make it to an altar? The other three loves of my life eventually moved with their subsequent significant others to Canada, Boston and Orlando. In reflecting on all four flawed attempts, eventually and painfully I learned I could never have restored what I wrongly thought each pairing had when together. Eventually I accepted folly in my fantasy.

All four were fantasies in which the parties participated. And without casting any aspersions on their and my rights to be who they and I really are, when I now observe them from afar and myself up-close, and what they and I are doing with our respective lives, it is clear none of us would have survived pledges we made for spending our lifetimes together. We were dead wrong. Restoration, therefore, is impossible. It took me years to get to this realistic truth. Love hurts.

In 1956 psychologist Erich Fromm published The Art of Loving, from which I learned new words for love, and four basic elements of love: care, responsibility, respect and knowledge. Love became hard work. Now I fear I may have worked too hard at making love work.

Restoration of four inherently flawed love relationships would be exercises in restoring myopia for which I have forgiven myself. Love was real. The relationships, however, were not as I experienced them.

Genuinely I doubt I will ever again enter a committed relationship. I needn't. Although highly socially active, since 1993 I do not formally date anyone. I remain somewhat at peace with the decision to remain a confirmed bachelor. Of course I remain open to divine providence.

Alfred, Lord Tennyson gives me comfort with his *"It is better to have loved and lost than never to have loved at all."* I need not love again, thanks to Tennyson. Forever, the types of love I experience remain with me.

Since 1973 I live hundreds of miles from family. Fortunately, a small handful of close friends keep their eyes on me, so I am hardly alone. Some abrogated relationships need to be restored, while others should remain as they are. Whenever I can, I am doing what I should.

Restoration of a Historic Home

A historic home that is restored is not really restored. Perhaps it is best to say it is refreshed to reflect an image of its original glory or an earlier state. A closest friend I love as a brother, and his wonderful wife, restored a large "Painted Lady" Victorian-style house on a sizable piece of prime real estate in Evanston, Illinois. Exactitude was required by the landmarks preservation mavens who approved and celebrated the many craftsmen's final work. On the outside, it was almost a new house, finished in the presumptive exact paint colors originally specified by architects or the other artisans involved in crafting its original whimsy and grandeur. I was privileged to observe a large percentage of the restoration. Yes, the family of six, and a truly blessed marriage, survived the major home-restoration project, with all its ups and downs; many successes and unforeseen failures along the way. The family seems to have become stronger because of the restoration project, though I've never posed that exact question.

Elsewhere in this book we dealt with the powerful word, "edification." Edification is used to build knowledge, wisdom, and value of people, and also applies to building edifices (*i.e.*, buildings of all types). If though edification fully responsible leaders can restore commercial and residential buildings, surely we can find ways to restore more business and personal relationships that may be more valuable now. Good judgment and great care are required.

Restoration in the Workplace

Restoring a business relationship, once I brought back on my management team a highly competent fellow who nearly destroyed a large project with client NBC News. When I returned to New York from Washington's NBC studios, on the spot I fired Carl. He knew he deserved it. With tears in his eyes and head held low, he walked out the door of our Park Avenue Pan Am Building (now Met Life Building) offices. The next week my attorney called to say Carl was contemplating suing me for wrongful discharge, and papers were being drafted. Yet oddly all Carl wanted was to speak to me over the telephone so he could apologize to me directly, and then he would drop plans for the law suit. Odd. Still smarting from this whole drama, I was not amused and very confused. I thought this was a cruel joke. Robert, my wise and empathic lawyer for HR matters, advised me to give Carl a call. It was worth a try. Carl assumed I would never again speak with him or see him. He was incorrect. His offer could not be refused.

During the strained telephone conversation I heard a very smart man review his culpability for the gargantuan error that cost me many thousands of dollars, and I sensed his atonement and great sorrow. He said he would drop pursuing the proposed law suit against me, as soon as we ended the call. I was never to worry about hearing from him again. My lawyer confirmed he dropped intention to sue, and he signed a General Release attorney Bob had ready for signature. The following week I called Carl and rehired him. Yes. He re-joined my team.

Carefully I had analyzed the value of having someone on-board who would never make the same mistakes, and who would monitor his performance in serious ways so he'd never take undue risks with our high-pressure production cycle. My wisdom, courage and patience would prove to be in vain.

In yet another melodramatic moment, two months later Carl resigned. He was wearing himself to a physical wreck by worrying about disappointing the man (yours truly) who gave him a second chance. He declared in his exit interview that he had never been treated so fairly in his life. The burden of my forgiveness, and demands of the second chance, weighed on him in ways he could not handle. I was stunned, hurt, angry, embarrassed, and yet somehow fully understanding. I felt his pain. The authentic forgiveness I offered was too great for him to bear. He felt undeserving. He was.

Restoration of Faith in Self

Thank you for allowing me to try to expand your horizon, while restoring our confidence in wisdom and value found within the mere thought or pursuit of restoration of any and all types. Please allow yourself to restore any confidence you may have allowed to wither or wane. At the very least this chapter allowed both of us to reflect back and dig a little deeper, and now we should be ready to reach a lot higher. I am. Let's climb further!

Restoration. Expound.

Result

Chapter Inspired by and Dedicated to
Yvonne B. (Shearer) Dallas

Insert or imagine seeing your first name: _____,

Seeing this chapter's title word, what immediately comes to your open mind? Do you already have a working relationship with this word? Somewhere inside of you does this word instantly appeal? As a response to a specific situation at-hand, will this word work to your and others' advantage? For this word to increase in real value, together we must dig, drill and think deeper, so we will reach, climb and soar higher.

You are likely to spend less time with this week's word chapter than in your reading of sports pages, business news, gossip, Facebook entries, Twitter's Tweets, blog postings, *etc.* As a primary result from experiencing this book, I am bold to trust that your favorable results at work, home and everywhere will increase and be of lasting value. A top result of reading this book will be to improve your results, plural.

> *"Your life is the sum result of all the choices you make, both consciously and unconsciously. If you can control the process of choosing, you can take control of all aspects of your life. You can find the freedom that comes from being in charge of yourself."*

> —Robert F. Bennett

In our personal and organizational pursuits, myriad results yield each sum result. Birth is a sum result and death is a sum result. In-between each sum result are lifetimes of interim results of all types and sizes. With economic and other pressure building in our homes, at work, in schools, and other institutions throughout the world, differentiating "results" (plural) from "result" (singular) merits these few moments of provocative focus.

"If necessity is the mother of invention, then surely greed must be the father.
Children of this odd couple are named: Laziness, Envy, Greed, Jr., Gluttony,
Lust, Anger and Pride." —JRDjr

This economic meltdown will fill historical volumes and business school case studies with accounts of both necessity (*e.g.,* onerously overdue reform for equal rights, education, healthcare, tax codes, politics, *etc.*) and greed (*e.g.,* dastardly deeds of the likes of Enron, Madoff, AIG, and a disgraced and unrepentant former governor of Illinois *et al*).

Only the unwise would pin root causative factors on a single tipping point, country, leader, religion, union, or political party. Collapse of this magnitude began decades or longer ago. Incessant *FORBES 400*-like glorification of personal wealth — over shared stewardship of resources for sustaining societal strength — fan flames of fires ignited years ago; internal combustion that compromises our free nation's resolve to think and act for the good of all God's people. A "Me Era" of selfishness began long before generations X, Y and M (Millennials). Baby Boomers and leaders of other ages are busy envisioning a global "We Era" of cross-cultural collaboration.

Are you?

On high seas of the U.S. free enterprise capitalistic way-of-life, shareholder insistence on never-ending short-term (*i.e.,* quarterly) growth dooms captains of business ships to hit icebergs. Many assumed indestructible vessels sink in shark-infested waters, and some skippers eventually hit rock bottom. Titanic or small, organizational wreckage often reveals prior character deficits and other bankruptcy. Ignoring or trivializing such navigational lessons seals fate of future crossings. Dire financial straits should serve to teach us why and how short-term gain can steer us toward long-term pain.

Let's drill a bit deeper before reaching a lot higher. Absence of deeper thought behind many household, business, and other leadership decisions creates fissures, cracks, chasms, and canyons of human emptiness and financial danger. Need-for-speed and wanton greed wreck havoc on nearly all the world's peoples, and allow untold damage to the earth's precious land, water and air. To secure and sustain — with random acts of mindfulness and un-tethered inventiveness — the only known inhabitable planet and its people, we each must work to envision, invent, align and implement an ever-steady stream of viable ideas and solutions.

"Economics is a subject profoundly conducive to cliché,
resonant with boredom. On few topics is an American
audience so practiced in turning off its ears and minds. And none
can say that the response is ill-advised." —John Kenneth Galbraith

Wages, salaries, commissions, or bonuses set way beyond logical economic worthiness for work actually performed became (1) desirable aspiration taught in MBA education, (2) bait used in white-collar recruiting, and (3) one of many lures for lifetime union membership. "Getting away with working as little as possible" while "earning as much as possible" is a dirty on-the-job secret of economic imbalance some perpetrators don't even admit to themselves. Others know full well what they are not doing, and knowingly continue in their high-risk role in a lopsided value exchange.

Employees earn negotiable currency for eight or more of the 24 nonnegotiable hours in each day that includes work. Someone who cumulatively *really* PRODUCES value for only seven, six, or fewer of eight paid hours, is walking toward budgetary quicksand. Eventually laggards fall-in and sink, often pulling down with them innocent dutiful earners. New workers are closely watching veteran employees, and some are willingly learning the slippery ropes.

"Character is the result of two things: mental attitude and
the way we spend our time." —Elbert Hubbard

When cuts have to be made, most alert bosses know who is pulling weight commensurate with their pay. Many low-performing workers are laid-off without bosses telling the displaced workers exculpatory evidence used in the decision. Risks of costly employee litigation against defensible truth about worker productivity grew too high, and so lies are told in termination proceedings. In this transaction, culprits are on both sides of the desk. Yes, all-around this is a bad scenario. Our economy suffers with such endemic weakness in human effort and organizational ethics.

For board rooms and collective bargaining tables, an *"All hands on deck!"* alarm is blasting a call for urgent strategic re-alignment of thoughts, people, plans, money, and performance. Pause to think about quantity and quality of results from your own daily productivity, and each day's measurable result. Are you steadily working at your personal best and earning for your employer at least three times more than you are taking out of their checkbook? Do you know for sure? Dare you ask your immediate supervisor?

Even in your most private reflection, do you assume any responsibility for thoughts or actions that might have contributed to economic circumstances and challenges we face? Are you at least looking beyond sensationalistic words of biased pundits and ratings-weighted news reports toward weeds in your own backyard? In drought conditions, grass-roots response starts with pruning and re-seeding our own fertile minds and hearts. The harvest in-mind will be plentiful, with enough surplus to store for life's dry periods ahead.

The trickle-down economic effect of our spending today what may be needed for tomorrow has become pop-culture rationalization for pursuing at all costs The American Dream. The house, vehicle, jewel, vacation, school, or any addiction purchased beyond ones means signals trouble ahead. How did The American Dream become The American Scheme? Is it time to re-dream, re-align, re-design, and name The Global Dream?

"There is nothing more exhilarating
than to be shot at without result." —Winston Churchill

Ten or so years ago an old Chicago company was occasionally chided by certain stockholders for stashing away for a rainy day approximately $2 billion in cash equivalents. The economically and otherwise conservative controlling shareholders felt duty-bound to their 12,000+ employees. The thoughtful and wise owners delayed rightful access to their share of company earnings, in favor of praiseworthy obligation to keep the business afloat if someday a *perfect storm* should hit. Without any lay-offs, fail-safe plans called for up to 18 months of belt-tightening and strategic re-alignment.

On a similar track of fiduciary responsibility, should public and private companies be required by law to save (*i.e.*, retain earnings) for funding at least a full year or more of rainy days, not unlike employees being coached to hold for possible career or health emergencies at least six months worth of necessary funds? For decades Government mandates workplace health and safety imperatives. To keep businesses afloat as a collision course is corrected or stormy seas grow calm, is it too far-fetched to federally regulate companies' retention of adequate contingency funding? With hundreds of billions of recent bail-out dollars in-mind, logic and forward-looking prudence dictate thoughtful consideration of this far-reaching solution. Imagine what such mandated across-the-board organizational financial stability would do for our nation's shaky standing in the now wary world of international commerce.

Philosophy and legislation for restitution through entitlement programs are often blamed for illogical and imprudent lending decisions in favor of commercial and human borrowers with questionable ability to pay. Among historically upper-income families, similarly unflinching expectation of higher and constant stock dividends creates a sense of entitlement, does it not? Corporate dividend entitlements are declared and paid-out even in troubled times. Announcing decisions to retain earnings would be more truthful and fiscally responsible. Independently wealthy people I know speak freely about receiving their Social Security payments, to which they brag about feeling entitled. Are they correct?

> *"Columbus did not seek a new route to the*
> *Indies in response to a majority directive."* —Milton Friedman

For his life's crowning result, Christopher Columbus gave credit to beneficent Queen Isabella, and thus guaranteed Spain a still questionable place in accurate world history. We surmise later-named Native Americans had not yet set out to discover Spain. Somehow Spaniards did not sustain to their flag's long-term advantage the claim to new-found land. Native Americans had not yet learned to withhold fiduciary trust until it is earned. One could ask if the Spanish queen's short-term PR gain clouded her vision toward long-term economic value in the asset in which she so trustingly invested? Did Native Americans have even a slight clue about unprecedented economic value they were about to yield to cunning opportunists? Did they study and learn from their results, and also accurately measure each result? We can safely guess.

Thinking back toward centuries of royal and other high-brow patrons of art, music, literature, exploration and exploitation, modern-day thinkers find in extra roles and expanded voices of academicians more than hints of stultifying arrogance of ancient aristocracy. Today's privileged few determine foundational alignment of focus for students, media, investors, board members, consulting clients, and theory-dependent managers. Do top professors of business, accounting, economics, or other fields of fiscal accountability own-up to any percentage of the global meltdown?

With MBAs more-than-ever in decision-making posts and places around the world, how could we have fallen so low? What was lacking in education or experience of those on whose watches calamity struck? In favor of teaching and testing rote knowledge, was student pursuit of nuanced wisdom, philosophy, and ethics set aside? Are historically boastful MBA schools bragging as much as before about their competitive preeminence? I notice welcome quiet on the graduate education front. Behind their closed doors and mouths introspection and course-correction are probably underway. They know what happened. So do some of us. Much good will come from this reassessment of principles, priorities and practices of schools of all levels and types.

What about *how-to* business lessons taught by immodest Donald Trump, iconic Jack Welch, deliberative Jim Collins, or other self-anointed czars of commerce and leadership education? In significant ways did these and other best-selling authors' vaunted prescience fail us readers? Or because of our hunger and thirst, did we grab any morsel or droplet they offered and felt it was a complete meal? Books, classes, and courses are career appetizers. Front-line leadership and personal productivity are the main course for us carnivores of meaty results. Dessert is what you might call a sum result.

As market forces dramatically shift, nearly every business school and information dissemination program is turning to frontline business leaders and asking "What went wrong?" Almost every major MBA program is being revamped, and many Deans of top business schools have been replaced. Most of this is being done rather quietly to avoid assigning blame to the teachers who have pushed so hard for monetization of our minds. Money first, people second.

The better question is, "What has been right all along?" From the 2005 beginning of Hillview's consulting, coaching, and speaking business, the answer remains the same:

"Put people first, put people second, put people third. Sustainable profit of many types will follow people, people, people." First: People who buy. Second: People who sell. Third: People who somehow benefit by efforts of those who buy and sell in a free-market economy.

Business professors and their students who put (1) making money above all else, (2) counting money in second position, and (3) manipulating money in third place, have caused immeasurable types of real harm to our global *ethos* and the world's economies. "It's all about the money" is how one overly celebrated business school professor starts his classes for entrepreneurship. Mere disagreement with this misguided fellow's ego can cost students grade points, derail alumni their job opportunities, cancel vendors' contracts, and inflict harm for everyone for whom he denies peace-of-mind. Even his more scholarly colleagues dare not disagree (publically) with his bombast and other forms of insecure belligerence. In private they bemoan his tenured stupidity.

Strip away what's left of Wall Street's formerly impenetrable metallic suit of armor with its Las Vegas Casino-like PR-polished patina, and the rust and weakness that's revealed usually comes from prioritizing money over people. People drive business success. Not money.

> *"Trust matters. Every day, in every person,*
> *and in everything, trust matters."* —Noreen J. Kelly

Fully responsible leaders look past pat answers. With today's reality and tomorrow's promise in view, let's collaboratively work toward sustainable new truth — any advantageous societal result worth the journey. Small steps for humankind allow more minds to engage in the journey. Moon and Mars landings unleashed generations of innovators. Fully responsible leaders nurture those who trust inherent potential in pursuit of results geared toward an ultimately favorable sum result.

Exit strategies for careers (*e.g.*, retirement fantasies), and liquidly events for companies (*e.g.*, record-breaking IPOs) forecast pockets-lined-with-gold results. Paradoxical impatience with ultimate value in mortality motivates many to hedge their bets with extra focus on earthly gain.

In 1976 I was introduced to Harold "Hal" Sydney Geneen (1910–1997), then Chairman and Chief Executive Officer of International Telephone and Telegraph Corporation (ITT), one of the largest-ever corporations, and perhaps once the world's most influential private-sector entity. When he asked me what my company was "doing for ITT," my response earned his wholly uncharacteristic arm around my shoulders as he said words a 26-year-old business owner could never forget, "John thanks for bringing us up-to-date. I never heard of such a 'thing.' I'm glad you're here."

For months or longer, I used that fleeting and unexpected moment of affirmation to keep my team's and my spirits high. The great Mr. Geneen gave me what felt like a Good Housekeeping Seal of Approval, an AAA rating from Standard & Poors, an A+ grade, or at least a gold star for my sweating forehead — for entrepreneurial results. He would always greet me with a big smile, and occasionally say hello, but we never again had any truly substantive conversation.

"In business, words are words; explanations are explanations, promises are promises, but only performance is reality." —Harold S. Geneen

Mr. Geneen's carefully chosen words, extended explanations, and sometimes startling promises were big parts of his performance as a command-and-control leader. Often his sense of ROI reality was reduced only to numbers tied to performance of some variety. Yet Mr. Geneen's rather steady stream of orchestrated or off-the-cuff performative words often caused eyebrows to rise, throats to clear, and heads to be scratched. With clarity as a result, ITT's stock price could rise. With muddle regarding the giant, shares could lose value.

Shortly after the so-called Year 2000 Problem, also known as Y2K or the Millennium Bug, I was involved in a software start-up with the results-driven Honorable Donald H. Rumsfeld as a lead investor and board member. His voice was the loudest and brightest of all. During a board meeting he openly and dramatically admonished me for thinking small. I wasn't. He heard wrong. His well-intentioned diatribe — against my not thinking big enough — still speeds-up my adrenaline. From the moment's embarrassment, I salvaged more than key lessons he directed squarely at me regarding one of his favorite big-thinking economists and philosophers, F.A. Hayek. Over 10 years later, I feel that result. Shortly thereafter he was called back to public service, and we would never again talk about results of big thinking.

More than only focusing on the difference between plural and singular, thank you for pausing to differentiate "results" (*i.e.,* milestones) from "result" (*i.e.,* destinations). These differences can realign thoughts, people, technology, plans, money and performance.

Result. Expound.

Success

Chapter Inspired by and Dedicated to Carl-Johan Hellner

Insert or imagine seeing your first name: _____,

Seeing this chapter's title word, what immediately comes to your open mind? Do you already have a working relationship with this word? Somewhere inside of you does this word instantly appeal? As a response to a specific situation at-hand, will this word work to your and others' advantage? For this word to increase in real value, together we must dig, drill and think deeper, so we will reach, climb and soar higher.

Headlines of populist rage toward Wall Street's wayward ways with investor trust and millions of taxpayer dollars, and desperate competitive pleas for consumer pennies in retail advertising, are extremes of downside reminders of economic importance of understanding success. Not unlike perception of beauty, what one person calls success, another might call something else. Success is also in the eyes of the beholder. How do you see success?

"Strive not to be a success, but rather to be of value." —Albert Einstein

In board rooms or the Oval Office, do today's fully responsible leaders define success differently and adequately? How do you identify or determine success for yourself and others? Are these definitions and descriptions aligned with your faith, core values, ethics, knowledge, and accrued wisdom? How do others characterize you in terms of success? Do those who matter most to you know how you define and measure success?

Success evolves and emerges from ones nature and nurture. Ask someone how she or he truly defines success, and immediately you will glean remarkable insight about the other person and yourself. Carefully question children and young adults about their personal relationship with success. Yes, success is very personal. Today's changed political landscape and pressing financial realities are dramatically influencing minds of all ages.

Words and ways of family, neighbors, teachers, writers, lyricists and pastors formed my early conflicting views of success. Mrs. Edith Cleland, an essentially memorable eighth-grade reading teacher, said she knew me well from topics I raised for hours of after-class discussion. So she offered me Ralph Waldo Emerson's words as a rather unconventional road map for a teenage boy's adult life ahead:

"Success. To laugh often and much; to win the respect of intelligent people and affection of children; to earn the appreciation of honest critics and endure the betrayal of false friends; to appreciate beauty, to find the best in others; to leave the world a bit better, whether by a healthy child, a garden patch or a redeemed social condition; to know even one life has breathed easier because you have lived. This is to have succeeded."

Still I am occasionally asked why I smile so much and laugh so easily. And I surround myself with best brains and hearts . . . love the sound of children's voices . . . appreciate respectful criticism . . . grieve during discovery of disingenuousness or worse . . . revel in symphonic music, fine art, clever food, fresh flowers, and warm hospitality . . . pray for beloved daughter Jennifer's triumphs . . . celebrate true friendship . . . facilitate thought leadership, innovation and entrepreneurship . . . strive to share best practices and hard lessons of front-line experience with health and wealth . . . and humbly attempt to breathe oxygen into rooms I am privileged to enter. Emerson's road map adds to my life's journey real-world milestones. For your life's upward climb, do you agree with these mile markers? No milestone is as important as the journey.

Money is not a barometer against which I measure any individual's personal success. Friendships and career ties, with billionaires and broke folk, erased common misconceptions about success. From a young age my career included considerable and yet erratic financial reward. So doubting souls might say it is easy for me to preach and teach such high-minded views about success. My 40-plus high-risk entrepreneurial years occasionally included debilitating periods of virtually no personal compensation. Gain and pain left on me their respective good marks and deep scars. Because of abiding faith in Emerson's "Success" lessons, when finances failed, deep down I felt sufficiently successful — and eventually grateful for it all.

In the wake of economic adversity, understanding and pursuing success is difficult and sometimes painful. No pain? No gain. Fear of gain's pain is fear of success. Ideally with professional support of executive coaches, fear of failure and fear of success must be addressed head-on by all fully responsible leaders.

In testing resonance of a draft of this chapter, a mid-20s reader could not set aside his long-held notion that success was measured by the amount of money one earns, saves, invests and spends. I was startled and annoyed by his intransigence. From his family life he was hard-wired to believe success and money are synonymous. So he was allowing his early-career financial worries to define him as a failure. Only money would make him a success. Still others and I try to sufficiently redirect his focus to see alternative views toward success.

IBM's visionary founder offered this view from his mind's hill:

"Would you like me to give you a formula for success? It's quite simple, really. Double your rate of failure. You are thinking of failure as the enemy of success. But it isn't at all. You can be discouraged by failure or you can learn from it. So go ahead and make mistakes. Make all you can. Because remember that's where you will find success." —Thomas J. Watson

What definitions, descriptions or illustrations of success come to your agile mind? What types of success warm your heart? Who in your close circles do you consider successful. Why? How?

Wherever you are you successfully arrived. The good, bad or other qualities of where you are do not influence the logic that you successfully landed at this point in time and in this place. Choosing to be at a different place, you can start with a clearer sense of possibility.

Do these additional insights about success motivate you to continue to move toward more successful outcomes for yourself and others? Are you becoming aware of an increase in your desire to succeed?

"Always bear in mind that your own resolution to succeed is more important than any other." —Abraham Lincoln

Thank you for allowing this book of letters to you from me support your quest for success. Allow nothing to stand in your way. Succeed.

Success. Expound.

Team

Chapter Inspired by and Dedicated to Kenneth C. Hicks

Insert or imagine seeing your first name: _____,

Seeing this chapter's title word, what immediately comes to your open mind? Do you already have a working relationship with this word? Somewhere inside of you does this word instantly appeal? As a response to a specific situation at-hand, will this word work to your and others' advantage? For this word to increase in real value, together we must dig, drill and think deeper, so we will reach, climb and soar higher.

"There is no 'I' in TEAM" — but there sure is 'M' and 'E' for ME. Do cliché-bound athletic coaches and project team leaders still miss how 50% of TEAM is about ME? Yes, M and E for me and my collaborative thoughts ("T") and cooperative actions ("A"). Connectivity with teammates is based on others' and my very own Thoughts, Empathy, Actions and Measurement — T.E.A.M. — all learned, practiced, and delivered for the good of the whole team and its parts, including *ME; me, myself and I.*

"If it's going to be, it's up to me," remains a motivational adage I've felt and followed since childhood days in *Braveheart*-like fullness-in-faith communities in urban and suburban Pittsburgh. The future of this great city, state, nation and world was up to me, I was told. I believed. I wish I could remember when I first heard this truth and from whom, as I am ever-certain of its lasting impact on my sense of self and duty. Under peer or other pressure, have you yielded your "ME," essentially subordinated your own sense of fullness in the pursuit of the team's goals and objectives? I have. Now on every team I serve and lead, I do not lose my sense of "ME."

With and without others you are complete. *Psychobabble* might tell you that you are more complete with the team. Complete is complete. Your faith in your Creator is all you need to grasp the paradoxical mystery, majesty and magnitude of your snowflake-like uniqueness and completeness. With or without the team, you are completely you. You can complete the team.

The much-admired "I Am Only One" motivational reading (which is still magnetized on my refrigerator's door) was adapted from Edward Everett Hale: *"I am only one, but I am one. I cannot do everything, but I can do something. And because I cannot do everything, I will not refuse to do the something that I can do. What I can do, I should do. And what I should do, by the grace of God, I will do."*

A well-formed team is made up on "Only Ones" (*i.e.*, "MEs") who know their unique gifts and limitations, and find greater strengths and potential in working with others who are similarly aware of their self-agency. Self-agency is defined as the conceptual understanding of self as an agent capable of shaping motives, behavior, and future possibilities (Damon & Hart, 1991). Multiply by the number of "MEs" on each team the psychological, emotional, societal and economic value to your organization of strategically aligned individuals with self-agency.

Steelers City's south suburban Baldwin High School's swimming pool had a bulletin board reserved for our late 1960s swim team members. I was startled and somehow saddened when confronting a posted notice's attempt at pithiness: *"If you think you are an indispensable member of Baldwin's swim team, go dive in the pool, climb back out, and then turn around and look at the hole you left in the water."* Ouch! I belly-flopped in an empty pool and hit concrete bottom.

Team became another four-letter word to erase from my vocabulary. For years I avoided thinking about or using the word "team." I was leading teams without using the word. "Task force" was the term I used to avoid "team." On this matter, eventually I grew-up. Thank heavens!

"The whole is greater than the sum of its parts." —Aristotle

Hillview's "ME Factor" for strategic team alignment and sustainable success focuses on how high degrees of strengths-based self-agency, and exceptionally strong PERSONAL commitment between and among fellow team members, create and fuel high-performance teams. Personal connection with the ME of others and of oneself allows the whole to be greater than the sum of the team's parts.

Respectfully I disagree with this outdated quote attributed to a man whose work I truly treasure, Peter F. Drucker: "The leaders who work most effectively, it seems to me, never say 'I,' and that's not because they have trained themselves not to say 'I.' They don't think 'I.' They think "we;" they think "team." They understand their job to be to make the team function. They accept responsibility and don't sidestep it, but "we" gets the credit. This is what creates trust, what enables you to get the task done."

Times are changing. Change is ceaseless. So, especially for today's and tomorrow's "me generation," it's unwise to ignore the "M" and "E" for ME in TEAM. Fully responsible leaders accomplish better results with teams by acknowledging strengths, weaknesses, opportunities and threats (S.W.O.T.) of each individual on a team, and strategically aligning people in ways to accentuate positives while ameliorating negatives — seizing opportunities while eliminating threats. Ultimate team success depends on intentional and masterful strategic alignment of people, money, and other mission-critical resources.

Are you a team player? Really? For the purpose of our digging deeper so together we can reach higher, it's important for you to be brutally honest with yourself. Again — are you a team player? Are you regarded, respected, and revered by others for your steadfast commitment to cooperation, collaboration, collegiality, and other continuity in team-centric thoughts, words, deeds and rewards? Do you feel your connection to the teams on which you serve?

Are you a team leader? Really? For the purpose of our digging deeper so together we can reach higher, it's important for you to be brutally honest with yourself. Again — are you a team leader? Are you regarded, respected, and revered by others for your steadfast commitment to leading with and through cooperation, collaboration, collegiality, and other continuity in team-centric thoughts, words, deeds and rewards? Do you feel connection with your teammates?

Are you answering, *"yes, no, maybe, not sure, or why in the world is he asking such seemingly impertinent questions in such an uncharacteristically dramatic fashion?"* Well, for you and me teams and teamwork may not be all they are cracked up to be. There, I said it; a hint of tough talk about trials and tribulations of teams. This reality check is why we are asking ourselves these invasive yet basic questions. Not unlike leadership, too often definitions and understandings of teams and teamwork are reduced to cosmetics of PR efficacy (*i.e.*, *blue smoke-and-mirrors*); form over substance, with public appearance camouflaging private truth of inefficiency. In more than the obvious way, for some of us team is a four-letter word.

In 1993 Harvard Business School Press first published McKinsey & Company's *The Wisdom of Teams, Creating a High-Performance Organization*, authored by Jon R. Katzenbach and Douglas K. Smith. I still have my 1994 copy (the pages are already quite yellow). I remember being lost in what I considered gobbledygook. I needed (and still need) more direct language about teamwork. I suppose I had not yet learned a nuanced style of writing that allows thinking readers to find between lines and paragraphs what they need, even if only to allow them to form Socratic questions for further investigation. Now I grasp more of the type of thinking William Safire-like authors are asking of us.

Called "Uncommonsense Findings" in the above book, writers point out how teams are not teams just because someone declares a team to be formed or otherwise uses the word. Once leaders articulate and make clear performance expectations of individuals, sometimes teams form essentially on their own. Teams can rise out of strategic alignment of people.

Authors Katzenbach and Smith also point out how high-performance teams are rare; precious few teams actually outperform other teams. Teams work, and yet few teams work over-abundantly better than others. This is good, bad and neutral news.

From thoughts and tasks of defining and describing teams, to formally forming teams based on agreed upon definitions and descriptions, perhaps most organizational leaders have taken too lightly esoteric and pop culture perceptions and facts about teams, team players, team leaders, and their composite performance. I have.

If I can possibly influence adaptation of deeper formative thinking and sharper definitions for teams, I will and do. Sadly, some clients still practice principles of Keeping It Short and Simple (K.I.S.S.), and less than desirable team outcomes often seem tied to oversimplification.

Going toward essential complexity, I see team rooted within *koinonia* (koy-nohn-ee'-ah), the Anglicization of the Greek word κοινωνία, which includes ancient definitions of joint participation, sharing, contribution, and other deeper meaningfulness for working together.

Team Members and Leaders
R.E.A.C.H. and R.E.A.C.T.

Students, practitioners, and other aficionados of Hillview's High-Impact Leader Lens (HILL) Model for Viewing Strategic Alignment (The HILL Model) know the triangular model's three cornerstones: wisdom, courage and patience. Wise, courageous, and patient teams and team leaders are best seen with HILL perspective. From HILL views, members of teams are observed on their true-north journeys toward set worthy destinations. Team members and leaders are seen to R.E.A.C.H. with Reality, Energy, Ascendancy, Commitment and Humility. And they are encouraged, empowered and otherwise enabled to R.E.A.C.T. with Respect, Empathy, Authenticity, Clarity and Trust. Please memorize words behind these Hillview acronyms.

To fortify strengths of teams and leaders, The HILL Score measures 36 vectors for viewing Level of Consciousness (LOC), Level of Engagement (LOE), and Level of Performance (LOP), including the 10 measurements above: (1) reality, (2) energy, (3) ascendancy, (4) commitment, (5) humility, (6) respect, (7) empathy, (8) authenticity, (9) clarity, and (10) trust. Other vectors include five each for relevant-to-performance personal and organizational strengths, weaknesses, opportunities and threats (HILL S.W.O.T. Vectors 11-30), and subjective and objective observations for: (31) knowledge, (32) skill, (33) collaboration, (34) wisdom, (35) courage, and (36) patience.

With these vectors and other HILL criteria related to clearly stated imperatives, Return on Leadership (ROL) is measured before Return on Investment (ROI) is calculated in monetary and other terms. Imagine defining or describing a team, team players, team leaders, or team performance without taking into account all of the above and more. It would be unwise, uncourageous and impatient to forge any vision or plan without such a robust view of teams — one team player and team leader at a time, please.

There is, of course, a shadow side of teams and team leaders. You may know all too well how passive-aggressive, excessively proud, dangerously self-absorbed, hostile, arrogant, belligerent, bellicose, and other types of misaligned personalities assigned to teams can turn teams into deadly tornadoes. Reflect for a moment on teams on which you serve or lead, and identify by name people who fit with any of the above or more warning signals of trouble ahead. Your team's success depends on such clarity about risk and what you can and cannot do to reverse it.

On a global scale, The Olympics are designed as bigger-than-big showcased examples of teams composed of MEs. ME+Team Effort begins many years before any city's Olympic extravaganza begins. Again, my much beloved Chicago seems to have thought itself more important than the world's teams we appear to crave. From the 2016 committee's overly celebrated kickoff, when the internationally patented Olympic torch was co-opted by Chicago's ill-advised PR advisers (to the dismay of all higher-ups in the Olympic movement, and then brought down [at high cost] from billboards, and off of bus stop shelters) — fiery flames within which Sears/Willis Tower, Aon Center, and Hancock Tower were shown fully ablaze; burning in horrific 9/11-style in the flames of the plagiarized torch. The ill-fated graphic image was explained as designed to tell the world we survived the 1871 Chicago Fire — as if today anyone outside of our region knows or, frankly, cares about "the fire." My snapshot of this view may seem to be overexposed. It's not. Allow a bigger picture to form.

Did windy-city (*i.e.*, those thought to be overly brash, boastful and proud) Chicagoans approach the 2016 Bid as if the world would be coming to play on Chicago's stage, instead of more wisely envisioning Chicago being privileged and humbled — yes, humbled — to play on the world's much bigger stage? This traditional convolution in grasping Chicago's place in the global marketplace cost Chicago The Bid. Rio got it. By thinking locally *and* globally, Rio won The Bid.

Do Chicago leaders and others continue to learn fire-starting and fire-fighting lessons from the misappropriated torch and other missteps? Does such costly experience help to extinguish rampant perilous pride? Team 2016 earned many accolades, yet The Games were lost. One wonders how team-like things were in the locker rooms of decision-making. Who was calling which shots? As Chicago is a perfect city to host any Olympiad, suspicions are that all wise voices were not heard or respected. Hillview's "T6 Game Plan" is a solution — **T**eams **T**hinking **T**hings **T**hrough **T**horoughly **T**ogether.

Asking team leaders "Where do things stand?" is the wrong question. Nothing stands still. Change is ceaseless. Ceaseless change means non-stop motion. Who is moving true-north, almost, or not even close? Measurable strategic team alignment (STA) data help to forecast outcomes. Team misalignment invites and ignites disaster. Too frequently and too late organizational misalignment is seen with 20/20 hindsight. Failures from early misalignment are often falsely attributed to external factors: market conditions, competition, bad timing, *etc*. Diligent bosses, board members, advisers, investors, lenders, partners, and others are asking hard questions about accountability for strategic team alignment.

"There is always some [S.O.B.] at table who doesn't get it." —JFK

Imagine a table with 10 people gathered to hear their team leader explain the dream of a new project. There are detailed handouts, charts, graphs, slides, and other exhibits. Heads nod in assent, copious notes are taken, cogent questions are asked, considered responses are given, and the discussion is robust. The meeting ends with a sense everyone is on parallel tracks — per Plan — and about to move forward. Are all individuals fully aligned?

Did a percentage of the participants inadvertently miss some of the leader's specifically stated — and unstated — alignment imperatives? What percentage of the group really got it? How many did not get it? Among the 11 individuals at table, even one or two out of alignment adds unacceptable risk to Plan. More c-level executives and other team leaders are admitting and addressing the likelihood of team misalignment.

Leaders want and need to believe they and their teams are aligned. Most know odds are simply not in their favor for 100% strategic team alignment.

"Teamwork makes the dream work." —John C. Maxwell

It is wise to use the word "team" more judiciously, more accurately, and more infrequently. Use "team" when the "MEs" at table are strategically aligned for best-effort personal and team outcomes. This takes work. It's more than well worth it.

Thank you for rethinking and reworking your "ME" and other "MEs" on each team you lead. There is no "I" in team, yet YOU and they are!

Team. Expound.

Trial

Chapter Inspired by and Dedicated to William D. Becker (1947-2011)

Insert or imagine seeing your first name: _____,

Seeing this chapter's title word, what immediately comes to your open mind? Do you already have a working relationship with this word? Somewhere inside of you does this word instantly appeal? As a response to a specific situation at-hand, will this word work to your and others' advantage? For this word to increase in real value, together we must dig, drill and think deeper, so we will reach, climb and soar higher.

Do you feel you are almost always on trial? Are you the judge and jury? Who else in your life makes everything a trial? Are fully responsible leaders always on trial? Are they themselves their toughest judicial system? Have your trials made you wiser, more courageous, and more patient with yourself and others? Mine have. Almost unbearable personal and career trials have made me stronger. Do you identify with this logic?

In an admittedly weakness-obsessed U.S. culture, we the free have been programmed by default to think ourselves guilty until proven innocent. Feelings of guilt intentionally infused in our young psyches by certain well-meaning (we hope) parents, pastors, and other teachers can last unchecked for a lifetime. For mature functionality in self-efficacy and other mental health, early detection and correction are essential.

Scholar Albert Bandura advanced the notion of cyclical psychological interdependencies between a person and her or his environment. For our purposes, we take Bandura's work a step further, suggesting a positive home or work environment will allow people to yield more positive outcomes, while negative environments virtually guarantee failure and other misalignment. Is your home a positive or negative environment? Is your workplace measurably positive or negative?

Would you agree an unexpected neutral response to either question would probably skew more toward negative than positive?

A child bringing home a report card with all As and one F experiences more guilt of failure with the F than success with the As. Most parents admit they would focus on the F more than the As. This is knee-jerk unwise parental focus on weakness instead of strength. The student is on trial to prove the F is not a reflection of diminished capacity to perceive (*i.e.*, I.Q.) or learn. Childhood trials and tribulations can eventually yield to smiles and celebrations. The toddler or youngster who is a trial for her or his parents may be demonstrating early propensity toward greatness.

In the grown-up world, where do you see this upside-down focus mostly on weakness — from your boss, spouse, significant other, elected officials, family *et al*? Think deeply about this. If you can, you may need to remove from your circle those misfits and naysayers who pull or push you down into the muck of negativity. "Misery loves company," my Grandmother Shearer would intone. Positive and successful people thrive amidst other positive and successful people.

While you are out on your own for a relaxing evening with same-sex friends, and your spouse calls your mobile telephone (perhaps more than once), instantly do you feel you are on trial? Do wives call husbands more often than husbands call wives? Either way, when the phone is answered, the look on the recipient's face suggests possibility that a mini-trial is about to begin.

As a divorced man — now what they used to call "a confirmed bachelor" — I marvel at the vulnerable and sad faces I see when caller I.D. tells a visitor to my home his wife is calling. Perhaps these wives are mischievously envisioning the grimace crossing their husbands' faces, and even imagining silent or expressed views about the short leash. Hearing grown men justify their time away from their homes saddens them and me. Too often I note the change in the comfort and joy of the dutiful husband who was just put on trial. Some are sentenced with stopping at the 7-11 store for a loaf of bread and gallon of milk the wife wants but does not need. Forget infractions in courtesy toward the spouse's host, where is the marital trust in these trials?

When your boss or client calls you to her or his office, does it feel like a trial is about to begin? When the IRS leaves a voicemail message, are you expecting a trial of an audit? With whom and where else in your life do you expect and feel a trial almost always in-the-works? Clergy? Houses of worship? Are these feelings justified? Are these trials real or imagined?

When bosses, clients, consultants, coaches, lawyers, pastors, doctors, dentists, therapists, significant others, parents, co-workers, family, friends and others point out more errors and problems than they celebrate successes and strengths, brains of perpetrators and victims become wired to fail more than to succeed. Yes, even professional practitioners paid to protect us from our weaknesses serve themselves and others better by prioritizing sharp and vocal focus on their and our strengths.

As an example, remember to ask your trusted physician to tell you what you are doing correctly before telling you what to do better. Top-ranked Rush University Hospital internist Steven K. Rothschild, M.D. begins every medical exam with observation of things he can tell are going right for me. This approach makes easier to swallow any bitter pills he might need to dispense or prescribe.

Before the dentist or dental hygienist admonishes you for not flossing three times each day, ask her or him to tell you what's at least okay with your teeth, gums, mouth, and other health signs related to oral care. Why must so many dentists and hygienists prove their mastery over mouths by first telling patients how stupid we are about the way we manage our gums and teeth?

Does your attorney pat you on the back for your lawful actions, or does your auditor commend your mastery of QuickBooks? With your paid resources, insist on at least some positive feedback before any negative. Intentional focus on strengths allows us to overcome trials in our weaknesses. Positive words open and strengthen parts of our brain that are needed for problems.

When was the last time your city's traffic court wrote to commend your safe driving record, or honor a full year or more without a parking violation or other citation? Does your landlord or mortgage lender thank you for paying on-time, or do you only hear from the front office when the check is six days late? Does your place of worship tell you when they have surplus funds, or do you only hear calls for increased contributions? Are we always being tried? Well, yes.

Hillview clients are requested to take Gallup Organization's online assessment of strengths within Tom Rath's StrengthsFinder 2.0 (strengthsfinder.com). Knowing and living up to your strengths is a different type of trial. Hillview's High-Impact Leader Lens (HILL) Model (The HILL Model) is calibrated to focus on strengths. Weaknesses come into view within the framework of strengths. This nuance is profound in its promise, passion and other potential.

Indeed life is a trial. This is a good thing. Imagine living without a sense of trial-and-error. Etymologically the "tri" of trial refers to three (3). Three seems to be a notion deeply embedded in the human experience. Wives and husbands eventually realize there are three (not two) sides to every story; her story, his story, and the probably truer story found somewhere in-between. Three was the number for the foundational relationships set between two sinful humans and their sinless Creator. Even non-believers know New Testament teachings reveal a triune (three-part) God: Father, Son and Holy Spirit; one in three, three in one. All of the above and more mystery is intellectual trial for our thinking brains and feeling hearts.

The geometrically strongest triangle depicting Hillview's High-Impact Leader Lens (HILL) Model has three cornerstones: Wisdom, Courage, and Patience. Exploring "trial" is, in itself, a bit of a trial requiring extra measures of wisdom, courage, and patience. To facilitate thinking deeper to support reaching higher, this word's great significance requires extra measures of care, thought, feeling and action. For these few minutes we're together with this HILL Word, please allow me to climb with you as we explore the high risk, potential, and reward of "trial."

Trial is a word we probably hear more than once each day. Does trial-and-error by name skew minds toward the negative? Why not shoot for "trial-and-success?" Trial-by-fire stands on its own. Fair trials are in the eyes of the beholder. Trial-by-jury suggests desirability thereof — and even hints at infallibility of peers. Deeper thought provides obscure context for the crime-deterrent factor in a would-be criminal's thinking about a trial by a jury of his or her peers. In other words, what wily convict would want to be tried by other wily convicts; would Wall Street Ponzi Scheme thieves want to be tried by a jury of similarly untrustworthy Ponzi Scheme thieves? Imagine how trials would run if a jury was filled with the plaintiff's true peers.

A mentor once told me, "There's no such thing as a free lunch." He was 100% correct. And there's no such thing as a free trial. At some point someone pays something. It may not be the end user, but someone is paying. One way or another there is a value exchange in every ethical transaction between and among moral individuals.

Trial runs run out. From January 2009 through June 2010, on a weekly basis (without fail) I offered to a carefully selected roster of thought leaders a free trial of weekly e-mailings of draft preview chapters and other content for We Need to Have a Word. The extra steps required to process and post reformatted text cost me considerable time and effort (many hundreds of hours). Readers responded. Their in-kind cost is measured in time, interest, trust, and actions taken as a direct or indirect result of their focus on the featured HILL Word. Together we were in this not-so-free free trial.

Let's think about the upside potential within the trial of a nearly shattered U.S. economy; a world that revealed unbridled hubris behind revelry of the wealthiest. Also blue-collar complicity and complacency are still attributed to the misdeeds of the rich. From billionaires being rather certain they can buy their way out of any legal problem they cause, to workforce borrowers with over-the-top mortgage balances and credit card debt, We the People are on trial.

"We are known by the challenges we keep." —JRDjr

In closing this chapter, let's dive extra deep and then we'll be able to reach extra high. In Hillview's HILL Model, understanding (1) goodness, (2) ethical pursuits, and (3) moral behavior is reduced to these three-part trials.

Goodness, Ethics and Morals

(1) A good person wants to do the right thing. (2) An ethical person works to learn the deeper differences between right and wrong things. (3) A moral person does right things for right reasons.

Good Leader, Responsible Leader, and a Fully Responsible Leader

(1) The good leader wants to do the right thing. (2) A responsible leader knows deep difference between the right and wrong things to do. (3) The fully responsible leader actually does the right things, for the right reasons, in the right way, and at the right time.

Ethics require I mention the tsunami of memories of personal and professional trials that flooded my brain and heart as I drafted this letter to you. Great was the temptation to continue writing and writing. From trials I witnessed in my toddler years, to today's and tomorrow's trials I'll navigate, I am blessed to trust the communion of saints in and around my world. During times of essential focus on trials, occasionally fully responsible leaders may feel lonely, but always they know they are not alone.

Keith is my favorite Chicago waxologist for shining my shoes, mind and heart. He works from the shoe repair shop in the lower level of The John Hancock Tower on The Magnificent Mile. I sense more than I hear about Keith's lifetime of trials. When genuinely I told him how much I appreciate his perspective on life, he responded, "You see my glory but you don't know my story." Can you relate? I can.

Perhaps most battle scars from trials are invisible to the naked eye. Post-traumatic stress disorder (PTSD) is commonplace for veterans of battle fields, complicated childbirth, fractured relationships, career catastrophes, and a host of other trials. Seeking professional support is a wise course for PTSD and other negative impact of life's trials.

Trial is a word worth understanding at deeper levels, more for the good than the bad. It takes time and effort to discern the good that comes from each trial. Right can go wrong, and wrong can go right. Our knowing what to do in virtually any trial scenario influences favorable or other outcomes. These are constants: deeper thought, deeper feelings, deeper prayer, and deeper faith.

> *"Great spirits have always encountered violent opposition*
> *from mediocre minds." —*Albert Einstein

Thank you for being emboldened, empowered and enriched by trials.

Trial. Expound.

Trust

Chapter Inspired by and Dedicated to Noreen J. Kelly

Insert or imagine seeing your first name: _____,

Seeing this chapter's title word, what immediately comes to your open mind? Do you already have a working relationship with this word? Somewhere inside of you does this word instantly appeal? As a response to a specific situation at-hand, will this word work to your and others' advantage? For this word to increase in real value, together we must dig, drill and think deeper, so we will reach, climb and soar higher.

> *"If there's not trust, there's basically nothing,*
> *no foundations, nothing."* —Kiara

Trust is a precious and dangerous word. What child or adult forgets the empty feeling when a parent or significant other said, "I can't trust you anymore?" Trust is about fullness. A glass of trust is never half-full. Trust drained always makes the glass half-empty or less. For life between a baby's instinctive trust of a nursing mother and an adult's ultimate trust in a higher power, trust is fertile farmland with hidden minefields. Understanding the full-range of trust is economically, socially and spiritually significant, yet too few of us pause to adequately define, describe or exemplify it.

Global economic reality requires unprecedented levels of trust in oneself, others, institutions, and organizations. Especially in navigating the U.S. correction economy, measurable trust must be at the center of strategic re-alignment of thoughts, people, plans and performance. We already entrust our money to technology and algorithms we don't understand. People we'll never meet protect or destroy our assets; operatives to whom we are account numbers linked to dollar signs and tax filings. Why do we trust with our assets so many people and things? Well, we must. The economics of trust include faith in many. With "In God We Trust" emblazoned, the U.S. Treasury set the bar at the highest level.

Perhaps for too many, investment risk begins with greed. Trusting a big pay-off from a hunch or a stock tip are camouflage terms for explaining away unwarranted risk. Trust in Wall Street's fabled masters of the universe is predicated on our knowing they will line their own pockets with our low-hanging dollars. If our dollars produce offspring when matched with investments, everyone more-or-less wins. When the marriage doesn't produce results, some money masters default to cheating — mostly so they alone win, at least for the short-term. Madoff's crimes against the very nature of trust are unfathomable. AIG's decades of blindness to reasonableness continue to astound. For when fiduciary trust is mishandled, employment contract law may have already been set against ethics and populist logic. Although on unsure legal and political footing, President Obama appeared to be determined to do the right thing with trust busters.

"If you once forfeit the confidence of your fellow citizens, you can never regain their respect and esteem. It is true that you may fool all of the people some of the time; you can even fool some of the people all of the time; but you can't fool all of the people all of the time." —Abraham Lincoln

Trusted friend and colleague Noreen Kelly is President of Trust Matters Group. Of course I invited her perspective: "Trust plunged in the United States while resilient across the globe, according to the 2011 Edelman Trust Barometer, the firm's 11th annual trust and credibility survey (the survey sampled informed publics in two age groups [25-34 and 35-64] in 23 countries). U.S. trust in business fell by eight points to 46% and decreased in government by six points to 40%. The U.S. was the only country to see trust fall in all four institutions: business, government, NGOs, and media. Trust in all credentialed spokespeople is higher this year, signaling a desire for authority and accountability — a likely result of the skepticism wrought by last year's string of corporate crises. CEOs are now in the top tier of trustworthy spokespeople, a 19% increase over 2009. Fifty percent say CEOs are credible spokespeople about a company."

The survey also measured how trust hits the bottom line: 85% of respondents said they bought a product or service from a company they trusted, while 73% had refused to buy products or services from a company they distrusted. To cultivate a culture of trust within your organization, follow these 10 actions: (1) Live the values, (2) Tell the truth, (3) Communicate, communicate, communicate, (4) Be in integrity, (5) Be authentic, (6) Be accountable, (7) Be transparent, (8) Respect the individual, (9) Share information, and (10) Do the right thing.

In effect, New York City remains the Economic Trust Capital of the world. For its massive volume of trading in derivatives and commodities, Chicago has been called by pundits the Economic Risk Capital of the World. Is it time to forge The New York-Chicago TRUST Exchange (NYCTE) bridging with wise minds and state-of-the-art technology — to ensure statutory compliance and full accountability — the 791.25 miles between Chicago's Willis Tower (formerly Sears Tower) and Freedom Tower at World Trade Center?

Think about strengths, weaknesses, opportunities and threats these two great cities could identify, then collaboratively manage to mutual advantage. New York and Chicago could set world records for economic productivity and trustworthiness. Listen to your immediate response to this big idea. What just happened in your mind? Did any of your response involve trust? Was the idea too small or far-fetched?

For Main Streets and Wall Streets, things new, things big, and things trustworthy have to emerge from the smoldering ruins of this trust-busting era. From the turn-of-the-century dot com collapse, Enron's horrors, and other economic implosion, changes then may not have been commensurate with need. Instead of innovating for new ways of earning and sustaining investor trust, we spent our time resuscitating old thoughts and ways. It is time for new models, means and methods for measuring, trusting and investing in our country's true long-term economic strength — steady funding and other support for small and mid-size businesses. Let's start with defining, building, measuring and sustaining new levels of trust in entrepreneurship for the Americas and the world.

Misalignment in life or an entire enterprise may be based on mistrust of a leader's self. Undetected, undeclared, yet ultimately corrosive lack of internal trust scuttles careers, projects, organizations, and lives of the young and older among us. Indeed this chapter's big word commands extra space, time and attention. Please allow the word to stay in the front of your mind. Do all you can to build instead of shake trust. Talk about trust with your teams, please. A leader's purposeful word or act builds trust, while a careless expression or deed could crush trust. Fully responsible leaders — including parents, teachers, and other standard-bearers — define, describe, and exemplify trust for children and others.

From age eight (1958) I was trusted to travel on my own — *via* a Mister Rogers-like "trolley" rail car (a streetcar) — from Pittsburgh's Mt. Washington to the city proper, where I would ride *big* elevators to the top of the Gulf Oil Building, then the city's tallest. The view from the observation deck was mesmerizing. My showing up so often seemed to amuse the trusting ladies who worked there.

"Relationships and trust. This is the bedrock of life." —Mukesh Ambani

Indeed trust is front-and-center when you allow someone else to drive any vehicle in which you are a dependant passenger. In 2004 I was in a back-seat trusting a physician pal's driving. Rather firmly I asked him to slow down on a wickedly icy highway. He admonished me for being as ignorant to the road we were traveling as he was familiar. Truly within seconds of his misguided temerity, the car spun out of control and "flew" down into a deep snow-filled ditch — firmly packed snow that probably saved all three lives and the car. Emergency vehicles arrived. Badly shaken yet physically unharmed, within 30 minutes we were back on the road — slowly driving back to Chicago for perhaps 50 more miles.

The egocentric driver's apologies were accepted, but his braggadocio could not be forgotten. That night trust in his mature judgment was shattered. Trust-busting types of shenanigans to come disappointed me, but they were hardly surprising. My misplaced trust had been withdrawn. Since then the trust-starved friendship withered and died.

"But it is impossible to go through life without trust; that is to be imprisoned in the worst cell of all, oneself." —Graham Greene

Strategic alignment is about trusting true-north movement toward vision, mission, objectives, goals, and other worthy destinations. Trust fuels the journey.

"Trust only movement. Life happens at the level of events, not of words. Trust movement." —Alfred Adler

Trust. Expound.

Vision

Chapter Inspired by and Dedicated to Linda Bryant Valentine, Esq.

Insert or imagine seeing your first name: _____,

Seeing this chapter's title word, what immediately comes to your open mind? Do you already have a working relationship with this word? Somewhere inside of you does this word instantly appeal? As a response to a specific situation at-hand, will this word work to your and others' advantage? For this word to increase in real value, together we must dig, drill and think deeper, so we will reach, climb and soar higher.

> *Vision without action is a daydream.*
> *Action without vision is a nightmare.*
> —Japanese Proverb

Dictionary definitions for Vision: Noun (1) the faculty or state of being able to see, (2) the ability to think about the future with imagination or wisdom, (3) a mental image of what the future will or could be like, (4) an experience of seeing something in a dream or trance, or as a supernatural apparition, (5) the images seen on a television screen, (6) a person or sight of unusual beauty. Latin origin from *videre* — "to see." Synonyms: revelation, prophecy, dream, hallucination, apparition, concept, idea, mental picture, image, visualization, foresight, farsightedness, imagination, forethought, prescience, eyesight, sight, ability to see. (Drawn with permission from onelook.com.)

Questions for Leaders: Did President Obama's first years in office narrow or broaden your view of where people and things are moving? Are you thinking, saying and doing things the same way as before the President's game-changing inauguration? From what vantage point are you keeping watch? Surely you are not standing exactly where you were. What's new and in-view for you?

Panoramic view from The HILL: Getting to any favorable outcome from this gut-wrenching correction economy will be painful before gainful. Today's truly visionary leadership thinking and action will contribute to tomorrow's unprecedented turnaround success. Hillview's vision for fully responsible leaders is a journey that ends with a start.

Reality in-view and beyond will test to-the-max our collective visionary strengths, challenge the globe's multicultural societal norms, shift Wall Street's outdated economic paradigms, and otherwise correct endemic global misalignment of people, money, and other mission-critical resources.

Change is ceaseless. Change for the better is long overdue. Favorable change requires positive vision. Viable vision requires wisdom, courage and patience.

> *"The final wisdom of life requires not the annulment of incongruity but the achievement of serenity within and above it."* —Reinhold Niebuhr

When facts and numbers sound economic warning alarms, fully responsible leaders do not panic. To build bridges, pave pathways, and re-surface potholes in minds and matter, fully responsible leaders are more attentive, intentional, realistic, nimble, vigilant, empathic, emphatic, communicative, proactive, adventuresome, in-touch, investigative, innovative, analytical, predictive, preemptive and positive.

Worthy vision must be a true-north destination that you and your teams want and need to reach. Vision clearly seen is then effectively communicated. Effectiveness in communication is measured — *i.e.,* tested — by levels of comprehension, retention, engagement, motivation, and other results.

Test, Test and Re-Test Vision

Dream it. Test it. Glimpse it. Test it. Sketch it. Test it. See it. Test it. Write it. Test it. Say it. Test it. Hear it. Test it. Set it. Test it. Communicate it. Test it. Do it. Test it. Feel it. Test it. Smell it. Test it. Recalibrate it. Test it. Celebrate it. Test it. Never stop dreaming or testing. Vision commands and demands our non-stop vigilance. Test.

> *"Vision looks inward and becomes duty.*
> *Vision looks outward and becomes aspiration.*
> *Vision looks upward and becomes faith."* —Stephen S. Wise

This 52-chapter year-long vision journey seeks to rekindle child-like excitement you surely felt when words first became parts of your identity. Words leaders choose to use are strengths of our *brand me*; electrifying and invigorating elements of our essence. Words are used to define, describe and illustrate our brand's vision. It is too bold to say your vision is your identity? Defining, improving and protecting your leader brand supports movement toward each worthy vision.

Thinking about, applying and monitoring immediate, short-term, and long-range results from Language for Leading™ supports adult you. With these luminous words ignite neural receptors to stimulate success.

Imagine blank space below, or anywhere else in this book, as an unused artist's canvas, empty picture frame, or a big-screen monitor — all waiting to be filled with your mind's bright light of images, illustrations and words. Sketch or at least imagine filling free space with your vision of a better moment ahead. Every word in this book is offered to ignite, support and affirm your vision. See, feel and trust your panoramic, innovative, evocative and constructive vision, please.

Immediately after you finish reading this letter to you from me about vision, you may want to write emerging visionary thoughts forming in your mind and heart. Let those thoughts, feelings, images and words flow freely. Allow yourself to see, hear and feel your true brilliance.

"If you do not breathe through writing, if you do not cry out in writing, or sing in writing, then don't write, because our culture has no use for it." —Anais Nin

Vision is expressed in all parts of this book. So this section is particularly brief yet sufficiently evocative. In the spirit of author Ian Fleming's reader-engagement strategies, especially for his James Bond 007 character's use of laser-locked specificity to get right to the issue of the moment, I encourage you to shake things up in your mind and soul. With this book's shorter chapters minds are shaken *and* stirred. Oxygenate your brain. Rattle your thoughts. Recalibrate your vision.

If you had planned to read for a longer period, perhaps this would be a good time to read again an earlier chapter or two that stimulated your vision toward a brighter tomorrow. Choose to add at least one twist to your visionary cocktail. In 007's style, shake things up a bit.

"The end in mind is always another new beginning." —JRDjr

Vision. Expound.

Wisdom

Chapter Inspired by and Dedicated to Peter Koestenbaum, Ph.D.

Insert or imagine seeing your first name: _____,

Seeing this chapter's title word, what immediately comes to your open mind? Do you already have a working relationship with this word? Somewhere inside of you does this word instantly appeal? As a response to a specific situation at-hand, will this word work to your and others' advantage? For this word to increase in real value, together we must dig, drill and think deeper, so we will reach, climb and soar higher.

"The doors of wisdom are never shut." —Benjamin Franklin

Wisdom. Definition Highlights: 1. good sense: the ability to make sensible decisions and judgments based on personal knowledge and experience, 2. wise decision: good sense shown in a way of thinking, judgment, or action, 3. accumulated learning: accumulated knowledge of life or of a sphere of activity that has been gained through experience. 4. opinion widely held: an opinion that almost everyone seems to share or express, 5. sayings: ancient teachings or sayings. Thesaurus Synonyms: understanding, knowledge, sense, insight, perception, astuteness, intelligence, acumen, prudence, sagacity. (Used with permission from onelook.com)

To more clearly see from your mind's hills where people and things are moving, this book invites your continuing focus on words from the language of strategic alignment for people and things. From definition, description and application, to relevant philosophy, interpretation and practicality, this is a word-by-word journey upward.

Today's audible global cry for fully responsible leadership is addressed by applying deeper definitions and descriptions of words related to key functions of leaders. So-called bad leadership can often be traced to root misunderstandings of what it means to be a fully responsible leader. Philosophers Bertrand Russell and Peter Strawson taught restraint in accepting fullness in any definitions or descriptions. Accordingly, The HILL Model refers to meaning more so than it asserts absolutes.

With great respect for subtleties of ordinary linguistic usage, The HILL Model offers evocative thoughts associated with carefully selected words. Actionable understanding evolves from reverence for certain old words. In climbing The HILL toward linguistic alignment, we will reach higher heights and see clearer sights. Wiser and better thoughts and actions should follow.

Of all words in this collection of letters to you from me, wisdom requires we put our toes in at least the comparatively shallow end of the pool of philosophy and science about the word.

Scottish philosopher James Frederic Ferrier (1808-1864) needed a word to characterize the study of knowledge. Yes, one word for all of that. Epistemology. Expound. Imagine the essay!

For this extended purpose, epistemology is the word attributed to Ferrier. Under the umbrella of this single word, he chose to study interconnectivity between and among beliefs and truth, and scholarly justification for both. Logically he overlaid skepticism related to claims of knowledge.

Somewhat paradoxically, epistemological thinking grew to represent critical thinking; essentially characterizing one's thought order that is mapped to methodology. It seems Mr. Ferrier was moving in a different direction. Unlike critical thinking's requirements for topics, methods, mechanisms, specific propositions, logical fallacies, deceptions, and bias, epistemology allows for claims to perception of truth. Epistemology, in the word's pure form, appears to reach above real-world deductive processes (*i.e.,* what is generally accepted practice for problem solving).

For grasping even the basic of physics, epistemology is vital to grasping today's interpretation of quantum mechanics. Reviewing and analyzing how physicists came to their conclusions requires epistemological thinking. Your epistemologically seeking wisdom is a wise, courageous, and patient philosophic pursuit. Enjoy expounding on epistemology.

It seems the more bravely and boldly one studies knowledge about so-called truth and beliefs, the greater the wisdom that emerges.

Looked at separately or together, Dr. Koestenbaum's The Leadership Diamond®, and your author's High-Impact Leader Lens (HILL) for Fully Responsible Leadership (The HILL Model™), allow explorers to dig, drill and think deeper about knowledge, so our minds can reach, climb and soar a lot higher — with more wisdom.

Naming our internalism and externalism regarding identification and acquisition of knowledge — and ideally our contemporaneous pursuit of wisdom — allows us to value higher our many suspicions and occasional conclusions about both knowledge and wisdom. What is known independently of actual experience (*i.e., a priori* knowledge), and empirical encounters (*i.e., a posteriori* knowledge) fuel many of us to never stop trying to move beyond knowledge of either type toward wisdom of ever-greater depth and height. This is not as confusing as it may appear.

In one of many of the world's holy texts, the word "wisdom" appears in 165 of the 1,362 chapters within the 81 books of The King James version of The Bible; found in 36,819 verses with just under one million words (exactly 930,243). A woman was first to identify value in seeking wisdom. We know the rest of the "first apple" story. The first Biblical reference to wisdom:

"When the woman saw that the fruit of the tree was good for food and pleasing to the eye, and also desirable for gaining wisdom, she took some and ate it. She also gave some to her husband, who was with her, and he ate it." —Genesis 3:6

Women often bring to their leadership posts a more holistic sense for leading. Men are learning, I'm biased, bold and brave to suggest.

For a deeper dive about the roles of wisdom in leadership, I believe there is no better submersible vehicle than The Leadership Diamond®. To see where people and things are moving — with the freewill embodied in Dr. Koestenbaum's lessons — I stand strong atop The HILL Model™.

Standing atop The HILL you too will want to hear, see, think, and feel differently about your never-ending quest for wisdom. Especially when you are leading people and managing things, discipline yourself to think deeper to reveal greater clarity in what you are seeing and sensing. Always look beyond the obvious. Peer behind the curtain of accrued knowledge and experience. Steer clear of taking any easy-way out. And just when you think you see it all and have it all figured out, remind yourself you probably do not. Look. Ask. Listen. Lead. Learn.

Repeat. Do you feel "the spirit of wisdom?" Let this question resonate for a lifetime. Feel it.

"The limits of my language are the limits of my mind.
All I know is what I have words for." —Ludwig Wittgenstein

Seen from The HILL, "The end in mind is always a new beginning." Beyond knowledge and experience wisdom can be found. Usually it takes work. And wisdom discerned might be true wisdom. There's always more. Beneath perceptions more wisdom remains to be discovered. I believe ultimate wisdom is unattainable in this realm. This humbling reality reminds empathic leaders to always (1) pursue wisdom, (2) personify courage, and (3) practice patience.

Doing Wisdom's Work

Following his mid-2011 about-face vote in favor of same-sex marriage rights, New York State Senator Mark Grisanti said from his perspective of being an attorney, "I would not respect myself if I didn't do the research, have an open mind and make a decision, an informed decision, based on the information before me. A man can be wiser today than yesterday, but there will be no respect for that man if he failed in his duty to do the work." He was doing wisdom's work.

When a wise leadership decision is to be taken, have confidence in your intentional alignment of: thoughts, people, things, knowledge, experience, wisdom, wants, needs and deeds. Think alignment. Alignment is a word that works as a guidepost on the never-ending journey toward greater wisdom. Alignment is wisdom's work. Wisdom's work is alignment. Alignment Teams are Wisdom Teams.

Wise words we choose to express wisdom's work touch our minds and souls at levels of depth and height we might not otherwise reach. The 400th anniversary of the publication of the King James Bible did not pass without notice in the English-speaking world. Only four centuries ago, wisdom's work was given new linguistic context within which to operate and promulgate.

This chapter is intentionally among the book's shorter offerings. Perhaps wisdom is the word with the longest reach. You already know this word has been addressed rather illustratively in all prior 51 chapters. Yet, even as we close this 52-week reading and thinking journey, you and I both know there is so much more to learn about and experience with each featured word. Perhaps you also think wisdom is the word that commands the most attention and effort.

Three of the most influential deeper thinkers in European History emerged during the Scottish Enlightenment: James Hutton, David Hume and Adam Smith. From one of the three came:

> *"In order to be able to know something, or even believe it,*
> *we must first be able to think it. We must first be able to entertain it*
> *as a hypothesis, to suppose it might be true."* —David Hume

Abundant wisdom, courage and patience are required. Which is your favorite word of the three? If you are where you can do so, please slowly read aloud these three words, perhaps three times.

Now, please breathe-in deeply — and slowly exhale — three deep breaths: The Wisdom Breath. The Courage Breath. The Patience Breath. Pause. After experiencing We Need to Have a Word, enjoy the exhilarating feeling you allow yourself following this climb to higher ground. With each breath and word invite wisdom's wonders.

After you read the next few final pages of this book, you may feel compelled to start rereading all or some of the 52 chapters. Do it. Please. Read again Preface and Content and feel increased electricity. Enjoy deep satisfaction for wisdom you allow to take root and grow.

> *"Knowledge comes, but wisdom lingers."* —Alfred, Lord Tennyson

Consider writing your own list of your 52 top words for unblocking and unlocking deeper thoughts, higher views, and greater accomplishments. Let wisdom be your word for action in conference rooms, war rooms and family rooms. Allow this word to be your depth finder. With this book and other wisdom readings, you are doing wisdom's worthy work.

> *"Language is the house of Being. In its home man dwells.*
> *Those who think and those who create with words*
> *are the guardians of this home."* —Martin Heidegger

Wisdom. Expound.

Courage. Expound.

Patience. Expound.

You are doing wisdom's work.

Acknowledgment

Immediately I acknowledge your trust. Thank you for allowing time and space for these words to take root in your mind and heart. They will continue to grow in value. I appreciate you and your wise words.

In alphabetical order, I thank these exemplary individuals for encouraging words and other specific actions related to development and distribution of this book: The Reverend Dr. Joanna M. Adams, Benjamin Angel, Kevin Bendle, Clyde O. Bowles, Jr., Esq., Eric R. Broughton, Philip and Jill Calian, The Honorable James Cappleman, Patrick Chantelois, Sandra Craig, John J. Dallas, Yvonne B. Dallas, Adam Daniels, Dr. Dennis Deer, Kerry Grady, Nancy Hablutzel, Ph.D., J.D., Philip N. Hablutzel, Esq., Kenneth C. Hicks, Douglas Hinderer, Craig Jackson, Jason P. Jacobsohn, Noreen J. Kelly, Dr. and Mrs. Peter Koestenbaum, Jan Kostner, Andrew R. McGaan, Esq., Scott McPherson, Douglas W. Pemberton and his parents Donna and Scott, Gary Punzi, Kelly Redmond, Todd A. Rickel, Ph.D., Steven K. Rothschild, M.D., Jeffrey L. Russell, Michael G. Russell, Richard and Martha Sabol, Geoffrey Dallas Snyder, James and Karina Sweeney, Terri Winfree, Ph.D., Michael Werbowsky, and Ava Youngblood.

From the start, Timothy R. Courtney and David E. Turner provided highly valued time and effort. Peter and Patty Koestenbaum offer nonstop encouragement. Clyde Bowles adds another moral compass. Noreen Kelly infuses a mandate to establish and sustain trust. Family members gauge relevance of personal detail. Long before publication, Rick Sabol placed the first bulk order. Jason Jacobsohn finds many ways to draw attention to the book. Kevin Bendle adds his expertise as a bookseller. Scott McPherson offers guidance for PR and events. Michael Werbowsky manages the Facebook page and other social media messaging. Douglas Hinderer applies to his work insight he gleans.

Truly I am grateful to many deep thinkers whose wise words I insert as supportive quotes throughout the book. Forever I am in their debt.

Beyond those to whom chapters are dedicated, words from other good souls remain with me: James Logan Abernathy, Leonard E. Ancona, M.D., Ted D. Anders, Ph.D., William M. Barnard, M.D., Ph.D., Jonathan T. Bateman, Edith Cleland, Matthew Cooleen, James Curry, Andrew J. Derks (1983-2007), Joan Emrich, Peter Englert, Robert M. Eppinger (1943-2009), Mark K. Farley, Gary F. Frye, James A. Galli, Patrick Hall, Kurt Hansen, H. Eugene Hile, III, The Reverend Dr. Robert J. Lamont (1920-2012), Joseph Lay, Ronald F. Madden, Corey Makrush, Daniel J. McEvoy, Marianne Michaelis, David Lynn Morrow (1945-2009), Brent Pawlecki, M.D., Gary Punzi, Juvenal Reis, June Scobee-Rodgers, Ph.D., Ovetta Sampson, Scott E. Squillace, Esq., Wayne Swift, Ph.D., Eric C.P. van Ginkel, Esq., James Weaver, Ph.D., Theodore J. White, Jr., and Jeffrey A. Wilson.

Several word-wise souls influence my lexicon for abundant living. Daughter Jennifer is truly omnipresent in my thoughts and prayers. Cynthia Gray Norris, Christopher Sorg, Phillip L. Petree, and Kevin E. Organ each contributed pivotal words to my heart's vocabulary.

The legacy of the Rev. Dr. Clarence Edward Macartney (1879-1957), my first Pastor, influenced earliest interest in language and writing. He was a prolific author. From vivid memory of my cradle church, First Presbyterian of Pittsburgh, I always draw value. The Church of Scotland-based faith community enriches my King James vocabulary.

It would be disingenuous to avoid acknowledging real value for this book derived from relationships that became fractured beyond repair. Several unnamed individuals know I still value them and their words, and how much I regret unexpected and irreparable developments.

Certainly I may have unintentionally neglected to list or otherwise acknowledge someone for specific contributions to the development of this book. If I overlooked anyone, here I express my gratitude, and my regret for any oversight. Quickly please let me know if I omitted someone who contributed to the book's 2009-2013 writing and publication process. Future editions may include additional names.

Thank you. Thank you. Thank you.

Acknowledgment. Expound.

Author

For many years John R. Dallas, Jr. is known as "a man of his words." He is Founder and Chief Alignment Officer (CAO) of Hillview Partners Network LLC, a team of independent consultants, executive coaches, and public speakers; credentialed individuals preeminent in fields related to strategic alignment of people, money, technology, and other resources. John aligns people with plans. His clients range from *Fortune 500* companies to owners of sole proprietorships and other individuals. Among other affiliations, John is associated with a global leadership development firm that provides organizational development consulting, team facilitation, and executive coaching.

John is formerly President of five technology-based national service companies in New York, suburban Washington, D.C., and Chicago. His prior CEO post was President and Chief Executive Officer of Chicago Title Credit Services, Inc., then the nation's largest big-data aggregator of consumer credit information for banks and other financial institutions. Before moving to Chicago, in Virginia he was the lead co-founder and served as President of CreditComm Services, now known as Intersections, Inc., a Nasdaq-listed public company.

John's entrepreneurial roots run deep. While majoring in journalism at Pittsburgh's Duquesne University, John started a student-run publicity service for high-profile nonprofit groups. After for-profit companies started to hire his award-winning young team, in 1972 a regional advertising agency acquired his start-up business. At age 22 John was named the buyer's Vice President, Public Relations. One year later he was recruited to a totally new career in New York City. At New York's Columbia University he continued his studies.

In Manhattan, he led three pacesetting tech-based national service companies: National Business Intelligence Corp. (renamed ETX Corporation), Group Concepts Capital Corp., and Market Access Resources Corp. (MARCOR). His work continues to allow him to participate in various types of training, education and information events in business, finance, law, journalism, politics, and leadership. For over 40 years John has been on the front line building businesses.

Worldwide John ranks among the top 100 of over 1,500 mentors for Silicon Valley's Founder Institute, a global entrepreneurial support organization for technology start-ups. He is a frequent featured presenter and panelist for San Francisco-based E-Factor, regarded as the world's largest entrepreneurial community. For Teach for America's entrepreneurial initiative for educators, he is a presenter and mentor. For other groups John also serves in various leader roles.

While Chairman for two years of Technology Leadership Forum (TechForum) at the Union League Club of Chicago, he was voted by peers as one of the region's Top 100 Technology Leaders. He was the first Chairman of the Advisory Board for the Leadership Arts Certificate Program of The University of Chicago's Graham School. John remains a highly regarded guest lecturer at schools.

On Fox TV-Chicago John frequently appeared on an Emmy Award-winning series featuring entrepreneurial success stories. Locally and nationally, he has been interviewed on ABC, CBS and NBC. Frequently he appeared on CAN-TV as a guest and host for an etiquette foundation's weekly call-in community television series. He has appeared on radio talk programs, and has been included in newspaper articles, blogs, podcasts, and online information resources.

He held elected posts in large urban churches in Pittsburgh, New York, and Chicago. In 2001 he was elected and ordained as an Elder for Fourth Presbyterian Church of Chicago (with over 6,500 members) where for two years he chaired the Congregational Life Committee, and moderated lay leadership development workshops.

A life-long early adopter of computing technology, in 1960, at age 10, John requisitioned from his parents a Think-a-Tron® toy computer. Only three years earlier, in 1957 the first book was published about computers. In the mid-1970s he acquired five first-generation PCs.

Directly as a result of these very early interests, for 12 years John ran ETX, a truly pioneering electronic publishing company. ETX supported Wall Street communication objectives of large publicly traded corporations. Aligning telephony and computing in ways that had never been monetized if ever attempted, John personally developed a system to facilitate real-time remote processing of professionally edited printed records of corporate, financial, and media events held worldwide (*e.g.,* stockholder meetings, securities analysts sessions, press conferences, *etc.*). Standards were being set.

The ETX client roster included 27 of top 50 Fortune 500 companies, such as IBM, GE, GM, Ford, Exxon *et al.* His company served top news media including ABC, CBS, NBC, The New York Times, The Washington Post, Fortune, Business Week, and others. Leaders in academia, law, auditing, finance, advertising, and politics were clients.

In 1976, 1980 and 1984, John negotiated to win exclusive contracts for ETX to electronically publish the only official transcriptional records of the historic United States Presidential and Vice-Presidential Debates, and also several high-profile Congressional debates. This body of work resides in the U.S. Library of Congress. Related published work with ABC-TV News and NBC-TV News focused on the purpose, function and future of the Electoral College.

John is the unconditionally loving father to Jennifer Gray Dallas, an independent thinker, brilliant writer, accomplished poetess, talented actress, and an entrepreneur. He enjoys an exceptionally strong paternal bond with adoptive son Geoffrey Dallas Snyder, Jennifer's half brother. In addition to beloved Mother, two sisters, numerous nieces, nephews, cousins, and spouses among the above, other friends are John's cherished extended family. Additional information:

johnrdallasjr.com/about-john-r-dallas-jr/

John R. Dallas, Jr.
Founder and Chief Alignment Officer (CAO)
Hillview Partners Network LLC

1133 North Dearborn Street | Suite 3201 | Chicago, Illinois 60610-7197

Business inquiries: 1.312.643.8000 | Skype: JRDallasJr

johnrdallasjr@hillviewpartners.com

linkedin.com/pub/john-r-dallas-jr/0/3b/668/

facebook.com/JohnRDallasJr

twitter.com/JohnRDallasJr

weneedtohaveaword.com | hillviewpartners.com | johnrdallasjr.com

Exhibit 1

The HILL Model™

High-Impact Leader Lens™ (HILL) for Viewing Alignment | The HILL Model™

Hillview

View to Align Vision with Viability < **👤** > View to Align Viability with Vision

Left Brain for Viability:

Uses logic
Detail-oriented
Defines "it"
Knows object's name
Facts rule
Words and language
Present and past
Math and science
Comprehends
Knowing
Acknowledges
Order/pattern perception
Reality-based
Forms strategies
Practical
Risk-averse
Humble by deduction

Right Brain for Vision:

Uses feeling
Big-picture oriented
Describes "it"
Knows object's function
Imagination rules
Symbols and images
Present and future
Philosophy and religion
Senses intrinsic value
Believing
Appreciates
Spatial perception
Imagination-based
Presents possibilities
Impetuous
Risk-ready
Hubris-prone (high risk)

Courage

Trust

Wisdom   **Patience**

Copyright © Hillview Partners Network LLC

Fully responsible leaders choose to view movement of people and things after climbing in their minds to just-right HILL-height, instead of looking from flat plains, lofty mountaintops, or stale ivory towers.

Wisdom	**Courage**	**Patience**
✓ Beyond knowledge	✓ To think differently	✓ With oneself
✓ Beyond the obvious	✓ To act decisively	✓ With others
✓ Beyond boundaries	✓ To dare boldly	✓ With process
✓ Beyond life's stages	✓ To fail insightfully	✓ With distraction
✓ Beyond history's pages	✓ To succeed humbly	✓ With roadblocks
✓ Beyond trusted sages	✓ To accept consequences	✓ With providence

Exhibit 2

The Leadership Diamond®

Author's Tribute to Peter Koestenbaum, Ph.D.

Outer Leadership Diamond® =
Leadership Capacity

Ethics
Be of service

Reality
Have no illusions

Greatness

Vision
Think big and new

The Leadership Diamond®
Copyright © Peter Koestenbaum, Ph.D.

Courage
Act with sustained initiative

(Used with Permission)

The Leadership Diamond® was created by Peter Koestenbaum, Ph.D. It is a model of the leadership mind and a methodology for expanding leadership. The Leadership Diamond® distinguishes four interdependent leadership imperatives, or "orientations:" Ethics, Vision, Courage and Reality. These orientations are your inner resources, always available to help you if you access them. The relationship among the four orientations determines the shape and size of the space within your

Leadership Diamond®. The space within The Leadership Diamond® is your leadership capacity, which is called "Greatness."

Dr. Peter Koestenbaum is a unique asset in the minds, hearts and lives of leaders working around the globe. I am richly blessed to have him in my life as a cherished personal friend, attentive colleague, trusting thinking partner, and esteemed mentor. Between us we are nearing 100 years of combined frontline experience in exploring, expressing, and practicing what we now both call **fully responsible leadership**. Forever humbly I remain grateful for having Peter in my life.

As our respect for each other's work is strategically aligned and highly complementary, herein I invited Peter to showcase his Leadership Diamond® and reveal other aspects of his unique insightfulness. I am privileged to commend to you Dr. Koestenbaum's work. I encourage you to visit amazon.com *et al* to order Peter's books. Allow me to connect you with Peter to discuss any high-impact services he offers.

In addition to visiting online booksellers to purchase Peter's books, you may want to search *via* Google or Bing for Peter Koestenbaum, Ph.D. and The Leadership Diamond®. You will be greatly enriched.

Specifically for this book and my own public talks, on the next page you'll see my interpretative graphic view of Peter's Leadership Diamond®. With his permission I offer you a glimpse at this work-in-progress. Because of Peter, this "open-corridors" graphic is how I see his luminescent model unfolding. Graphically and functionally, it is a situational *out-and-in* approach to guiding leaders and their followers.

Hillview encourages clients to consider alternative views, bridges and pathways toward personal and professional success. For day-to-day front-line functionality of leading and following, Dr. Koestenbaum's brilliant work is re-envisioned as a diagram for leaders to reach their attentive followers, and for engaged followers to reach their accessible leaders. Hillview graphically illustrates corridors of accessibility through which leaders reach out to their followers. And followers are encouraged to consider which access points of The Leadership Diamond® are best choices; inbound corridors that ideally relate to the leader's needs for clarity related to any person or thing being addressed. The Leadership Diamond® illuminates all pathways.

— JRDjr

The Leadership Diamond®

With Dr. Koestenbaum's Encouragement, Permission and Underwriting
Graphically Re-Envisioned by John R. Dallas, Jr. Specifically for this Book
Copyright © Peter Koestenbaum, Ph.D. | All Rights Reserved

Introductory narration is essential for this open-corridors model. The illustration below is the first version of more refined graphic work-in-progress. To retain and schedule Dr. Koestenbaum and John Dallas for a Rapid-Immersion Excursion Workshop with The Leadership Diamond®, please call 312.643.8000. Thank you for your interest.

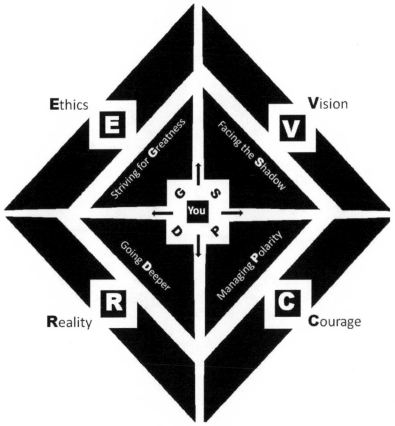

The Leadership Diamond® | Copyright © Peter Koestenbaum, Ph.D.

Ethics refers to the importance of people and integrity. It means caring about people, being sensitive and of service to them, and behaving in accordance with moral principles.

Vision means applying analytical skills, thinking big, looking at situations in new ways, and being inspirational.

Courage is defined as taking charge, using power wisely, acting with sustained initiative, managing anxiety, and being free and responsible.

Reality refers to a no-nonsense approach to facing life without illusions, relying on data that is factual rather than emotional, and being tough, task-oriented and results-focused. It also means being able to understand other people's perceptions of what is actually true.

By assessing the relative strengths and weaknesses of your Diamond® orientations, you can identify where your increased efforts can be best leveraged, giving you the maximum impact from the least effort. Your weakest orientation is your Leverage Corner. Cultivating your Leverage Corner, while continuing to value your stronger orientations, is key to breaking through your "stuck points," so that you can experience lasting leadership transformation. —PK

"There are three things extremely hard:
steel, a diamond, and to know one's self."
—Benjamin Franklin

Exhibit 3

Clear Views from Hills — instead of Flat Plains, Lofty Mountaintops, or Stale Ivory Towers

Hillview Partners Network LLC
Alignment Strategists

In the Business of Reversing Risk in Misalignment

Person-Plan Alignment
Seller-Buyer Alignment
Work-Life Alignment

Consulting | Coaching | Speaking

A Vantage Point to Your Advantage ™

Since 2005 Hillview is a collaborative network of independent consulting, coaching and speaking specialists; individuals preeminent in various fields related to facilitating strategic alignment of people, money, technology, and other mission-critical resources.

Consulting to Align Team Views toward Greater Productivity:

1. Focusing on what buyers truly value and sellers truthfully sell

2. Focusing on team engagement, efficiency, and measurable results

3. Focusing on where minds are moving during planning, execution and measurement stages of projects and other work

Coaching to Align Leader Views toward Higher Performance:

1. Executive development aligned with organizational growth

2. Career acceleration, stabilization, enrichment, or on-boarding

3. Career transition (value far exceeds that of outmoded and misnamed "outplacement" services)

Speaking to Align Audience Views toward Broader Perspective:

1.   Building buyer-centric cultures, plans, operations, and sustainable revenue streams

2.   Igniting fully responsible leaders to maximize their Return on Leadership™ (ROL)

3.   Digging, drilling and thinking at least somewhat deeper — to reach, climb and soar a lot higher

Today there are 68 separate and customizable talks and titles in Hillview's repertoire for retained speaking engagements. Among the talks are 52 hour-long modules based on key words features in this volume, drawn from Hillview's Language for Leading™ curriculum.

Language for Leading™ Roundtable is a structured program, of varied length, offered for on-site or other locations for clients and audiences to explore what specific words mean to the past, present and future of the sponsoring organization or other groups of minds. The Language for Leading™ Roundtable program includes readings from We Need to Have a Word and other leadership development texts.

All Hillview efforts encourage clients and others to choose clear views from hills in their minds, instead of observing people and things from flat plains, lofty mountaintops, or stale ivory towers. It works.

Inquires are invited from all types and sizes of fully funded organizations interested in exploring upside potential of retaining Hillview. All Hillview work is paid for on an advance-retainer basis. Terms may vary depending on nature and scope of work required.

You will be pleased with special accommodations that are offered to readers of this book who eventually become clients of Hillview, or who attend an event where John Dallas is a featured participant.

Contact John Dallas by writing to jrdallasjr@hillviewpartners.com. In the subject header for the e-mail please insert "New Business Opportunity for Hillview." If you do not hear back within one week, your message may not have made it through overly aggressive spam filtering. At any time, please free welcome to call John: 312.643.8000.

Thank you for expressing interest in features, benefits, attributes, and other value offered through the highly adaptive programs, systems and services delivered by Hillview and Hillview-certified affiliates.